THE LABOUR GOVERNMENTS 1964–70
volume 2

MANCHESTER
UNIVERSITY PRESS

THE LABOUR GOVERNMENTS 1964–70

Series editors   Steven Fielding and John W. Young

THE LABOUR GOVERNMENTS 1964–70
volume 2

International policy

John W. Young

Manchester University Press

Manchester and New York

distributed exclusively in the USA by Palgrave

Published by Manchester University Press
Oxford Road, Manchester M13 9NR, UK
and Room 400, 175 Fifth Avenue, New York, NY 10010, USA
www.manchesteruniversitypress.co.uk

Distributed exclusively in the USA by
Palgrave, 175 Fifth Avenue, New York,
NY 10010, USA

Distributed exclusively in Canada by
UBC Press, University of British Columbia, 2029 West Mall,
Vancouver, BC, Canada V6T 1Z2

British Library Cataloguing-in-Publication Data
A catalogue record for this book is available from the British Library

Library of Congress Cataloging-in-Publication Data applied for

ISBN   0 7190 4365 4   *hardback*

First published 2003

11 10 09 08 07 06 05 04 03   10 9 8 7 6 5 4 3 2 1

Typeset by R. J. Footring Ltd, Derby
Printed in Great Britain by Biddles Ltd, Guildford and King's Lynn

For Helen, Frazer and Jacob

Contents

Series foreword

Before the Labour Party entered government in October 1964 its leader, Harold Wilson, raised hopes of creating a 'new Britain', based on furthering the 'white heat' of technological change and aiming to pursue egalitarianism at home and abroad. In June 1970 Labour was ejected from office having lived up to few of these aspirations. Most analysts of the party's period in power consequently characterise it as a miserable failure. The majority focus on the Labour leadership's lack of ambition and reserve much of their censure for Wilson's strategic shortcomings. Present-day 'New' Labour, for which the 1960s are clearly an embarrassment, effectively endorses this glum assessment.

The three volumes in this series tackle different aspects of the 1964–70 Wilson governments' record and assume contrasting approaches to their subjects. Each, however, benefits from access to recently released government files housed in the Public Record Office, as well as other documents lately made available to historians. Together the volumes constitute the most complete record of these governments currently obtainable. While not denying Labour in office was a disappointment when measured against party rhetoric, the authors assume a more nuanced view compared with most previous accounts. In particular, they highlight a wider range of reasons for the governments' relative lack of achievement. If the disposition of Labour's leaders played its part, so did the nature of the party, the delicate state of the economy, the declining place of Britain in the world order and the limited ambitions of the British people themselves.

In testing some well entrenched assumptions about these governments in light of new evidence, the authors dispute their status as the black sheep of Labour history and establish some new perspectives. In this respect, these volumes therefore mark an important stage in the permanent revisionism to which all historians should subject the past. It is hoped they will encourage more research on Labour's period in office and challenge their overly grim reputation among both academics and lay readers alike.

Preface

In *The Governance of Britain* Harold Wilson recalled that, when he became Labour leader in 1963, nuclear weapons and British relations with the European Economic Community (EEC) 'took the centre of the political stage' and that, as Prime Minister in the 1960s, he was 'much involved, personally, in the Rhodesian problem, South Africa, Vietnam, Anglo-American and Anglo-Soviet relations and, later, the Nigerian civil war'.[1] In providing a broad analysis of the international policy of the Labour governments of 1964–70 that exploits recent archival releases, this study focuses on the most significant international questions, guided in part by Wilson's list. There are chapters on the EEC, southern Africa and Nigeria, while relations with the USSR are treated in a chapter that also discusses the Atlantic alliance, and nuclear armaments problems feature in the chapters on the Atlantic alliance and on defence. Anglo-American relations figure in most chapters but with a general discussion as part of Chapter 1. The government is probably best remembered, in its international dimension, for the strategic withdrawal from bases 'east of Suez', especially from South-East Asia and the Middle East, and three chapters are dedicated to this subject. The term 'international policy' is used in this volume to reflect the fact that the concerns that shaped Britain's role in the world went beyond traditional 'foreign policy'. Defence strategy, colonial problems and economic factors also had a significant impact.

Of course, isolating particular international questions from one another can give a false impression about how decisions were made. Events on any number of issues were unfolding simultaneously and often affected each other, as well as the domestic scene. The retreat from east of Suez, for example, pleased many backbenchers, contributed to spending cuts and thereby helped the economic situation, but upset Commonwealth members in the region, provoked concern in Washington and was criticised by the opposition. At any given point, policy-makers might have to deal with a number of developments on different fronts. Thus, in early 1969 the arrival of a new administration in Washington coincided with a bleak period in Anglo-Soviet relations following the invasion of Czechoslovakia, a crisis in Anglo-French relations (the 'Soames affair') and rising pressure to dissociate Britain from the actions of the Nigerian government in its war against Biafra. Yet, discussing issues simultaneously, following a chronological structure, would make them impossible to follow. So, while making references to the interconnection of events when appropriate, this book looks at the key problems separately. First, however, Chapter 1 sets out the broader context of how policy was made. Inevitably, in a single study, many issues have to be either touched upon only briefly or omitted altogether. Commonwealth immigration, the 1968 Non-Proliferation Treaty, the Cyprus problem, negotiations with Argentina over the Falklands, policy on information and propaganda, attitudes towards the non-aligned movement, environmental concerns and co-operation with France on the Concorde airliner are just a few issues on which whole chapters could have been written. On bilateral problems, it has been possible to sum up British dealings with the USA and the USSR, France and Germany, but many important relationships are virtually absent. Anglo-Irish questions are an obvious example.[2] This does not reflect any wish to ignore issues, but has been dictated by the need to be selective about material and to provide a coherent rather than a comprehensive account.

There are many people without whom this project would not have come to fruition, not least the British Academy, who provided me with a generous grant. Financial support was also given by the Universities of Nottingham and Leicester. Academics who had a direct impact on the arguments include Richard Aldrich, Nigel Ashton, Stephen Ashton, Stuart Ball, Geoffrey Berridge, Nicholas Cull, Oliver Daddow, Anne Deighton, Saki Dockrill, James Ellison, Steven Fielding, Peter Hennessy, Matthew Jones, John Kent, Donna Lee, Piers Ludlow, Spencer Mawby, Philip Murphy, Gillian Staerck, Philip Taylor, Jim Tomlinson and Chris Wrigley, as well as the anonymous reviewer who read the final version for Manchester University Press. I am also grateful to Bob Borthwick, David Clarke, David Easter, Geraint Hughes, Nelson Lankford, Helen Parr, Raj Roy and the staff at Manchester University Press. Jeremy Wiltshire and my daughter, Linda, acted as research assistants. I am grateful to the following archives and libraries: the Public Record Office, London; British Library, London; Churchill College Archive, Cambridge; Bodleian Library, Oxford; British Library of Political and Economic Science, London; Institute of Historical Research, London; Leicester University library; Liddell Hart Centre at King's College, London; Labour History Archive, Manchester; National University of Wales, Aberystwyth; Nottingham University library; US National Archives, Washington, DC; Lyndon B. Johnson Library, Austin; Harry Truman Library, Independence; and the Virginia Historical Society, Richmond.

Those who gave permission for me to see specific collections of private papers are acknowledged in the bibliography, but I would like to repeat my thanks to them here. Finally, I am deeply grateful to my wife, Helen, for reading over the manuscript and to her, my children – Julie, Linda, David, Frazer and Jacob – and my mother for their support.

Rothley

Notes

1 Harold Wilson, *The Governance of Britain* (Weidenfeld and Nicolson, London, 1976), 119.
2 Anglo-Irish relations in the Wilson years are too often overshadowed by the sectarian 'troubles', on which see Peter Rose, *How the Troubles Came to Northern Ireland* (Palgrave, London, 2001). But the earlier years saw some success for Wilson's efforts at improving relations, notably with the return of the body of Roger Casement and improved trade co-operation: see Christopher Reeves, 'Britain, Ireland and the exhumation of Sir Roger Casement', *Irish Studies in International Affairs*, vol. 12 (2001), 151–78; Jane Toomey, 'Ireland and Britain's second application to join the EEC', in Oliver Daddow, ed., *Harold Wilson and European Integration: Britain's second application to join the EEC* (Frank Cass, London, 2002), 227–42.

Abbreviations

MOD	Ministry of Defence
MP	Member of Parliament
NATO	North Atlantic Treaty Organisation
NIBMAR	no independence before majority rule
NLF	(South Arabian) National Liberation Front
NPT	Non-Proliferation Treaty
OAU	Organisation of African Unity
ODM	Overseas Development Ministry
OPD	Overseas Policy and Defence Committee
PKI	Indonesian Communist Party
PLP	Parliamentary Labour Party
RAF	Royal Air Force
SALT	Strategic Arms Limitation Treaty
SAS	Special Air Service
SEATO	Southeast Asian Treaty Organisation
UDI	unilateral declaration of independence
UKUSA	British–American post-war intelligence agreements
UN	United Nations
USA	United States of America
USSR	Union of Soviet Socialist Republics
WEU	Western European Union

In the notes

BL	British Library
CAB	Cabinet papers
Cmnd	Command papers
COS	Chiefs of Staff
CRO	Commonwealth Relations Office (Commonwealth Office 1966–8)
DBPO	*Documents on British Policy Overseas*
DEFE	Defence papers
DOHP	Diplomatic Oral History Project
FCO	Foreign and Commonwealth Office
FO	Foreign Office
FRUS	*Foreign Relations of the United States*
LBJL	Lyndon B. Johnson Library
NA	National Archives (of USA)
NSF	National Security File (at LBJL)
PLP	Parliamentary Labour Party
PREM	Prime Minister's Office
PRO	Public Record Office
RG	(US National Archives) Record Group
USNA	US National Archives

1

Policy-makers and policy-making

Labour took office in October 1964 on a wave of hope under a young leader promising social reform, better planning and the greater application of technology to improve Britain's economic performance. The programme would be kick-started by 'a hundred days of dynamic action'. Electoral success was tainted by the narrowness of the victory, but there was a clear victory at the next general election, in March 1966, after which the 'Labour benches were pervaded by a gala atmosphere'. Almost immediately, however, economic problems blighted Harold Wilson's second administration. A deflationary package in July 1966 failed to stave off devaluation in November 1967. The following years saw an abortive attempt to reform the House of Lords, a botched proposal for trade union reform and the rise of sectarian strife in Northern Ireland. Many supporters were disillusioned and not just on the left. David Owen, who entered the Commons in 1966 inspired by the Prime Minister's leadership, felt by New Year 1968 'as if an age has passed' and wished 'fervently that we could get rid of him'. During the following year the established political order was called into question on both sides of the Iron Curtain. Referring to 'the American defeat in Vietnam', the Prague Spring and the Paris riots, Richard Crossman wrote of 'new forces from below ... in revolt against ... parliamentary democracy'. In Britain, there were large-scale anti-Vietnam War demonstrations and student disruption of universities. Yet the danger of disorder soon receded and an economic upturn provided Wilson with a chance of winning the next election. Defeat in June 1970 came as a surprise.[1]

On the international side there was a real sense of disappointment with Labour, even if, during the 1966 and 1970 elections, Wilson prevented failures abroad from looming large in voters' minds. Despite a tradition of bipartisanship in foreign policy, Labour in 1964 seemed to differ from the Conservatives in its strong condemnation of apartheid in South Africa, its faith in the Commonwealth and United Nations (UN), its opposition to membership of the European Economic Community (EEC) and doubts about the British nuclear deterrent. In power,

1

however, Wilson retained the nuclear deterrent, sold warplanes to South Africa, presided over bitter divisions within the Commonwealth, upset the UN over British policy in Aden and launched a 'second try' to enter the EEC. Rather than coming to terms with Britain's relative decline in world affairs, the government at first tried to maintain the existing value of sterling against the dollar and refused to initiate an early withdrawal from military bases east of Suez. One self-confessed Labour supporter, writing ahead of the 1970 election, portrayed an administration that was humiliated in Rhodesia and Aden, ineffective in its foreign aid programme and confused about its role in the world. On the Labour right, Desmond Donnelly MP wrote an unforgiving account of Wilson's performance, highlighting his failure to get into the EEC, his vainglorious performance over Rhodesia and his surrender of the world role, while the left-wing journalist Paul Foot argued that Wilson had betrayed socialist principles by allying with the USA, turning towards the EEC and letting the Commonwealth wither.[2]

Contemporary left-wing criticisms have been sustained by many writers since, and for years it was almost a truism that Wilson betrayed Labour's ideals at home and abroad. John Pilger has written that 'the Wilson government ... supported the American invasion of Vietnam, sold arms to racist South Africa and ... conspired with the Nigerian military regime to crush Biafra', while Clive Ponting accuses Labour of giving 'a low priority to moral issues as a matter of clear political choice', citing cuts in the aid budget, purchases of US military aircraft and a halfhearted sanctions policy against Rhodesia. In the 1990s a number of historians portrayed Wilson as a more complex figure than the left allow. He was not lacking in principle or idealism but faced genuine problems and exhibited considerable skill, both in holding his party together and in winning elections. But even Chris Wrigley, in a quite sympathetic analysis, argues that Labour followed a 'very traditional foreign policy' that showed 'essential continuity' with previous governments, apart from the cosmetic novelty of 'newsworthy sudden initiatives by Harold Wilson'.[3]

Wilson

Ted Short, Wilson's first Chief Whip, found that his leader 'knew more about the nitty-gritty of foreign affairs than the rest of the Government put together' and dominated decision-making in this area. In itself, prime ministerial interference in foreign policy was not unusual: all Conservative premiers since 1951 had engaged in personal diplomacy, upstaging their Foreign Secretaries. Wilson regularly intervened in foreign policy matters, took action without full reference to the Foreign Office and became adept at announcing personal diplomatic efforts to solve problems like Rhodesia and Vietnam. These were easily dismissed as publicity exercises, but Wrigley points out that they usually 'had a multi-faceted tactical aspect to them', with Wilson playing to several constituencies at once, from allies and enemies abroad to the media, Labour Party and opposition at home, and he usually achieved some aim, even if only transitory. As Austen Morgan notes, however, 'Wilson began to fade on the international stage in 1968'. Around that time the devaluation of the pound and withdrawal from east of Suez reduced Britain's role in the world and the Prime Minister's personal interest in Rhodesia receded.[4] But in the early years he took a keen interest in many of the most important international questions – particularly Anglo-American relations, Vietnam, Anglo-Soviet matters and Rhodesia – and, as will be seen in the next chapter, down to 1967 the future of Britain's world role was of central importance to the story of the government.

Wilson's predominance initially rested on his being one of only three ministers to have served in a Cabinet before, as President of the Board of Trade in 1947–51. He came from a modest, middle-class, Yorkshire background but had excelled in economics at Oxford. In 1951 he resigned from Clement Attlee's Cabinet alongside the radical Aneurin Bevan, partly over the issue of defence expenditure, thereby establishing a reputation as a left-winger that was undeserved. In February 1963 he became the leader of the Labour Party after the death of Hugh Gaitskell. Where world affairs were concerned, Wilson had family in Australia and he seemed to be a strong believer in the Commonwealth. He had first visited the USA in 1943, when working as a wartime civil servant and, while not uncritical of US policy, was quite 'Atlanticist' by 1963. He was also known for his enthusiasm over détente and expanded trade with the Eastern bloc, and had served for a time as shadow Foreign Secretary.[5]

One of the most balanced pictures of the Prime Minister came from Lord Longford, who served him as Leader of the House of Lords. Longford criticised Wilson as a schemer, obsessed with conspiracies and lacking in settled convictions, yet also praised him for his powers of assimilation, analysis and exposition, for his remarkable memory, his determination, ambition and stamina, as well as more human qualities: his sense of humour, fertile wit and personal kindness. David Owen also recognised that it was easy to become either too critical or too laudatory of Wilson, who was clever, articulate, hard-working, well informed and a sensitive party manager, but who could be indecisive, overly concerned by minutiae and absurdly optimistic. Some of the contradictions are particularly striking. His suspicion of plots grew apace after July 1966 and there was much genuine plotting against him in 1968–9, yet he insisted on promoting rivals and critics to key positions, including two to Foreign Secretary, Patrick Gordon Walker and George Brown. Wilson came to Downing Street with considerable bureaucratic experience yet has been described by Peter Hennessy as 'the untidiest of all the post-war premiers in administrative terms', as he created a myriad of ministerial and official committees, and opened and closed whole ministries. While portraying himself as a British Kennedy, he would let meetings 'talk themselves out', with conclusions being reached through sheer boredom, sometimes after several sessions.[6]

Christopher Mayhew, who had known Wilson since Oxford, once told journalists that 'his ambition was always to get to Number 10 but, now he's there, he has absolutely no idea what to do with it'. That Wilson was a political virtuoso, adept at wrong-footing the opposition yet also an arch pragmatist lacking in long-term outlook or ideological belief, was a common view. Even Bevan once remarked that his friend was 'all facts and no bloody vision'. Yet Wilson held some beliefs strongly, being a patriot and a monarchist who believed in government action to improve social conditions. His foreign policy was also affected by his odd mix of conservative and progressive principles, the former shown especially in his desire to maintain a world role for Britain, the US alliance and the position of sterling, the latter in his dislike of racism and his wish to avoid war and to relax East–West tensions.[7] A more serious flaw, perhaps, was what has been called his 'Walter Mitty' side, a reference to the frustrated mediocrity who daydreamed about being a superman. Wilson had an almost pathetic desire to boast about his influence over foreign leaders, especially those in Moscow and Washington, which was far removed from reality. One early biography of Wilson was subtitled *Yorkshire Walter Mitty*, and argued that the Prime Minister's fantasies affected his foreign policy directly, especially his belief that he could end the Vietnam War and bring down Rhodesia's Ian Smith.[8]

In Downing Street, Wilson relied on a handful of key advisers. Two civil service appointments that proved important on international issues were the Secretary to the Cabinet and the Private Secretary for foreign affairs. The former post was held throughout the 1964–70 governments by Burke Trend, the archetypal senior civil servant, highly intelligent, diligent and self-effacing. Anyone who works through the papers of the Prime Minister's office will be struck by the value of Trend's minutes to the Prime Minister, with their succinct summaries of memoranda from other departments, their advice on how to handle meetings and recommendations on the decisions to be reached, all done in an objective, disinterested style so that Trend's personal view can be discerned only in the odd turn of phrase. While he was a convinced Atlanticist and 'Commonwealth man', the Cabinet Secretary recognised that Britain could no longer play a world role and came to terms, albeit reluctantly, with the move towards EEC membership.[9] Wilson relied heavily on his

Private Secretaries for foreign affairs. He had three in succession, all highly successful mid-career diplomats seconded from the Foreign Office (FO): Oliver Wright, who was inherited from the former Conservative premier, Alec Douglas-Home, and who became ambassador to Copenhagen in March 1966; Michael Palliser, formerly head of the FO Planning Department, a 'pro-European' who later became Permanent Under-Secretary at the Foreign and Commonwealth Office (FCO);[10] and, in 1969–70, Teddy Youde, a China expert who later became ambassador to Beijing.

There was a small group of personal–political advisers, the so-called 'kitchen cabinet', at Number 10. An important figure was his long-serving secretary, Marcia Williams, with whom he was maliciously – and falsely – accused of conducting an affair. But her interventions in foreign policy seem to have been few, partly because of her 'unofficial' status. Derek Mitchell, Wilson's Principal Private Secretary, would let her accompany Wilson on his first Washington visit only if she travelled as a maid and she was not allowed into formal meetings with President Johnson.[11] Other members of the 'kitchen cabinet' included the economist Thomas Balogh, who had particularly strong views on defence and the EEC, and George Wigg, in Cabinet as Paymaster General in 1964–6, who had special responsibilities for intelligence matters. Someone else who regularly spoke out on defence was the government's Chief Scientist, Solly Zuckerman. Wilson also used a number of friends on diplomatic missions, including the MP Harold Davies (sent to Hanoi in 1965) and his lawyer, Arnold Goodman (used as an envoy to Rhodesia in 1968). The use of such 'special envoys' and 'trouble-shooters' would become a trademark of Wilson's diplomacy alongside his own overseas missions.

Key ministers

Patrick Gordon Walker, Wilson's first Foreign Secretary, had been Commonwealth Secretary in 1950–1 and strongly believed in the Commonwealth as a durable institution and an effective voice in the world. In this, as well as his Atlanticism and indifference towards the EEC, he seemed to have much in common with Wilson, except that Gordon Walker was a Gaitskellite. He lost his seat in the 1964 election but Wilson generously appointed him Foreign Secretary anyway, and sought a 'safe' constituency for his return to the Commons. Inevitably Gordon Walker had to devote considerable time to his re-election fight. This led his Permanent Under-Secretary, Harold Caccia, to begin daily meetings of senior officials to review overseas problems and provide a quick overview for the Foreign Secretary, a practice that proved so valuable that it was continued thereafter. Inevitably, too, the Foreign Secretary was unable to appear in the Commons, where Wilson, in the first major foreign affairs debate, of 16–17 December 1964, undertook the daunting task of opening and closing the government case. Gordon Walker did play an active role in policy: he made several overseas visits and was particularly active in developing ideas on nuclear co-operation within the North Atlantic Treaty Organisation (NATO). But on 21 January 1965 he failed to win a second 'safe' seat in three months and resigned. One study considers that, while it is difficult to judge adequately on such a short term of office, he was 'a potentially sound, if not particularly outstanding, foreign secretary'.[12]

The term 'safe pair of hands' might have been invented for Michael Stewart, who replaced Gordon Walker and who returned as Foreign Secretary when George Brown suddenly resigned in March 1968.[13] More dynamic figures were available in January 1965 but Stewart's appointment was not a complete surprise. He had been Under-Secretary of War under Attlee, regularly spoke on foreign policy in the Commons and had accompanied Wilson to the USSR in 1963. Judgements on him are seldom inspiring: a junior diplomat described him as 'rather dull but competent'; Roy Jenkins disliked his return to the FO in 1968 because 'it seemed likely to perpetuate both the greyness and the stubborn traditionalism of the government'; and another Cabinet colleague, Barbara Castle, felt him 'sadly miscast as Foreign Secretary. He was a decent, honourable man who had good radical views on a number of social service issues … but in foreign affairs all his radicalism disappeared'.[14] A former schoolteacher with a pedantic streak, Stewart inspired little affection and could be very shy. His memoirs provide only the blandest understanding of his policies. The factors that guided him were, apparently, a belief that British trading interests were best served by the preservation of world peace, an understanding that the country was now in the 'second rank' and loyalty to the Western alliance, alongside a readiness to explore détente. He had some admirable qualities. He was a capable, convincing public speaker, diligent in mastering his briefs and principled in his dealings. To his first Private Secretary, Nicholas Henderson, Stewart was 'an unsung Foreign Secretary', someone with a deadpan sense of humour, an inner self-confidence and sound grasp of human nature, who dealt calmly with an array of difficulties. In contrast to Gordon Walker, Stewart was loyal to the Prime Minister and one observer felt that as the government progressed Wilson 'probably depended more on his advice than any other minister's'.[15]

The contrast between Stewart and Wilson's third Foreign Secretary could hardly be more pronounced. A temperamental alcoholic, insecure and anxious in himself but assertive and bullying towards others, George Brown could alternatively be a charming entertainer or an ill-mannered braggart, skilful in establishing a rapport or utterly tactless. Although lacking much formal education, he had a natural intelligence, an original mind and a quick wit; he was able both to dominate Cabinet discussions and to woo a public meeting. While determinedly pro-European, he was also an intense patriot; despite having a Jewish wife, he had a reputation as a pro-Arab on Middle Eastern issues; his pro-Americanism did not prevent him questioning their presence east of Suez and criticising their policy in Vietnam. In many ways his appointment, on 11 August 1966, was surprising. His behaviour seemed particularly ill-suited to the world of diplomacy and his dislike of Wilson, who had beaten him in the 1963 Labour leadership contest, was well known.[16] But Brown was the deputy Labour leader, was increasingly frustrated in his position as head of the Department of Economic Affairs and, following the July 1966 economic crisis when he favoured a devaluation of the pound, was likely to resign if he was not given the FO. He also had real vision about Britain's international role, favouring an early withdrawal from bases east of Suez and entry to the EEC. His drive and imagination, linked to his clear strategy, should have made him a good Foreign Secretary – if they had not been cancelled out by his volatility, arrogance and inability to stay sober.

Among diplomats Brown was loved by some, loathed by others. Even after Labour lost office, his memoirs continued to stir up strong feelings, because he criticised the working practices of 'bowler-hatted chaps' in the FO. Paul Gore-Booth, the Permanent Under-Secretary at the FO in 1965–9, spent a section of his own memoirs rebutting Brown's complaints.[17] The Foreign Secretary had not much liked Gore-Booth, who came from a landowning family and had been educated at Eton. To succeed him Brown (only shortly before quitting the FO) chose Denis Greenhill, whose father had worked on the railways.[18] Brown's worst misbehaviour in front of a foreign leader came with the state visit of President Sunay of Turkey, when, during a performance by the Royal Ballet, he turned to his guest and said, 'You don't want to listen to this bullshit – let's go and have a drink'. The unpleasant side of his character was most starkly revealed through his dealings with British ambassadors, whom he treated virtually as servants when on foreign visits. Once in Brussels, on being welcomed by ambassador Roderick Barclay to 'my embassy', Brown retorted, 'It's not your bloody embassy, it's mine'. It was common knowledge that he told Lady Reilly, whose husband held the Paris embassy, 'You are not fit to be an Ambassador's wife'.[19]

So difficult were relations between Downing Street and the FO while Brown was there that Wilson tried to conduct areas of foreign policy without him. The FO Minister of State, Lord Chalfont, acted as 'George's unofficial minder' and Michael Palliser developed what he called a 'private line' to the FO, which meant 'pirate' documents being

passed to Downing Street without Brown's knowledge, sometimes before
he had read them himself.[20] The 'private line' continued to operate after
Brown's departure.[21] He finally resigned in March 1968 after Wilson
failed to consult him about a decision to close the Stock Exchange and
London 'gold pool'. Brown later argued his resignation was a principled
protest against Wilson's 'presidential' style, but at the time he seemed more
upset about the personal affront.[22] Brown continues to divide opinion.
So, while one historian judges 'that, given more time, he might well have
proved … one of Britain's better foreign secretaries', another believes
he was 'surely one of the worst Foreign Secretaries of the century'.[23]

Oliver Wright argued in January 1966 that the 'real problems' of
international policy facing the government involved colonial and
Commonwealth matters – Aden, Indo-Pakistani conflict, Rhodesia –
rather than FO concerns.[24] But the ministers who headed the Colonial
Office (CO) and Commonwealth Relations Office (CRO) in this period
were of secondary importance to the Foreign Secretary in the Cabinet.
Wilson's first Colonial Secretary, Anthony Greenwood, was a left-winger,
popular on the backbenches, who survived as a minister throughout
1964–70. His progressive views, especially on policy towards Aden, put
him at odds with the CO and he was replaced in December 1965 by
Lord Longford; Greenwood was moved to the Overseas Development
Ministry (ODM). Longford had wanted a proper administrative department for some time but even his official biographer admits he lacked
the application needed for the CO, which he ceded to Fred Lee after
barely four months.[25] Lee was distinguished only by being the last
Colonial Secretary, the post being abolished in August 1966. Wilson's
first Commonwealth Secretary, Arthur Bottomley, had been a junior
minister in the old Dominions Office in 1946–7. Like Greenwood, his
forthright approach to a colonial problem (this time Rhodesia) put him
at odds with Wilson; like Greenwood too, he was moved on to the ODM,
replacing Greenwood there in August 1966. Bert Bowden, the next
Commonwealth Secretary, was formerly Leader of the House of Commons
and a close ally of the Prime Minister, but he too differed with Wilson
over Rhodesia and was a convinced opponent of the EEC application.
He left the Cabinet in August 1967, being succeeded by George
Thomson, previously Minister of State at the FO. Another Wilson loyal-
ist, Thomson was most notable for working to fuse his ministry with the
FO in October 1968, thereby putting himself out of a job; but he continued to work on international issues as Minister without Portfolio and,
from October 1969, Chancellor of the Duchy of Lancaster.

The ODM was one of the new ministries set up by the incoming
government in 1964. Designed to draw together responsibilities that
had previously been scattered around Whitehall, it was placed under a
leading left-winger, Barbara Castle, who had a seat in Cabinet. She

hoped 'to establish a revolutionary new principle: that the purpose of
aid was to promote the development of the backward countries of the
world' rather than to promote the trading interests of donor countries,
but she soon found it 'impossible to challenge the Treasury veto on our
policies'. As Clive Ponting has argued, it never really did become a
'development' ministry in a full sense, which would have involved
responsibilities in the trade, defence and immigration fields. Instead, it
primarily became an agency for sharing out a decreasing amount of
aid. Castle was promoted to the Ministry of Transport in December
1965 and only thirteen months later the Minister for Overseas Development ceased to hold Cabinet rank.[26]

Two other new appointments were promised in the 1964 manifesto
and, like the ODM, were designed to demonstrate Labour's commitment to international peace and justice. Both were based in the FO.
One was the Minister for Disarmament, a post filled by Alun Gwynne
Jones, a former soldier and defence correspondent of *The Times*, who
was ennobled as Lord Chalfont. His brief was 'to represent Britain at
international disarmament negotiations not, as some of the dottier
elements in the peace movement seemed to assume, to disband this
country's armed forces'.[27] He served in the role until May 1967, when
the job passed to Fred Mulley, with a reduced profile. Ministerial rank
was also given to the ambassador to the UN, Hugh Foot, who was made
Lord Caradon. An advocate of decolonisation and a former colonial
administrator, who had served at the UN before, he seemed the ideal
figure to raise Britain's reputation with the newly emerging nations.
But he could not single-handedly end the tirades against Britain in New
York, especially on southern African issues, nor could he compensate
for the fact that the government's initial commitment to a strong UN
waned, alongside its determination to produce a meaningful overseas
development policy and take a high profile in global disarmament efforts.

Of greater importance in shaping international strategy, if only for
their insistence on spending restraint, were Wilson's two Chancellors of
the Exchequer. The first, James Callaghan, was a party moderate, a
former spokesman on colonial affairs and another 'Commonwealth
man'. He soon found his personal sympathy for the role of Britain east
of Suez was at odds with the need to control expenditure and his
defence of sterling made resignation inevitable when devaluation came
in November 1967. Roy Jenkins, who then swapped the post of Home
Secretary with Callaghan, was only a junior minister when the government began. A right-winger, 'pro-marketeer' and critic of the presence
east of Suez, he had an important role in accelerating the end of
Britain's world position in 1968–70. Another major player on international policy was the larger-than-life figure of Denis Healey, Secretary
of State for Defence throughout the government. A Communist in his

youth but now on the centre-right, he had specialised in foreign policy
and defence since the 1940s. Intelligent and efficient, energetic and
tough, he grasped all areas of his department's work, from the complexities of nuclear strategy to the technicalities of logistics. He secured
his reputation as a great Defence Secretary despite presiding over
average cuts in spending of 0.7 per cent per annum.[28]

The creation of the FCO
and problems of the Empire/Commonwealth

The most important administrative development in international affairs
under Labour was not the creation of new ministerial posts but the
fusing of old ones. The CO and CRO merged into the 'Commonwealth
Office' on 1 August 1966. This in turn merged with the FO to form the
FCO on 17 October 1968. Such mergers had been discussed since the
1940s and the February 1964 Plowden report had accepted the in-
efficiencies of having more than one ministry trying to define policy
towards the outside world. Under the Conservatives in 1962–4 the CO
and CRO had been put under one minister, even though the role of the
former in colonial administration was very different from that of the
latter, which was essentially concerned with diplomacy among Commonwealth countries. In 1965 the CO was still responsible for thirty-three
territories but only Hong Kong (with 3.7 million inhabitants) and South
Arabia (with 1.1 million) had more than a million inhabitants. The process of decolonisation was now well under way and Labour was deeply
committed to it. Colonial Secretary Anthony Greenwood told ministers
that even territories deemed too small for independence must have
democratic rights that left them without any sense of 'colonial status'.
The larger dependent territories, apart from Hong Kong, were independent by 1970 and the remainder were mostly small islands scattered
around the world.[29] Thus the role of the CO was shrinking anyway and
it was something of a surprise that Wilson appointed separate ministers
to head the CRO and CO in 1964. Keeping the FO and CRO separate
was more understandable and Plowden had set no fixed target for their
merger, but the departments began to plan for common management
and filing systems. It was typical of Wilson's unpredictable methods that,
when merger was finally announced, it came as a surprise: Downing
Street took advantage of George Brown's resignation to announce it
and the final process was quite rushed.[30]

Labour's plans to fuse the FO, CO and CRO did not imply any wish
to run down the Commonwealth. Indeed, if the 1964 manifesto laid
emphasis on anything in the international field, it was the need to reinvigorate it. At Houghton-le-Spring in May 1963 Wilson had set out a

programme not only for the development of trade but also Common-wealth higher education, scientific exchange and social development.[31] Yet, whatever Labour's original hopes, the Commonwealth was declin-ing in significance and not just because of any Conservative neglect. In general, since 1945, hopes of wielding influence over former possessions had been disappointed, as Britain's own power declined, national interests diverged and ex-colonies showed themselves determined to throw off the vestiges of imperialism.[32] In trade, for example, the Commonwealth still accounted for over 40 per cent of British exports at the end of the 1950s, but this proportion shrank rapidly thereafter. The British them-selves focused in the mid-1960s on developing freer multilateral trade, with negotiations through the General Agreement on Tariffs and Trade (GATT) to reduce tariff barriers, in the so-called 'Kennedy round', then turned to EEC membership. In the March 1966 election the Common-wealth barely featured in the Labour manifesto. By 1973 exports to the Commonwealth were a modest 17 per cent of the total. Most Common-wealth states remained members of the sterling area until 1967, but many withdrew balances thereafter, forcing Britain to shore up the position of the pound in September 1968 by giving financial guarantees, by which time the area had only a few years of life left. There were some joint Commonwealth development schemes but, as seen above, the scale of British overseas aid was not large, and while the total value of invest-ment in the Commonwealth was increasing, up from £2.4 billion in 1965 to almost £3.4 billion in 1970, the figures were artificially boosted by the devaluation.[33]

On the political side, an important step for the Commonwealth was the establishment of a permanent secretariat in 1965, with a Canadian diplomat, Arnold Smith, as its first head. But Labour could not claim the credit for this since discussions had begun under Douglas-Home.[34] The Commonwealth was particularly scarred by the Rhodesia problem in 1965–6. The September 1966 Prime Ministers' conference was a depressing event, with Wilson declaring in one meeting that 'Britain is being treated as if we were a bloody colony', a remark that only made matters worse.[35] Indeed, after agreeing to three Commonwealth con-ferences in 1965–6, Wilson avoided another until 1969. After the September 1966 conference Cabinet ministers even asked for a study of the value of the Commonwealth. The CRO remained positive about the organisation, and emphasised the Commonwealth's role as a vehicle for British influence, a continuation of historical ties and a link between races. But FO planners argued the Commonwealth was a wasting asset, of limited economic importance, which did not help British dealings with the EEC or the USA; its demise would at least stop Britain being blackmailed by those who threatened (especially over Rhodesia) to quit the Commonwealth unless they got what they wanted.[36] Then again, opinion polls taken in Britain in 1969 still suggested that people saw the Commonwealth as a viable and valuable organisation. When asked with which group Britain's future best lay, respondents to an NOP poll even put the Commonwealth first (with 30 per cent), ahead of the EEC (24 per cent) and the USA (11 per cent).[37]

Whatever the popular perception of Britain's future and however slow Wilson was to accept that the world role must end, the government became focused in 1967 on a withdrawal from east of Suez and an EEC application. FO planners helped draw up a Cabinet paper, submitted in February 1968, which argued that, despite global trading interests, Britain's ability 'to influence events outside the Atlantic area will be considerably less' in future. The main aim of policy should be a strong, cohesive Western Europe with Britain in the EEC, but as a partner of the USA, alongside a strong NATO.[38] In July 1969 a study was published on the future shape of British diplomatic representation overseas that reflected the new priorities. It was written by a committee headed by Val Duncan, the chairman of Rio Tinto Zinc. In contrast to the Plowden report, which wanted to maintain global influence and improve staffing levels, the Duncan report was launched with the purpose of reducing expenditure in line with the withdrawal from east of Suez. Wilson set the tone in Cabinet on 12 January 1968, by stating 'that it wasn't necessary to have massive political intelligence when you hadn't got the power to make use of the information, and he urged that we group our embassies and concentrate … upon commercial work'. The Duncan report saw Britain as 'a major power of the second order', which must come to terms with its diminished presence in the world by reducing its embassies in the 'outer' area, where Britain was judged to have limited interests, and concentrating on a 'core' of Western Europe and North America, where economic, political and cultural ties were deepening. There was faint praise for the Commonwealth. Yet, while it reflected the recasting of international ambitions at this time, the report was deeply flawed in its inclusion of vast areas, including China and Japan, in the 'outer' area. It was never fully implemented, although there was a greater FCO focus on commercial work.[39]

Despite the shift from an imperial role, colonial problems continued to demand attention. Michael Palliser, in December 1966, noted a 'tendency to let … residual colonial problems drift until some kind of crisis flares up and takes everyone by surprise'.[40] Two examples were the Falklands, where a crisis eventually occurred in 1982, and Anguilla. In the Falkland Islands dispute in the South Atlantic, Wilson and the FO hoped for a diplomatic settlement with the Argentineans, who claimed the islands, but the islanders themselves were determined to remain British. Intelligence experts did not expect an early Argentinean invasion, but feared that this could change under public pressure, especially if no diplomatic solution seemed possible.[41] Under UN pressure, talks were held in 1966–8 but, whereas the British hoped to encourage a gradual change in the islanders' attitudes, the Argentineans wanted to secure a rapid transfer of sovereignty.[42] A visit by Lord Chalfont to the Falklands in late 1968 focused media and parliamentary attention on a possible 'sell-out'. Riding low in the opinion polls, and already facing intense criticism over the Nigerian civil war, Wilson was reluctant to make an issue of what seemed a marginal problem. In Cabinet on 11 December 1968, Michael Stewart urged that a 'memorandum of understanding' be signed with Argentina, but most ministers rejected this. Stewart then assured the Commons that 'we are not prepared to make any settlement which would oblige us to hand over the islands against the wishes of the inhabitants' and the dispute remained a potential future flashpoint.[43]

The British invasion of the Caribbean island of Anguilla, in March 1969, provoked considerable criticism of the government for a time. In 1965 London had devised the status of 'associated state' for islands too small for independence: they received internal autonomy while Britain kept responsibility for external relations and defence. Anguilla (with a population of only 6,000) was part of such an associated state, but resented its subservience to the larger island of St Kitts and, in April 1967, threw out the St Kitts police force. The British encouraged talks on the future of the island, but the islanders declared their independence in January 1969. On the basis of unreliable intelligence, Stewart warned the Cabinet that 'elements from the underworld in the United States might move in' and Bill Whitlock, a junior FCO minister, was sent to assess the situation, only to be bundled off the island the day he arrived, 11 March.[44] The FCO feared that the population had been forced into independence by their new leader, Ronald Webster, backed by 'gangsters', and at a ministerial meeting on 14 March Stewart pressed for armed intervention. Healey was sceptical, wanting more time to collect intelligence, but it was decided to launch a quick invasion, which went ahead four days later, the full Cabinet not being consulted for fear of leaks.[45] A 350-man force was despatched, spearheaded by paratroops. It encountered no resistance and discovered an island quite at peace. One rifle was found – but no 'gangsters'. Considerable concern was expressed in Cabinet about the invasion being launched at all and in his memoirs Stewart conceded that Webster 'represented the real feelings of the Anguillans'.[46] Faulty intelligence, hastiness and a failure to listen to local concerns had produced a comic-opera episode that an experienced government ought to have avoided, even if it resulted in no bloodshed and was soon forgotten.

Intelligence

As Prime Minister in the 1970s, Wilson learnt of the suspicions harboured against him within the counter-intelligence service, MI5. His visits to the USSR in the 1950s had made him a potential security risk in the eyes of 'spycatchers' like Peter Wright. Only a generation later did the papers of Vasili Mitrokhin confirm that, while the KGB had entertained hopes of employing Wilson, these never bore fruit.[47] Wilson was probably unaware of suspicions against him in 1964, and he was happy to exploit MI5 reports on Communist activities during the seamen's strike of 1966.[48] But he was well aware of the security scandals that had engulfed the Macmillan administration in the early 1960s and, to prevent similar difficulties, gave George Wigg special powers in the intelligence field, so as to spot potential scandals and tighten security procedures.[49] Spy cases existed under Labour but never on the scale of the Macmillan years. The highest-profile embarrassment was the escape from Wormwood Scrubs, in 1966, of the Soviet spy George Blake. But not all threats originated with the Soviet bloc. It has been rumoured that a Cabinet minister passed information to the USA, most likely George Brown.[50] Wilson also faced a rare example of right-wing subversion against the elected government in May 1968, when there was a plot to replace him by some kind of coalition government. The scale of the plot is still far from clear.[51]

For the British espionage agency, MI6, the 1960s were a decade of uncertainty. Like MI5, it needed to recover from spy scandals of the past and doubts about its efficiency. There were also adjustments forced by the retreat from Empire and expenditure controls. In the context of both the strategic analysis of intelligence in Whitehall and the relationship with the USA, MI6, with its declining volume of assessments, lost influence to the signals intelligence body, Government Communications Headquarters (GCHQ).[52] MI6 had difficulty obtaining information from behind the Iron Curtain, especially at a high political level, but Wilson was more exasperated with failures in Africa. Not only was it difficult to penetrate the Smith regime in Rhodesia, but there was a failure to predict military coups in Ghana and Nigeria in early 1966, the last only days after Wilson had visited it. In contrast to MI5, however, MI6 had, in Dick White, an effective head. Encouraged by Burke Trend but at the cost of some resentment within MI6, White replaced many senior staff in 1966 and strengthened coverage of Africa.[53] British espionage operations against allied states are understandably difficult to uncover, but London seems to have been very well informed about Germany's negotiating position on the EEC in 1967.[54]

Information on GCHQ is similarly difficult to obtain, although the general nature of its work is clear. With a global network of listening stations as far afield as Hong Kong, Oman and Gibraltar, it intercepted signals and other communications traffic and broke the codes of foreign powers. Under the 1947 UKUSA agreements on the sharing of intelligence it also liaised closely with other signals intelligence organisations in America, Canada, Australia and New Zealand.[55] One of Wigg's reports into departmental security covered GCHQ. Among other things it reveals that the organisation employed about 8,000 staff, with another 3,500 (many seconded from the armed forces) involved in signals intelligence collection. This made it about the same size as its parent department, the FCO.[56] It is also rare to discover what precisely GCHQ's activities revealed or how particular pieces of information affected decisions. In a study of the Malaysian–Indonesian 'Confrontation', however, David Easter has shown that signals intercepts probably encouraged the British to undertake more aggressive raids across the Indonesian border in 1965, because they had a good idea of how their opponents would react.[57] Eavesdropping on diplomatic conversations and messages was probably commonplace, but few references exist to examples. An exception is the tapping of the telephone of Soviet premier Kosygin, at Claridge's Hotel in London in 1967, which has been revealed from US sources. Visiting delegations were well aware of the dangers of being 'bugged'. When Ian Smith, the Rhodesian premier, visited London in late 1965 his delegation held one conversation in the ladies' lavatories, where it was felt that even British agents would not be so indelicate as to eavesdrop.[58] In February 1967 a *Daily Express* journalist, Chapman Pincher, revealed that the British government routinely intercepted overseas cable traffic and thereby sparked the celebrated 'D notice affair'. Wilson argued that the story broke a defence ('D') notice, under which the press agreed not to comment on certain security issues, but his eagerness to pursue the *Express* raised questions about his own good judgement. Incredibly, GCHQ was never named in the affair and its activities remained unknown to the public.[59]

The most important body in Whitehall to co-ordinate activity in the field was the Joint Intelligence Committee (JIC). Meeting weekly, it approved reviews of intelligence for limited distribution, set up studies on particular problems and discussed current issues, using a range of sources, both covert and overt. It had a number of sub-committees, relied on a 'Joint Intelligence Staff' to carry out assessments and had contact with agencies in allied countries.[60] Its papers, while largely open before 1968, have been carefully weeded and its minutes are written in an elliptical way. It began life under Labour in difficult circumstances, as it had to report that the fall of Khrushchev in Moscow 'had occurred without warning' and that, in light of the first Chinese nuclear test, 'our intelligence on the production of Chinese fissile material had proved inadequate'.[61]

The main reform of the Wilson years in this area was to create a new post of Intelligence Co-ordinator, based in the Cabinet Office, in April 1968, with a simultaneous attempt to strengthen intelligence on the economic, industrial and technological side through the creation of a JIC(B) committee (the original JIC now becoming the 'A' committee). The key mover behind this was Burke Trend and the first Intelligence Co-ordinator was Dick White, who was in the unique position of having led both MI5 (1953–6) and MI6 (1956–68). The new system faced an early setback with the failure to predict the Soviet invasion of Czechoslovakia. Moreover, the JIC(B) committee seems to have been treated as a poor cousin of JIC(A) and White's transfer had the unfortunate side-effect of bringing MI6 under the direction of John Rennie, who was not too popular with his staff. Arguably the reforms did not go far enough. In particular, there was a case for removing the JIC chairmanship from the FCO, to improve its objectivity, something that was eventually done after the Falklands War.[62]

Policy co-ordination and the Cabinet

Under the British system, policy co-ordination across relevant ministries in Whitehall is through a pyramid of committees, with the Cabinet at the top, under which are ministerial committees, committees of officials, and various sub-committees and working groups, with members drawn from relevant departments. At ministerial level *ad hoc* 'miscellaneous' committees (or MISCs) are set up to deal with a particular problem and exist for a limited time. Others are more permanent, 'named' committees, recognised by their initials. The most significant of these in the international field under Wilson was the Overseas Policy and Defence Committee (OPD), set up in 1963 and chaired by the Prime Minister. As its name suggests, it had responsibility for defence matters and other overseas issues, though not all of them. Policy on European integration, for example, rarely came before it but rather had its own dedicated committees. The OPD was serviced by an inter-departmental group of officials, the OPD(O), some of whose studies were of a long-term nature. The Whitehall system sounds rational and tidy, but it does not prevent overlap, confusion and disagreement. Official committees often failed to resolve differences or produce compromise positions and appeal was possible from ministerial committees to the full Cabinet, though Wilson tried to restrict the frequency of this. On some questions the sheer scale of the problem and the breadth of its institutional impact led to a plethora of committees. On Rhodesia, for example, there were regular Cabinet discussions, a ministerial 'Rhodesia' committee, certain other ministerial committees (such as 'Rhodesia X', set up in 1965 to look at negotiations with Ian Smith, but which developed a broader remit), a steering committee of officials, a large committee concerned with sanctions and a host of others dealing with specific points like aid to Zambia or information policy.

One problem, apart from co-ordination on specific issues, was to give the machine an overall sense of direction. In addition to the studies set up by the OPD(O), the JIC kept some long-term issues under review, and the FO had its own Planning Department. The overlap between these bodies does not seem to have provoked serious problems, but planning in international affairs was notoriously difficult, thanks to the array of factors at work and the unpredictability of world events. The problems with producing a single view of the 'national interest' were further complicated by the wide range of departments that could have an impact, not only those discussed above but also, for example, the Board of Trade and Department of Economic Affairs (on international economic issues), Ministry of Technology (on multinational technological projects), Ministry of Agriculture (on the EEC's Common Agricultural Policy) and Home Office (on issues of asylum). All these departments inevitably developed their own views on what was best for Britain. At the Ministry of Technology, for example, Tony Benn held his own 'foreign policy' meetings.[63]

In a sense, all Cabinet ministers could influence foreign policy, which was regularly the second item they discussed (following parliamentary business), though it tended to slip down the agenda once the withdrawal from east of Suez was decided. But in practice there was no more than an oral update by the Foreign Secretary on the latest developments and at least one minister considered it 'more than a little pointless'. Gordon Walker admitted that, as Foreign Secretary, he often 'had a previous word with the Prime Minister about what to disclose or to keep quiet about' and that after the report there were only 'brief questions and answers'.[64] Major issues were meant to appear as a specific item on the agenda, but here too the Prime Minister could manipulate the situation. Even important topics, like the Vietnam War, rarely saw a detailed discussion. Others, such as nuclear weapons, were shunted off into ministerial committees. Furthermore, even an outspoken minister like Castle found that, especially in the early years, 'I was so absorbed with departmental work that I only superficially followed what was happening in government. Other ministers experienced the same phenomenon.'[65] This is not to say that there were no difficult moments for Wilson and his Foreign Secretaries in Cabinet. On Rhodesia, Nigeria and the Falklands they faced serious opposition at times, while in May 1967 the Cabinet forced Wilson and Brown into a reversal of policy on the Middle East. But the last proved a unique event and there were ways of reducing the dangers of such an embarrassing defeat.

Parliament, public, press and party

Beyond the machinery of government were a range of influences on
policy-making, though in the case of public opinion, press attitudes and
parliamentary votes these were generally less significant for foreign
policy than on domestic issues.[66] Foreign affairs and defence had little
impact on any of the elections in this period. In 1964, even on nuclear
defence, which the Conservatives tried to turn into a major issue, only
13 per cent of respondents expressed strong views in an NOP pole. In
1966 the resignation the Navy minister, Christopher Mayhew, only weeks
before the election, failed to focus attention on the 'east of Suez' question
in the way he hoped. The 1970 election saw quite frequent mentions of
the EEC but, since all three main parties favoured membership, there
was little controversy on the point.[67] Yet policy-makers were aware that
international matters could stir up popular concern, especially around
1967–8. Gore-Booth remembers that 'public emotion sometimes took
almost hysterical form over Vietnam, over Nigeria and Biafra, over security,
over student power'.[68] In parliament, supposedly the 'sovereign' body
in the constitution, British governments traditionally experience only
spasmodic difficulties over foreign policy. Government secrecy and day-
to-day control of international policy, lack of appropriate expertise
among most MPs and the general dominance of the executive over the
legislature are important factors creating this situation. Furthermore,
there was no Select Committee for Foreign Affairs until 1979.[69] Wilson
began with a slim majority in 1964 but was much safer after the 1966
election and the Conservatives were never a very effective opposition.
Repeatedly their leader, Edward Heath (after 1965), took a line close to
the government on the most important foreign policy issues.

Wilson became obsessed with press attitudes and 'leaks' to the newspapers, while also briefing journalists himself at times against political
rivals. Media stories, including 'instant' television images, were becoming increasingly difficult to control, even without the move to a less
deferential press–government relationship in the 1960s. This was particularly evident over Vietnam but was also true of the Nigerian civil
war, where images of starving children bred sympathy for the Biafran
secessionists. The BBC, though funded by the government, was viewed
as being 'unhelpful' on Nigeria and other issues and the FCO tried to
strengthen its methods of influencing the Corporation's news coverage.[70] But the government could generally rely on certain newspapers,
such as the *Daily Mirror* and the *Guardian*, and it is difficult to sense the
media forcing a change of policy except when it combined with parliamentary and ministerial concern, as over the Falklands. The impact of
pressure groups is similarly difficult to measure. The Confederation
of British Industry may have encouraged the move towards an EEC

application but it could not force a change in government restrictions on arms sales to South Africa in 1967, even with such allies in government as Healey and Brown. Promotional groups, dedicated to a particular 'cause', were vocal on the EEC (the European Movement), Nigeria (the Committee for Peace in Nigeria being the best known) and Vietnam (with a number of anti-war groups) but again none had a discernible impact on policy decisions, even if they did make the government careful about the way policy was presented.

By far the greatest problem for Wilson outside the government machine was his own party, especially the left. While they did not want to replace Wilson, who had been 'their' candidate to succeed Gaitskell, they did want him to follow a more internationalist, anti-capitalist, even anti-American policy. There were also some right-wingers who were critical, especially of the failure to withdraw from east of Suez more quickly. The 1960s saw several revolts against government policy by the party conference, and votes went against Wilson on Vietnam, defence expenditure, Biafra and continued links to Greece after the military coup of 1967. But the conferences were intermittent events, whose resolutions could easily be ignored by the government. As to Labour's National Executive Committee, it was effectively dominated by a mixture of government ministers and pro-Wilson trade unionists, while Labour's head office at Transport House was sidelined on international subjects. The real headache was the Parliamentary Labour Party (PLP), where backbenchers regularly attacked the government in meetings. Sometimes the Prime Minister himself stepped in to try to stem the discontent. Thus, in early February 1966 – with a general election looming – he addressed the PLP for forty-five minutes on Vietnam, having insisted that all the Cabinet be present to support him.[71] Party discipline worsened after the 1966 election, partly because MPs felt they could indulge in dissent when there was a larger majority. In March 1967 Wilson became so exasperated with revolts over Vietnam, the EEC and defence that he reminded the PLP of his right to call a general election.[72] In the event, on none of these issues were Labour rebels willing to risk bringing the government down, mainly because this could have benefited only the Conservatives.

The US connection

'Almost every British policy will react in one way or another upon our relations with the USA', wrote Gordon Walker in the August before the 1964 election. He believed that, 'If we are dependent upon US for ultimate nuclear protection, we must so arrange our relations with the US that our share in the pattern of US alliance is as indispensable as we

can make it'. That same month, a paper by the FO Planning Department called the alliance with Washington 'the most important single
factor in our foreign policy'.[73] The USA's influence on particular areas
of policy will be dealt with in individual chapters but, given its importance,
some general points are appropriate here. The existence of the 'special
relationship' is subject to considerable debate, touching on such complex
issues as belief systems, cultural ties, linguistic and emotional links.[74] It
may have existed during the Second World War but even then it was
more important to London, as a way of dealing with US power, than it
was to Washington. After 1945 there were grave problems over the Korean
War in 1950 and Suez in 1956 but co-operation on nuclear, monetary
and intelligence matters was generally close and differences on Atlantic
defence were usually overcome without grave divisions. The Macmillan
government conceived a policy of 'interdependence', by which the USA
would be led to consult with Britain on international questions because
of a web of common interests and institutions. Despite some anti-
Americanism on the left, much of the Labour Party was well disposed
to Washington. In part this was due to the legacy of the Attlee years,
when the Atlantic alliance had been founded, and in part it reflected
the moderate nature of Labour's socialism and the bipartisan approach
to foreign policy in Britain since 1945, but it was also because Labour
leaders hoped to influence US policy. Steven Fielding has shown that
the USA was particularly influential on Labour right-of-centre 'revisionists'
like Healey and Jenkins, as well as Gaitskell. Whereas the left criticised
US capitalism and Cold War policies, the revisionists admired America
for its liberalism.[75]

By the mid-1960s Britain was becoming merely one US ally among
many and was far less powerful than its transatlantic partner. Several
countries, such as Germany and Israel, could claim a 'special relationship'
of sorts and, from the US perspective, British claims to a privileged
position were embarrassing in dealings with other allies. With good
reason, C. J. Bartlett sees a marked decline in the relationship in 1966–8
owing to the British refusal to fight in Vietnam, their retreat from east
of Suez and the devaluation of the pound. It is a point echoed in other
accounts and supposedly symbolised by the singing of 'I've Got Plenty
of Nothing' when Wilson visited President Lyndon Johnson in February
1968.[76] Alan Dobson shares the approach, but makes an interesting distinction between the declining *importance* of the relationship, as Britain
became less significant in world affairs, and its *quality*, which could still
be considered good given the continued willingness of individuals to
work together closely. It is an idea echoed in Johnson's remark to the
journalist Henry Brandon, in February 1968, that Britain and the USA
'will always remain friends. But, of course, when our common interests
shrink, the flow of communications and common business shrinks too.'

Yet Henry Kissinger, appointed President Richard Nixon's National Security Adviser in 1969, believed that 'the special relationship with Britain was peculiarly impervious to abstract theory', or to particular crises, and he told the President, 'we do not suffer from such an excess of friends that we should discourage those who feel that they have a special friendship for us'.[77]

Ritchie Ovendale considers that Wilson began to redefine the relationship in late 1964, by publicly stating that there was 'not ... a special relationship but ... a close relationship'. But John Baylis judges that the Prime Minister's change to the description of the relationship was 'more verbal than substantive'. Wilson wanted regular meetings with the President and at one point was rumoured to have discussed the idea of Britain becoming the 'fifty-first state'.[78] Where leading personalities are concerned, the real controversy surrounds Johnson's view of the Prime Minister. There is general agreement that Wilson's relations with Johnson were much less good than the former believed them to be.[79] When Labour was elected, the reaction of US officials was hardly ecstatic and the President may have been influenced by reports to the effect that Wilson was devious and untrustworthy, and that he was a security risk because of his supposed affair with Marcia Williams.[80] Then again, a detailed study by Saki Dockrill suggests that the first Wilson–Johnson summit, in December 1964, went well.[81] It is difficult to disagree with the judgement that 'no personal rapport developed between the rough-spoken Texan and the wily British Prime Minister' but Johnson's precise attitude to Wilson is hard to fathom.[82] Under-Secretary of State George Ball believed 'Johnson took an almost instant dislike to [Wilson]', but the President, a touchy individual, more at home in domestic politics, did not much like the process of negotiating with any foreign leaders. Compared to many of them, Wilson was treated well enough. Canada's Prime Minister Lester Pearson in April 1965 found himself bitterly criticised by Johnson over a speech that urged negotiations on Vietnam. The President also abruptly cancelled summits with the Indian and Pakistani leaders in 1965 and upset King Faisal of Saudi Arabia by arriving late for a reception the following year.[83]

It should also be noted that personal relations between Johnson and Downing Street had deteriorated before Wilson took office, when Douglas-Home visited Washington in February 1964 and publicly differed with an outraged Johnson over the sale of British buses to Cuba.[84] Under Wilson they may even have improved, even if they always fell far short of the intimacy the Prime Minister craved. Sylvia Ellis, despite tending towards a negative view of the personal relationship, acknowledges that their summits often proved successful. The first went well partly because Vietnam was not yet pressing; the next, in April 1965, saw Johnson agree to let Wilson explore the possibilities of a

Vietnam peace; and, following their December 1965 meeting, relations
looked 'quite rosy'. The President even took his guest to the switching
on of the White House Christmas tree lights. The last British leader to
have that honour was Churchill, back in 1944. US ambassador David
Bruce reported that Johnson was 'favourably impressed' by Wilson on
the December visit. Ellis sees the chance of a friendly relationship
evaporating in June 1966, when Wilson criticised US bombing of North
Vietnam, and yet it was during their July 1966 summit that Johnson
compared his guest (indirectly) to Churchill. Afterwards, Johnson was
reported to have said of Wilson, 'I really do like that man'.[85] In their
short June 1967 summit their views were close on the pressing issue of
the day, Arab–Israeli tension. And at their sixth, and final, summit, in
February 1968, Johnson avoided mention of Britain's decision to hasten
its retreat from east of Suez, even though the USA had spoken against
this for years. Mrs Johnson's diary of the February visit suggests a warm
occasion in which the President, though preoccupied with Vietnam, insisted
that Wilson have an impromptu lunch at the White House.[86] Furthermore, in 1971, when both leaders were out of office, Wilson was invited
to stay at Johnson's Texas ranch, hardly an act that suggests personal
animosity. Meanwhile, whatever the truth about the personal relationship, there are US documents that suggest the inter-governmental
relationship was still significant. 'At no time in the post-war period have
our relations with the United Kingdom been closer … since Labour
took office in … 1964', declared a State Department memorandum in
1967, which emphasised that this was due to common interests world-
wide, not mere sentiment. In early 1968 another memorandum noted
that, 'The special relationship has been pronounced dead as often as
Martin Bormann has been reported alive. Indeed, perhaps the best
evidence that it is still alive is the fact that its detractors feel obliged to
re-announce its death every few months.'[87]

    There is general agreement that the Wilson–Nixon relationship was
quite good, though it may have been no better than that between Johnson
and Wilson. Certainly there was no great warmth between Nixon and
Wilson. The President recoiled from the latter's suggestion, made at
their first meeting, that they use first names.[88] Relations almost got off
to a bad start because, before Nixon's victory could be predicted, Wilson
had decided to appoint an old political ally, John Freeman, to be ambassador to Washington. But in 1962 Freeman had described Nixon as 'a
man of no principle' and it was feared the latter would now reject the
appointment. When Nixon visited London in February 1969, however,
he said that worse things had been written about him and that the past
was best forgotten. Wilson passed a note to the President describing
this as 'one of the kindest and most generous acts I have known in a
quarter of a century in politics'. The Prime Minister had every right to

be relieved. He had done all he could to get the new relationship off to a good start, inviting Nixon to a meeting with ministers in the Cabinet room, as well as one-to-one talks at Chequers.[89] The two leaders maintained the frequency of summits of the Johnson years, with the difference that Nixon did not at all mind foreign travel. As well as visiting London in February, he stopped at Mildenhall airbase to see Wilson in August, when en route to Washington from Romania. Downing Street does seem to have sensed a lack of warmth from the new administration, but this may have been due to oversensitivity on Wilson's part, since Freeman took a very different view. Delays to a prime ministerial visit to Washington in 1969 were mostly due to Wilson's inability to make suggested dates.[90] When he finally visited Washington in January 1970 Nixon repaid him handsomely for the Downing Street talks by having him attend a National Security Council meeting. Wilson told the Cabinet that it was 'by far the best visit I have had to the US' and that he had deeply impressed the President, though some ministers felt he was only engaging his Walter Mitty side.[91] In the 1970 election Kissinger was determined not to be seen taking sides but Nixon was evidently pleased with the Conservative victory.[92]

Two examples of the inter-relationship of British and US interests, not discussed elsewhere in this volume, are British Guiana and Diego Garcia. They are evidence of the geographical scope of the Anglo-American connection and of the importance of defence and intelligence links. They also illustrate the point made by William Louis and Ronald Robinson that, as it declined, the British Empire, rather than fading away, was reshaped under US pressure and sometimes 'internationalised' as part of an Anglo-American condominium.[93] The US government was concerned at what might occur in the wake of a British withdrawal from its remaining colonies in the Caribbean, especially with Cuba already presenting a regional problem. British Guiana had been promised independence in 1960, but there were ethnic divisions, which led to sporadic violence between the African-American and East Indian communities. More important, the radical leanings of the East Indian leader, Cheddi Jagan, aroused the suspicions of the US government. As Prime Minister in 1961–4 Jagan developed ties to Cuba and the British Conservative government, goaded by Washington, introduced a new electoral system based on proportional representation, designed to boost the election chances of his opponents.[94] The Americans pressed Wilson to maintain Conservative policy, including close co-operation with the US Central Intelligence Agency (CIA) to undermine Jagan by covert means. Minutes of a meeting in November 1964 show that senior ministers were well aware of CIA activities and that Wilson 'was unhappy that these American operations could take place on British territory'; but it was argued that Jagan was receiving money from Cuba, that the

CIA operations were unobtrusive and that, 'Since the CIA would run agents in British Guiana whatever the British might do, it was better to work with them rather than break off contact'.[95] London would have faced a real crisis if Jagan had won the general election in December 1964; the government would have been caught between its commitment to grant independence and its desire to please the Americans.[96] As it was, the election brought to power an African-American coalition under Forbes Burnham and the country became independent in May 1966. To Jagan, who had hoped for a change of policy when Wilson took office, there had been a 'cynical betrayal of our cause'; Labour had 'completely succumbed to US pressure based on cold war and anti-Castro fears'.[97] But, for the British, facing dire colonial problems in Aden and Rhodesia, the independence of Guyana can only be deemed a success given the potential problems of inter-ethnic violence that had been evaded.

Another way in which Britain helped to meet US security needs was to develop the Indian Ocean island of Diego Garcia as an air base, which filled a significant gap in the USA's global communications. The idea of a base had been explored under Douglas-Home. To the OPD, meeting in April 1965, it made perfect sense because it was desirable to get the USA committed, alongside Britain, to the defence of the Indian Ocean. Washington agreed to share the costs of setting up the base by waiving part of the cost of the Polaris missile system, a fact that was kept secret from Congress.[98] In September 1965 Britain ended the island's status as a dependency of Mauritius (a colony that became independent in March 1968), paying the Mauritian government compensation in return for its accommodating the islanders. Two months later, London turned Diego Garcia and the rest of the Chagos Archipelago into a new colony, the 'British Indian Ocean Territory', which also included islands detached from the Seychelles. In 1968 it was confirmed that the USA wanted to use Diego Garcia and a base was constructed in the 1970s. US interest in the Indian Ocean increased as the British withdrew.[99] Yet this decision, relatively minor at the time, would be remembered long after most of the Wilson governments' other international actions were forgotten. For the islanders were viewed as virtual 'un-people' and were removed against the will of many. Diego Garcia was remote and its population only about a thousand. But there can be no doubt that the expulsion breached the UN Declaration on Human Rights because, while London and Washington tried to pretend the population were all temporary workers on plantations, some families had lived there for two generations.[100] It led to the British government's embarrassing defeat in a court case in November 2000.

Notes

Unless otherwise stated the place of publication is London.

1 Quotes from: Anthony Shrimsley, *The First Hundred Days of Harold Wilson* (Weidenfeld and Nicolson, 1965), xi; James Griffiths, *Pages from Memory* (Dent, 1969), 193; David Owen, *Time to Declare* (Michael Joseph, 1991), 91; Richard Crossman, *The Diaries of a Cabinet Minister, Volume II: Lord President of the Council and Leader of the House of Commons 1966–8* (Hamish Hamilton and Jonathan Cape, 1976), 76–7.

2 Brian Lapping, *The Labour Government, 1964–1970* (Penguin, Harmondsworth, 1970), 59–108; Desmond Donnelly, *Gadarene '68* (William Kimber, 1968), especially chapters 5, 6 and 8; Paul Foot, *The Politics of Harold Wilson* (Penguin, Harmondsworth, 1968), especially chapters 7–9. On policy in opposition see Peter Catterall, 'The Labour Party', in Wolfram Kaiser and Gillian Staerck, eds., *British Foreign Policy, 1955–64* (Palgrave, 2000), chapter 5.

3 John Pilger, *Hidden Agendas* (Verso, 1998), 139; Clive Ponting, *Breach of Promise: Labour in power 1964–1970* (Hamish Hamilton, 1989), 397–406 (quote from 399); Chris Wrigley, 'Now you see it, now you don't: Harold Wilson and Labour's foreign policy', in P. Coopey, S. Fielding and N. Tiratsoo, eds., *The Wilson Governments, 1964–70* (Pinter, 1993), 123–32.

4 Edward Short, *Whip to Wilson* (MacDonald, 1989), 21; Wrigley, 'Now you see it', 125–7; Austen Morgan, *Harold Wilson* (Pluto, 1992), 339.

5 There are three substantial biographies: Morgan, *Wilson*, is quite critical; Ben Pimlott, *Harold Wilson* (Harper Collins, 1992), is quite sympathetic; and Philip Ziegler, *Wilson: the authorised life* (Weidenfeld and Nicolson, 1993), benefits from access to Wilson's papers.

6 Frank Longford, *The Grain of Wheat: an autobiography* (Catholic Book Club, 1974), 68–73; Frank Longford, *Eleven at Number Ten* (Harrap, 1984), 119–20; Owen, *Time*, 100–1; Peter Hennessy, *The Prime Minister* (Allen Lane, 2000), chapter 12 (quote from 310).

7 Sandy Gall, *Don't Worry About the Money Now* (Hamilton, 1983), 202; Michael Foot, *Harold Wilson* (Penguin, Harmondsworth, 1964), 16; Wrigley, 'Now you see it', 133.

8 Andrew Roth, *Harold Wilson: Yorkshire Walter Mitty* (Macdonald, 1977), 6 and 53.

9 Peter Hennessy, *Whitehall* (Secker and Warburg, 1989), 212–18; Hugo Young, *This Blessed Plot: Britain and Europe from Churchill to Blair* (Macmillan, 1998), 176–7 and 225.

10 The merger of the Colonial Office with the Commonwealth Relations Office, and the subsequent merger with the Foreign Office to become the Foreign and Commonwealth Office, are outlined below.

11 Hennessy, *Whitehall*, 189; George Ball, *The Past Has Another Pattern* (Norton, New York, 1982), 336.

12 Patrick Gordon Walker, *The Commonwealth* (Secker and Warburg, 1962), especially chapters 23–24; FCO historians, *The Permanent Under-Secretary* (FCO, 2002), 37–8; quote from Avi Shlaim, Peter Jones and Keith Sainsbury, *British Foreign Secretaries Since 1945* (David and Charles, 1977), 190.

13 From August 1966 to March 1968 Stewart was Secretary for Economic Affairs.

14 Bryan Gould, *Goodbye To All That* (Macmillan, 1995), 54; Roy Jenkins, *A Life at the Centre* (Macmillan, 1991), 234–5; Barbara Castle, *Fighting all the Way* (Weidenfeld and Nicolson, 1993), 382–3.

15 Michael Stewart, *Life and Labour* (Sidgwick and Jackson, 1980), chapters 7 and 9; Nicholas Henderson, *Inside the Private Office* (Academy, Chicago, 1987), chapter 8; Short, *Whip*, 33.

16 Peter Paterson, *Tired and Emotional: the life of Lord George Brown* (Chatto and Windus, 1993), chapter 7; Pimlott, *Wilson*, 329–32.

17 George Brown, *In My Way* (Gollancz, 1971), 129–34 and 155–66 (quote from 163); Paul Gore-Booth, *With Great Truth and Respect* (Constable, 1974), 407–12. And see Geoffrey Moorhouse, *The Diplomats: the Foreign Office today* (Jonathan Cape, 1977), 165–7; John Dickie, *Inside the Foreign Office* (Chapmans, 1992), 96–101.

18 Paterson, *Tired*, 207; Young, *Blessed Plot*, 198; FCO historians, *Permanent Under-Secretary*, 38–40.

19 Alun Chalfont, *The Shadow of My Hand* (Weidenfeld and Nicolson, 2000), 127–8; Paterson, *Tired*, 195–7 (on Sunay), 208–9 and 213–15.

20 Chalfont, *Shadow*, 126; and, for example, the following Palliser notes to Wilson in 1967: Public Record Office (PRO), PREM 13/1476 (26 January); PREM 13/1482 (13 May); PREM 13/1484 (20 July); and PREM 13/1487 (2 December).

21 For example, PREM 13/2517, Halls to Wilson (16 March), forwarding plans to invade Anguilla.

22 For reviews of the evidence: Paterson, *Tired*, chapter 13; Pimlott, *Wilson*, 494–503.

23 Shlaim *et al.*, *British*, 220; Anthony Adamthwaite, 'Anglo-French relations and Britain's second EEC membership bid,' in Oliver Daddow, ed., *Harold Wilson and European Integration: Britain's second application to join the EEC* (Frank Cass, 2002), 169.

24 PREM 13/905, Wright to Wilson (28 January); PREM 13/1984, Palliser to Wilson (23 December).

25 Peter Stanford, *Lord Longford* (Heinemann, 1994), 347–51.

26 Castle, *Fighting*, 344 and 352; Ponting, *Breach*, 215–18; and see D. J. Morgan, *The Official History of Colonial Development, Volume IV: changes in British aid policy, 1951–70* (Stationery Office, 1980), chapter 2.

27 Chalfont, *Shadow*, 88–9.

28 On Healey's performance see: Peter Nailor, 'Denis Healey and rational decision-making in defence', in Ian Beckett and John Gooch, eds., *Politicians and Defence* (Manchester University Press, Manchester, 1981), 154–77; Geoffrey Williams and Bruce Reed, *Denis Healey and the Policies of Power* (Sidgwick and Jackson, 1971), chapters 8–11; Edward Pearce, *Denis Healey* (Little, Brown, Boston, 2002), chapters 30–41.

29 PRO, CAB 148/18, OPD(65)28th (2 June); CAB 148/21, OPD(65)89th (31 May) and see CAB 148/22, OPD(65)127th (14 September). Statistics from Morgan, *Colonial Development*, 1–2. For a brief review of colonial policy under Labour, see W. David McIntyre, *British Decolonization, 1946–97* (Macmillan, 1998), chapter 5.

30 On the mergers see: Joe Garner, *The Commonwealth Office 1925–68* (Heinemann, 1978), 406–21; J. D. B. Miller, *Survey of Commonwealth Affairs: problems of expansion and attrition, 1953–69* (Oxford University Press, Oxford, 1974), 401–7; and Gore-Booth, *Great Truth*, 386–91.

31 Gerard Noel, *Harold Wilson and the 'New Britain'* (Gollancz, 1964), 149–50 and 158.

32 In general see John Darwin, *Britain and Decolonisation* (Macmillan, 1988), 297–307.

33 Miller, *Survey*, 293–4, 296 and 300–6; Yusuf Bandura, *Britain and*

Commonwealth Africa: the politics of economic relations 1951–75 (Manchester University Press, Manchester, 1983), 78–82, 111–13, 181 and see chapter 6.

34 On the formation of the secretariat see: Garner, *Commonwealth Office*, 351–4; Miller, *Survey*, 397–401; Arnold Smith, *Stitches in Time* (Andre Deutsch, 1981), chapter 1; and David McIntyre, 'Britain and the creation of the Commonwealth secretariat', *Journal of Imperial and Commonwealth History*, vol. 28, no. 1 (2000), 135–58.

35 Smith, *Stitches*, 65; Bandura, *Commonwealth Africa*, 107–11.

36 PRO, FCO 49/7, *passim*, especially SC(67)92nd (2 February). The eventual report was a compromise: CAB 129/129, C(67)59 (24 April).

37 Miller, *Survey*, 363–5.

38 CAB 129/135, C(68)42 (23 February); and see FCO 49/13.

39 CAB 128/43, CC(68)5th (12 January); *Report of the Review Committee on Overseas Representation* (Cmnd 4107, 1969). For discussions see: Geoffrey McDermott, *The New Diplomacy* (Plume Press, 1973), 85–90; Moorhouse, *Diplomats*, 25–29; Dickie, *Inside*, 62–5.

40 PREM 13/1984, Palliser to Wilson (23 December).

41 CAB 158/54, JIC(64)79th (16 November 1964), CAB 158/66, JIC(67)21st (20 January 1967) and CAB 158/71, JIC(68)43rd (5 June 1968).

42 See especially FCO 7/140, record of a meeting on 12 January 1967 (dated 17 January), and Buenos Aires to FO, 14 May 1967; CAB 128/43, CC24(68), 28 March.

43 *House of Commons Debates*, vol. 775, columns 607–13. The Cabinet record has been withheld but see: Tony Benn, *Office Without Power: diaries 1968–72* (Hutchinson, 1988), 133–4; Barbara Castle, *The Castle Diaries 1964–70* (Weidenfeld and Nicolson, 1984), 568–9.

44 CAB 128/44, CC11 and 12(69) (6 and 12 March).

45 CAB 148/91, OPD(69)3rd and 4th, confidential annexes (14 and 18 March); Richard Crossman, *The Diaries of a Cabinet Minister, Volume III: Secretary of State for Social Services 1968–1970* (Hamish Hamilton and Jonathan Cape, 1977), 415–16.

46 CAB 128/44, CC13 and 14(69) (20 and 25 March); Crossman, *Diaries III*, 421–3; Stewart, *Life*, 246–7.

47 Christopher Andrew and Vasili Mitrokhin, *The Mitrokhin Archive* (Allen Lane, 1999), 528–9. And see David Leigh, *The Wilson Plot* (Heinemann, 1988), especially chapters 5–9; Stephen Dorril and Robin Ramsay, *Smear! Wilson and the secret state* (Fourth Estate, 1992).

48 Keir Thorpe, 'The 1966 state of emergency and the Wilson government's response to the seamen's strike', *Twentieth Century British History*, vol. 12, no. 4 (2001), especially 482–4.

49 John W. Young, 'George Wigg, the Wilson government and the 1966 report into security in the diplomatic service and GCHQ', *Intelligence and National Security*, vol. 14, no. 3 (1999), 198–208.

50 Chapman Pincher, *Inside Story* (Sidgwick and Jackson, 1978), 160; Tom Bower, *The Perfect English Spy* (Heinemann, 1995), 356. But see Dorril and Ramsay, *Smear!*, 165–6 and 355, note 19.

51 Barry Penrose and Roger Courtiour, *The Pencourt File* (Secker and Warburg, 1986), 316–18; Dorril and Ramsey, *Smear!*, 173–85.

52 Nigel West, *The Friends* (Weidenfeld and Nicolson, 1988), 167–8.

53 Bower, *English Spy*, 341–58; Stephen Dorril, *MI6* (Fourth Estate, 2000), 724–5.

54 It is probably best not to specify where this evidence can be found.

55 See James Bamford, *The Puzzle Palace* (Houghton Mifflin, Boston, 1982),

xii–xxiii and 331–5; and Jeffrey Richelson and Desmond Ball, *The Ties That Bind* (2nd edition) (Allen and Unwin, 1990), especially chapters 2, 7 and 8.

56 Young, 'George Wigg', 203–8.

57 David Easter, 'British intelligence and propaganda during the Confrontation, 1963–6', *Intelligence and National Security*, vol. 16, no. 2 (2001), 88–90.

58 Philip Kaiser, *Journeying Far and Wide* (Scribner's, New York, 1992), 221; George Herring, *The Secret Diplomacy of the Vietnam War* (University of Texas Press, Austin, 1983), 468–9; Andrew Skeen, *Prelude to Independence* (Nasionale Boekhandel, Bloemfontein, 1966), 70.

59 Matthew Creevy, 'A critical review of the Wilson government's handling of the D-notice affair 1967', *Intelligence and National Security*, vol. 14, no. 3 (1999), 209–27.

60 Percy Cradock, *Know Your Enemy: how the Joint Intelligence Committee saw the world* (John Murray, 2002), 262–4.

61 CAB 159/42, JIC(64)52nd (22 October).

62 John W. Young, 'The Wilson government's reform of intelligence co-ordination, 1963–6', *Intelligence and National Security*, vol. 16, no. 2 (2001), 133–4; Cradock, *Enemy*, 264–7.

63 Benn, *Office*, 285.

64 Richard Marsh, *Off the Rails* (Weidenfeld and Nicolson, 1978), 90–1; Patrick Gordon Walker, *The Cabinet* (Jonathan Cape, 1970), 115.

65 Castle, *Fighting*, 348.

66 In general see: David Vital, *The Making of British Foreign Policy* (George Allen and Unwin, 1968); James Barber, *Who Makes British Foreign Policy?* (Open University Press, Milton Keynes, 1976).

67 D. E. Butler and Anthony King, *The British General Election of 1964* (Macmillan, 1965), 128–31; D. E. Butler and Anthony King, *The British General Election of 1966* (Macmillan, 1966), 117–18; D. E. Butler and Michael Pinschinsky, *The British General Election of 1970* (Macmillan, 1971), 438 and 442.

68 Gore-Booth, *Great Truth*, 394–5, 416–17 and 424–5.

69 See Peter Richards, *Parliament and Foreign Affairs* (George Allen and Unwin, 1967); Charles Carstairs and Richard Ware, eds., *Parliament and International Relations* (Open University Press, Milton Keynes, 1991), introduction and chapters 1–4.

70 For example, FCO 26/473, Johnston minute (3 April 1969).

71 Labour History Archive, Manchester, PLP minutes, 1962–71 file, minutes of 2 February 1966; Richard Crossman, *The Diaries of a Cabinet Minister, Volume I: Minister of Housing 1964–66* (Hamish Hamilton and Jonathan Cape, 1975), 444; Castle, *Diaries*, 214; and in general, Craig Wilson, *Rhetoric, Reality and Dissent: the foreign policy of the British Labour government, 1964–70* (PhD, Washington State University, 1982).

72 Vital, *Foreign Policy*, 76–7.

73 Robert Pearce, ed., *Patrick Gordon Walker, Political Diaries, 1932–71* (Historians' Press, 1991), 299; FO 371/177830/7A, SC(64)30 (21 August).

74 See especially John Dumbrell, *A Special Relationship: Anglo-American relations in the Cold War and after* (Macmillan, 2001), chapters 1–2.

75 Nigel Ashton, *Kennedy, Macmillan and the Cold War: the irony of interdependence* (Macmillan, 2002); Peter Jones, *America and the British Labour Party* (Tauris, 1997), 124; Steven Fielding, 'Labour revisionists and the imagining of America', in Jonathan Hollowell, ed., *Twentieth Century Anglo-American Relations* (Macmillan, 2001), chapter 5.

76 C. J. Bartlett, *The Special Relationship* (Macmillan, 1992), 109–18; David Dimbleby and David Reynolds, *An Ocean Apart* (BBC Books, 1988), 256; Dumbrell, *Special Relationship*, 72;

77 Alan Dobson, *Anglo-American Relations in the Twentieth Century* (Routledge, 1995), 138; Henry Brandon, *Special Relationships* (Macmillan, 1988), 231; Henry Kissinger, *The White House Years* (Little, Brown, Boston, 1979), 90–1.

78 Ritchie Ovendale, *Anglo-American Relations in the Twentieth Century* (Macmillan, 1998), 132; John Baylis, *Anglo-American Defence Relations* (Macmillan, 1984), 151–2; Dumbrell, *Special Relationship*, 63–4.

79 For example: Raymond Seitz, *Over Here* (Phoenix, 1998), 316; Jones, *America*, 172–4; and see Sylvia Ellis, 'Lyndon Johnson, Harold Wilson and the Vietnam War,' in Hollowell, ed., *Anglo-American*, 182–3.

80 Ellis, 'Vietnam War', 189–90; Leigh, *Wilson Plot*, 69; Anthony Summers, *Official and Confidential: the secret life of J. Edgar Hoover* (Corgi, 1994), 427–8.

81 Saki Dockrill, 'Forging the Anglo-American global defence partnership: Harold Wilson, Lyndon Johnson and the Washington summit, December 1964', *Journal of Strategic Studies*, vol. 23, no. 4 (2000), 107–29.

82 Dimbleby and Reynolds, *Ocean Apart*, 247.

83 Ball, *Past*, 336; Elmer Plischke, 'Lyndon Johnson as diplomat in chief', in Bernard Firestone and Robert Vogt, eds., *Lyndon Baines Johnson and the Uses of Power* (Columbia University Press, New York, 1988), especially 265–9; Lester Pearson, *Mike: the memoirs of Lester B. Pearson, Volume III, 1957–68* (Gollancz, 1975), 138–43.

84 Ovendale, *Anglo-American Relations*, 136; John Dickie, *Special No More: Anglo-American relations* (Weidenfeld and Nicolson, 1994), 133–4.

85 Ellis, 'Vietnam War', 184–7 and 192–200; Pimlott, *Wilson*, 366; Virginia Historical Society, Richmond, David Bruce diary (17 December); PREM 13/1262, Dean to Maclehose (3 August).

86 CAB 128/43, CC13(68) (15 February); Lady Bird Johnson, *A White House Diary* (Weidenfeld and Nicolson, 1970), 629–32.

87 Truman Library, Independence, Philip Kaiser papers, box 8, research memorandum (7 February 1968); US National Archives (USNA), RG59, State Department, Office of the Executive Secretariat, Conference Files, box 444 (lot 67 D 586), Scope Paper (April 1967).

88 Kissinger, *White House*, 92. For discussions see Dickie, *Special No More*, 143–4; Bartlett, *Special Relationship*, 127–30; Robin Renwick, *Fighting with Allies* (Macmillan, 1996), 202–7.

89 Richard Nixon, *The Memoirs of Richard Nixon* (Book Club Associates, 1978), 370–1; CAB 128/44, CC10(69) (27 February); Kissinger, *White House*, 89–96.

90 See especially PREM 13/3428, Wilson to Freeman (5 November) and reply (17 November).

91 CAB 128/44, CC6(70) (5 February); PREM 13/3428, records of meetings (27–28 January); Castle, *Diaries*, 759 (including quote); Crossman, *Diaries III*, 807; Kissinger, *White House*, 416–18.

92 USNA, Nixon Presidential Materials Project, White House Central Files, Subject Files, box 80, C160 (UK), Kissinger to Hullin (28 April); Kissinger, *White House*, 418–19.

93 William Roger Louis and Ronald Robinson, 'The imperialism of decolonization', *Journal of Imperial and Commonwealth History*, vol. 22, no. 3 (1994), 462–512.

94 See especially Cary Fraser, 'The new frontier of Empire in the Caribbean: the transfer of power in British Guiana, 1961–4', *International History Review*, vol. 22, no. 3 (2000), 583–610.

95 Fraser, 'British Guiana', 606–7; USNA, RG59, State Department, Central Policy Files 1964–6, box 2777, POL 7 UK, London to State (23 October); PRO, DEFE 25/135, record of meeting (25 November).
96 FO 371/178907/162, brief for Gordon Walker (21 October).
97 Cheddi Jagan, *The West on Trial* (Michael Joseph, 1966), 372.
98 CAB 148/18, OPD(65)21st (12 April); CAB 148/30, OPD(67)20th (25 May 1967); *Foreign Relations of the United States* (*FRUS*), 1964–8, vol. XXI (US Government Printing Office, Washington, DC, 2000), 83–97.
99 PREM 13/2565, Stewart to Wilson (25 July 1968); *FRUS*, vol. XXI, 103–17.
100 See especially PREM 13/2565, Stewart to Wilson (21 April 1969); Ponting, *Breach*, 234–7.

2

Economics, defence and withdrawal from east of Suez

On defence, the Wilson governments appear in retrospect as lacking in direction, forced from one round of expenditure reductions to the next, vainly resisting pressures to abandon the world role until overwhelmed by monetary crisis in 1967. This paralleled the economic situation, where there were recurrent monetary crises, with sterling in trouble from the day the government entered office, until devaluation was reluctantly accepted. David Reynolds has described the period as 'a last, desperate effort to maintain Britain's global role, or at least the status symbols of that role – the parity of Sterling and the commitment east of Suez'. This chapter focuses on the broad shape of defence policy, especially from the perspective of the withdrawal from east of Suez. While there are references to the political situation in South-East Asia, Aden and Europe, detailed events in those regions are covered in subsequent chapters. A separate volume in this series surveys economic policy in detail but it is essential to provide some background on economic policy in order to understand the defence decisions. As Michael Palliser once said, 'one cannot understand the Wilson government's conduct of its foreign policy without constantly remembering that it had to be done under a permanent economic thundercloud' that 'restricted the ... room for manoeuvre ... and complicated ... external relationships'.[1] The USA in particular was asked to bolster Britain's financial position and this in turn gave Washington a degree of influence over British policy.

While treating economics and defence together, it is essential to recognise that non-economic motives also influenced the withdrawal from east of Suez. European empires were in retreat generally and there was a specific aversion to colonialism in the Labour Party. Such political factors may have made leaders less willing to resist economic pressures to reduce commitments. Some may interpret this as a lack of 'will', others as a timely adjustment to realities. Throughout 1964–70 the link between defence spending and economic performance was taken as axiomatic, but so too was the need to reduce the dangers of conflict and rely more on allies in the defence field, while somehow safeguarding those elusive

31

elements 'influence' and 'prestige'. An over-hasty retreat could lead to regional instability, offend allies and harm Britain's reputation. These various pressures had been recognised under previous Conservative administrations, under which defence spending came to absorb 7 per cent of gross national product. Overseas expenditure in a wider sense included diplomatic representation and foreign aid as well. Not only did it represent a demand on the Treasury, but it was also a balance of payments burden of about £400 million per year because of the expenditure in other countries that was involved. Some Cabinet ministers wanted to reduce this burden, retreat from global military commitments and make a bid for membership of the European Economic Community (EEC), arguing that membership would benefit the economy and allow Britain to arrest the decline of its global influence.

Most studies see the withdrawal from east of Suez as a gradual process, but some see particular moments as more important than others. Jeffrey Pickering has emphasised the January 1968 decision to pull out of South-East Asia and the Persian Gulf by the end of 1971 as the real turning point. This is supported by George Thomson, the Commonwealth Secretary at the time, who once said that 'the moment of truth came in the 1967–8 period following the devaluation'. But in an early account David Greenwood, a former Ministry of Defence (MOD) official, argued that what occurred in 1968 was an 'acceleration' of earlier decisions, notably those of the July 1967 White Paper, which aimed at withdrawal from east of Suez by the mid-1970s. This argument is powerfully supported by Saki Dockrill, who, in the first book-length study based on archival evidence, shows that some ministers interpreted that White Paper as implying a complete withdrawal as early as 1973. Others emphasise the precursors even to the 1967 White Paper. Matthew Jones points out that the Macmillan government was already looking at withdrawal from South-East Asia in the early 1960s, before calculations were upset by the Indonesian–Malaysian 'Confrontation'. Again, there is a contemporary witness to support this line: C. W. Wright, another MOD official, recalled that withdrawal was a serious issue 'before the Confrontation but it had to be dropped' while Indonesia remained a threat.[2] Before proceeding, it is also important to grasp that Britain's world role depended not just on holding military facilities, but also on appropriate types of equipment, such as aircraft carriers and long-range aircraft. Also, there was always the possibility of remaining east of Suez at a lower cost, using limited defence facilities, nuclear weapons and improved co-operation with allies.

The 'battle for the pound', 1964–6

It is easy to argue that, with a current balance of payments deficit estimated at £400 million but actually almost twice as high, sterling ought
to have been devalued in 1964. Even at the time the 'battle for the
pound' seemed a forlorn hope, the centre of government disappoint-
ments because monetary weakness damaged growth, trade and spending
plans. Under the system of fixed exchange rates, often called the
'Bretton Woods system', the pound had been pegged at $2.80 since
1949, becoming overvalued as Britain's trade and growth slackened
relative to those of other Western countries. Britain's gold and currency
reserves were too low to mount a confident defence of the pound, whose
position was undercut by persistent balance of payments problems. Aside
from the burden on the domestic economy, the attempt to maintain the
value of sterling had a detrimental impact on overseas policy, forcing
cuts in defence, complicating attempts to enter the EEC and leading
Britain to require support from other countries.

In 1964 devaluation could have been blamed on the inheritance from
the Conservatives and would have freed Labour from years of sterling
crises and deflationary packages. But there were strong arguments
against it. Devaluation would have pushed up import costs, could be
negated by 'competitive devaluations' of other currencies and would
have meant a loss to overseas holders of sterling, including Commonwealth governments. Since Labour was responsible for the change of
value in 1949, it could have been tarred with a reputation as 'the party
of devaluation'. There was also a belief that Britain gained global prestige
from possessing a major currency and the USA was strongly opposed to
devaluation because the pound was seen as a first line of defence for
the dollar, whose own position was being undermined by trade deficits.[3]

Key ministers took the decision not to devalue unanimously and
quickly. Problems soon followed.[4] The decision was accompanied by an
alternative step to improve the balance of trade – a 15 per cent import
surcharge but this was illegal under the rules of the General Agreement
on Tariffs and Trade (GATT). While Washington condoned it, seeing it
as preferable to devaluation, the surcharge upset many trading partners,
especially those in the European Free Trade Association (EFTA). During
an EFTA ministerial meeting in Geneva in mid-November 1964 the
other members threatened to introduce counter-measures, forcing the
government to promise that it would remove the surcharge as quickly
as possible.[5] It was reduced to 10 per cent in April 1965 and terminated
in November 1966, a step that, while it eased relations with allies, removed
one line of defence for the pound. The first 'run' on sterling under the
new government came in late November 1964, triggered by the increased
social spending in James Callaghan's first budget. A rise in interest rates

failed to halt the speculators but it was possible to save the pound through a $3 billion support package from the other central banks, after Washington pressured the Europeans to help. The episode raised doubts in Washington about Labour's ability to manage the economy.[6]

After November 1964 devaluation became 'unmentionable' in Whitehall for fear of a leak throwing the markets into panic. Nonetheless, in 1965 the Treasury's Permanent Secretary, William Armstrong, along with the Bank of England secretly initiated contingency plans for devaluation with Wilson's approval. This has been seen as evidence that, typically, he had an 'exit strategy' in case the initial policy failed.[7] In mid-1965 a number of economists became concerned that the value of sterling was inhibiting growth and at this point George Brown, head of the Department of Economic Affairs (DEA) and hitherto an opponent of devaluation, became sympathetic to the idea. In his memoirs Callaghan revealed that various ways of escaping the currency problems were studied, including 'floating' or, more dramatically, a merger of the pound and dollar. But no viable option emerged. Other ministers quickly discovered how the 'battle for the pound' inhibited Labour's original ambitions. Barbara Castle complained that 'we were all prisoners of the government's commitment to maintain the value of Sterling at all costs'.[8] The Americans had a hand in backing the Treasury demands for spending restraint. They urged tax increases and spending cuts in Callaghan's second budget, in April 1965, and drilled the Chancellor on the need for continuing toughness when he visited Washington in late June. There was another US-led support package for sterling in September, in which a number of European countries, Canada and Japan took part.[9] After that, helped by rising exports, the pound largely remained stable until mid-1966, carrying Wilson through the all-important election period.

Remaining 'east of Suez', October–December 1964

Alongside balance of payments problems and its status as a 'reserve' currency, the third main reason for pressure on the pound was overseas expenditure, especially on defence. Under the Conservatives there had been repeated attempts to match defence policy to worsening economic circumstances. The 1957 defence White Paper underlined the change in emphasis in strategic thinking from large, conventional forces to small, mobile units and nuclear weapons. But that same year a 'profit and loss' analysis of the Empire repeatedly referred to the loss of prestige and economic opportunities that might result from premature withdrawals, as well as the danger of vacuums being filled by hostile, Communist powers. In 1962 Polaris had been ordered from the USA to provide a strategic nuclear deterrent and, to fit the new thinking, conscription was ended, despite warnings of recruitment problems and evidence – from 'emergencies' in Brunei, East Africa and Kuwait – that many threats could not be met by nuclear weapons. Britain still had commitments scattered around the world, but particularly in Europe and 'east of Suez'. In the Far East, these included Malaysia (with the Singapore base) and Hong Kong. In the Middle East several Persian Gulf states were under British protection and there was an important base at Aden, essential for intervention in the Gulf and Africa. There were also alliance commitments through the Southeast Asia Treaty Organisation (SEATO), Central Treaty Organisation (CENTO, in the northern Middle East) and the North Atlantic Treaty Organisation (NATO). Yet even getting to some key areas was a problem. The 'east-about' route to the Far East was reliant on the agreement of countries like Turkey and the Sudan, whose co-operation could not be guaranteed in future. The 'west-about' alternative, reliant on the USA and Canada, was safer but covered an enormous distance.[10]

Conservative governments had thus tried to have the best of all worlds, ending conscription while retaining a global presence, purchasing a US strategic weapon (Polaris) while pretending it was independent, paring down costs but making no major reductions in theatres of operation. Concerned at the situation, the Cabinet Secretary, Burke Trend, established a 'Long-Term Study Group' in May 1964 to look at alternatives to Britain's existing array of commitments. But there were difficulties in reconciling the opinions of the various departments represented on this group, with the Foreign Office (FO) keen to retain the world role while the Board of Trade and the Treasury questioned it. It was still at work in October.[11] Furthermore, despite some apparently radical ideas in opposition, there were signs the incoming administration might repeat old errors. Labour's manifesto attacked the Conservatives for a failure to prioritise, but was thin on how to achieve its aim of 'value for money'. It was critical of the Polaris purchase but did not categorically state that it would be cancelled. Leading ministers also seemed set on maintaining the world role. Preparing for office, Patrick Gordon Walker wrote some 'Thoughts on Foreign Policy' in August that emphasised the need for facilities around the Indian Ocean, including Singapore and Aden, together with transport aircraft, ships and elite troops that gave Britain both mobility and effectiveness.[12]

Despite the retrospective sense of a policy lacking in direction, Wilson actually got off to a brisk start on defence, hoping to carry through a swift and comprehensive review. In November he held a weekend discussion among key ministers at Chequers. A joint paper from the Treasury and DEA successfully pressed for a ceiling of £2 billion (at 1964 prices) to be placed on defence expenditure, a target to be achieved by 1969–70, implying cuts of £360 million on the predicted budget for that year. The decision was meant to lay the basis for an affordable policy and set a vital parameter for the defence review that followed. Another paper was the final report of the Long-Term Study Group. This accepted that Britain was bearing an overseas burden disproportionate to its economic strength and that this was harming its competitiveness and forcing it to rely on financial support from others, but there was disagreement about whether, on balance, the presence east of Suez was damaging British influence because, as the FO argued, any reduction of commitments would also reduce Britain's impact on world affairs, especially its voice in Washington. If forced to choose between commitments, officials believed European defence must have priority, because it was so vital to Britain's own security as well as to Western economic and political stability, and there were clear commitments to NATO. The Group placed the retention of the Aden base above that of Singapore, largely on grounds of cost but also because British economic interests in the Middle East, especially oil, were of greater importance than investments in South-East Asia. Another highly significant point, however, was the belief that neither Singapore nor Aden could be held in the long term in the face of local nationalist feeling. Thus, as soon as the new government began its term of office, withdrawal from east of Suez was a definite option, even if no timetable for it could be set.

The ministerial discussion at Chequers, however, came close to reversing the officials' priorities. It was argued that there was currently little chance of war breaking out in Europe, so that spending on the British Army of the Rhine (BAOR) could safely be reduced. Beyond Europe, especially in South-East Asia, areas were less stable and it was in these that Britain played a unique role. As a result of this unwillingness to cut commitments, the focus for financial savings was put on equipment, specifically military aircraft. Britain was currently involved in a number of projects, including the development of the tactical, strike and reconnaissance jet TSR-2, the P-1154 fighter and the HS-681 transport aircraft. All might be replaced by cheaper purchases 'off the shelf' from the USA. The Chequers meeting agreed to study cuts in aircraft development over the next two months and there would be separate studies by officials on wider defence cuts, to be completed by June 1965. It was implied that the nuclear deterrent would remain. Therefore, while agreeing an important spending 'ceiling', this opening debate showed a preference for cutting back on resources while maintaining geographical commitments, and it suggested incremental changes in strategy rather than a revolutionary leap into the future.[13]

How is the reluctance to reduce commitments to be explained? The Malaysia–Indonesia Confrontation was undoubtedly an important, practical factor in preventing a rapid retreat from South-East Asia, since it forced London to deploy troops to defend Malaysia. The Defence Secretary, Denis Healey, was plain in his memoirs that 'so long as we were engaged in the ... Confrontation ... we could not reduce our forces in the Far East'. Nor did unrest in Aden allow for an easy withdrawal. Such short-term, specific dilemmas are important to any historical study of the 1960s.[14] Yet they cannot explain a persistent reluctance of some policy-makers to retreat from east of Suez. Cold War considerations – a reluctance to abandon positions that might fall to Communism – have already been mentioned. Tradition and status were probably other factors. Philip Darby has argued that the east of Suez role 'was too deeply rooted in Britain's outlook and history' to be questioned easily. At the time, writers like Paul Einzig argued that retreat from east of Suez was a mistake because it alienated Britain's allies, put its investments at risk and weakened the West's defences. Robert Holland has suggested that the decision to remain east of Suez, as well as those to maintain the parity of sterling and retain the nuclear deterrent, were all wrapped up in the desire to make the Labour Party appear a patriotic, dependable party of government. More generally, Holland argues that, across much of the twentieth century there was a compromise at the heart of the British body politic, whereby governments of any party sustained both large-scale spending on welfare at home and on a 'great power' role abroad, thus trying to please the main constituencies in the electorate. It was Wilson's misfortune to preside over the period when this compromise began visibly to fall apart.[15]

Just as important for the key decision-makers, it seems, were Commonwealth ties and the 'special relationship'. Like Gordon Walker, Wilson was eager to work closely with the USA and to protect Commonwealth allies such as Australia, New Zealand and Malaysia. Gordon Walker made clear to the Cabinet after his first official visit to Washington that British influence on the USA depended on maintaining a global presence. America did not want to see Britain quitting positions east of Suez, partly because this would lead to pressure on the USA to expand its own commitments.[16] Another point is that, to some experts, remaining east of Suez made perfect sense, given global realities. It even represented a forward-looking element in policy. Ahead of Wilson's first Washington summit, Oliver Wright drafted a memorandum on the 'Chequers philosophy' that had emerged from the defence weekend. The 'shape of the world to come' was of the 'East–West conflict stalemated in Europe and thus less acute'; the 'points of danger [were] shifting Eastwards and Southwards' into the Third World, while there was also the 'danger of North–South conflict with poverty tending to divide the world on racial lines'. In this situation the USA and Britain must grasp that the West had 'won the battle for Europe', work for an end to the arms race and 'devote ... military and economic resources ...

to the problems of the late 60s rather than relive the problems of the 50s'. The fact is that, rather like the debate over devaluation, there seemed good reasons to maintain a role east of Suez. Indeed, in surveying post-war British policy in Malaysia–Singapore, Karl Hack has argued that the British had quite a clear grasp of the dangers of overstretching themselves and tried to adapt by, for example, relying more on regional allies.[17]

Yet, as Wyn Rees argues, in addition to the all-important financial constraints, 'there were powerful factors that were steadily undermining the extra-European role'. The first, as recognised by the Long-Term Study Group, was nationalism in the less developed world, which suggested that the days of military bases were numbered, even if some locals (as in Singapore) did not yet urge Britain's expulsion. Second, it was clear that other Western countries, like Germany and Japan, were economically successful without maintaining a global defence presence. It was even arguable that overseas bases were detrimental to Britain's commercial interests because they were a focus for anti-imperialist discontent. Rees also highlights what he calls the 'logistical impracticability' of the world role, as the Empire shrank and various countries denied Britain 'over-flying rights' for military aircraft. Finally, in the event of war with the USSR, it was quite evident that Britain would have to focus its military effort in Europe.[18] Nevertheless, Wilson's early rhetoric suggested a deep commitment to remaining east of Suez. One of his most famous statements, made in his first Guildhall speech in November 1964, was that 'We are a world power and a world influence or we are nothing', while in the Commons a month later he insisted Britain should retain a triad of responsibilities – nuclear weapons, the presence in Europe and the world role. As Darby says, 'Wilson introduced a new emotional content to discussions about the East of Suez role', which made the subsequent withdrawal seem very much a reversal of intentions, notwithstanding the government's determination to cut defence spending.[19]

The defence review delayed, January–June 1965

The February 1965 defence White Paper, very much an 'interim' statement while the defence review took place, reflected the contradictions in policy. Spending would be cut, the P-1154 and HS-681 were cancelled and there were hopes of savings in Europe, but the east of Suez role would remain.[20] Rather than deciding on the future of all aircraft issues at this time, it was not possible to announce the cancellation of the TSR-2, the most important case, until April. This was because the sophisticated multi-role aircraft, while it was expensive and had a US substitute (the F-111) available 'off the shelf', was also important to the future of the British aerospace industry. A range of other arguments entered the equation and different departments took different sides: the Minister of Technology, Frank Cousins, believed that if it was a choice of buying British or American, then spending should go to Britain; Roy Jenkins, the Minister of Aviation, feared that, 'The massive scale on which we are proposing to "go American" ... will not improve our relations with France'; and the Board of Trade was concerned that purchasing the F-111, while it could save around £280 million over several years, would adversely affect the balance of payments. But Healey, keen to focus savings on aircraft projects while also safeguarding the world role, was able to win a generous deal from the USA on the F-111 and the Royal Air Force (RAF) was more than happy with this alternative to the TSR-2. The government considered such alternatives as a mixed purchase of F-111s and TSR-2s, or even avoiding a purchase of either. The last idea was pressed by George Wigg and won some support from those ministers who wished to focus expenditure cuts on defence. Two lengthy Cabinet meetings were needed on 1 April before the option – and it was only an option – of purchasing F-111s was accepted. The Conservatives condemned the cancellation of TSR-2 but, in retrospect, given the subsequent withdrawal from east of Suez, the decision can hardly be faulted.[21]

Even with the decisions on aircraft, £200 million in cuts still had to be found and the Overseas Policy and Defence Committee (OPD) began studying these in earnest only in March 1965. It was soon clear that the defence review would not be completed until early 1966. The problem was that cuts in force levels and equipment risked making it impossible to defend commitments. Hence even the Chiefs of Staff, the professional heads of the armed services, argued that ministers must be prepared to cut commitments. An inter-departmental working party was established to study this but the idea of withdrawal from the world role was still unpopular with the FO. There were grave problems with cuts in Europe, because of the impact on NATO, or in the Far East, thanks to the Confrontation. Indeed, in a change from the November 1964 position, Aden now seemed the best option for savings, partly because of local opposition to the British presence. Further savings on equipment were also considered but this provoked a growing divide between the Navy and RAF, because substantial savings could be achieved only through the cancellation either of a new generation of aircraft carriers or of the F-111. In fact, although issues of commitments and equipment were treated somewhat separately in official studies, in the last analysis they had to be linked. The F-111, for example, largely made sense as an 'east of Suez' weapon. The US Defense Secretary, Robert McNamara, even called the F-111 purchase 'the best evidence that [the British] intend to maintain their commitments east of Suez'.[22]

Ministers met at Chequers again in June for an initial discussion of officials' studies. These included a covering paper proposing that, whatever the uncertainties in the Confrontation, Britain should plan for an eventual departure from South-East Asia. Savings might also be made by withdrawal from Aden, adjustments in NATO and planning future land operations only on the basis of allied support. Healey put his own memorandum forward suggesting withdrawal from Aden, the South Atlantic and the Caribbean; getting a better financial deal from Germany and Hong Kong for forces based there; abandoning plans to defend Kuwait and Libya from invasion; and the development of joint planning with Australia and New Zealand for the defence of South-East Asia, including the building of a base in Australia to replace Singapore. The last idea had already been raised under Macmillan. Healey recognised that cutting the number of forces and equipment would be difficult unless commitments were reduced, but he also feared that a poorly managed retreat could breed local crises that might drag British forces back in to deal with them. In discussion Callaghan and Brown pressed strongly for savings and it was generally conceded that the days of the Singapore base were numbered. Agreeing on meaningful steps was difficult at this stage and the official studies would continue. Yet even an implied decision to make cuts east of Suez was a significant one, if only because it marked a departure from the Chequers meeting of November 1964.[23]

The debate over US influence

If Britain did decide to quit Singapore it would need to prepare its allies for this. But when Callaghan went to the USA in June 1965 he was warned by McNamara not to change defence commitments in any way or else America would re-examine its whole relationship with Britain.[24] One major theme in the literature – and perhaps the most hotly discussed issue about Wilson's foreign policy – is the argument that Britain remained east of Suez and maintained the value of sterling thanks to US pressure. There can be no doubt that Washington came to see the pound as a first line of defence against the dollar or that, especially as it became mired in Vietnam, the USA had little desire to see Britain retreat from South-East Asia. The Americans thus pressed Britain to overstretch its resources and to focus spending cuts on the domestic sphere. But the exact nature of the Anglo-American arrangement on finance and defence is subject to debate for at least two reasons. First, was there an actual, explicit, perhaps secret agreement? And second, did it mean that Washington 'dictated' British policy? On the first question, Clive Ponting has claimed that in the summer of 1965 the need for US financial support led Wilson to 'accept a deal that allowed American dictation of British policy' on sterling and defence. Ben Pimlott, on the other hand, feels there was only an 'implicit' arrangement, while Chris Wrigley argues that there was neither a deal nor a US diktat. Wilson gave the USA only 'commitments in line with the policies he intended pursuing anyway'. It made sense to remain east of Suez and avoid the devaluation of sterling until the next general election and, even if reluctant, the government's subsequent decision to devalue and retreat from east of Suez showed the Prime Minister's ultimate readiness to act against US wishes. John Dumbrell, while accepting that 'economic troubles were now driving Britain's relationship with the US', also feels that the British played a limited hand well and that 'Washington did not hold all the cards' in the relationship. The USA could not treat Britain as a 'satellite'. The American historian Diane Kunz agrees: the British 'sacrificed over £1 billion … in a vain attempt to maintain the pound's stability' not 'because of American pressure but because it was their chosen road'.[25]

Until firm evidence of a formal 'deal' emerges it is safest to assume that none existed and that Wilson did ultimately keep his hands free. But in 1964–7 the British government was well aware that US goodwill depended on maintaining the value of sterling and the world role, and that this acted as a restraint on London's independence. There were numerous occasions in 1965 when US officials made the links plain. The clearest was in September, when George Ball, the Under-Secretary of State, told Wilson that 'the American effort to relieve Sterling was inextricably related to the commitment of the UK government to maintain its commitments around the world'. The Prime Minister replied that 'there was no misunderstanding on this point'.[26] A few months before this, President Johnson was told by his National Security Adviser, McGeorge Bundy, that 'it makes no sense for us to rescue the Pound in a situation where there is no British flag in Vietnam and a threatened British thin-out in both east of Suez and in Germany'. Raj Roy is among those who doubt that such arguments ever produced a formal 'agreement', but he has chronicled the economic links between the two countries and shown how closely the USA was able to influence British policy in this field, especially down to July 1966. He argues that a combination of US economic might, the growing inter-dependence of the world economy, ties between US and British officials, and Wilson's personal desire for a close relationship with Johnson gave Washington enormous influence over British economic policy. This endorses Robin Renwick's point that, during the Wilson years, 'the relationship was one of greater dependence on the United States than at any other point in peacetime'.[27]

Increasingly, however, as Jeremy Fielding points out, the Americans' 'definition of an acceptable British foreign policy contradicted their own understanding of Britain's financial fragility'. In July 1965 Francis Bator of the National Security Council staff warned that Britain could not do all the USA expected: staying east of Suez, maintaining the BAOR, avoiding devaluation, taking tough domestic economic decisions, maybe even committing itself to Vietnam. It was all too much; Washington must prioritise what it wanted from Britain. Similarly, Dean Acheson, the former Secretary of State, complained in September 1965 that 'this wizened island is expected to bear world-wide burdens.... We expect it to do this, partly, because of the persistent illusion [that Britain remained powerful] and, partly, because the alternative, bearing them ourselves, brings the chill of loneliness.' There were, according to Fielding, 'conceptual lags' in US thinking, centred on a belief that Britain would remain a world power and that the money markets could be faced down in the battle for sterling. Ultimately, in 1967, both beliefs broke down. Where Roy tends to emphasise the US ability to shape British policy, Fielding sees a web of economic and political–security interactions in which the Anglo-American relationship was far from one-sided. Britain's very weaknesses, the threat that it might devalue and retreat from global involvements, gave it influence in Washington and, in the last analysis, 'London acted according to its own proclivities'. Tore Petersen has taken this line of thinking to extremes and postulated that Labour was far freer than the USA in this period. He sees the Wilson government as exploiting its trade deficit from the start: 'Failures could be blamed on its predecessor, economic problems used to squeeze money out of the United States, and ... any predisposition to liquidate the empire hidden behind the fig leaf of financial exigency', while the US '[u]nable, or unwilling, to take over Britain's military commitments east of Suez ... had little choice ... except to continue to support the pound until Britain devalued it'.[28]

A 'two-faced' policy? The February 1966 White Paper

Petersen overstates the case perhaps, but even in the second half of 1965 the debate surrounding defence showed that large-scale cuts could be expected east of Suez. In August, the separation of Singapore from Malaysia due to internal friction hardened the view in London that the Confrontation must be brought to an early end, that the days of the Singapore base were numbered and that alternative facilities might be developed in Australia. Both John Subritzky and Saki Dockrill see the discussions in autumn 1965 as especially significant. Contradicting many earlier studies, it is clear from declassified documents that the government became increasingly committed to a disengagement from the Far East and began to plan on this basis. Subritzky believes that

Wilson was 'employing a very "two-faced" policy', planning withdrawal for the sake of Britain's long-term interests but unable to declare this openly because he required US, Australian and New Zealand support while the Confrontation lasted. These countries argued against Britain's thinking on a withdrawal from Singapore, when they were first made aware of it in September 1965, but won only a short respite. In December Wilson told President Johnson that the 'provisional' results of the defence review pointed to substantial cuts in the Far East and the Prime Minister wrote to the Australian and New Zealand premiers about Britain's intention to reduce its presence in Malaysia–Singapore. The message was driven home uncompromisingly when Healey and Foreign Secretary Michael Stewart visited allied capitals in the New Year. By then internal developments in Indonesia had weakened its leader, Sukarno, and there were signs that the Confrontation might soon end. If it did, the main reason for keeping large troop numbers in the Far East would disappear.[29]

In the light of the archival evidence it is difficult to deny that, in late 1965, government rhetoric about remaining east of Suez was out of line with actual plans. But this is not a rare position for governments and it was due as much to the genuine dilemma Britain faced as to any calculated deceit. Having come into office genuinely convinced of the desirability of the world role, Wilson had been forced to admit that reductions were inevitable but a precipitate announcement could have demoralised Malaysia–Singapore and brought defeat in the Confrontation. It must also be recognised that a reduction of forces in South-East Asia did not necessarily mean a complete withdrawal from east of Suez. The idea of an Australian base was evidence of that, as was the planning for various Indian Ocean 'staging posts', such as Gan in the Maldives and the Aldabra Islands near Madagascar. These were on isolated islands, free from the nationalist pressures that threatened other bases and with a minimum need for 'over-flying rights' between them. An 'island strategy' offered the chance to maintain a presence in the Indian Ocean at low cost and there were plans to develop the Aldabras, as well as Diego Garcia, as joint projects with the USA. As Healey later told the OPD, the Aldabras were useful for preserving an 'east-about' route to the Far East, would allow aerial surveillance over a wide area of the Indian Ocean and would provide a base for operations in Africa, including any intervention in Rhodesia, which many left-wingers (who otherwise criticised the world role) hoped to see.[30] Wilson also talked about basing Polaris submarines east of Suez and, even if few others took the proposal seriously, it is difficult to account for his persistent advocacy of the scheme unless he saw this, too, as a way to wield power in the Indian Ocean at a reduced cost.[31] Another important argument, of course, was that Britain could maintain a global presence more easily in co-operation with allies. Stewart laid special emphasis on this in a general review of foreign policy for the Cabinet in September, while conceding that withdrawals from the Middle and Far East were now the aim.[32]

When ministers on the OPD took preliminary decisions about the defence review on 24 November it was clear that spending in the Mediterranean and Middle East would be cut most dramatically, at least in proportional terms. If Aden were abandoned, and forces in Cyprus, Libya and Malta reduced, expenditure there could be halved. In South-East Asia, on the other hand, thanks to the Confrontation and allied opposition to British withdrawal, the exact level of savings was hard to predict.[33] In the MOD some were increasingly exasperated at the failure to match commitments to tightening resources and the Navy minister, Christopher Mayhew, was prepared to dramatise the issue through resignation. To Mayhew, the endless paring down of the defence budget, linked as this now was to a proposed abandonment of the aircraft-carrier programme, made no sense. He preferred to end the presence east of Suez; it certainly could not be maintained without carriers. But the budget for such vessels was substantial, estimated at an average of £140 million per annum for the next decade, whereas the F-111 could provide a capability for rapid, long-range intervention using island staging posts. The Royal Navy currently had four carriers, but two were old and the Conservatives had already planned to build a new one, the CVA01. Healey and most of the MOD favoured scrapping this project, but the Navy found support from the government's Chief Scientist, Solly Zuckerman, who argued that a carrier force was a far more formidable weapon than the F-111. Healey later described it as 'my most difficult equipment decision', but carriers were always an expensive way to provide air power and, with a force of three, only one could be kept permanently on station in the Far East. The cancellation of the CVA01 became inevitable. In fact, for a time, Healey also had to fight against those who, in view of the likely withdrawal from the Far East, wanted to cancel the F-111 as well. He eventually had to accept a cut in the number of these aircraft from 110 to 50.[34]

In early 1966 the OPD held an exhausting series of meetings to finalise the next White Paper. Mayhew presented his case on the carrier question, Callaghan made predictable calls for economies and Healey, supported by Stewart, insisted that Britain must remain in South-East Asia at least for a while, an argument aided by continuing uncertainty about the Confrontation.[35] On 14 February the Cabinet held two meetings on the defence review. There was some feeling, especially from Castle and Richard Crossman, that the world role should be drastically reduced and the F-111 slashed altogether, but general acceptance that neither was feasible in current circumstances. It would have been difficult for the Cabinet to overturn the package devised by the OPD, given the time that had been invested and the fact that most Cabinet ministers were also on that committee. The decision not to build a new aircraft carrier was easily taken and it led Mayhew and the First Sea Lord, David Luce, to resign. If Mayhew expected that the sacrifice of his political career would cause a political earthquake he was mistaken: he made a dull, overlong resignation speech that was quickly forgotten.[36]

The main elements of the White Paper, published on 23 February, were: to keep forces in Europe stable, while hoping for German help in covering costs; to make substantial savings in the Mediterranean and Middle East, especially through withdrawal from Aden in 1968; and to reduce spending in the Far East once the Confrontation was resolved. In future, Britain would not 'undertake major operations of war except in co-operation with allies'. On the equipment side, the F-111 order remained but at its reduced level and the new aircraft carrier was cancelled, making the RAF the backbone of the presence east of Suez. The decisions on Aden and the carrier marked a significant erosion of the world role. However, the cuts would not quite achieve the £2 billion target for 1969–70 and South-East Asia would continue to absorb around 40 per cent of defence spending. The need to tread cautiously, not least with regard to allied feelings, meant that the White Paper was worded in such a way that Britain could stay in Singapore indefinitely. Even with the archival evidence it is difficult to disagree with Darby's judgement that, on a sympathetic interpretation, the White Paper was 'a reasonable compromise between political exigency and economic necessity' but that, more critically, 'it might be described as the final monument to the inability of post-war British governments to bring commitments into line with capability'.[37] The archives, however, show that more dramatic decisions had already been contemplated.

Announcing withdrawal, March 1966–July 1967

By the 1966 election Britain's willingness to remain east of Suez was clearly fading but still there was a reluctance or an inability actually to liquidate commitments and, even if the days of the Aden and Singapore bases were numbered, it was possible to see Britain remaining in the Indian Ocean as part of a low-cost policy for many years. In March Labour won the election and by June the end of the Confrontation was definitely in sight, though Britain still could not put a date on withdrawal from Singapore. Yet the economic pressure to retreat remained. The government had escaped a full-blown monetary crisis in 1964–6 but in May a long seamen's strike began and in July a severe 'run' on sterling occurred. Brown, Castle, Crossman and Jenkins were among the senior ministers open to devaluation. Brown was most outspoken, telling

Castle, 'We've got to break with America, devalue and go into Europe'. Others, including Wilson, Healey and Stewart, as well as Callaghan, wished to rely on deflation alone, although even the beleaguered Callaghan toyed with 'floating' the pound. There was a particularly bitter Cabinet debate on 19 July, but the Prime Minister secured a clear majority for a mixture of spending cuts and a wage/price freeze. On 20 July, in addition to £500 million cuts at home, Wilson announced reductions of nearly £100 million on the overseas budget, largely through accelerating the reductions agreed in the February White Paper (helped by the imminent end of the Confrontation), paring down overseas aid and securing a better deal from Germany on the 'exchange costs' of the BAOR (see Chapter 5).[38] Once again the USA backed the tough deflationary package and continued to support the pound in the currency markets, although some US officials were beginning to consider that a sterling devaluation might be unavoidable in future.[39]

The July crisis harmed Wilson's reputation for sound economic management, ruined ambitions for sustained growth and made defence an obvious target for further savings. In August the Treasury pressed for a reduction in defence expenditure to £1,850 million per year by 1970–1 at 1964 prices. The defence review was therefore revived, with a new round of studies soon established.[40] Pressure to make cuts east of Suez came from others across the political spectrum. Actually it had been growing for some time but now there was 'a sustained attack'.[41] Lord Gladwyn, the Liberal defence spokesman, had been arguing for years that retreat from the world role would do no harm to British economic interests.[42] Perhaps more surprisingly the Conservative defence spokesman, Enoch Powell, told his party conference in October 1965 that Britain should concentrate on defending Western Europe rather than east of Suez. Powell was a maverick in his own ranks, but at a meeting of the shadow Cabinet following his speech 'there was fairly general agreement that we should not attempt to maintain in the long-term a military presence on the continent of South-East Asia'.[43] More important for Wilson was pressure for defence cuts in his own party. The September 1965 Labour Party conference carried a resolution 'that military expenditure … should be drastically reduced' in order to 'apply the savings to the urgent economic and social needs of the nation'. In May 1966 Mayhew and others attacked the world role at a meeting of the Parliamentary Labour Party (PLP) and in June the Prime Minister made a long speech defending the east of Suez role in ways that Labour back-benchers might approve, as a contribution to peace and stability under the United Nations, a service to Commonwealth countries in the area and a means to provide support to India against China. Then, at the party's Brighton conference in October 1966, Frank Cousins, who had resigned from the Cabinet in early July, moved a resolution that the

government should 'make a decisive reduction in military commitments
East of Suez, including the withdrawal from Malaysia, Singapore and
the Persian Gulf, by 1969–70'. The right-wing Mayhew spoke in support,
thus highlighting the strength of feeling across the party, and the
resolution was carried.[44]

The appointment of George Brown as Foreign Secretary in August
1966 added to the pressures for change. It brought to the centre of
overseas decision-making someone who wished to withdraw from east
of Suez and enter the EEC, a dual decision which, if taken with determination, would have seemed a decisive turning point in British policy.
'I was clear in my mind,' he later said, 'that that was a deliberate choice.'
In September Brown raised with Wilson the possibility of a complete
withdrawal from east of Suez, but the Prime Minister was not ready for
such radicalism.[45] In his memoirs Brown said he did not want a
precipitate retreat and, from the archival evidence, it appears that the
longer he was at the FO the more he was prepared for withdrawal to be
gradual. But he did temper his department's desire to retain the world
role and his arrival probably led to greater urgency about entering the
EEC, which in turn influenced thinking about a withdrawal from the
world role. Such thinking even seems to have influenced Healey. The
Defence Secretary was no 'pro-marketeer', but he was someone who
discerned the significance of shifts in policy and adapted accordingly.
He told Robert McNamara in May 1967 that 'a decision ... to join
Europe inevitably means a turning away from other parts of the world'.[46]
Another important event, in August 1966, was that a formal settlement
was reached to the Confrontation.

When a group of ministers discussed defence economies on 22
October 1966, Healey posed the question starkly of whether they wished
to retreat from Europe or east of Suez, only to advise limited cuts across
the whole range of geographical commitments. Wilson backed Healey,
and Brown was evidently too drunk to mount a coherent opposing case.
Arguments about contributing to Western defence and preserving influence in Washington still held sway. Thus Helen Parr judges that the
immediate 'aftermath of July 1966 was a bid for renewed stability:
managing the crisis without a radical transformation of Britain's conventional outlook'.[47] Then again, Brown, Callaghan and Crossman all
remained dissatisfied and Healey had conceded at the meeting that
savings could most easily be made by focusing on South-East Asia.
Pressures for change from within the government continued and, at an
OPD session on 9 December, quite dramatic options for commitment
reductions were put forward by Healey and Stewart. Callaghan and
Crossman urged that some theatres should be cut altogether and it was
then agreed to study a total withdrawal from South-East Asia. This allows
Matthew Jones to conclude that 'the 'Rubicon of a pull-out from the

Far East had actually been crossed by key figures ... in the latter part of
1966' with 'few signs of ... sentimental and romantic attachment to a
world role'.[48] Nonetheless, the February 1967 defence White Paper was,
as Healey told the Cabinet, 'essentially a progress report'. It retained
the presence east of Suez, pending the completion of expenditure studies,
and sparked a fresh outburst of discontent from backbenchers. Over
sixty backbenchers abstained in a vote on the White Paper, which led
Wilson to make an embittered speech to the PLP, in which he compared
the rebels to dogs in danger of losing their licence.[49]

   A month after the White Paper came a significant breakthrough. In
one of his decisive personal initiatives, Healey put forward a proposal
for a 'peripheral' strategy east of Suez. This would remove virtually all
land forces from Malaysia–Singapore by 1970–1, and air and naval forces
would be relied on to defend remaining commitments; this promised a
saving of £200 million. A complete withdrawal of land forces from South-
East Asia would take place by 1975–6, with a reduction of Britain's
political commitments in the region. Officials did not even have time
to discuss this fully before the OPD held a provisional discussion of cuts
on 22 March but ministers, including Brown and even Wilson, were
sympathetic to Healey's idea.[50] In Cabinet on 11 April Healey's strategy
was approved, despite opposition from the Commonwealth Secretary,
Bert Bowden, who warned of its impact on Commonwealth allies.
According to Crossman only six ministers opposed drastic cuts and many
wanted to go further than Healey, with Jenkins especially outspoken.[51]
Consideration was given, in March, to an equally dramatic but very
different route out of Britain's difficulties when certain US officials
proposed giving a substantial loan, of $4 billion over thirty years, to
stabilise the British economy. But the USA's own economy was increasingly troubled, thanks to poor trade figures, inflationary pressures and
expenditure in Vietnam. The proposal was never officially put to Britain,
although London learnt of it. Even had it become a formal suggestion,
the signs are that the British would have rejected it. They were reluctant
to add a substantial loan to their liabilities: they feared that Washington
would demand that, in return, Britain should remain east of Suez; and
ministers felt that such evidence of financial reliance on the USA would
now complicate their efforts to get into the EEC.[52]

   The US, Australian and New Zealand governments were deeply unhappy with the course of British thinking on withdrawal when Brown
explained it to them at a SEATO meeting in April 1967. The Malaysian
and Singaporean governments appeared more sanguine when Healey
visited them shortly afterwards, but they wanted the withdrawal to be
gradual and expected an aid package to help them cope with the
impact on their economies and to provide them with their own defence
forces.[53] When Wilson met Johnson at the funeral of Konrad Adenauer,

the President even asked if the British were 'going crazy' by planning to quit South-East Asia while war was raging in Vietnam. But Wilson, for all his previous desire to remain east of Suez, would not give way.[54] There was some debate in May about how to placate the allies, with Healey proposing that Britain should retain a 'capability' to intervene in the Far East – from bases in Europe – after 1975–6, an idea the Cabinet accepted after some debate. As Dockrill says, the 'difference between presence and capability was indeed significant', as it allowed Britain to argue that it could still act in South-East Asia in an emergency, thus pleasing its allies while nonetheless slashing forces in the region.[55] Wilson put the proposal to Johnson in early June and the Americans greeted it with resignation.[56]

After further debate in which some ministers continued to press for more drastic cuts, a supplementary White Paper was published in July. Its key element was the reduction of Britain's presence in the Far East to a small naval amphibious force plus the Hong Kong garrison by the mid-1970s, but with a 'capability' to send units out from Europe in a crisis. There were currently 80,000 personnel in the British forces in Malaysia–Singapore; by 1971 this figure would be halved. The government also planned to end the presence in the Persian Gulf by the mid-1970s but, because of the current uncertain political situation in the region, this was not specifically stated in the White Paper. There was undoubted drama in the statement that Britain would 'cease to play a worldwide military role…. We shall increasingly become a European power'. The White Paper was also supposed to mark the end of the government's major defence review, which had been taking place since 1964. Furthermore, the term 'mid-1970s' was deliberately chosen to leave open the possibility of withdrawing before 1975, maybe as early as 1973. Even some of those who had wanted to go further recognised it as a turning point. Tony Benn told Crossman it was 'the death knell of the British Empire east of Suez'. Castle more bluntly wrote that 'East of Suez is dead'.[57]

Accelerating withdrawal, July 1967–January 1968

For a year following the July 1966 crisis the pound was stable, but in June 1967 the Six Day War closed the Suez Canal to trade and highlighted Britain's dependence on oil imports. The application to join the EEC contributed to the air of economic uncertainty. Then, in October, a dock strike sparked a bout of currency speculation. Ponting has argued that by mid-1967 the USA's ability to shape British policy was in decline (as evidenced by the July supplementary White Paper) and that the Prime Minister was becoming more open to devaluation.

Yet Wilson and Callaghan continued to defend the existing value of sterling in early November and both Fielding and Roy have shown, on the basis of archival evidence, that Wilson still expected the Americans to bail Britain out. The cost, however, would have been $3 billion and Washington was now acclimatised to the prospect of devaluation. On 18 November the pound was devalued from $2.80 to $2.40 because, quite simply, the scale of speculation against it had become too great.[58] It was always understood that this would be accompanied by further spending restraint and overseas expenditure was bound to be a target. Devaluation had instantly added to the foreign currency costs in this area. Before leaving the Treasury for the Home Office in the wake of devaluation, Callaghan was looking for defence cuts of £100 million, which the Cabinet approved on 21 November. The main victim was the planned post on the Aldabra Islands. Even this apparently minor step was symbolic of a wider retreat. After all, the Aldabras had been an important element in the 'island strategy' that was meant to maintain Britain's presence in the Indian Ocean at a reduced level. Plans to build it had been confirmed by the OPD as recently as July.[59]

Callaghan's successor as Chancellor, Roy Jenkins, soon recognised that devaluation would work no instant miracle on the balance of payments. Further substantial spending restraint was essential and he was determined this should include further defence cuts. Wilson supported him. Having accepted earlier in the year that withdrawal from east of Suez was inevitable, he had little trouble in agreeing an accelerated timetable, especially if this was vital to the government's future. But considerations of personal survival were also in play. With Labour's hopes resting on a successful economic policy, Jenkins became the key figure in the government, a potential replacement for Wilson. The Prime Minister appears to have calculated that he must keep close to his Chancellor so that their fortunes rose or fell together. Jeffrey Pickering has argued that Jenkins' arrival at the Treasury was as vital as continuing economic pressure to the early withdraw from east of Suez that followed. However, it will be seen below that the decisions on defence included significant elements of compromise on Jenkins' part and that Wilson did much to shape the details. Jenkins himself, while critical of some of the Prime Minister's tactics, writes that the latter's 'quiet, almost resigned loyalty was impeccable'. Despite devaluation Wilson was no spent force and, while staying close to Jenkins, he planned to remove other rivals. In mid-December he told Alasdair Hetherington, editor of the *Guardian*, 'that he himself was going to make sure of really serious cuts in the defence budget' and that the cancellation of F-111 'was now almost certain to come', even if this led Healey to resign. The Prime Minister also intended to accept Brown's resignation next time it was offered.[60] Around this time he clashed bitterly in Cabinet with both

Healey and Brown over arms sales to South Africa and Edward Pearce has argued that this might have made him more eager to side with Jenkins against them on defence cuts.[61]

Jenkins met Brown, Healey and the Commonwealth Secretary, George Thomson, on 20 December 1967 and put forward a dramatic proposal to leave South-East Asia by 1971 and the Persian Gulf as early as 1968–9. Jenkins' account suggests an unpleasant meeting, a view confirmed by Healey's diary. Yet the official record suggests Jenkins' only outright opponent was Thomson. Healey complained that past cuts in defence had not been matched on the civil side but agreed that meaningful cuts should include whole theatres. Brown wanted an inter-departmental study to be carried out but, without committing the FO, 'said that his own personal view was that it might be possible to contemplate the proposed timetables' for disengagement.[62] In Cabinet meetings between 4 and 15 January Jenkins got much, but by no means all, of what he wanted. The first meeting took place, Tony Benn recorded, 'in an icy atmosphere'. The most divisive debate concerned the F-111, which was of personal importance to Healey. After all, he had persuaded the RAF to cancel the TSR-2 only on the understanding that the F-111 would be bought. He had strong allies in Brown, Stewart, Thomson and Callaghan but, with the Cabinet split down the middle, the Prime Minister cast the deciding vote for cancellation. Also, after a marathon discussion, a tentative date of March 1971 was decided for the withdrawal from both South-East Asia and the Persian Gulf, instead of March 1972 which the FO and MOD would have preferred, or an earlier withdrawal from the Gulf as Jenkins favoured. A 'capability' to send forces east of Suez would remain.[63]

Britain's allies had already come to terms with the principle of withdrawal but pressure for a later withdrawal date was strong when Brown and Thomson visited allied capitals to sound them out on the latest proposals. The Persian Gulf rulers also urged reconsideration. Brown had a 'bloody unpleasant' meeting with US Secretary of State Dean Rusk, who asked 'Why don't you act like Britain?', while President Johnson wrote to Wilson pleading for a rethink.[64] The Foreign Secretary related all this in emotional tones to the Cabinet on 12 January and complained, according to Castle, that the country was becoming 'neutralist'. When Healey and Brown talked of resignation Wilson said that would not change matters, but he did agree to defer a final decision until he had met the Singaporean premier, Lee Kuan Yew, who was about to arrive in London. At Chequers on 14 January Lee pressed for 1973 as a withdrawal date and, in Cabinet the following day, there was more heated debate before Wilson suggested a compromise of December 1971. The significance of this was that, while it extended the date only by nine months, there had to be a general election beforehand, giving a chance that the Conservatives might change policy. Significantly, it

was also much nearer to the original date, March 1972, preferred by
Brown and Thomson, than it was to Jenkins' earlier targets. Yet the
Cabinet agreed to the proposal without a vote.[65] Polaris was retained,
partly because most of the capital was now paid for, so that it cost only
£20 million per year. The Chancellor had argued, at a Nuclear Policy
Committee meeting on 5 January, for its cancellation. But Wilson supported Brown, Stewart and others in retaining the weapon, and Healey's
diary suggests that Jenkins did not press the issue.[66]

The January 1968 defence decisions have been placed 'among the
most momentous decisions in twentieth century British history' and
Jenkins himself suggested that they marked a radical departure from
Callaghan's policies, ending 'old-fashioned' beliefs in the world role.[67]
It is certainly possible to create the image of a 'revolution' by downplaying
previous shifts in policy, exaggerating Wilson's continuing commitment
to the world role in 1967 and overemphasising the impact of Jenkins'
arrival at the Treasury.[68] But it is questionable how dramatic a change
occurred at this point. The July 1967 White Paper had already pointed
towards a withdrawal from east of Suez and the January 1968 decisions
were defended by Wilson in parliament as an 'acceleration' of earlier
plans.[69] Brown made a telling argument in the opening discussion
on 4 January that 'it would be wrong to suppose that any new major
change of policy was now in question. That change had been made ...
in July 1967 when the decision had been taken to withdraw ... from
East of Suez and, although it had not been announced at the time,
from the Persian Gulf.' His own doubts in January 1968 very much
focused on the pace of withdrawal and its impact on allies rather than
on the principle, which he had long upheld. Jenkins had secured the
cancellation of the F-111 but was forced to compromise on withdrawal
dates and could not rid Britain of Polaris. Indeed, the overall package
was very much shaped by Wilson's interventions. Also, one of the key
changes in defence thinking at this time actually came not under Jenkins
but in Callaghan's last days, when the Aldabra project was abandoned
and with it any notion of remaining an Indian Ocean power at minimal
cost. There were no resignations over the acceleration and allies soon
adapted to the new reality. Johnson, who had questioned British sanity
in the last round of cuts, did not even raise the latest reductions with
Wilson when they met in February.[70]

A European, nuclear power, 1968–70

Devaluation did not mark the end of monetary instability. In the weeks
following it, Britain lost another $1.5 billion in gold and currency reserves.
Washington organised another support package, worth $1.4 billion, and,

as Jeremy Fielding has revealed, it also, in a highly secret operation, flew $500 million of gold to London to calm demands on the multi-national 'gold pool' based there.[71] In March 1968, however, Britain faced a potentially worse crisis than it had in November. The focus of specu-lation on this occasion was not the pound but the dollar, which had now lost sterling as its first line of defence. The crisis revealed the continuing inter-dependency of Britain and the USA, because on 14 March Johnson asked Wilson to close the London 'gold pool'. It was at this point that Brown resigned, because Wilson did not consult him over the decision to agree to such a controversial step. The British feared that speculation against the pound might mount when the gold pool reopened and they even toyed with suspending its convertibility through 'Operation Brutus'. But such extreme action proved unnecessary. William Armstrong, the Permanent Secretary of the Treasury, went to Washington and secured another $4 billion in support for sterling from US and European central banks.[72] The crisis led in July to the Basle agreements, by which twelve central banks provided a stand-by credit of $2 billion, to prop up sterling while its role as a reserve currency was wound down. After that the focus of speculation shifted to the franc and Deutschmark, although there was always the danger that Britain could be caught up in the turmoil. In mid-November there was a crisis in Anglo-German relations when Wilson called in ambassador Herbert Blankenhorn to lecture him about the 'irresponsible' nature of German policy in refusing to revalue the Deutschmark.[73] The franc was eventually devalued in August 1969, by which time British trade figures were consistently safe.

In the area of defence, the main challenge after January 1968 was to carry out the cuts east of Suez. In contrast to the uncertainties of previous years, the withdrawal largely went to plan. The 1969 defence estimates were the first for eleven years to be lower at current prices than the previous year. When briefing Wilson on the 1970 defence White Paper, Trend informed him that there was little contentious in it.[74] British influence east of Suez would now be exerted by non-military means, using development aid, defence sales, cultural work by the British Council, traditional diplomatic efforts and commercial–financial ties. Involve-ment in local political disputes was to be shunned. The OPD discussed this strategy in July 1968, on the basis of extensive studies by planners at the FO and Commonwealth Relations Office. It was understood that the mix of non-military methods would have to be adjusted to local circumstances. In South-East Asia, for example, the focus should be on trade promotion and technical assistance. Crossman dismissed it all as 'a schoolboy essay on diplomatic relations': lacking military power, Britain had little choice other than to fall back on what were actually well estab-lished alternative methods of wielding influence. But Stewart, now back as Foreign Secretary, was quite proud of the exercise.[75]

A defence decision that the government maintained consistently was the purchase of Polaris. This was despite Labour's scepticism about nuclear defence before 1964, the withdrawal from the world role and the impossibility of using nuclear weapons independently of Washington. The first Polaris submarine, HMS *Resolution*, became operational in June 1968 and in July 1969 the Navy took control of strategic nuclear defence from the RAF. The full force of four submarines, the minimum necessary to keep one on station at any time, was available only after Labour lost office. Having effectively removed the nuclear issue from public controversy by 1966, Wilson did not choose to reopen the debate by purchasing the next generation of US submarine-launched ballistic missiles, Poseidon, when the question was raised in 1967–8. But there was concern by then over the Soviet development of an 'anti-ballistic missile' (ABM) system, which could blunt the effectiveness of a single-warhead weapon like Polaris. A lively debate developed in the ministerial Nuclear Policy Committee about whether to improve Polaris by 'hardening' it and deploying 'penetration aids' like decoy missiles, so as to negate the effect of ABMs. The costs of such improvements were difficult to predict and the discussion became embroiled in another, about whether to cut spending on the Atomic Weapons Research Establishment at Aldermaston. But there were familiar arguments in favour of maintaining the nuclear deterrent, more concerned with political influence than military effectiveness. Supporters claimed that Britain needed an effective deterrent to have a voice in Washington, maintain its standing in the Western alliance and preserve equality of status with France. Healey was at the forefront of those urging improvements to Polaris; Solly Zuckerman, the Chief Scientist, was a determined opponent. While research work was carried out under Labour, a decision on improving Polaris, through the 'Chevaline' project, was left to the Heath government.[76]

Conclusion

'I imagine', wrote Healey, 'historians will best remember my six years at the Ministry of Defence for the liquidation of Britain's military role outside Europe'. After the withdrawal from east of Suez, Britain was still a nuclear power and the USA's closest ally in the intelligence field, and had a scattering of global bases, from Gibraltar to Hong Kong. But, as the February 1970 White Paper said, 'The main function of British forces in the future will be to help in guaranteeing peace and security for Europe through the … Atlantic Alliance'. Wyn Rees points out that the focus on Europe was not something pre-planned by a visionary administration. Labour had begun by putting the world role above the European one and it long sought to reduce the costs of the BAOR; after 1968 Europe was left as the main theatre of military activity by a simple process of elimination.[77] There are important questions about why the withdrawal from east of Suez occurred, when it was decided upon and how it was managed. It is difficult to disagree with Dockrill's conclusion that 'economic imperatives drove the defence debates', with 'a strong conviction' that high defence spending was contributing to Britain's poor economic performance compared with its competitors. As Brown wrote in July 1967, 'The overriding need for us is to get our economy straight and bring our defence expenditure into line with our resources.'[78] But a number of political factors were also at work in the field of ideas (anti-imperialism), shifting diplomatic aims (the EEC application) and personnel changes (notably the arrival of Brown and, later, Jenkins in key positions), while particular problems, notably the Confrontation and the need to placate allies, influenced the precise timing of retreat. The importance of the July 1966 and November 1967 economic crises should not be overstated. These were only the most dramatic reminders of the country's precarious financial position. As much as anything it was the November 1964 decision to restrict defence spending to £2 billion that set the tone for the whole administration, for it was clear, within months, that achieving that target might involve cuts in commitments, unless resources were stretched beyond breaking point.

This is not to say that the commitment to an east of Suez role was always a deceit on Wilson's part. When, in May 1965, Brown complained about the strain that the presence east of Suez put on the balance of payments, the Prime Minister scribbled curtly over the letter, 'One day I will reply'. Questions of prestige, anti-Communism, alliance commitments and Commonwealth responsibilities all helped justify a global presence. Ministers took time to adjust to the realities of the debate, and even in January 1968 some resisted Jenkins' wish for a rapid withdrawal. Nonetheless, it was the *pace* of retreat, as much as the principle, which was significant by then. Even before the end of 1965 there were clear signs that the government was eager to liquidate the Aden base and drastically reduce costs in South-East Asia. In March 1967, when Healey put forward his radical ideas on a rundown east of Suez, Palliser warned Wilson, 'we should be under no illusion that it is anything but the end of Britain's "world role" in defence'.[79] By mid-1967 Britain's Far Eastern allies were well aware that its days as a regional military power were numbered and the January 1968 decisions accelerated final withdrawal from South-East Asia and the Gulf by only a few years. Britain still retained a general 'capability' to intervene in these areas but even the idea of an Indian Ocean 'island strategy' fell by the wayside. If anyone deserved the blame for urging the British to cling on to the world role while simultaneously refusing to devalue, thus over-stretching their resources, it was the USA. But in 1964–6 Wilson's aims probably coincided with Washington's, without any need for a formal 'deal' between them, and in 1967 he was quite happy to push through the withdrawal from South-East Asia in the face of US doubts. The USA could not 'dictate' British policy, it came to appreciate that Britain was unable to sustain the world role and it adjusted quickly to the decisions of July 1967 and January 1968.

Gordon Walker later argued that the withdrawal from east of Suez was a 'revolutionary decision, taken at the earliest possible time'. This puts too positive a gloss on affairs. Frank Cooper, one of Healey's senior officials, was more honest in saying, 'there was an amazing process of muddling through but it came out quite well'.[80] Policy-makers were beset by uncertainties – not just specific uncertainties, like when the Confrontation would end, but broader ones about how to extricate themselves from Aden, Singapore and the Gulf without sparking new crises, upsetting allies and damaging British influence. And there was one towering uncertainty, through which few contemporaries saw clearly. The financial upheaval of 1966–9 was a reflection of global economic developments that no single government could control. West European growth, the rise of Japan, the relative weakening of the US economy and the inability of the central banks to control the ever-growing volume of currency and capital exchanges all combined to put enormous pressure on the system of fixed exchange rates. There were daunting inflationary pressures that Western governments, dominated by Keynesian thinking on state expenditure, were ill-prepared to face and which would make the 1970s a decade of stagnation, inflation and further currency upheaval. In a sense, the Wilson governments were dealing with the opening phase of an irresistible, but unfamiliar and unwelcome, change in economic conditions. Their reaction to the changes left something to be desired in speed and decisiveness, but they somehow contrived to put the British economy back on an even keel and, beyond Aden, to conduct quite an orderly imperial retreat. Furthermore, the Conservatives did not choose to reverse the withdrawal from east of Suez, the most important decision the Wilson governments took in the international field.

Notes

Unless otherwise stated the place of publication is London.

1 David Reynolds, *Britannia Overruled* (Longman, 1991), 226; Michael Palliser, 'Foreign policy', in Michael Parsons, ed., *Looking Back: the Wilson years* (University of Pau Press, Pau, 1999), 23.

2 Jeffrey Pickering, *Britain's Withdrawal from East of Suez* (Macmillan, 1998); also his 'Politics and "Black Tuesday": shifting power in the cabinet and the decision to withdraw from "East of Suez"', *Twentieth Century British History*, vol. 13, no. 2 (2002), 144–70; David Greenwood, *The Economics of the East of Suez Decision* (Aberdeen University Press, Aberdeen, 1973); Saki Dockrill, *Britain's Retreat from East of Suez: the choice between Europe and the world?* (Macmillan, 2002), especially 211–12; Matthew Jones, 'A decision delayed: Britain's withdrawal from Southeast Asia reconsidered, 1961–8', *English Historical Review*, vol. 67, no. 472 (2002), 569–95; Thomson and Wright quoted from 'The East of Suez Decision', Institute of Contemporary British History seminar, 16 November 1990.

3 For contemporary accounts see: Henry Brandon, *In the Red* (Andre Deutsch, 1967); William Davis, *Three Years Hard Labour* (Andre Deutsch, 1968). For retrospective studies see: B. W. E. Alford, *British Economic Performance, 1945–75* (Macmillan, 1988); Alec Cairncross, *Managing the British Economy in the 1960s* (Blackwell, 1996). On the US dimension see Rajarish Roy, *The Battle of the Pound: the political economy of Anglo-American relations, 1964–8* (PhD, London School of Economics, 2000), 61–76.

4 James Callaghan, *Time and Chance* (Collins, 1987), 163 and 168–9; Kenneth Morgan, *Callaghan: a life* (Oxford University Press, Oxford, 1997), 212–13.

5 Public Record Office (PRO), CAB 128/39, CC10(64) (24 November); Douglas Jay, *Change and Fortune* (Hutchinson, 1980), 297–9 and 308–11.

6 Callaghan, *Time*, 173–6; Morgan, *Callaghan*, 215–18; Roy, *Battle*, 80–95; Jeremy Fielding, *The Currency of Power: Anglo-American economic diplomacy and the making of British foreign policy, 1964–8* (PhD, Yale University, 1999), 90–101.

7 Morgan, *Callaghan*, 213; Fielding, *Currency*, 87–8.

8 PRO, PREM 13/255, Brown to Wilson and Callaghan (23 July); Roy, *Battle*, 141–3; Callaghan, *Time*, 185–6; Barbara Castle, *Fighting all the Way* (Weidenfeld and Nicolson, 1993), 352.

9 For full discussions see: Fielding, *Currency*, 107–27; Roy, *Battle*, 109–90.

10 On the background to defence policy see: Dockrill, *Britain's Retreat*, chapters 1 and 2; C. J. Bartlett, *The Long Retreat: a short history of British defence policy, 1945–70* (Macmillan, 1972), chapters 5–6; Phillip Darby, *British Defence Policy East of Suez, 1947–68* (Oxford University Press, Oxford, 1973), chapters 6–8. 'Profit and loss' memorandum, CAB 134/1551, CPC(57)27 reproduced in Ronald Hyam and William Roger Louis, eds., *The Conservative Government and the End of Empire, 1957–64, Part 1* (Stationery Office, 2000), 4–28.

11 Dockrill, *Retreat*, 50–54; Hyam and Louis, *Empire*, 298–307.

12 Robert Pearce, ed., *Patrick Gordon Walker: political diaries, 1932–71* (Historians' Press, 1991), 298–9.

13 CAB 130/213, MISC 17/1st and 2nd (21 November), and papers 1–3 (13 and 18 November); Saki Dockrill, 'Britain's power and influence: dealing with three roles and the Wilson government's defence debate at Chequers in November 1964', *Diplomacy and Statecraft*, vol. 11, no. 1 (2000), 215–27 and 232–4.

14 Denis Healey, *The Time of My Life* (Michael Joseph, 1989), 279, also 290 and 293; Patrick Gordon Walker, *The Cabinet* (Jonathan Cape, 1970), 133.

15 Darby, *Defence Policy*, 330; Paul Einzig, *Decline and Fall?* (Macmillan, 1969), 63–73; Robert Holland, *The Pursuit of Greatness* (Fontana, 1991), 318–21, 328–33 and 336–8; also John Darwin, *Britain and Decolonisation* (Macmillan, 1988), 290–8.

16 Richard Crossman, *Diaries of a Cabinet Minister, Volume I: Minister of Housing 1964–6* (Hamish Hamilton and Jonathan Cape, 1975), 93–5 and 116–17; Jones, 'Decision delayed', 576–83.

17 PREM 13/103, Wright to Wilson (2 December) and handwritten Wilson minute; Karl Hack, *Defence and Decolonisation in South-East Asia, 1941–68* (Curzon, Richmond, 2001), *passim*.

18 Wyn Rees, 'British strategic thinking and Europe, 1964–70', *Journal of European Integration History*, vol. 5, no. 1 (1999), 60–2.

19 *The Times*, 17 November; *House of Commons Debates*, vol. 704, columns 421–4; Darby, *Defence Policy*, 284–5.

20 *Statement on the Defence Estimates 1965* (Cmnd 2592, 1965); Michael Carver, *Tightrope Walking: British defence policy since 1945* (Hutchinson, 1992), 73–4.

21 Sean Straw and John W. Young, 'The Wilson government and the demise of TSR-2', *Journal of Strategic Studies*, vol. 20, no. 4 (1997), 18–44; quote from PRO, AVIA 65/1744, Jenkins to Wilson (21 January). See also: Dockrill, *Retreat*, 77–94; Edward Pearce, *Denis Healey* (Little, Brown, Boston, 2002), chapter 32.

22 Dockrill, *Retreat*, 95–100; David Easter, *British Defence Policy in South East Asia and the Confrontation, 1960–66* (PhD, London School of Economics, 1998), 267–72 and 282–5; McNamara quoted in Cyrus L. Sulzberger, *An Age of Mediocrity* (Macmillan, New York, 1973), 265.

23 CAB 130/213, MISC 17/5th, 6th and 7th (13 June) and papers 17/8, 9 and 10 (9–11 June); CAB 128/39, CC(65)33rd (15 June); Dockrill, *Retreat*, 100–4; Easter, *Defence*, 282–9.

24 PREM 13/216, Callaghan–McNamara meeting (30 June); Callaghan, *Time*, 186–8.

25 Clive Ponting, *Breach of Promise: Labour in power 1964–1970* (Hamish Hamilton, 1989), 53; Ben Pimlott, *Harold Wilson* (Harper Collins, 1992), 383; Chris Wrigley, 'Now you see it, now you don't: Harold Wilson and Labour's foreign policy', in R. Coopey, S. Fielding and N. Tiratsoo, eds., *The Wilson Governments, 1864–70* (Pinter, 1993), 131–2; John Dumbrell, *A Special Relationship: Anglo-American relations in the Cold War and after* (Macmillan, 2001), 64 and 66–9, and see his 'The Johnson administration and the British Labour government: Vietnam, the pound and east of Suez', *Journal of American Studies*, vol. 30 (1996), 230–31; Diane Kunz, 'Anglo-American defence and financial policy during the 1960s', *Journal of Imperial and Commonwealth History*, vol. 27, no. 2 (1999), 228. For other discussions see: Dockrill, *Retreat*, chapter 5; Alan Dobson, 'The years of transition: Anglo-American relations 1961–7', *Review of International Studies*, vol. 16 (1990), 239–58; Diane Kunz, *Butter and Guns: America's Cold War economic diplomacy* (Free Press, New York, 1997), chapter 8; and Pickering, *Britain's Withdrawal*, 136–74.

26 PREM 13/2450, records of meetings (8–9 September); *Foreign Relations of the United States* (*FRUS*), 1964–8, vol. XII (US Government Printing Office, Washington, DC, 2001), 506–9; Matthew Jones, *Conflict and Confrontation in South East Asia: Britain, the US, Indonesia and the creation of Malaysia, 1961–5* (Cambridge University Press, Cambridge, 2002), 289–90.

27 Lyndon Johnson Library, National Security File, Bundy files, box 10, Bundy to Johnson (28 July); Roy, *Battle*, especially 155–9, 181–3 and 331–40; Robin Renwick, *Fighting with Allies* (Macmillan, 1996), 200.

28 Fielding, *Currency*, introduction (quotes from 5, 7 and 9), 70–1 and 196–7; *FRUS*, vol. XII, 501–2 (Bator memorandum); Acheson papers, Sterling Library, Yale, draft memorandum to Schaetzel (10 September 1965) – which

I am grateful to Dr Donna Lee of Birmingham University for pointing out; Tore Tingvold Petersen, 'Crossing the Rubicon? Britain's withdrawal from the Middle East, 1964–8', *International History Review*, vol. 22, no. 2 (2000), 330, 335 and 338.

29 John Subritzky, *Confronting Sukarno: British, American, Australian and New Zealand diplomacy in the Malaysian–Indonesian confrontation, 1961–5* (Macmillan, 2000), 199–201; Dockrill, *Retreat*, chapter 6 and 148–51. Key British documents are: CAB 148/18, OPD(65)41st (23 September); CAB 148/22, OPD(65)131st (20 September); and PREM 13/889, records of Healey's talks (1–4 February). On the Washington talks: PREM 13/686, record of meetings (16–17 December) and PREM 13/801, Washington to FO (28 January); *FRUS*, vol. XII, 512–28.

30 CAB 148/18, OPD(65)21st (12 April); CAB 148/24, OPD(65)185th (22 November);CAB 148/25, OPD(66)28th (10 June).

31 See pages 64–5 below.

32 CAB 128/39, CC49(65) (23 September).

33 CAB 148/18, OPD(65)52nd (24 November); CAB 148/23, OPD(65)174th (22 November); CAB 148/24, 180, 181 and 183 (19–22 November); Dockrill, *Retreat*, 124–31; Easter, *Defence*, 324–7, 329–34, 341–2; Pearce, *Healey*, 281–3.

34 Dockrill, *Retreat*, 138–48; Pearce, *Healey*, 297–302; quote from Healey, *Time*, 275; Christopher Mayhew, *Time to Explain* (Hutchinson, 1987), 169–72; and see his *Britain's Role Tomorrow* (Hutchinson, 1967); Solly Zuckerman, *Monkeys, Men and Missiles: an autobiography 1946–88* (Collins, 1988), 378–80.

35 CAB 148/25, OPD(66)3rd–13th (9 January–13 February); Pearce, *Healey*, 283–6.

36 CAB 128/41, CC8 and 9(66) (14 February); Crossman, *Diaries I*, 455–6; Barbara Castle, *The Castle Diaries 1964–70* (Weidenfeld and Nicolson, 1984), 106–8; Pearce, *Healey*, 289–90; Edward Short, *Whip to Wilson* (Macdonald, 1989), 225–6.

37 *Statements on the Defence Estimates, 1966: Part 1* (Cmnd 2901, 1966); Pearce, *Healey*, 303–9; Darby, *Defence Policy*, 304.

38 CAB 128/41, CC37 and 38(66) (19–20 July); Castle, *Diaries*, 147–51 (Brown quoted on 147); Crossman, *Diaries I*, 576–8; *House of Commons Debates*, vol. 732, columns 627–9.

39 Fielding, *Currency*, 299–303; Roy, *Battle*, 204–31 and 254–63.

40 PREM 13/802, Callaghan to Healey (11 August) and reply (16 August).

41 Bartlett, *Long Retreat*, 215 and see 215–18.

42 Lord Gladwyn, *Halfway to 1984* (Weidenfeld and Nicolson, 1966), 34; Lord Gladwyn, *Memoirs* (Weidenfeld and Nicolson, 1972), 354.

43 Enoch Powell, *Freedom and Reality* (Paperfronts, 1969), 223–30; Bodleian Library, Oxford, Conservative Party papers, Leaders' Consultative Committee, LCC(65)71st (27 October 1965).

44 Labour Party, *Conference Report, Blackpool, 1965*, 186–201; Labour History Archive, Manchester, PLP minutes, 25 May and 15 June; Labour Party, *Conference Report, Brighton, 1966*, 249–52 and 271–3; Geoffrey Goodman, *The Awkward Warrior: Frank Cousins* (Davis Poynter, 1979), 492–5.

45 British Library of Political and Economic Science, London, Brook Publications' 'Seventies Archive', Brown interview, 29; PRO, FO 800/961, Maclehose minute and Brown–Wilson meeting (4–5 September).

46 George Brown, *In My Way* (Gollancz, 1971), 141; Jones, 'Decision delayed', 585–7 on Brown, and 588 (quote from Healey).

47 CAB 130/301, MISC 129(66)1st (22 October); Richard Crossman, *The Diaries of a Cabinet Minister, Volume II: Lord President of the Council and Leader of the House of Commons 1966–68* (Hamish Hamilton and Jonathan Cape, 1976), 85–6; Easter, *Defence*, 392–97; Helen Parr, *Harold Wilson, Whitehall and British Policy Towards the European Community, 1964–7* (PhD, Queen Mary College, London, 2002), 170.

48 CAB 148/25, OPD(66)48th (confidential annex, 9 December); Crossman, *Diaries II*, 155–6; Jones, 'Decision delayed', 594–5.

49 CAB 128/42, CC6(67) (3 February); *Statement on the Defence Estimates* (Cmnd 3202, February 1967); Philip Ziegler, *Wilson: the authorised life* (Weidenfeld and Nicolson, 1993), 275–6.

50 PREM 13/1384, unsigned letter to Nairne (14 March) and Palliser to Wilson (21 March); CAB 148/30, OPD(67)14th (22 March).

51 CAB 128/42, CC19(67) (11 April); Crossman, *Diaries II*, 308 and 313.

52 CAB 130/313, MISC 140/1st (9 March) and 3rd (20 March); PREM 13/1525 and 1526, *passim*; Callaghan, *Time*, 211–12. For discussions see: Fielding, *Currency*, 313–15; Ponting, *Breach*, 105–6; Roy, *Battle*, 275–84.

53 CAB 148/30, OPD(67)17th (21 April); CAB 128/42, CC23(67) (27 April); PREM 13/1456, Lee to Wilson (26 May); Dockrill, *Retreat*, 187–9.

54 PREM 13/1528, Palliser to Maclehose (25 April).

55 CAB 148/30, OPD(67)19th (12 May); CAB 128/42, CC34(67) (30 May); Dockrill, *Retreat*, 190.

56 PREM 13/1906, Wilson–Johnson meeting (2 June); Jones, 'Decision delayed', 589–90; Fielding, *Currency*, 366–9.

57 CAB 148/30, OPD(67)25th (3 July); CAB 148/32, OPD(67)46th (21 June); CAB 128/42, CC45(67) (6 July); Castle, *Diaries*, 273–4 and 285; Crossman, *Diaries II*, 403 and 411–12; *Supplementary Statement on Defence Policy* (Cmnd 3357, July 1967); Dockrill, *Retreat*, 193–9 and 211.

58 Ponting, *Breach*, 288–9; Fielding, *Currency*, 323–32; Raj Roy, 'The battle for Bretton Woods: America, Britain and the international financial crisis of October 1967–March 1968', *Cold War History*, vol. 2, no. 2 (2002), 37–47. For discussions see Callaghan, *Time*, 218–22; Morgan, *Callaghan*, 268–75; Pimlott, *Wilson*, 473–84; Harold Wilson, *The Labour Government 1964–1970: a personal record* (Weidenfeld and Nicolson, 1971), 447–61.

59 CAB 128/42, CC68(67) (21 November); CAB 148/30, OPD(67)28th (28 July).

60 Roy Jenkins, *A Life at the Centre* (Macmillan, 1991), 211–12; Pickering, 'Black Tuesday', *passim*; British Library of Political and Economic Science, London, Alastair Hetherington papers, 13/1, meeting with Wilson (13 December 1967).

61 Pearce, *Healey*, 344–8; and see pages 167–8 below.

62 PREM 13/1999, record of meeting (20 December); Jenkins, *Centre*, 213–14; Pearce, *Healey*, 348; Pickering, 'Black Tuesday', 157–62.

63 CAB 128/43, CC1(68) (4 January); Tony Benn, *Office Without Power: diaries, 1968–72* (Hutchinson, 1988), 2–4; Castle, *Diaries*, 348–50; Crossman, *Diaries II*, 634–5; Pearce, *Healey*, 349–50.

64 PREM 13/1999, New York to FO (11 January, including Brown quote); PREM 13/2081, Thomson telegrams to CRO (7–12 January); PREM 13/2209, Roberts to FO (8–9 January); *FRUS*, vol. XII, 603–11.

65 CAB 128/43, C5, 6 and 7(68) (12 and 15 January); PREM 13/1999, Johnson to Wilson (14 January); PREM 13/2081, Lee–Wilson meetings (14 February); Benn, *Office*, 16; Castle, *Diaries*, 354–8; Crossman, *Diaries II*, 646–8 and 650; Healey, *Time*, 273; Lee Kuan Yew, *From Third World to First* (Harper Collins, 2000), 40–3.

66 Official minutes are withheld but see Benn, *Office*, 5–6; Pearce, *Healey*, 350.

67 Pickering, 'Black Tuesday', 145; Castle, *Diaries*, 349.

68 Pickering, 'Black Tuesday', 148–9, *passim*. For a contrast see Jones, 'Decision delayed', 593–5.

69 *House of Commons Debates*, vol. 756, columns 1579–83; *Statement on the Defence Estimates, 1967* (Cmnd 3540, 1967); Dockrill, *Retreat*, 206–7.

70 CAB 128/43, CC1(68) (4 January); PREM 13/2455, record of meeting (8 February).

71 Fielding, *Currency*, 333–6.

72 Peter Hennessy, *The Prime Minister* (Allen Lane, 2000), 316–19; Fielding, *Currency*, 344–50; Roy, 'Bretton Woods', 52–4.

73 PREM 13/2586, Wilson–Blankenhorn meeting (20 November); Jenkins, *Centre*, chapter 14, especially 264–5; Herbert Blankenhorn, *Verstandnis und Verstandigung: Blatter eines politischen Tagebuchs, 1949–79* (Propylaen, Frankfurt, 1980), 543–4.

74 CAB 148/91, OPD(69)1st (12 January 1969); PREM 13/3122, Trend to Wilson (20 January).

75 CAB 148/35, OPD(68)14th (26 July); CAB 148/37, OPD(68)44th (24 July); Richard Crossman, *The Diaries of a Cabinet Minister, Volume III: Secretary of State for Social Services 1968–1970* (Hamish Hamilton and Jonathan Cape, 1977), 159; and, generally, FCO 49/15–19.

76 CAB 134/3120, PN(67)2nd (3 April), 3rd (18 May) and 4th (5 December, for arguments on retaining Polaris); PREM 13/1316, Zuckerman to Wilson (8 December 1966) and Trend to Wilson (6 January, 17 May and 1 December 1967); PREM 13/2493, Trend to Wilson (1 December 1967, 4 January, 24 June and 28 November 1968); Lawrence Freedman, *Britain and Nuclear Weapons* (Macmillan, 1980), 37–40; Zuckerman, *Monkeys*, 386–97.

77 Healey, *Time*, 277; *Statement on the Defence Estimates, 1970* (Cmnd 4290, 1970); Rees, 'Strategic thinking', 64–71.

78 Dockrill, *Retreat*, 217; PREM 13/1457, FO to Washington (13 July 1967).

79 PREM 13/1890, Brown to Wilson (19 May 1965) and undated Wilson minute; PREM 13/1384, Palliser to Wilson (21 March 1967).

80 Gordon Walker, *Cabinet*, 130–3; Cooper, in 'East of Suez' seminar, 16 November 1990.

3

South and East Asia

The Vietnam War, the best-remembered conflict of the 1960s, presented a range of challenges to the Labour governments, touching on the Anglo-American 'special relationship', Britain's role in South-East Asia, Commonwealth unity and domestic stability. Michael Stewart called it 'the most difficult and the most agonizing of all the problems I had to face'.[1] But when Labour entered office in October 1964, Vietnam was not a priority and Britain was already involved in another conflict, the so-called 'Confrontation' between Malaysia and Indonesia. Malaysia, which at that time included the island of Singapore, was a former colony, central to British investment and military interests in the Far East. Singapore was an important air, army and navy base. Furthermore, in 1965 Britain was also concerned with a war between two Asian Commonwealth nations, India and Pakistan. In all three conflicts a significant background factor was Communist China.

Generally in East Asia since 1945, London had been less willing to take risks than had the USA in facing the Communists. Britain wanted to see Communism defeated and, as seen in the counter-insurgency campaign against Malayan Communists (1948–60), could be ruthless in defending its own interests. The British position east of Suez was closely wrapped up in their self-image as a great power. But the colony Hong Kong was vulnerable to Chinese pressure and Britain did not want to be dragged into a general war in the region by American bellicosity. Despite US unhappiness, London supported the division of Vietnam at the 1954 Geneva conference, when a Communist state was formed in the north. Britain and the USSR were co-chairs of the Geneva conference, which was recalled in 1961–2 to help settle a civil war in one of Vietnam's neighbours, Laos. The unhappiness was not one-sided: when Indonesia's Ahmed Sukarno launched the Confrontation, it was London that was upset by the Americans, who favoured a conciliatory approach, fearful of driving Indonesia into the arms of Beijing. But Anglo-American differences should not be exaggerated. Washington had little liking for Sukarno and sometimes tried to undermine him;

whereas, during the Kennedy years, the British Conservative government generally supported US policy on Vietnam and sent a military
advisory mission to Saigon.[2] Britain needed to work as closely as
possible with the USA if only to restrain its ally when it came to a crisis
and the USA wanted Britain to retain an active role in the Far East so as
to share the burdens of defence. London also knew that two Commonwealth states, Australia and New Zealand, saw the defeat of Communism
in South-East Asia as a priority.

China, India and Pakistan

While in opposition, Labour had an ambiguous policy on Communist
China, favouring its admission to the United Nations (UN) (which the
USA opposed) but condemning its attack on India in 1962. Just as
Labour entered office, China exploded its first atomic bomb, raising
fears of a nuclear attack on India. Once in office Wilson, keen to co-
operate with the USA, agreed not to press Chinese membership of the
UN.[3] At this point China seemed more threatening, and certainly more
irrational, than the USSR. Patrick Gordon Walker had written in April
that 'an isolated China is a wild ... force in a very dangerous part of the
world' and that it would be wrong to play 'China off against Russia. In
the conflict between Russia and China our sympathies must be with
Russia.'[4] The Sino-Soviet split had grown apace in recent years and the
Joint Intelligence Committee (JIC) judged that relations had reached
'the verge of rupture. Each country is now likely to pursue its national
interests independently of the other.' But the split, by weakening the
world Communist movement, also made a Chinese confrontation with
the West less likely. One JIC report argued that Beijing would 'maintain
the status quo in Hong Kong for the time being'; another felt that,
thanks to economic and military weaknesses, there was 'a discrepancy
between the militancy of China's language and the caution of her actions',
although it did wish to regain lost territory, including Hong Kong.[5]

Hong Kong had been built up since the nineteenth century as a commercial and financial centre. There was no question of handing it back
to the Communist regime yet, but neither could it be given independence, because the Chinese had leased most of the territory to Britain
and the lease would expire in 1997. In 1966–7, however, Chinese policy
became increasingly unpredictable as Mao Zedong initiated his Cultural
Revolution, in which youthful Red Guards tried to reinvigorate Communism by attacking traditionalist elements and foreign interests.
There were several demonstrations outside the British mission in Beijing
before it was ransacked in August 1967. Trouble began in Hong Kong
in May 1966. In its colonies Britain was responsible for internal and

external security, and in this case the two were closely linked. In May 1967 there were riots in Hong Kong and from June to August there was a series of border incidents, forcing the British to reinforce the colony with a warship and troops. In July relations with China were also strained by the arrest of a British journalist, Anthony Grey, in Beijing. In the Commons on 20 July 1967 George Brown accused the Chinese of challenging 'the normal civilised means of communication between governments' and insisted 'we cannot allow ourselves to be intimidated by threats from China, or by violent outbreaks of local Communist sympathisers'. Yet the JIC did not depart from its opinion that Chinese actions would not match their rhetoric. A report in October 1966 concluded, 'The Chinese are unlikely to attack Hong Kong during the next few years', although 'if they did, they could bring overwhelming force to bear, and we might have no effective warning'. The JIC stuck to this view through 1967. In September the Cabinet was assured that the security situation in Hong Kong was 'under control' and by 1968 the troubles in Hong Kong receded as Chinese policy became saner.[6] However, a real improvement in relations, mirroring the USA's 1971–2 'opening to China', had to await the Heath government.

When Wilson took office one of Britain's main concerns was Chinese intentions towards India, the most populous democracy in the Commonwealth. But support for India was complicated by the position of another Commonwealth member, its neighbour Pakistan. The two had fought an inconclusive war over the Kashmir in 1948 and tension over this had continued. Pakistan's military leader, Mohammad Ayub Khan, had moved closer to China after 1962, while remaining allied to the West; whereas India, though non-aligned, had improved its relations with the USSR. China's explosion of an atomic bomb made Wilson eager to provide India with a guarantee against Chinese aggression, partly to prevent a regional arms race by showing the Indians that there was no need to build an atomic bomb themselves. Britain took an interest in ideas for a US–Soviet–British nuclear 'umbrella' to protect India from Chinese nuclear attack but, despite some soundings in early 1965, it was difficult to produce a form of words that gave the Indians sufficient reassurance while leaving the nuclear powers with the freedom to decide their own response to a crisis.[7] With the worsening of US–Soviet relations over Vietnam in 1965, any joint guarantee by the superpowers became even less likely and the Indians would not accept a Western-only guarantee. Rising tension between India and Pakistan also made a guarantee problematic, since the Pakistanis disliked the idea of guarantees to their rival by outside powers.[8]

Meanwhile, Wilson developed some remarkable ideas for a British nuclear 'umbrella' in the Indian Ocean, through the use of Polaris submarines. Andrew Pierre has shown that this proposal made sense for several reasons: war with China seemed more likely than war with the USSR; Labour was still committed to remain east of Suez; and, given the sympathy for India in left-wing circles, such a policy might persuade the Labour Party to retain the British deterrent. But Pierre questions whether Britain could ever realistically have deterred the might of Red China.[9] Official papers show that ministers, other than Wilson, had little enthusiasm for the project but that the Prime Minister did not easily give it up. In August 1966, in the Overseas Policy and Defence Committee (OPD), he again argued the case for sending Polaris to the Indian Ocean: apart from reassuring India, this 'might also enable us to make substantial economies on our other forces in the Far East'.[10] A month later, once Brown had become Foreign Secretary, Wilson pressed him to support the proposal and in January 1967 it went before the ministerial Nuclear Policy Committee. The record is withheld but the relevant memorandum shows that the whole Polaris force would be placed east of Suez (splitting it between theatres would ruin its effectiveness) and that it could not be deployed there before 1972, because it would require special facilities, like a depot ship. Nonetheless, despite the problems, ministers left the possibility open until mid-1968, by which time the withdrawal from east of Suez had been decided. Even then, Wilson was told it could be reactivated, albeit at enormous cost.[11]

Long before that, Labour's hopes of a close relationship with India faded, due to Indo-Pakistani tensions. In late April 1965 border clashes began in the Rann of Kutch, a marshy area far removed from Kashmir. The Americans feared the crisis 'could build up to a real mess' but the British were soon accepted as mediators and a cease-fire was agreed on 6 June. Following talks between Wilson and the Indian and Pakistani leaders, Lal Bahadur Shastri and Ayub Khan, at the 1965 Commonwealth conference, an agreement was reached on 29 June to end the border clashes and put the dispute to arbitration. US Secretary of State Dean Rusk told President Johnson that the British 'worked like Trojans, under the most complicated and frustrating circumstances, to hammer out … an agreement', and Johnson sent a letter of congratulations to Wilson.[12] The success proved short-lived. The Rann of Kutch episode had helped rekindle tensions in Kashmir and at the end of August full-scale war began. Britain, like the USA, suspended arms deliveries to both sides. In early September the Pakistanis were having the best of the fighting in Kashmir but, around 6 September, the Indians launched an offensive towards Lahore. Pakistan argued that, in contrast to its own actions in the disputed region of Kashmir, India had launched an attack across an internationally recognised border. The argument won some sympathy in London and led Wilson to issue a statement which, while he claimed to be even-handed, was specifically critical of India's conduct. The Indians were furious.

In his memoirs Wilson blamed the statement on poor advice from a
'pro-Pakistani faction' in the Commonwealth Relations Office (CRO)
but he subsequently conceded this was inaccurate. He was actually fore-
warned by the CRO that the messages to Shastri and Ayub Khan were
'rather stiff' and that one aim was 'to shake the Indians' confidence in
their rectitude'. His Private Secretary for foreign affairs, Oliver Wright,
told the Americans that there had been 'a pretty tough statement.... We
fully expect India to react strongly'.[13] Joe Garner, the Permanent Under-
Secretary at the CRO, continued to defend the statement years afterwards:
such 'forthright action achieved its purpose of bringing home to both
parties the seriousness of the situation'. But Garner also acknowledged
that 'relations between Britain and India were strained so long as Wilson
remained PM'. Thanks to the statement the British were not seen as
potential arbitrators in a post-war settlement, as they had been over the
Rann of Kutch. Britain's ambassador, John Freeman, was told by the
Indian President that 'relations were more strained than at any time
since independence'.[14] After a cease-fire was achieved it was the USSR
which took the lead in trying to broker an Indo-Pakistani settlement.
British ministers were not too distressed, in that the USSR took on a
difficult task and, at Tashkent in January 1966, achieved no more than
a return to the pre-war situation. But Stewart conceded it was a blow to
London's *amour propre* and Brown suggested that Tashkent, by showing
the limited value of Commonwealth ties, pointed Wilson towards an
EEC application.[15] China, it should be noted, made bellicose noises
about the Sino-Indian border, but made no attempt to intervene in the
war despite British concern that it would do so.

The Malaysian–Indonesian Confrontation, 1963–5

The Confrontation was triggered by the creation in September 1963 of
the federation of Malaysia. This comprised a number of former British
territories: Malaya; the island city of Singapore, reckoned to be economically non-viable on its own; and the territories of north Borneo and
Sarawak, both on the island of Borneo and viewed as too small for self-
government. The creation of Malaysia gave London the opportunity to
lose direct responsibility for running these possessions and yet retain
use of the all-important Singapore base. But London also hoped that
creating a stable Malaysia would allow a reduction of force levels east of
Suez. The Malayan government of Tunku (Prince) Abdul Rahman had
signed a defence agreement with Britain in 1957 and was happy to see
its forces remain for the moment. Singaporean premier Lee Kuan Yew
saw membership of Malaysia as a way to satisfy popular demands for
independence while providing the island with income from the British

base. There was no love lost between the Tunku and Lee, however. Both had ambitions of dominating the federation. Another difficulty was that Sukarno had long been critical of Britain's colonial presence in South-East Asia, and that Indonesia had claims on northern Borneo, which bordered on its own territory. On 20 January 1963 he formally condemned plans for 'Malaysia' and launched the Confrontation, a propaganda campaign accompanied by border clashes.

All at once the security of Malaysia was called into question. At almost a thousand miles in length, the border with Indonesia in Borneo was difficult to defend, while Singapore was literally minutes away from a potential Indonesian air attack. British hopes of reducing their force levels in the Far East were ruined. Nonetheless, London favoured a robust response and looked to regional allies – the USA, Australia and New Zealand – for support. The allies were not keen to enrage Sukarno, however, and saw Malaysia as a British responsibility. The Indonesian leader, though radical and unpredictable, seemed popular with his people, had no obvious rival for power and was at least able to keep the Indonesian Communist Party (PKI) in check. Indonesia, with about 100 million people, was too important to drive into the Eastern bloc. When Malaysia formally came into being, in September 1963, the Indonesians reacted violently. The British embassy in Jakarta was burnt down and the Confrontation intensified. The Conservative government deployed extra troops to protect Malaysia, launched counter-incursions into Indonesia and again sought to persuade Washington that Sukarno was a menace. The last had some success after Johnson became President. In February 1964 he and Douglas-Home agreed to reciprocate political support over the Confrontation and Vietnam, a most significant understanding in view of later events. A negotiated settlement proved impossible because, while Malaysia would negotiate only on the basis of its territorial integrity, this was the very point Sukarno questioned.[16]

Ahead of the 1964 British general election, there was an increase in border incidents and even an infiltration of guerrillas into mainland Malaya. No British government could welcome an all-out war with Indonesia, which would absorb huge resources and perhaps stir up China. But Labour was committed to the defence of Commonwealth states in the region and had supported a robust line in opposition and continued this in office. Australian and New Zealand forces were now providing troops and Edward Peck, the Assistant Under-Secretary for the Far East, told a US official in November that the British were not finding the Confrontation too much of a strain. They doubted Sukarno was genuinely interested in diplomacy, although he had put out some peace feelers, and they believed in maintaining pressure on him for the time being.[17] Indeed, militarily, the Confrontation was going well for Britain: it had superiority in the air and at sea, while on the ground the British carried the fighting into Indonesian-ruled Borneo. In January the government extended, to 10,000 yards (up from 3,000), the distance to which local commanders could make 'deniable' infiltrations across the border. These were spearheaded by the elite Special Air Service regiment (the SAS), the ideal military unit for small-scale operations, such as those in Borneo and Aden, where large-scale offensives would have aroused the ire of the UN.[18] Casualties in the Borneo campaign were light, at 114 killed in 1963–6, while Indonesian losses were five times as high. Also, there was little domestic opposition in Britain, where the moral case for resisting intimidation was widely accepted. But the drain on resources was substantial, with jet fighters and eighty naval vessels deployed in the area, as well as a peak presence of 17,000 British troops in Borneo.[19] The Americans were concerned at the situation, especially given Sukarno's growing dependence on the PKI, his increasing friendliness with China and his erratic behaviour, seen in his walking out of the UN. In late January, Johnson even suggested he might meet the Indonesian leader to try to exert a moderating influence, but Wilson resisted and the idea was dropped. Significantly, the British were more confident than Washington that the Indonesian army would prevent any Communist takeover if Sukarno were removed. Peck even looked forward to a showdown between the PKI and the army.[20]

On taking office, Labour initiated its review of defence expenditure, which resulted in the decision to reduce defence spending to £2 billion. But of course this was difficult to achieve. Arguments that Britain's overseas bases should be retained in order to safeguard prestige, defend Western commercial and security interests, and retain influence over Washington were particularly significant for South-East Asia, because the Singapore base was central to the position east of Suez. In any case, with the Confrontation between Malaysia and Indonesia at its height, Britain had little choice other than to remain in the region for the time being. Nonetheless, South-East Asia was absorbing far more resources than was desirable and it was believed that the Singapore base was untenable in the long term because of rising Asian nationalism. In a sense, the British had nothing to gain in the long term from resisting Sukarno, in that they were always likely to cut their local presence once the Confrontation ended. The planning staff at the Foreign Office (FO) produced a paper in November 1964 that highlighted the contradictions in Britain's position. Economically, South-East Asia was of little importance, taking only a few per cent of British trade, and the retention of a Western military presence risked driving local nationalists towards the Communist bloc, so that 'the ultimate neutralization of the area ... between the West and the Communist powers' was desirable. But the Chinese threat, the Confrontation and the need for good relations with the USA, Australia and New Zealand all meant that rapid British withdrawal was impossible. Indeed, no date for it could be set. The idea of a long-term 'neutralisation' of South-East Asia remained popular among diplomats in early 1965. As John Subritzky has noted, this interest in withdrawing from the region in order to prevent Asian nationalism becoming too anti-Western shows that arguments for a 'retreat' from east of Suez were not all about economics.[21] But then hopes of 'neutralising' the region were undermined by a serious new development, the direct involvement of the USA in a South-East Asian war.

Escalation in Vietnam, 1964–5

In opposition Wilson had sometimes criticised US policy in Vietnam, but even by the time he became Labour leader such disagreements had been toned down.[22] During the August 1964 Gulf of Tonkin crisis, when the USA first bombed North Vietnam for a short time, Tony Benn noted two serious constraints on Labour's policy: 'The British government needs American support against Sukarno ... and Wilson is particularly anxious not to upset Johnson'.[23] These factors would continue to operate for some time. Actually, when Wilson took office the Vietnam situation did not seem pressing. Lyndon Johnson even portrayed himself as the peace candidate in the 1964 presidential election campaign. The President did ask Wilson for a military commitment in Vietnam when they met for the first time in December, but the Prime Minister was easily able to resist on that occasion. He depicted Britain's military commitment in Malaysia as being equivalent to US efforts in Vietnam and argued that they must not compromise Britain's role as co-chair of the Geneva conference, which might soon be recalled to discuss the conflict.[24] In early February 1965, when the war began to intensify, with Communist attacks on US 'advisers' in Vietnam, Wilson became concerned, telephoned Johnson and offered to go to Washington for discussions. But the President flew into a temper and told Wilson, 'I won't tell you how to run Malaysia and you don't tell us how to run Vietnam'. Fredrik Logevall, in one of the few US accounts of the Vietnam War to utilise British sources, has argued that Johnson was too determined upon escalation in February 1965 to listen to British doubts. 'He rejected a Wilson visit because it would cause publicity and thus interfere with his plan to keep the escalation secret' from the American people at this stage.[25] The telephone call seems only to have harmed the President's view of British resolve. In the months following, his advisers repeatedly said that Wilson was doing all that could be expected: Under-Secretary of State George Ball believed that British support 'has been stronger than that of our other major allies' and the National Security Adviser, McGeorge Bundy, said 'every experienced observer has been astonished by the overall strength and skill of Wilson's defence of our policy'. But the very fact that these assurances frequently had to be repeated suggests that Johnson was never convinced.[26]

In late February the USA began its 'Rolling Thunder' bomber offensive against North Vietnam and, in public certainly, Wilson's line was sympathetic. Thus, in the Commons on 1 April 1965 he made 'absolutely plain our support of the American stand against the Communist infiltration in South Vietnam'. Given Wilson's desire for a close relationship with Johnson and previous promises of mutual support over Vietnam and the Confrontation, he could hardly do otherwise.[27] But behind such utterances there were limits to the government's support for US tactics in Vietnam. In late March, when the Americans announced that they were using gas in Vietnam, Stewart followed it up with critical public remarks in Washington. It is significant that he had gone there to clarify US aims in Vietnam and was instructed by Wilson to say Britain would not be 'the tail-end Charlie in an American bomber'.[28] The various Vietnam peace initiatives that Wilson made in 1965–7 have frequently been castigated as hopelessly pro-American, the products of Wilson's vanity,[29] but in fact the Americans did not welcome them with any enthusiasm and Wilson had several, quite hardheaded, if selfish, reasons for taking them: they helped counter US pressures for British involvement, provided the Prime Minister with a meaningful international role as a peacemaker, and helped him deal with backbench dissent. The significance of backbench criticism in driving Wilson's peace initiatives has been questioned, because only six or seven MPs regularly spoke out on it.[30] Yet it is surely no coincidence that Wilson's most intense, public attempts at mediation came in 1965, when he had a wafer-thin majority in the Commons. As early as March 1965 the Chief Whip, Ted Short, was pressing the Cabinet for a public initiative of some sort to placate backbench opinion, as he had found that Vietnam 'caused … more party problems than any other issue'.[31] After winning a clear majority in March 1966 Wilson's peace efforts would slacken even though, paradoxically, the scale of backbench revolt increased.

Britain's first peace effort was an approach to the USSR in early 1965, as co-chair of the Geneva conference, to arrange exploratory talks with each conference member. But Moscow rejected any initiative, insisting that the USA must first call off its war against the North.[32] The Soviets took a hard line probably because they were competing with China for influence in Hanoi. Hope for a settlement was provided by Johnson's speech at Johns Hopkins University on 7 April, when he insisted that he was ready for talks, but an analysis by the British ambassador, Patrick Dean, argued that the speech was designed mainly to impress neutral opinion, with 'no expectation of any results in the immediate future'.[33] A week later Wilson arrived in Washington and his meetings with Johnson went well. Wilson even claimed, retrospectively, that they had agreed on a 'division of function': 'The American government would not be deflected from the military task; but, equally, he would give full backing to any British initiative which had any chance of getting peace-talks on the move.' The official record is less dramatic but, for public relations reasons, Johnson could hardly stand in the way of any peace initiatives.[34] One had already been planned: Gordon Walker was sent on a fact-finding tour of East Asia in April to explore local views on the war. But, as the FO predicted, the key Communist players, in Hanoi and Peking, refused to see him.[35]

In June 1965 Wilson, in addition to the contrary pressures from the US President and the Labour left, faced the challenge of a Common-wealth conference. The Commonwealth included countries that sent contingents to fight in Vietnam – Australia and New Zealand – as well as critics of US policy, like Julius Nyerere of Tanzania. In his search for a way to keep the organisation united, Wilson proposed that the Common-wealth despatch its own four-man peace mission to the relevant capitals. As Chris Wrigley notes, the initiative 'worked at several levels': it took the focus off an even more divisive Commonwealth issue, Rhodesia; it again showed that Wilson was doing something to achieve peace; it was difficult for the Conservatives to attack; and it both appeared indepen-dent of the USA yet in fact had their prior, if unenthusiastic, approval. The desire to meet various aims in a single initiative was typical of Wilson.[36] The radical Kwame Nkrumah of Ghana agreed to join, which gave some hope that the mission would appear genuinely neutral, but it never had much chance of success. As with Gordon Walker's effort, all the Communist capitals refused to accept the mission. In an attempt to persuade Hanoi to change its mind, Wilson then hit on the novel idea of sending a junior minister, Harold Davies, to see Ho Chi Minh. A moderate left-winger and close ally of Wilson, Davies had met Ho on a visit to Vietnam in 1957. The FO was again sceptical and, although Davies reached Hanoi, he was unable to meet Ho.[37] That ended Wilson's serious peace attempts for the time being and, in retrospect, the failures had occurred at a crucial time. At the end of July the President agreed to a massive increase in US troop levels in Vietnam, after which both sides seemed set on securing a military edge before entering negotiations.

The British sensed Johnson was being dragged into a quagmire in Vietnam. Thus Oliver Wright wrote, in March 1965, 'that the Americans cannot win and cannot yet see any way of getting off the hook' – a statement oddly in tune with the President's own complaint: 'I can't get out. I can't finish it with what I've got. So what the hell can I do?'[38] Even in late 1964 there had been a pessimistic debate among British officials about the chances of the USA 'saving' South Vietnam. But a paper drawn up for the OPD in November argued that it was in Britain's interest to save South-East Asia from Communism and that London should support US policy if only 'to use the influence which this will give us towards restraining them from the graver risks of escalation'.[39] Once US troops were committed, British experts had little faith in the tactics of 'big unit' warfare, linked to massive aerial bombardment; the British preferred a pacification campaign in the South to tackle what was expected to be a drawn-out guerrilla war.[40] Officials could also be frank about weaknesses in America's political case. Thus, in July 1965, an FO memorandum admitted that 'the 1954 Geneva settlement, had it been applied, would have produced substantially the same result' as Hanoi wanted, namely a united, Communist Vietnam. A study by the FO planning staff, finalised in September, guessed that the Communists, rather than negotiating or broadening the conflict to Laos, would keep up the guerrilla war in the South. Another study, in December, was even more striking in its prediction that, if the USA failed to secure a military ascendancy, 'the most to be expected from negotiations would be a settlement enabling the United States to withdraw ... but offering the South Vietnamese little chance of maintaining a non-Communist independence'.[41]

The end of the Confrontation, 1965–6

Meanwhile, as 1965 progressed, all the main parties in the Confrontation faced difficulties. The Labour government increasingly wished to reduce defence costs, but could not do so until the Confrontation ended. The government's freedom was so restricted that it could not even announce an intention to cut spending in South-East Asia because such a declaration, while it might please the financial markets, would encourage Sukarno and alienate Britain's regional allies. As Stewart wrote in June 1965, the 'situation in Southeast Asia is mainly shaped by forces over which Britain has ... little or no control'.[42] This point was underlined on 10 August when Chinese–Malay tensions, reflected in the rivalry between Lee and the Tunku, led Singapore suddenly to become independent of Malaysia. The Tunku pushed the separation on Lee: Malays became the dominant ethnic group in Malaysia once Chinese-dominated Singapore was lost. The British had been worried for months about such an event, but the timing and degree of the separation were unexpected. Singaporean independence sparked grave concern in London. It called into question the viability of what remained of Malaysia and threatened to undermine international support for resistance to Sukarno, whose claims about the federation being 'artificial' now appeared justified. Separation also made the campaign in Borneo seem even less desirable, given that Britain's prime military interest in the area – the Singapore base – was no longer part of Malaysia, whose creation had sparked the Confrontation in the first place. Within days of the separation Healey told Wilson that the 'key issue is not whether or when we leave Singapore, but ... how to end our commitment under confrontation as soon as possible'. However, this would require allied support and some peacetime presence would need to be maintained, because any hint of a precipitous retreat might 'lead to the withdrawal of American support for Sterling'.[43]

At the end of August, the OPD agreed it was best to plan for an early end to the Confrontation, albeit in such a way that there was no 'surrender' to Sukarno and, in early September, Britain informed the Americans, Australians and New Zealanders of its hopes for a negotiated end to the Confrontation and a withdrawal from Singapore. Although there was also talk of setting up a British base in Australia, the proposals drew a frosty response.[44] A British departure from South-East Asia at this point would have been particularly disturbing to the Americans. Their own relations with Sukarno were now very poor and they did not want him bolstered by victory in the Confrontation. But Johnson could hardly tackle Indonesia forcefully at the same time as escalating the war in Vietnam. For the moment compromise was possible. George Ball visited London, urged Wilson not to reduce the presence in South-East Asia and promised continued US support for sterling. The British then backed off from any thought of an early with-drawal, even if their long-term hopes were unchanged.[45]

For all the problems it caused, the Malaysia–Singapore separation did not lead to defeat in the Confrontation because within a matter of weeks, quite fortuitously, Indonesia underwent its own domestic up-heaval. Ironically, in late September, unable to persuade their allies of the need for a negotiated settlement, the British considered increasing covert operations against Sukarno, including psychological warfare operations and support for dissidents so as to stir up domestic division. Some covert aid to separatist groups had probably been given since 1964.[46] Then, on 30 September 1965, pro-Communist elements in the Indonesian army, possibly encouraged by Sukarno, murdered several leading generals. Anti-Communists, led by General Suharto, quickly struck back. The Americans were both determined to prevent any PKI takeover and reluctant to intervene directly in the country, so they provided covert aid to the army. In the ruthless purge that followed, up to 500,000 suspected Communists were killed. Meanwhile, to allow the army to deal with the PKI, the British refrained from escalating the Confrontation. Instead, the FO approved a clandestine propaganda campaign against the Communists.[47] By March 1966 the PKI was effectively destroyed and General Suharto became the real power in Indonesia, though Sukarno remained President until 1967.

The defeat of Sukarno did not guarantee an end to the Confrontation. A US analysis in November 1965 judged such a step as 'unlikely' because of the army's own involvement in the campaign, patriotic feeling in Indonesia and the temptation to use the Confrontation to divert attention from the country's dire internal problems.[48] In December the OPD looked at plans to increase military pressure on the new regime if it continued the Confrontation and Andrew Gilchrist, in his valedictory telegram as ambassador to Indonesia, in April 1966, still feared the conflict would run on.[49] British troops still had to remain in large numbers. It soon became clear, however, that the new regime's anti-Communism and need for financial assistance pointed towards reconciliation with Malaysia. Under the foreign minister, Adam Malik, Indonesia distanced itself from China, re-entered the UN and began secret contacts with Malaysia. In late April, despite doubts from the Ministry of Defence, Stewart took the risk of securing Indonesia's goodwill by offering £1 million in aid. On 1 July, in another calculated risk by the FO, there was a successful visit by Stewart to Jakarta.[50] These initiatives continued a tradition of generally timely and successful British policy-decisions where Indonesia was concerned. The Confrontation was finally called off by an agreement of 11 August 1966. A year later Indonesia, Malaysia and others formed the Association of South-East Asian Nations (ASEAN), to foster stability and economic growth in the region.

The OPD agreed on 17 June to withdraw troops from Borneo as rapidly as possible once the Confrontation formally ended, a decision that was entirely in line with earlier hopes of reducing force levels in South-East Asia. There was no thought at this meeting of moving troops to Vietnam, where an increasingly bloody conflict was raging: indeed, Stewart led the way in saying this must not be done and that Britain's long-term goal in the region still remained 'neutralisation'. As Matthew Jones has said, by 'closing down the option of a more active British involvement in ... Vietnam during 1964–5, Indonesian policy, though it created immediate dilemmas ... of its own, may also have saved Britain from a far more costly exercise ... in the jungles of South East Asia'.[51] In July 1967 the British announced their decision to withdraw from South-East Asia by the mid-1970s. It seemed, perhaps, poor timing to announce British withdrawal when the future of Vietnam was so uncertain. But as George Brown, now Foreign Secretary, told the Commons in July, there was more to South-East Asia than America's war. In Indonesia, Sukarno's power was broken; the Confrontation had ended; there were signs of greater regional co-operation with the dawn of ASEAN; and Britain could exert influence through non-military means, such as aid policy and relief for Indonesian debts.[52] This was part of a general policy of focusing on non-military means of influence in the world, now that military withdrawal was underway, and a similar process will be seen when the Middle East is discussed. Yet, even while transforming its own policies, Britain had to continue dealing with the problems generated by Vietnam.

Vietnam, 1966–7

British policy on Vietnam could not easily escape contradictory pressures: to back the USA while seeking a peaceful settlement and placating backbench critics. In December 1965, during another trip to Washington, Wilson urged on Johnson the idea of a 'bombing halt' to give North Vietnam a chance to come to the peace table.[53] A previous halt had come to nothing, but pressure was building on the President from several quarters to try again. The January 1966 suspension of bombing lasted several weeks but again won no response from Hanoi and its ending, on 31 January, triggered a crisis in London. When the FO issued a statement in 'support' of the USA's resumption Labour backbenchers were furious and Wilson, presumably worried by the up-coming election, sent a stern rebuke to Stewart.[54] Yet a visit by Wilson to Moscow in late February only confirmed the impossibility of opening meaningful negotiations. Alun Chalfont, the FO Minister of State who accompanied Wilson, managed to talk to North Vietnamese representatives but neither they nor the Soviets backed away from insisting on a US withdrawal.[55] Fortunately for Wilson, Vietnam did not impact significantly on the general election, but thereafter feelings in parliament and the country sometimes ran high. The first major crisis came at the end of June, when Washington extended its bombing campaign in North Vietnam to targets near the main population centres, Hanoi and Haiphong. Many Labour MPs were outraged and Wilson publicly expressed 'regret' at the US action. This has been seen as an important moment in alienating Johnson from Wilson and, certainly, there can be little doubt that the President was exasperated at this point.[56] Yet all was not as it seemed, for Wilson was warned of the bombings well in advance and had even given advice on the precise wording of his 'dissociation' from the US action.[57] Neither did the incident prevent Johnson comparing Wilson to Winston Churchill only weeks afterwards.[58]

In August 1966 Brown became Foreign Secretary, determined to play a more forthright role in world affairs and to take the initiative in foreign policy away from Downing Street. The general aims of Wilson and Brown were similar where Vietnam was concerned. Both wanted Britain to play a major diplomatic role and to work for a settlement, while staying close to the USA. But Michael Palliser has commented that, while Stewart genuinely believed in the American cause, Brown was more critical. He warned one US official that another escalation of bombing 'might well lose you the support of all your friends in Europe, like me, who are trying to help'. At the Labour conference in October, without consulting the Americans, Brown launched a plan for a cease-fire in Vietnam, followed by peace talks on the basis of the 1954 settlement. He repeated this at the UN shortly afterwards.[59] But an embarrassment followed when Brown visited Moscow to sound out the Soviets out on peace talks. Unknown to the British, the USA had recently tried to establish a secret link to Hanoi via a Polish diplomat, Janusz Lewandowski. When the Soviets – who did know about Lewandowski – started asking Brown detailed questions, it became obvious to them that the British were not fully in Washington's confidence. On discovering this shortly afterwards, Wilson and Brown were aghast.[60] Yet, ironically, the failure of the Lewandowski initiative paved the way for Wilson's most significant peace effort.

Of all the attempts by Wilson to the end the war, only the February 1967 effort, codenamed 'Sunflower' by the Americans, features regularly in accounts of the conflict.[61] The complexities of what transpired in London that month were of Byzantine proportions, but basically the situation was this: there were signs that both Washington and Hanoi wanted to prepare for negotiations; a formula for achieving this already existed, involving both an end to US bombing (Phase A) and a de-escalation by the Communists of the war on the ground (Phase B); Kosygin, the Soviet premier, who had close contacts with the North, was visiting London for talks with Wilson, who, of course, could be considered a close ally of the USA; and it was hoped that these two could help to secure an agreement. Given what had happened in the Lewandowski episode, Wilson was determined to be briefed on Johnson's position and to this end a US official, Chester Cooper, was sent to London. The talks continued for several days and were accompanied by another US bombing pause, but they became hopelessly compromised when Washington altered the precise wording of the Phase A–B formula. Instead of a US bombing halt being followed by Communist de-escalation (as Wilson originally explained it to Kosygin), Johnson now insisted that the USA would permanently end the bombing only *after* North Vietnamese infiltration of the South ended. The North did not respond, the Soviet premier left London empty-handed, bombing was resumed – and Wilson was furious, certain that a 'historic opportunity had been missed'.[62] Support for the belief in a 'historic opportunity' comes from a study based on Soviet sources, which suggests that Moscow had been asked by Hanoi to clarify the US position, that Kosygin did seriously try to persuade the Kremlin that the Phase A–B plan might work and that the resumption of US bombing ended all chance of progress. There is no direct evidence from Hanoi that the initial A–B formula would have been acceptable but it seemed, even to Chester Cooper, that Johnson never expected anything from the Kosygin visit and did not treat it seriously.[63]

The impact of Vietnam on Britain

There is considerable debate about whether Washington used its economic power to encourage a British military contribution to the Vietnam War. As Philip Kaiser, the US number two in London, noted, the 'President deplored the failure to support us militarily even if the aid was essentially symbolic. "A platoon of bagpipers", Johnson said, would have been enough.'[64] The so-called 'Hessian option' of getting British troops into Vietnam in return for US support of sterling, just as Britain had hired Hessian mercenaries in the American War of Independence, was certainly discussed in Washington. A particular advocate was McGeorge Bundy, who once put a figure of $1 billion on the value of a British contingent. But he was opposed by George Ball, who argued that it was in America's own interest to back the pound and that maintaining the British position east of Suez in general was more important than getting a few extra troops into Vietnam.[65] In March 1965, Wilson told Stewart, regarding Vietnam, that 'Should the President try to link this question with support for the Pound I would regard this as most unfortunate', and almost a year later, in Cabinet on 14 February 1966, Wilson 'repeated time after time that the Americans had never made any connection between the financial support they gave us and our support for them in Vietnam'. Yet, at the same time, 'he was saying, "Nevertheless, don't let's fail to realize that their financial support is not unrelated to the way we behave in the Far East"'. Richard Crossman deduced 'that there was no understanding because there was no need of one: the President could reckon on ... Wilson'.[66] This may have been true in terms of diplomatic support for the USA, but it was certainly not true of a military commitment on the ground. If there was any specific Anglo-American 'deal' over South-East Asia it was one in which they gave each other general political support over the Confrontation and Vietnam, as agreed by Johnson and Douglas-Home in 1964. Johnson, indeed, seems seldom to have raised the issue of a troop contribution with Wilson directly. An exception was in April 1967 when, with the Confrontation drawing to a close, the President said Britain's financial worries would be over if two brigades were sent to Vietnam. Wilson replied that it would also mean his fall from office.[67] Yet, even if few Americans expected Wilson to contribute a 'platoon of bagpipers', resentment about his behaviour persisted. In late 1967 Secretary of State Dean Rusk 'was caustic, even bitter, about the British ... not sending troops to help us in Vietnam'.[68]

Whatever Rusk's feelings, there was British assistance of sorts to the Americans. On the clandestine side, Britain's consulate in Hanoi – set up in 1946 in French colonial days and maintained despite Britain's non-recognition of the Communist regime – was used to gather intelligence, not least on morale in North Vietnam. Britain provided material under the UKUSA agreement on signals intelligence, with the communications monitoring station in Hong Kong proving particularly valuable.[69] Several accounts have mentioned service by the British special forces unit, the SAS, in Vietnam. Individuals operated as part of Australian and New Zealand units and certain SAS soldiers, involved in training Thailand's special forces, may have taken part in reconnaissance missions into Laos.[70] Open assistance included arms sales, the use of Hong Kong as a port facility, the provision of army engineers to maintain airfields in Thailand (freeing US engineers to work elsewhere) and the training of South Vietnamese troops and US dog-handlers in the Jungle Warfare School in Malaysia. The British Advisory Mission set up under Macmillan ended in early 1965, its leader Edward Thompson having become disillusioned with the South's anti-insurgency campaign. But it was replaced by a small 'Police Advisers Team' focusing on civil policing.[71] There was also technical and medical assistance to South Vietnam. However, none of this was sufficient to prevent US complaints in 1965 over trade with North Vietnam on British ships. The ships, generally chartered by Chinese businesses in Hong Kong, carried exports from the North rather than imports useful for the war and the trade was worth a paltry £190,000 in 1965, but it provoked an outcry from Congress and the media.[72] There was a similar outcry in June 1966 when, to satisfy parliamentary opinion, Healey hastily announced that Britain would no longer provide arms for use in Vietnam. British ministers soon retreated: military matériel would still reach Vietnam, but would take the form of 'non-lethal' items.[73]

Ben Pimlott has pointed out that for 'many people in Britain in the mid-1960s … Vietnam was the most important matter facing the government, because of … the moral responsibility of the United Kingdom as an ally of the United States'.[74] In early 1965, as measured by opinion polls, there were more Britons who supported the US war effort in Vietnam than opposed it, but by December 1966 a majority (51 per cent) were critical of US actions, and only 30 per cent approved them.[75] Pacifists, Christians, idealistic university students – many joined with left-wing activists to blame Johnson for starting the war and calling for the USA to quit. A British Council for Peace in Vietnam was formed in April 1965 and large-scale demonstrations against the war began in October–November 1965. Press criticism of the war ranged from the *Daily Mirror* on the left, through the liberal *Guardian*, to the right-wing *Spectator*. The US embassy in Grosvenor Square – 'Genocide Square' to the protesters – was the focus of many demonstrations and the scene of some violence in

1967–8. The Home Secretary, Jim Callaghan, came under pressure to cancel a big demonstration in London in October 1968, but decided that such a denial of democratic rights was out of the question.[76] Yet the anti-war movement in Britain never achieved truly 'mass' appeal across society, its supporters were frequently divided between themselves – between, for example, those who merely wanted peace and those hard-line anti-Americans who wanted a Communist victory – and it soon declined in intensity, being replaced as a moral cause by Biafra in 1968–9.

In parliament, Wilson's main worry was not a defeat at the hands of the Conservatives, who generally sympathised with US policy, but a defection by his own supporters. As seen above, Wilson was especially keen to placate his critics before the 1966 election. Thereafter he did not seriously expect a defeat in the Commons, but the scale of revolt could be embarrassing. In July 1966, after the US bombing of Hanoi, thirty-one Labour MPs abstained in a vote on the government's Vietnam policy; and late in 1967 the Chief Whip warned that 'opposition on Vietnam was no longer the prerogative of the Left, but now spread across the centre and right'. The divisions ran straight to the centre of government, with several Cabinet ministers particularly critical of Michael Stewart. Crossman, who considered 'our attitude to Vietnam morally indefensible', wrote of Stewart's 'doctrinaire support for the Americans in Vietnam'.[77] But the Foreign Secretary's key argument against those who wanted him to criticise US policy – that this would 'have caused resentment in the US without altering their policy – was a difficult one to counter and he could rely on the support of key figures like Brown, Healey and, of course, Wilson. Few ministers were prepared to press their opposition to government policy very far and the only resignation that primarily involved Vietnam was that of Frank Allaun, a humble Parliamentary Private Secretary.[78] The Labour Party's broader divisions on Vietnam were exposed at the annual conferences in 1966 and 1967, both of which saw defeats for the leadership on the question.[79] A more regular concern was the Parliamentary Labour Party, where backbenchers regularly criticised the government's Vietnam policy. But, again, there were limits to the damage that was done. At a meeting in July 1966, following the US bombing of Hanoi, there was a motion of no confidence against Wilson, but such an extreme move succeeded only in dividing the left.[80] All in all, domestic discontent may have led Wilson to tone down his support for the Americans, but little more.

1968–70: Britain's withdrawal; America's 'unwinnable' war

In January 1968 came the decision to accelerate the withdrawal from east of Suez. An aid package was provided to Malaysia and Singapore

to help them cope with the economic impact, linked to assurances that
they would maintain their sterling balances, protect British investments
and use the aid to buy British goods as far as possible.[81] Beginning with
a five-power conference of Australia, Britain, Malaysia, New Zealand
and Singapore in June 1968, talks were held on the rundown of the
British presence, with the British determined to adhere to the December
1971 deadline while encouraging defence co-operation among the local
Commonwealth countries. There was also a determination to be rid of
the Anglo-Malaysian Defence Agreement and to minimise training exercises in the area so as not to encourage thoughts that the withdrawal
could be reversed.[82] By the end of 1971 the Malaysia–Singapore security
system had been transformed from one built around a substantial British
presence and written commitments to a form of consultation in which
Britain was one among several powers, including the USA, Australia
and New Zealand.[83]

Dismay over British withdrawal did not prevent Johnson from encouraging Wilson's last, vain efforts at a Vietnam settlement. The Prime
Minister went to Moscow in late January but found the Russians reluctant to pressure Hanoi, which was unsurprising after the 'Sunflower'
fiasco. Back in Washington in early February, Wilson found Johnson to
be at once 'extremely troubled' and yet 'optimistic about the future
course of the war'.[84] It was only in the following weeks that it became
obvious that the war had become 'unwinnable', in light of the Communist 'Tet' offensive. Johnson dramatically announced, on 31 March,
that he would not seek re-election as President and that he was restricting US bombing of the North. For a time, as if unable to absorb the
change, the debate in the British government over Vietnam continued
on its established lines. In the Cabinet, on 2 April, some ministers
argued the time had finally come to dissociate from the USA, but Wilson
and Stewart successfully resisted.[85] Downing Street had already issued a
statement applauding Johnson's statement and, in messages to the President, Wilson yet again offered to act as a go-between with the Soviets.[86]
For its part, the FO decided that its objective should now be 'to help
the United States find a way of retreating with the least possible stress
in Asia or in the United States itself'. The FO was concerned that, with
a US withdrawal, the 'whole region will become uneasy' and that local
regimes would try to come to terms with the Communists and 'our own
interests, both trading and political, are likely to suffer'.[87]

The British had little to do, directly, with Vietnam in 1969, and the
issue ceased to feature much in the Foreign Secretary's report to Cabinet.
A Foreign and Commonwealth Office brief noted that there was little
role to play now that Washington and Hanoi were conversing directly.[88]
There was an outburst of moral repugnance in November, when news
of the US massacre of Vietnamese civilians at My Lai was revealed. But

the only serious difficulty for Wilson over Vietnam after Tet came near the end of his administration, in April 1970, when US and South Vietnamese forces made a brief 'incursion' into Cambodia against North Vietnamese sanctuaries there. This was one of the few times the Cabinet had a proper discussion on Indochina, with a special meeting on 5 May at which Cambodia was the only subject. Castle, Crossman and others wanted to distance Britain from the US action but Stewart and Callaghan led the arguments against. Faced by a divided Cabinet, and with an election looming, Wilson predictably steered a middle course. Even Stewart acknowledges that the Cabinet was firm in its decision: 'it was agreed that we could not approve' the incursion. But later that day in the Commons, for the last time, Stewart again enraged many of his own backbenchers by emphasising that the Americans would not have acted but for the North Vietnamese presence in Cambodia. It was left to the Prime Minister to calm the situation with a skilful speech, which Castle described as perhaps his best ever demonstration of reserving his position without openly condemning the USA.[89]

Conclusion

Wilson's performance on Vietnam has drawn much comment and been a focus of criticism for various reasons. One biographer feels his peace initiatives were designed only 'to distract attention from Britain's continuing support for the United States'. Actually there was more to them than that. The motives in 1965 were, probably, quite parochial – to dampen backbench criticism, prevent a Commonwealth split, or raise Wilson's international profile – but the 'Sunflower' talks, being secret, were probably serious enough and there were always good reasons for Britain to seek peace in South-East Asia. There may be something in Peter Shore's argument that government support for the USA 'looked grubby and self-seeking to a whole generation of the young', but there were many other factors that contributed to youth alienation in the 1960s. Another line of attack, forcefully revived by Fredrik Logevall, is that Wilson could have had real influence if he had questioned Johnson's policies, especially in early 1965, before the commitment of large numbers of US troops.[90] But the wider context of British policy limited Wilson's options: apart from the need for US financial support, any readiness to criticise the USA was, as Matthew Jones says, 'muted by the desire not to lose Washington's support over confrontation with Indonesia'. Besides, even if Wilson had been more forthright, Johnson would most likely have ignored him.[91] Wilson's approach to Vietnam may not have brought peace but there was never much chance of that anyway, and the policy was no disaster. His verbal support for the war effort kept most US officials content, helped neutralise Johnson's pressure for British involvement and forestalled any argument with the Australian and New Zealand governments. It bears repeating that Britain had its own interests in seeing Communism contained in South-East Asia and no interest in seeing the USA suffer defeat. Indeed, one study takes the line that Wilson's policy *did* offend the President: according to Sylvia Ellis this contributed much to the decline of the special relationship in the 1960s.[92] Certainly, Wilson's willingness to criticise the USA at certain points, his refusal to become actively involved and his attempts to mediate a settlement helped to keep domestic opposition manageable and avoided a costly war.

There was more to British policy in Asia than Vietnam, however. In fact, the memoirs of most Cabinet ministers make only passing reference to that conflict and, while Vietnam may have featured regularly on the Cabinet's agenda, this was in order to keep ministers abreast of developments rather than to discuss policy. Vietnam, however difficult, was a day-to-day problem to be *managed*, rather than a pressing policy issue on which Britain could take decisive action. Philip Ziegler even criticises Wilson for devoting 'a disproportionate part of his time … to … Vietnam, in which the British interest was no more than peripheral'.[93] Far more important to the Cabinet and the OPD were the Confrontation, the future of Malaysia–Singapore and, of course, the problems of military withdrawal from the region. Viewed in this light, Wilson's decision to steer a middle course on Vietnam, avoiding a crisis with the Americans, seems even more sensible: he required Washington's sympathy on these other issues. Over both the Confrontation and the withdrawal from South-East Asia, British policy must be considered quite successful. There were elements of good fortune, notably the collapse of the Sukarno regime. But Britain's toughness with Sukarno in 1965–6, Stewart's readiness to court Malik in 1966 and the determination to withdraw from the region before nationalist opinion turned against Britain were brave as well as astute decisions. Despite some concern in August 1965, when Singapore became independent, the British saw the Confrontation through to an end, even though, once it was over, they intended to leave the region. The government also remained quite cool in the face of Chinese provocations in Hong Kong in 1966. Yet this was the same government that, in September 1965, unnecessarily alienated India, with a single ill-advised decision for which Wilson personally must bear the blame.

Notes

Unless otherwise stated the place of publication is London.

1 Michael Stewart, *Life and Labour* (Sidgwick and Jackson, 1980), 151. For a fuller discussion on Vietnam see John W. Young, 'Britain and "LBJ's War", 1964–8', *Cold War History*, vol. 2, no. 3 (2002), 63–92.

2 Peter Busch, 'Supporting the war: Britain's decision to send the Thompson Mission to Vietnam', *Cold War History*, vol. 2, no. 1 (2001), 69–94.

3 Victor Kaufman, 'The Anglo-American dispute over Chinese representation at the United Nations', *English Historical Review*, vol. 65, no. 461 (2000), 370–4.

4 Robert Pearce, ed., *Patrick Gordon Walker: political diaries, 1932–71* (Historians' Press, 1991), 298; Gordon Walker, 'Labour's defense and foreign policy,' *Foreign Affairs*, vol. 42, no. 3 (1964), 397.

5 Public Record Office (PRO), CAB 158/51, JIC(64)2nd (3 March); CAB 158/53, JIC(64)56th (11 February 1965); and CAB 158/54, JIC(64)71st (10 May 1965).

6 *House of Commons, Debates*, vol. 750, columns 2499–502; PRO, DEFE 4/217, COS 38th/67 (16 May); CAB 158/64, JIC(66)73rd (Final) (17 October); and CAB 158/67, JIC(67)51st (3rd revise) (14 December 1967); and see CAB 158/69, JIC(68)15th (12 January 1968); CAB 128/42, CC54(67) (7 September).

7 *Foreign Relations of the United States (FRUS)*, 1964–8, vol. XI (US Government Printing Office, Washington, DC, 1997), 80 and 177; PRO, PREM 13/973, Stewart to Wilson (3 March).

8 Lyndon B. Johnson Library (LBJL), Austin, National Security File (NSF), Country Files, India, box 129, State to New Delhi (5 May); PREM 13/1251, Wilson–Singh meeting (3 June); PREM 13/973, Maclehose to Wright (29 September).

9 Andrew Pierre, *Nuclear Politics* (Oxford University Press, Oxford, 1972), 285–7.

10 CAB 148/25, OPD(66)34th (5 August).

11 PRO, FO 800/961, note on 'Nuclear Policy' (13 September 1966); CAB 134/3120, PN(66)4 (14 December); PREM 13/2493, Trend to Wilson (1 December 1967) and Healey to Wilson (5 June 1968).

12 *FRUS*, vol. XXV, 234–5; LBJL, NSF, Country File, UK, box 208, Rusk to Johnson (30 June); and on the mediation, PREM 13/391 and 392, *passim*, but especially PREM 13/393, Freeman to CRO (30 July, including diary of events).

13 Harold Wilson, *The Labour Government 1964–1970: a personal record* (Weidenfeld and Nicolson, 1971), 133–4; PREM 13/393, Hughes to Wilson, Downing Street statement, and Wright to Bundy (all 6 September).

14 Joe Garner, *The Commonwealth Office 1925–68* (Heinemann, 1978), 403–4; PREM 13/394, New Delhi to CRO (16 September).

15 CAB 148/18, OPD(65)40th (22 September); Cecil King, *The Cecil King Diary, 1965–70* (Jonathan Cape, 1972), 55–6.

16 Greg Poulgrain, *The Genesis of the Konfrontasi* (Crawford House, Bathurst, 1998); Matthew Jones, *Conflict and Confrontation in South East Asia, 1961–5* (Cambridge University Press, Cambridge, 2002), chapters 1–9; J. A. C. Mackie, *Konfrontasi* (Oxford University Press, Kuala Lumpur, 1974), chapters 1–9; John Subritzky, *Confronting Sukarno* (Macmillan, 2000), chapters 1–5; David Easter, *British Defence Policy in South East Asia and the Confrontation, 1960–66* (PhD, London School of Economics, 1998), chapters 1–5.

17 *FRUS*, vol. XXVI, 192–4.

18 Tony Geraghty, *Who Dares Wins: the story of the SAS* (3rd edition) (Little, Brown, Boston, 1992), 373–80; Ken Connor, *Ghost Force: the secret history of the SAS* (Weidenfeld and Nicolson, 1998), 93–6.

19 Jones, *Conflict*, 272–3; Subritzky, *Sukarno*, 198–9; William Jackson, *Withdrawal from Empire* (Batsford, 1986), 207–10; Tom Pocock, *Fighting General* (Collins, 1973), chapter 6.

20 *FRUS*, vol. XXVI, 216–21; Subritzky, *Sukarno*, 125–6.

21 CAB 148/17, OPD(64)10th (19 November); Subritzky, *Sukarno*, 145–9.

22 Paul Foot, *The Politics of Harold Wilson* (Penguin, 1968), 204–5 and 211.

23 Tony Benn, *Out of the Wilderness: diaries 1963–7* (Hutchinson, 1987), 135.

24 Wilson, *Government* (Weidenfeld and Nicolson, 1971), 48; PREM 13/104, Wilson–Johnson meeting, 3.30 p.m. (7 December); *FRUS*, vol. I, 985–6.

25 PREM 13/692, telephone conversation (11 February); Fredrik Logevall, *Choosing War: the lost chance for peace and the escalation of war in Vietnam* (University of California Press, Berkeley, 1999), 340.

26 LBJL, NSF, memoranda to the President, vol. 4, Ball to Rusk (14 April) and Bundy to Johnson (3 June).

27 *House of Commons Debates, Fifth Series*, vol. 709, column 1981.

28 Rolf Steininger, '"The Americans are in a hopeless position": Great Britain and the war in Vietnam, 1964–5', *Diplomacy and Statecraft*, vol. 8, no. 3 (1997), 261–6; Wilson, *Government*, 85–6; quote from PREM 13/693, London to Washington (23 March).

29 Peter Paterson, *Tired and Emotional: the life of Lord George Brown* (Chatto and Windus, 1993), 222 and 224; Donald Maclean, *British Foreign Policy Since Suez* (Hodder and Stoughton, 1970), 324; Clive Ponting, *Breach of Promise: Labour in power 1964–1970* (Hamish Hamilton, 1989), 221.

30 Michael Donohoe, *The Wilson Government's Vietnam Peace Initiatives, 1964–7* (MPhil, Oxford University, 1997), 33–6.

31 Edward Short, *Whip to Wilson* (MacDonald, 1989), 160.

32 PREM 13/693, record of meeting (16 March); Steininger, '"The Americans"', 254–8, 260–1; Wilson, *Government*, 80–5; Christopher Twine, *Anglo-American Relations and the Vietnam War, 1964–7* (PhD, University of Wales, Aberystwyth, 2000), 122–7.

33 PREM 13/694, Washington to London (9 April).

34 Wilson, *Government*, 95–6; PREM 13/352, record of meeting (15 April); *FRUS*, vol. II, 557.

35 PREM 13/694, Gordon Walker report (7 May); Steininger, '"The Americans"', 267–74; Donohoe, *Peace Initiatives*, 29–61.

36 Chris Wrigley, 'Now you see it, now you don't: Harold Wilson and Labour's foreign policy', in R. Coopey, S. Fielding and N. Tiratsoo, eds., *The Wilson Governments, 1964–70* (Pinter, 1993), 125–6.

37 Based on John W. Young, 'The Wilson government and the Davies peace mission to North Vietnam', *Review of International Studies*, vol. 24 (1998), 545–62. See also: Sylvia Ellis, *Anglo-American Relations and the Vietnam War, 1964–8* (PhD, University of Newcastle, 1999), 196–214; Twine, *Vietnam*, 150–60.

38 PREM 13/693, Wright to Wilson (1 March); Lady Bird Johnson, *A White House Diary* (Weidenfeld and Nicolson, 1970), 248.

39 Steininger, '"The Americans"', 239–46; Logevall, *Choosing War*, 222–7, 262–5 and 276–9; CAB 148/17, OPD(64)10th (19 November).

40 Twine, *Vietnam*, 94–5 and 172–4.

41 PREM 13/696, 'Background Brief' by Peck (5 July); PRO, FO 953/2258/6, SC(65)28 (30 September) and FO 953/2258/9, SC(65)35 (6 December).

42 Stewart to Rumbold (22 June), quoted in Subritzky, *Sukarno*, 159–60.

43 Albert Lau, *'A Moment of Anguish': Singapore in Malaysia and the politics of disengagement* (Times Academic Press, Singapore, 1998); PREM 13/431, Healey to Wilson (13 August); Jones, *Conflict*, 287–8; and, for earlier worries about a separation, PREM 13/429, Trend to Wilson (4 and 18 February).

44 CAB 148/39, OPD(65)37th (31 August); CAB 148/22, OPD(65)123rd (25 August); Subritzky, *Sukarno*, 162–7; Easter, *Defence*, 300–12.

45 PREM 13/2450, records of meetings (8–9 September).

46 David Easter, 'British and Malaysian covert support for rebel movements in Indonesia during the Confrontation', in Richard Aldrich, Gary Rawnsley and Ming-Yeh Rawnsley, eds., *The Clandestine Cold War in Asia* (Frank Cass, 2000), chapter 9.

47 *FRUS*, vol. XXVI, 317–18; Easter, *Defence*, 319; Subritzky, *Sukarno*, 175–6.

48 *FRUS*, vol. XXVI, 371–3.

49 CAB 148/18, OPD(65)55th (22 December); CAB 148/24, OPD(65)191st (14 December) and 192 (20 December); Subritzky, *Sukarno*, 176–8; Churchill College, Cambridge, Andrew Gilchrist papers, GILC 13/C, Gilchrist to Stewart (18 April).

50 CAB 148/25, OPD(66)19th (6 April); Gilchrist papers, GILC 13/C, Philips to Stewart (11 July).

51 CAB 148/25, OPD(66)29th (17 June) and see 31st (5 July); Jones, *Conflict*, 304.

52 *House of Commons Debates*, vol. 750, columns 2497–8; and see PRO, FCO 49/9, for SC(67)15 (2 March 1967), advocating British aid and encouragement of regional co-operation.

53 Wilson, *Government*, 187 and see 191–3; Philip Ziegler, *Wilson: the authorised life* (Weidenfeld and Nicolson, 1993), 226.

54 PREM 13/1272, Wilson to Stewart (1 February); Ziegler, *Wilson*, 226–7; Richard Crossman, *Diaries of a Cabinet Minister, Volume I: Minister of Housing 1964–6* (Hamish Hamilton and Jonathan Cape, 1975), 443 and 445.

55 PREM 13/1216, Wilson–Kosygin meetings (22–23 February) and Chalfont meeting with North Vietnamese (23 February); Alun Chalfont, *The Shadow of My Hand* (Weidenfeld and Nicolson, 2000), 134–7; Wilson, *Government*, 213–14.

56 Sylvia Ellis, 'Lyndon Johnson, Harold Wilson and the Vietnam War', in Jonathan Hollowell, ed., *Twentieth Century Anglo-American Relations* (Macmillan, 2001), 196 and 199. There are full accounts in: Twine, *Vietnam*, 198–212; and Ellis, *Relations*, 280–314.

57 PREM 13/1083, Johnson to Wilson (14 June).

58 Ziegler, *Wilson*, 227–9. Wilson, *Government*, 263–4, expresses surprise at the friendly reception.

59 Churchill College Archive, Cambridge, Diplomatic Oral History Project, Michael Palliser interview, 18–19; US National Archives, RG59, State Department, Office of the Executive Secretariat, Briefing Books, London to State (7 November); Labour Party, *Report of the Annual Conference, Brighton, 1966*, 269–71; UN speech, 11 October, reproduced in *British and Foreign State Papers, 1965–6* (Stationery Office, 1975), 437–51.

60 George C. Herring, *The Secret Diplomacy of the Vietnam War* (University of Texas Press, Austin, 1983), part VI, chapter 2; Twine, *Vietnam*, 237–45.

61 See especially Herring, *Secret Diplomacy*, part VI, chapter 3, but also, for example: Stanley Karnow, *Vietnam: a history* (Viking, New York, 1983), 495–6; Thomas Zeiler, *Dean Rusk* (University of Indiana Press, Wilmington, 2000), 173; Robert Mann, *A Grand Delusion* (Basic Books, New York, 2001), 527–8.

62 Wilson, *Government*, 345–66 (quote from 365); George Brown, *In My Way* (Penguin, 1971), 141–7; Ellis, 'Vietnam War', 197–200. For detailed accounts: Ellis, *Relations*, 360–407; Twine, *Vietnam*, 246–72.

63 Ilya Gaiduk, *The Soviet Union and the Vietnam War* (Ivan Dee, Chicago, 1996), 100–6; Chester Cooper, *The Lost Crusade* (McGibbon and Kee, 1980), 367–8.

64 Philip Kaiser, *Journeying Far and Wide* (Scribner's, New York, 1992), 230.
65 John Dumbrell, 'The Johnson administration and the British Labour government: Vietnam, the pound and east of Suez', *Journal of American Studies*, vol. 30 (1996), 220–4; and on Bundy's valuation, *FRUS*, vol. XII, 506. See also John Dumbrell, *The Making of US Foreign Policy* (Manchester University Press, Manchester, 1990), 215–21.
66 Wilson to Stewart, 23 March 1965, partly reproduced in Ziegler, *Wilson*, 222–3; Crossman, *Diaries I*, 456 and 540.
67 PREM 13/1528, Palliser to Maclehose (28 April).
68 Virginia Historical Society, Richmond, David Bruce diaries (8 November 1967).
69 Simon Kear, 'The British Consulate-General in Hanoi, 1954–73', *Diplomacy and Statecraft*, vol. 10, no. 1 (1999), 215–39; Stephen Dorril, *MI6* (Fourth Estate, 2000), 719–20; David Leigh, *The Wilson Plot* (Heinemann, 1989), 151.
70 For a summary of the evidence see Dorril, *MI6*, 719.
71 Peter Busch, *Britain and Kennedy's War in Vietnam, 1961–3* (PhD, London School of Economics, 1999), 252–4.
72 PREM 13/1272, Southeast Asia Department memorandum (27 January), and FO to Washington (16 February 1966); PREM 13/1273, Dean to Gore-Booth (10 May 1966).
73 PREM 13/1275, Canberra to FO (26 June), Washington to FO (26 and 27 June), and CRO to Canberra (30 June).
74 Ben Pimlott, *Harold Wilson* (Harper Collins, 1992), 391.
75 For a summary of opinion polls see Caroline Page, *US Official Propaganda During the Vietnam War* (Macmillan, 1996), 190–225.
76 CAB 128/43, CC43 and 44(68) (24 and 29 October); James Callaghan, *Time and Chance* (Collins, 1987), 258–61; Kenneth Morgan, *Callaghan: a life* (Oxford University Press, Oxford, 1997), 314–16; Nelson Lankford, *The Last American Aristocrat* (Little, Brown, Boston, 1996), 337–9.
77 Ziegler, *Wilson*, 326, citing Falkender papers; Crossman, *The Diaries of a Cabinet Minister, Volume II: Lord President of the Council and Leader of the House of Commons 1966–68* (Hamish Hamilton and Jonathan Cape, 1976), 674 and 716.
78 Stewart, *Life*, 157; P. G. Richards, *Parliament and Foreign Affairs* (George Allen and Unwin, 1967), 141.
79 On the conferences see Craig Wilson, *Rhetoric, Reality and Dissent: the foreign policy of the British Labour government 1964–70* (PhD, Washington State University, 1982), 87–91, 105–7 and 114–16.
80 Labour History Archive, Manchester, PLP minutes, 1962–71 file, 6 July 1966; Crossman, *Diaries I*, 562–3.
81 See especially CAB 128/42, CC74(67) (21 December); CAB 148/35, OPD(68)1st (26 January).
82 CAB 148/35, OPD(68)10th (3 May); CAB 148/37, OPD(68)29th (29 April); PREM 13/2082, FO/CRO to posts (19 June).
83 Kin Wah Chin, *The Defence of Malaysia and Singapore, 1957–71* (Cambridge University Press, Cambridge, 1983), chapter 9; Christopher Hill and Christopher Lord, 'The foreign policy of the Heath government', in Stuart Ball and Anthony Seldon, eds., *The Heath Government, 1970–74* (Routledge, 1996), 288–91.
84 Wilson, *Government*, 489–93 and 496–503.
85 CAB 128/43, CC25(68) (2 April); Barbara Castle, *The Castle Diaries 1964–70* (Weidenfeld and Nicolson, 1984), 416–17; Crossman, *Diaries II*, 755–6;

Churchill College, Cambridge, Michael Stewart papers, STWT 8/1/5, diary for 2 April.

86 *Documents on British Policy Overseas (DBPO), Series III, Volume I, Britain and the Soviet Union, 1968–72* (Stationery Office, 1997), 32–5; Wilson, *Government*, 519–20.

87 PREM 13/2462, 'Vietnam Negotiations – British Interests' (covering note dated 17 May).

88 *DBPO, III, I*, 189, note 7.

89 CAB 128/45, CC20 and 21(70) (5 and 7 May); Castle, *Diaries*, 794–6; Crossman, *The Diaries of a Cabinet Minister, Volume III: Secretary of State for Social Services 1968–70* (Hamish Hamilton and Jonathan Cape, 1977), 909–11; Stewart, *Life*, 214.

90 Austen Morgan, *Harold Wilson* (Pluto, 1992), 277; Peter Shore, *Leading the Left* (Weidenfeld and Nicolson, 1993), 95; Logevall, *Choosing War*, 401.

91 Matthew Jones, 'US relations with Indonesia, the Kennedy–Johnson transition and the Vietnam connection, 1963–5', *Diplomatic History*, vol. 26, no. 2 (2002), 279; Subritzky, *Sukarno*, 155–9.

92 Wrigley, 'Now you see it', 128–9; Ellis, 'Vietnam War', 192.

93 Ziegler, *Wilson*, 219.

4

The Middle East and Mediterranean

The Middle East saw the most celebrated humiliation for Britain in the era of imperial retreat, the 1956 Suez crisis. This was followed two years later by the collapse of the pro-British monarchy in Iraq. Yet, simultaneously, an operation to stabilise the Jordanian monarchy, in tandem with US intervention in Lebanon, showed Britain was not finished as a Middle Eastern power, especially if it acted in concert with Washington. The region was vital to the British economy, because of oil and the trade that flowed through the Suez Canal; it remained one of the three principal areas of British military activity, alongside Europe and South-East Asia, and Britain had a diverse range of political and security responsibilities there, both formal and informal. In the mid-1960s London's attention focused locally on two security problems: the need to deter an Iraqi invasion of Kuwait, a former British protectorate; and the future of south-west Arabia, where Britain ruled Aden and had created protectorates in the surrounding territory. London also had responsibility for the defence and external affairs of nine small sheikhdoms in the Persian Gulf. There were military commitments to the Central Treaty Organisation (CENTO). Britain's ability to act in the Middle East relied on bases in the Mediterranean: Cyprus, Libya, Malta and Gibraltar. The main threat to the British was less Soviet Communism than the Arab nationalism espoused by Egypt's President Nasser, the 'victor' of 1956. He was opposed to the traditional elites who held power in Saudi Arabia, Jordan and elsewhere, and by 1964 his ambitions seemed to focus on the British position in southern Arabia, though 'Nasserism' was also a potential menace in the Gulf and Libya. This chapter looks at Britain's imperial responsibilities from Kuwait to Gibraltar, before dealing with policy towards the most serious conflict in the region, that between the Arabs and Israel. But it first considers the vexed problem of South Arabia.

South Arabia

There had been a British presence in Aden since 1839 and it became the only crown colony in the Arab world. Furthermore, 120,000 square miles of the hinterland had been turned into protectorates, where London relied on local rulers to preserve order. Aden was important for shipping, trade and oil storage and, especially after Britain's retreat from Egypt, it also became an important military base. It was the head-quarters of the Commander-in-Chief, Middle East, a 'staging post' to the Far East, and the starting point for intervention in various crises, including, in January 1964, East Africa, where there were army mutinies in Kenya and Tanzania.[1] Like Singapore, then, Aden was both a colony and an important military base, and the issue of decolonisation became inextricably wrapped up in Britain's desire to retain military facilities there. The Macmillan government tried to ensure political stability by doing what it did in Malaysia: it encouraged the rulers to form the Federation of South Arabia, and forced the reluctant Adenis to join this in January 1963; and it intended to retain the base. But British policy faced a daunting array of problems. Arab nationalist opinion was out of sympathy with the tribal rulers who dominated the federal government, and that government itself was poorly led, beset by internal rivalries and lacking stable leadership. Aden, a commercial centre of a quarter of a million people, had little in common with the poor, sparsely popu-lated protectorates and even in 1959 most Adeni voters boycotted the elections to the Legislative Council. Strikes had become frequent, a state of emergency was introduced and in 1963 militants founded the National Liberation Front (NLF), which aimed both to expel the British and to unite the Federation – often called 'South Yemen' by the nationalists – with republican North Yemen. It had a well organised paramilitary wing and, while initially seen as Nasserite, developed a Marxist–Leninist pro-gramme. The British were unable to gain much intelligence on the NLF and, to the end, failed to grasp that it really was Marxist.[2]

Internationally, the British position was criticised by the United Nations (UN), which, in December 1963, called on London to end the state of emergency and set a date for independence. Only in July 1964 did the Conservatives do so, with a date of 1968, and this did not impress radical Arab opinion, for two reasons: first, because London still intended to retain the base; and second, because it wanted to maintain the traditionalist federal government.[3] Arab nationalists were encouraged by developments in neighbouring Yemen, where civil war broke out in September 1962, when the army overthrew the royalist government and set up the 'Yemen Arab Republic'. Egypt backed the republicans, Saudi Arabia the royalists. The old regime, which had territorial claims on South Arabia, had been seen as a threat by the

British in the 1950s, but now they decided to aid the royalists. In 1964
British forces, alongside South Arabia's 'Federal Regular Army', were
increasingly active in the area known as the Radfan. Here, the Yemen
and South Arabian situations became fused because in October 1963
the NLF, whose very formation had been inspired by the Yemeni
'revolution', had launched an insurgency with Egyptian encouragement.[4] Meanwhile, there was a deteriorating security situation in Aden,
with an attempt to assassinate the British High Commissioner, Kennedy
Trevaskis, in December 1963.

Labour thus inherited a dismal situation and it is debatable how far
Wilson's administration can be blamed for the fiasco that followed. A
contemporary analysis held that, while the new government 'tried to
regain the initiative' in Aden, by seeking a more popular government,
'it was too late'. The Conservatives, 'obsessed with Britain's strategic
and economic interests', had irretrievably pushed the nationalists to
extremes. But in his memoirs Trevaskis launched a bitter attack on Labour,
accusing it of seeking the 'appeasement' of Nasser before an eventual
'surrender to anarchy'. Trevaskis believed that Labour should have fully
backed the existing federal government rather than trying to meet the
grievances of the nationalists. In common with other British officials,
he saw leading nationalists like Abd Allah Al-Asnag, General Secretary
of the Aden Trades Union Congress, as mere creatures of Nasser. Their
trouble-making would only be encouraged by concessions. The High
Commissioner had reason to be upset: he had been intimately involved
with the development of Conservative policy towards South Arabia and
was quickly removed from his post by the new Colonial Secretary, Anthony
Greenwood. Trevaskis was replaced by Hugh Turnbull, who had recently
overseen the independence of Tanzania.[5] But Trevaskis is not the only
writer to accuse Greenwood of delusion if he thought Adeni nationalists
could be brought to a compromise with the federal government. His
predecessor, Charles Johnston, also felt that, 'When the Labour government came in ... they overturned the table with the result that we had
to scramble out'.[6] Nonetheless, it has been argued in Greenwood's defence
that he had reason to question Conservative policies, that he brought a
welcome analytical approach to the question of South Arabian independence and that his efforts were undermined by Colonial Office (CO)
officials who thought like Trevaskis. Neither should the debate revolve
entirely around Greenwood and the CO. The Ministry of Defence (MOD)
also became favourable to retreat from Aden under Denis Healey and
the Foreign Office (FO) wanted to improve relations with Nasser.[7]

Labour entered office having criticised the decision to fuse Aden with
the protectorates, hopeful of working with leftists like Al-Asnag and
desiring a better relationship with the UN. In November 1964 Greenwood
visited Aden, consulted a range of political opinion and decided to back

the idea of a unitary South Arabian government, which would reduce the power of the sultans and so please the Adenis. Even the federal government appeared ready to co-operate and Greenwood seemed to have achieved a breakthrough that would create conditions for a stable, popular government in future.[8] In early March a nationalist politician, Abdul Makkawee, was appointed First Minister of Aden, and it was hoped to lay the foundations for an acceptable post-independence administration at a constitutional conference in London. Labour, still committed to the east of Suez role, wanted to retain the Aden base and, since the base was important to the local economy (as in Singapore), there was reason to believe local politicians would want to keep it. There were also hopes that a thaw in relations with Cairo would lead Nasser to accept an internal settlement in South Arabia. One advocate of this was George Wigg, Wilson's National Security Adviser, who believed 'Nasser was not anti-British' and that it was British behaviour that prevented a rapprochement. Another was Greenwood, who upset Wilson in Cabinet by pressing the point: 'I suppose', retorted the Prime Minister, with some exaggeration about what was happening in the colony, 'we mustn't be too discouraged when the Egyptian soldiers shoot ours down in Aden'. Wilson told the Commons in July of efforts to improve relations with Cairo, but also said that Britain was reluctant to go very far while Egypt backed the NLF terrorism campaign.[9]

It soon became clear that Greenwood's drive to win Adeni support was built on sand. The NLF, following setbacks in the Radfan, chose the last months of 1964 in which to initiate a sustained urban guerrilla campaign in Aden. Apart from the security problem this caused, moderate nationalist politicians now had to compete with the NLF for popular support, a necessity that did not tempt them to deal with London. The federal government was dismayed by the course of Labour policy, backed off from its support of a unitary state and bickered with Makkawee. Attempts to arrange a conference to prepare for independence collapsed because Makkawee and Al-Asnag insisted that UN resolutions on Aden should be implemented immediately. Makkawee proved quite unwilling to work with the British. He criticised their armed forces for conducting repression, demanded independence and called on London to recognise the Yemen Republic. Yet the danger that he might win popular support encouraged the NLF to condemn him as a British 'stooge'. Its own credentials as the leader of nationalist opinion were probably strengthened when Turnbull, on 5 June 1965, banned the organisation. 'It is a ludicrous position', Burke Trend told Wilson, 'that we are anxious to grant independence as soon as possible but cannot get the people concerned even to discuss the sort of independence they would like to have'. But Greenwood recognised that part of the problem was the British insistence on retaining the military base after independence.[10]

On 1 September 1965 the NLF claimed its highest-profile victim so far, when it assassinated the speaker of the federal parliament, Arthur Charles. Exasperated by an ever-deteriorating situation and encouraged by Denis Healey, on 23 September the Overseas Policy and Defence Committee (OPD) decided to resort to direct rule and Makkawee was sacked. This was supported by Turnbull, the federal government and many in the CO, but not Greenwood, who warned Wilson that 'repression is unattractive under any circumstances but it is quite unsupportable if … not accompanied by a political initiative'. The Colonial Secretary urged an early decision on the future of the base and suggested both advancing the date for independence and involving the UN. This, too, was out of line with his officials. His Permanent Under-Secretary, Hilton Poynton, had warned earlier that working with the UN 'never paid dividends…. The United Nations tuck the concession in their pockets and then embark on further demands'. Yet all Greenwood's policy recommendations were later attempted and he was correct that direct rule would ruin attempts to work with Nasser. Plans had been made for a junior FO minister, George Thomson, to visit Cairo but, incredibly, his visit coincided with the suspension of the Aden constitution. The OPD recognised that this might enrage Nasser but, on considering the matter, had decided to proceed. They reasoned that it would be even worse to introduce direct rule soon after the Thomson–Nasser meeting, because that would seem like duplicity.[11]

Greenwood was moved from the CO only three months later and direct rule, while bringing a short-term improvement in the security situation, led Adeni politicians to refuse to work with Turnbull. Lord Beswick, a junior minister who visited Aden in November 1965, found a depressing situation. The economy was in ruins, the political system seemed likely to 'disintegrate' and immense sums would have to be spent if the base were to be retained.[12] British forces were largely on the defensive, unable to rely on the local police, to block the local arms trade or to counter Arab nationalist feeling with an effective 'hearts and minds' campaign. The main counter-subversive body was the local Special Branch, but it suffered from assassinations and defections. By May 1965 the High Commissioner reported that, 'With an almost complete lack of an Arab element and faced by an unco-operative population, Special Branch is … meeting with little success'. Turnbull already feared that 'the present security situation is likely to continue at least until independence' and the Joint Intelligence Committee (JIC) warned that the federal government, with its ineffective (and sometimes disloyal) forces, could not achieve independence without British military support.[13] There was a general problem in recruiting staff to colonial Special Branches at this time, but the problem was particularly acute in Aden.[14] Terrorist incidents rose steadily, from 36 in 1964, to 286 in 1965, to 480 in 1966. After April 1967 there were hundreds each month. Unsurprisingly, shipping companies began to avoid using Aden and investment was further deterred by persistent labour unrest. Throughout 1964–7 more than 2,000 people were killed, including fifty-seven British servicemen and eighteen British civilians. Initially the Army supported the local police but in January 1967 it took over internal security in Aden. Morale held up but successful offensive operations were few, while searches for weapons and tough interrogation methods only alienated the local population.[15] Even the Special Air Service (SAS) found urban guerrilla warfare a novel challenge, being more used fighting in the jungles of Borneo or the mountainous Radfan. What they learned in Aden, however, would later prove valuable to them in Northern Ireland.[16]

Aden seemed to show what could happen in colonies where retreat was delayed, traditional elites supported and nationalist feelings ignored. Rather than being available to tackle emergencies elsewhere, troops became preoccupied with defending themselves. This undermined the whole purpose of the base and encouraged London to consider withdrawal. The broader debate over commitments east of Suez also impinged. Spending reductions were not easy in Europe or, thanks to the 'Confrontation', South-East Asia, so Aden was an obvious target for cuts. A date of January 1968 was set for withdrawal in the February 1966 defence White Paper, to coincide with South Arabian independence. When a similar announcement was made by the British in India in 1946, local political leaders had been keen to work together to ensure a stable new state. But the JIC already feared that, in South Arabia, it could lead the federalists to lose heart, renew Egyptian pressure and make local security forces even less co-operative.[17] For Trevaskis and others the White Paper was an ill-considered action. 'Having signified its intention to hand ... South Arabia over to its enemies', writes J. B. Kelly, 'the Labour government was now without a policy of any kind'.[18]

In fact Britain still hoped to leave a stable government behind. But, as Lord Beswick explained to federal ministers when he informed them about the decision, London did not accept that it had any obligation to defend South Arabia after independence. This placed the federal government and the British authorities in Aden in an unenviable position. The rulers were understandably angry at being abandoned by the British to face the NLF and maybe Egypt, especially since London had earlier fostered the Federation. Citing earlier Conservative promises, federal ministers asked both for military aid to build up their own forces and a long-term military guarantee. The CO argued that there was a moral obligation on Britain to help and there was bitter criticism of government policy from the Conservatives in parliament. But ministers prevaricated.[19] They were determined not to find themselves in their

own Vietnam, trapped into providing military support to a weak, unpopular government; yet neither did they want the federal government
to collapse before British forces left. Responsibility for South Arabia
was transferred in early 1966 from the CO, which was being wound
down, to the FO, and this may have weakened the pro-federal cause in
Whitehall. Actually the FO did try to secure a generous military aid
package for South Arabia but, after considerable wrangling with the
Treasury, only a limited amount was offered and no long-term security
guarantee. The federal government believed it had no alternative to
accept but, again, felt it was being put in a precarious position by British
policy-makers.[20]

One development that ought to have helped the British was a growing rift in the nationalist camp. During 1966 and into 1967 London
continued to see Nasser as the godfather of terrorism in South Arabia.
The JIC did not rule out an Egyptian military move against South
Arabia once it was given independence.[21] In fact, Nasser was concerned
about the radicalism of some elements in the NLF and tried to foster a
broader coalition of nationalist groups, including moderate politicians.
This led to the creation of the Front for the Liberation of South Yemen
(with the unlikely acronym of FLOSY). But not all NLF members were
ready to join the new umbrella organisation and in January 1967 the
two groups began to attack each other. In some ways this made Britain's
task harder: a political settlement became more difficult because neither
the NLF nor FLOSY would recognise the other as representative of the
nationalist cause. Yet George Brown, the Foreign Secretary, still told the
Commons in December 1966, 'Our aim is to leave behind a stable and
orderly country' and at the same time the OPD approved steps to end
the British presence on 1 January 1968.[22]

In March 1967, the JIC judged that the federal government would
probably survive down to independence but that broadening it to include
nationalists would be difficult and that its future beyond independence
was uncertain.[23] In order to extricate British forces while the regime
lasted, and so as to avoid being dragged into a long-term security operation, Brown now developed a plan to bring independence forward, to
1 November. This would allow the federal forces to take over internal
security at an early date and would pave the way for South Arabia to
enter the UN in 1967 (whereas a January 1968 independence date would
set back UN membership until the autumn of that year). Britain would
provide South Arabia with air and naval – but not ground – support as
a guarantee against external aggression for six months, thus deterring
any Egyptian invasion until the independent regime was established.
But efforts would also continue to broaden the base of the regime and
there was a readiness, now, to use UN help to achieve this. Brown also
wrote to Nasser, hoping for his co-operation.[24] However, when the policy

was explained to the federal government by George Thomson it reacted badly, arguing that it could not take over internal security so quickly. The British therefore decided to delay an announcement of an early independence date, pending the visit to South Arabia by a UN team.[25]

Initially, despite its general desire to support the UN, Labour had followed the Conservatives in denying the organisation any role in South Arabia. Now it asked for help with the transition to independence. A three-man UN delegation duly arrived in April but their visit ended in farce. They spent most of their time cowering in a hotel, unwilling to deal with the federal regime but unable to contact either of the rival guerrilla groups, who demonstrated their power in another bout of strikes and violent demonstrations. After five days the three departed, trying to blame the fiasco on the British, who had been so anxious to see the mission work. So another chance to escape the imbroglio disappeared. Wilson sent Lord Shackleton, Minister without Portfolio, to explore the situation but he could only recommend a 'determined initiative ... towards the Nationalists and United Nations', alongside the replacement of Turnbull.[26] In May, therefore, London appointed a new High Commissioner, Humphrey Trevelyan. He was not a colonial administrator but a veteran ambassador with experience of Cairo, in the run-up to Suez, and Baghdad, in the wake of the 1958 coup – someone, then, who had dealt with radical Arab leaders in difficult circumstances. From the outset he considered himself to be faced by 'an impossible task', but he nonetheless hoped to secure an orderly withdrawal and leave some stable political structure behind. On being offered the post he said there must be no 'scuttle' but Brown admitted complete disintegration was possible. Once he arrived in Aden, Trevelyan did try to negotiate, calling on nationalists to enter a 'caretaker' administration. But, well aware that independence was coming anyway, neither the NLF nor FLOSY was willing to compromise its reputation by dealing with him.[27]

The federal government, whose resistance had already prevented the independence date being accelerated, was still not quite without weapons of its own. In May, King Feisal of Saudi Arabia visited London and urged Britain to give South Arabia a long-term security guarantee. The Americans, too, while they generally backed London over Aden, were worried by the prospect of a pro-Egyptian regime there. The question was on the US National Security Council agenda for 24 May 1967, but was overtaken in importance by rising Arab–Israeli tensions.[28] Nasser's subsequent defeat by Israel in the Six Day War was a blow to Egyptian confidence, but Trevelyan believed it would only make Nasser more determined to win in Aden and British policy largely continued on established lines.[29] Brown told the Commons on 20 June that the withdrawal would be in January 1968, with naval and air support for the

federal government for six months after that and military supplies to
the federal forces. The federal government may have escaped a November
withdrawal date but the message was still that Britain's presence was
time-limited and that it would not get involved in a ground war, which
was hardly calculated to boost federal morale. Furthermore, to help
Trevelyan's efforts at an internal settlement, Brown also announced that
the ban on the NLF was being lifted. That same day, however, came a
shattering blow, with mutinies among the police and the federal regular
army, sparked by both anger over the Six Day War and tribal antagon-
isms within the forces. Once the mutiny subsided the army did not align
fully with the nationalists and it had to be kept in being by the British
if immediate anarchy were not to break loose. But it was now an unreliable ally at best and the federal government lost virtually all chance
of maintaining itself in power after independence. As British forces
concentrated on covering their own withdrawal, the protectorates were
abandoned to their fate, with the nationalists easily toppling the local
rulers. Embarrassingly, for several days after the mutiny the NLF even
took control of the Crater area of Aden, before Lieutenant-Colonel
Colin ('Mad Mitch') Mitchell led a contingent of Argyle and Sutherland
Highlanders to restore authority. In August Trevelyan argued that, with
the political situation out of control, the withdrawal date must be brought
forward, to avoid British forces being dragged into a morass.[30]

Between September and November the NLF defeated FLOSY in a
series of armed clashes and the demoralised federal administration
simply disintegrated.[31] Ironically, however, the long-feared decline into
anarchy did not create complete gloom in London. For one thing, there
were few British casualties at this time because the terrorists were so
busy killing each other. Also, as Brown told the Cabinet in September,
the disintegration of the federal regime conveniently disposed of
Britain's earlier promises of aid and a six-month defence guarantee. In
the OPD he baldly declared that Labour had never liked dealing with
the sultans anyway and (according to Crossman) that 'we want to be out
of the whole Middle East as fast as we can'. George Wigg was a lone
voice complaining that British allies were being betrayed and that the
traditional rulers in the Gulf would be demoralised.[32] In a sense, policy
continued unchanged: the British stuck to the priority of withdrawal
while hoping to avoid complete anarchy on their departure. The logic
of this was that power must now be handed to the radicals. Trevelyan
offered to do this in a broadcast on 5 September, without stating a
preference for the NLF or FLOSY, but the two groups were still fighting
for domination. In late October, hoping to minimise casualties, ministers
decided to bring withdrawal forward to the end of November and
Crossman was quite ecstatic: 'chaos will rule after we've gone, and there'll
be one major commitment cut – thank God'.[33]

In fact, chaos did not rule because the NLF, having eliminated its rivals, wanted to be recognised as the legal successor to British rule. Talks took place in Geneva in late November, where Britain agreed a handover of power and even an aid package to the new government. The last troops left on 29 November and the final transfer of power to the 'People's Republic of South Yemen' went surprisingly smoothly.[34] It should be noted that the NLF victory, apart from placing South Arabia under a vicious one-party state, created problems for another British client, the autocratic Sultan Said of Oman. His remote Dhofar province bordered on South Arabia and had been the scene of an insurgency since mid-1965. In April 1966 there had been an assassination attempt on Said. Now the NLF government, backed by the Soviets, was able to aid the rebels in Dhofar and by mid-1970 the security situation was worsening markedly, with most of Dhofar in rebel hands, their targets including the British service personnel who were aiding Said. This became a major problem just as Labour lost office, and plans were made to replace the unpopular Said with his more pliable son, Qabus, in a palace coup. The coup actually took place on 23 July, under Heath's Conservative government, and was followed by a successful six-year campaign to end the rebellion in Dhofar, spearheaded by the SAS.[35] There was also success of sorts in the Yemen, where, following Nasser's defeat in the Six Day War, the Egyptians and Saudis sought a peaceful settlement. In May 1970 a coalition government was formed there.

Aden had seen the same factors at work as propelled the British out of other colonies. Ronald Hyam has noted that in East Africa under Macmillan several 'fundamental imperatives' operated: 'fears of the country dissolving into chaos, worries about the whole situation going sour on them in the United Nations, the impossibility of holding the situation by force, the ineluctable impact of what was happening in neighbouring territories…'. All these were present in Aden. But the British did not fulfil two other 'fundamental imperatives', the 'desirability of pre-empting the growth of Russian and Chinese influence and the necessity always of acting upon … cold war considerations'. Instead, South Yemen became a Marxist outpost in the Middle East. J. B. Kelly doubts that there had ever 'been such a shameful end to British rule over a colonial territory as the abandonment of Aden', marked by the cynical betrayal of a client government. Like Trevaskis, Kelly's analysis suggests it would have been better to maintain the unrepresentative federal government, backed by British forces. In contrast, Trevelyan argued in his memoirs that London had no legal basis for maintaining an unpopular government against internal opposition after independence. Labour's policy was constrained by the errors of previous governments and was frequently at the mercy of events, such as the mutiny in the federal army, yet culminated in Britain leaving 'without glory but without

disaster'. Neither can Britain alone be blamed for the situation. The
ineffectiveness of the federal government, divisions in the nationalist
camp and NLF ruthlessness all helped reduce Aden to a wasteland. If
Greenwood's policy of broadening the federal government with Egypt's
co-operation had been given a real chance in 1965, then the outcome
would have been better, not only for the British but also for Makkawee,
Al-Asnag and even Nasser. Nonetheless, Labour cannot escape some
responsibility for the Aden fiasco. However distasteful ministers found
the federal regime, it had been built up as a British client and deserved
more generous support in 1966–7 to provide it with a real chance of
survival beyond independence. But outright support for the federal
government would have been difficult to justify internationally and
would have risked creating a Vietnam-style quagmire when British
interests in South Arabia in the long term had become minimal thanks
to the decision to liquidate the base. As with other elements of the
government's international policy, it was a case of the broad aim – withdrawal from the base and local political commitments – being difficult
to fault, even if the execution of decisions left much to be desired.[36]

Withdrawal from the Persian Gulf

When Britain left Aden its forces were redeployed to the Persian Gulf,
where, since the mid-nineteenth century, Britain had responsibility for
the foreign policy and defence of several small sheikhdoms. The decision
to move forces to the Gulf was also linked to the defence of Kuwait,
independent since 1961 but claimed by Iraq, which could have invaded
it at any time. Aircraft and troops were stationed in Bahrain (the base
of Britain's 'political resident' in the Gulf) and Sharjah (one of the
'Trucial States' at the base of the Gulf, which late became the United
Arab Emirates). As mentioned above, there was also a British military
presence in Oman, between the Trucial States and South Arabia. The
British position was not simply an imperial hangover. Ministers liked to
emphasise their role in preserving stability in the Gulf rather than selfish
interests, but the fact is that two-thirds of British oil imports came from
the Gulf, and Kuwait was one of the largest and cheapest producers.
Kuwait also had substantial investments in London.[37]

During 1965 the FO firmly resisted the readiness of the MOD to
jettison the commitment to Kuwait, but it was recognised that this commitment would be difficult to fulfil once the Aden base was lost. A study
by defence planners in 1966 showed it could take three weeks to reinforce Kuwait against a land invasion but that Iraq could act almost
instantly, perhaps exploiting a coup in Kuwait. The Chiefs of Staff
continued to prepare to assist Kuwait with aircraft from Cyprus, even

though such support might not be the best means to meet Iraqi action.[38] Well aware of the problems, Denis Healey, the Defence Secretary, told the OPD in January 1967 that Britain should 'narrow our commitment to Kuwait' and that in the Gulf 'our aim should be to remove all our forces as soon as consistent with our interests'. An official study five months later suggested it might be wise to leave the Gulf early because it was currently quite stable and both Iran and Saudi Arabia, whose policies were vital to regional security, were under pro-Western regimes. Such favourable circumstances might not last. But there was a counter-argument that local rulers should be allowed some time to prepare for Britain's departure, that the Aden situation must be settled first and that withdrawal should await Britain's departure from South-East Asia, since Gulf bases were part of the 'east-about' communication route.[39]

The British therefore hoped to strengthen the internal viability of the Gulf sheikhdoms and to improve their external security through co-operation with Saudi Arabia and Iran. This policy was particularly urged by William Luce, the political resident in the Gulf in 1961–6, who advocated 'Peninsula Solidarity' – tying the Trucial States, Bahrain and Qatar into a single political entity.[40] Bahrain, the most developed of these, seemed particularly susceptible to militancy and subversion and was a permanent worry for London. But the fears were exaggerated. Actual incidents in Bahrain were few, beyond some labour disturbances in 1965 and demonstrations during the Six Day War. As in Aden, the main threat to stability in the Gulf seemed to be Nasserite groups, encouraged by Radio Cairo. In May 1965 one official was driven by the latest propaganda claims and the arrest of some Yemenis in Dubai to minute that 'The Egyptians have started their long-awaited subversive effort in the Gulf'. But nothing dramatic followed. Some months later, while concerned over rebel activity in Oman and convinced that subversive activity would grow in the region, the JIC believed that the Trucial States would see only 'crude isolated attacks' in the immediate future. True, Iraq was also a potential menace, but no love was lost between Iraq and Egypt.[41] Indeed, so untroubled was the Gulf that in 1966 MI5 resisted pressure, from the FO and the military, to appoint a full-time officer to the Persian Gulf, arguing that there was not enough work.[42] As with Aden, some in London believed British interests might be served by co-operation with Cairo. In 1964–5 the Arab League offered a development package to the Trucial States and Barbara Castle, the Overseas Development Minister, suggested that an aid consortium should be formed that included Britain and Egypt. But Wilson and Stewart successfully resisted this, fearing it would become a vehicle for Egyptian subversion.[43]

In January 1968, when the Cabinet decided on an early withdrawal from the Gulf, a junior FO minister, Goronwy Roberts, was sent to inform the Gulf rulers, who were deeply unhappy. Some even offered to cover the British costs, which amounted to only £12 million per year, but they could win no changes.[44] As Paul Gore-Booth, the Permanent Under-Secretary of the FO, later explained, the FO felt 'some anxiety about an indefinite prolongation in the Gulf of a "special position" which might involve us in internal struggles in the Arab world'. Officials also feared the conditions that might be attached to any financial deal with the sheikhs.[45] Over the following weeks, in talks with foreign ministers from the region, George Brown argued that British withdrawal had been inevitable for some time and that the essential thing was to create a stable new system, which meant Iran and Saudi Arabia following a responsible and co-operative policy.[46] The Gulf rulers now hastily looked at a possible federation and signed an agreement on a 'Union of Arab Emirates' in February 1968. The British publicly supported the idea but privately doubted its workability and the attempts to create a feder-ation had little success before Labour lost office.[47] The failure was partly due to internal difficulties, especially the practical problems of sharing power and forming a single defence force, but also external factors, including an Iranian claim to Bahrain, which was not resolved until April 1970, and a territorial dispute between Abu Dhabi and Saudi Arabia. In 1971 Bahrain and Qatar both became independent, leaving the Trucial States to form the United Arab Emirates. The British com-mitment to assist Kuwait ended in May of that year.[48]

The Mediterranean

The term 'east of Suez' was something of a misnomer in relation to Britain's world role. Certainly, the key British bases of Aden and Singapore lay beyond Suez, but there were also important staging posts to the Middle and Far East in the Mediterranean Sea, with bases in Cyprus, Libya, Malta and Gibraltar. By 1965 there was general agree-ment in Whitehall that Britain's presence in the Mediterranean should be reduced. This seemed less problematic as a cost-cutting exercise than retreat from South-East Asia or the Gulf because the threat from external powers was less and naval forces of the North Atlantic Treaty Organisation (NATO) were based locally. Once a withdrawal from Aden was deemed likely, it made sense to wind down bases in the Mediter-ranean, even though there were treaty obligations to Libya and to the CENTO (for which the two British sovereign bases in Cyprus were sig-nificant). The OPD, meeting on 24 November 1965, decided to reduce units in Libya and Malta, and retain only one base in Cyprus.[49] It did not prove easy to carry this out, however. In Cyprus the savings from closing down one base turned out to be so small that it was decided to retain both, while in Malta the locals wanted the British base to remain because, as in Singapore, it brought income and employment. In 1966 the news that the base would be run down over three years to the level of a 'staging post' was greeted with anger by the Maltese government. Popular demonstrations and harassment of British forces followed. In OPD discussions there was a determination not to back off from the cuts but also concern that the Maltese might decide to end the British presence completely or even seek a security arrangement with the Eastern bloc.[50] In early 1967 Patrick Gordon Walker, back in government as Minister without Portfolio, was sent to negotiate with the Maltese. The talks were tough and the British were forced to slow the pace of withdrawal to five years. In March the talks moved to London and, despite a British offer of more economic aid, reached the verge of breakdown before the Maltese suddenly realised that there was no more on the table and agreed to settle.[51] Another crisis blew up a year later when, because of uncertainties over its future, it was feared that the naval dockyard might close, creating massive unemployment. Wilson sent out another of his 'trouble-shooting' ministers, Lord Shackleton, who soon struck a deal that kept the yards open.[52]

Another base that the locals wanted to remain was on Gibraltar. This was a special case where, like Hong Kong and the Falklands, external realities prevented decolonisation. Gibraltar was a colony of only a few square miles, with a naval base that commanded the western Mediterranean. Spain had ceded it to Britain in 1713 but now pressed for its return, taking the issue to the UN in 1963 and securing a vote for the termination of Gibraltar's colonial status. Just before the 1964 British general election the UN urged talks between the two countries and Spain had placed restrictions on traffic across the border. But the vast majority of Gibraltarians opposed a return to Spanish rule: only 44 people, out of more than 12,000, voted for this option when a referendum was held in September 1967. An added complication was that Spain was currently ruled by the dictatorship of General Francisco Franco, to whom it seemed impossible to hand over the territory. Faced by Spanish pressure, the incoming government had cancelled a naval exercise with Spain, which only inflamed the situation. In February 1965 the Cabinet agreed to stand by Gibraltar but without taking action that would antagonise Spain further.[53] Officials' talks during 1966 failed to achieve a settlement and in April 1967 the Spaniards created further problems by tightening restrictions on flights to Gibraltar. Despite the economic cost of supplying the colony, popular support in Britain for the Gibraltarians was strong and there was no bowing to the UN demand for talks.[54] By December 1967 the Madrid embassy saw little basis for negotiation, since Spain would negotiate only on the basis of a transfer of sovereignty, which Britain was determined to oppose. Unable to rely on diplomacy, the FO developed its propaganda to emphasise 'the seamy side of Spanish internal politics, as well as the vulnerable features of Spain's own colonial policy'.[55]

Libya's King Idris had signed a defence treaty with Britain in 1953, which gave the British a military presence in return for a military guarantee and financial assistance. The significance of this was dwarfed by the scale of US aid and the US base at Wheelus. Especially after the Suez crisis there was concern about popular Nasserite sentiment, but the autocratic Idris clung onto power. The JIC consistently believed that a change of regime was probable if Idris died and, while an invasion from Egypt (which borders on Libya) was deemed unlikely, a military coup was not ruled out.[56] Libya became a significant oil producer in the 1960s and the USA hoped the British would remain, yet Britain's ability to protect the country from external attack was reduced after the February 1966 defence White Paper and London had no desire to become involved in Libyan internal security.[57] In 1968, rather than offend Idris with a premature withdrawal, the British decided it was better to leave in 1973, when the 1953 security agreement ended. But it was not at all certain that the regime would survive until then. A number of plots were being hatched within the army and Idris himself was evidently giving thought to abdication. Denis Healey later admitted that a revolution was 'obviously inevitable' but Western observers failed to predict who exactly would carry it out.[58]

On 1 September 1969 a group of young army officers, led by Muammar Gaddafi, easily overthrew the government while Idris was abroad. Although Michael Stewart agreed to meet a royal emissary, the British quickly decided there was no point trying to save the decrepit monarchy. With precedents like Nasser, it seemed to make sense for the British to recognise Gaddafi, in the hope that he would co-operate with them. Stewart reminded the Cabinet that Shell and British Petroleum had £100 million invested in the Libyan oil industry.[59] Even when, on 29 October, Gaddafi asked them to quit their Libyan bases it did not seem an unreasonable demand, since the British were planning to leave in a few years anyway. Stewart told the Cabinet that the request was 'a natural and not unexpected consequence of the Libyan revolution itself'. An agreement was made to end the British military presence by 31 March 1970, with Stewart continuing to be as reasonable as possible, partly to prevent Libya turning to the Soviet bloc.[60] It was to no avail. Gaddafi began to nationalise the oil industry in 1971 and was soon a ruthless opponent of Western involvement in the Middle East.

The Six Day War

The Arab–Israeli war of June 1967 would have been difficult to predict even months before. Israel, which had proved its military superiority in the wars of 1948 and 1956, seemed secure and, with much of his army committed in the Yemen, Nasser was hardly in an ideal position to attack. The Soviets and Americans had too many other worries to focus on the Middle East. As to Britain's position, it was argued that, in order to minimise political and economic liabilities, 'our interests would be best served by our withdrawal from the Arab–Israeli dispute', to a position of impartiality.[61] Yet Arab–Israeli tensions were far from resolved and both sides were being armed by their respective superpower ally. Syria, in particular, supported attacks by Palestinian guerrillas on Israel. In early May 1967 Syrian fears of an Israeli invasion were fuelled by Soviet intelligence and Nasser, seeing himself as leader of the Arabs, mobilised his army. He also asked the UN to withdraw the force that it had installed in Sinai after the 1956 war. Secretary General U Thant felt he had no choice but to comply, but Foreign Secretary George Brown was appalled. The UN withdrawal gave Egypt control of the Straits of Tiran, on which Israel relied for access to the Red Sea, and through which its oil supply flowed. On 23 May the Israeli premier, Levi Eshkol, made clear Israel would treat interference with its shipping in the Straits as an act of war. These moves specifically affected Britain because, in March 1957, following the Suez crisis, the USA, Britain and France had promised to maintain Israeli access through the Straits and, on 21 May, Wilson had written to Eshkol supporting the principle of 'free passage'. The British were deeply concerned about the possible economic impact of a war and hoped to act via the UN to keep the peace.[62]

Britain had a long, complicated role in the history of the Arab–Israeli dispute. Having first promised the creation of a Jewish 'homeland' in Palestine, in the 1917 Balfour Declaration, London was blamed by the Arabs for foisting a Jewish state on their soil. But, when administering Palestine down to 1948, the British, fearing Arab opposition, had tried to limit Jewish emigration and so alienated Zionist opinion. If there was a consistent factor in British government policy it was that it was geared neither to pro-Arabism nor to pro-Zionism, but to the defence of British interests. Thus Stewart told the Cabinet in 1965 that policy in the dispute was based on maintaining a balance of arms supplies to both sides, while encouraging a peaceful settlement.[63] Then again, in Britain there was a great deal of sympathy for the Israeli cause and one pro-Arab MP complained that 'Harold Wilson was the most pro-Israeli Prime Minister the country had then seen'. Few MPs took much interest in the problem of Palestinian refugees and Wilson's pro-Zionist feelings were such that he later wrote a book on the subject.[64] Many of his ministers were members of the 'Labour Friends of Israel' group and the party had large number of Jewish MPs. Most of the British press also tended to be pro-Israeli.[65] In contrast, George Brown, although his wife was Jewish, once described himself as 'an Arab at heart'. On becoming

Foreign Secretary he told Wilson that the 'vendetta' with Nasser must end and he worked for the reopening diplomatic relations with Cairo.[66] These had been broken off in 1965 over Rhodesia but Brown, in a typically unconventional act, used a visit to Moscow in late 1966 to open contact with one of Nasser's ministers.[67] Then again, relations were not actually restored until December 1967, well after the Six Day War.[68] And during the war itself Brown's approach was far from pro-Arab.

On the morning of 23 May Wilson met Brown and Defence Secretary Healey, and Brown proposed an international naval force to keep the Straits of Tiran open, alongside a declaration by maritime states in support of 'free passage'. He was motivated by a need to dissuade Israel from going to war, to work with Washington, to act via the UN and to avoid any charges of 'imperialism'. At this point Healey agreed on the need for firmness.[69] But he was subsequently warned by the Chiefs of Staff that any naval operation was fraught with danger. A force in the narrow waters of the Red Sea would be vulnerable to air attack and must be kept small. It could be supported by a larger carrier force in the Mediterranean, but only if London and Washington were ready to contemplate air raids on Egypt in retaliation for any aggressive action.[70] There was a tempestuous Cabinet meeting that afternoon at which Wilson backed Brown, Brown became angry with Healey for raising difficulties, and both Wilson and Brown became angry with James Callaghan, the Chancellor, when he supported Healey by mentioning the likely impact of naval action on the pound. An array of ministers, from Castle on the left to Jenkins and Gordon Walker on the right, opposed a naval force. Finally it was agreed to send George Thomson to explore US thinking.[71] On 24 May the Israeli foreign minister, Abba Eban, arrived in London and was very pleased with Britain's attitude, which was far more pro-Israeli than that of the French.[72]

Diplomatic attempts to prevent the war came to nothing. On 23–26 May Brown visited Moscow, where it was evident that the Soviets strongly backed the Arab cause. While Brown was there, President de Gaulle proposed a four-power conference to discuss the situation, arguing that this was the best way to achieve a balanced settlement. The British had good reason to back such a proposal: it would give them a diplomatic role; co-operation with de Gaulle might help the EEC entry bid that had just been launched; and they were interested in any scheme that might keep the peace. A Cabinet discussion on 25 May, far more relaxed than two days earlier, agreed to back the French initiative and Wilson asked US President Johnson to consider the merits of a conference.[73] But the Soviets rejected it. Meanwhile, the Thomson mission discovered that the Americans had not seriously studied a naval force. Instead, they were expecting London to take the lead on what was seen as a 'British' plan, which was not at all what the British wanted.[74] On 30

May the Cabinet had another long meeting where, with the Americans pushing Britain to lead naval action and the Soviets opposed to four-power talks, Brown retreated further from his early bellicosity. His emphasis was now on achieving a declaration by the maritime powers on 'innocent' passage (rather narrower than 'free' passage) through the Straits of Tiran, which would remain under Egyptian control. A naval force should go ahead only if it won genuinely multinational support, which seemed unlikely.[75] A few days later Wilson was in Washington for a previously arranged summit. As US Defense Secretary Robert McNamara noted, 'the imminent Arab–Israeli war ... crowded all other issues off the agenda'. The 'Red Sea regatta', as the naval proposal had become known, was discussed but the problems seemed daunting. A declaration by a group of maritime powers still seemed possible, but would serve little purpose unless someone enforced it.[76] Wilson came home satisfied with a meeting where, for once, 'the US felt they needed us more than we needed them'. But the lack of meaningful action only increased Israel's belief that it must defend its own interests.[77]

On 5 June, the Israelis launched war. The JIC had long predicted that Israel would 'have the best of any conflict' with the Arabs and, sure enough, by 10 June its forces had captured Sinai, the Gaza Strip, the West Bank and the Golan Heights.[78] During the fighting Nasser claimed that US and British aircraft had aided Israel. This 'big lie' harmed Britain's standing in the Arab world and provoked a breach in diplomatic relations with some Arab countries, though the truth was soon exposed. In fact, London was no more than a helpless bystander to Israeli victory and adopted a neutral position. Even the ardently pro-Zionist Richard Crossman recognised that 'if we hadn't been neutral our oil would have been stopped and a large part of our sterling balances ... withdrawn'.[79]

For the British the war was a salutary lesson, not because they were involved, but because they were not. In reviewing its impact a month afterwards, ministers, taking their lead from Brown, concluded that they had played no worthwhile role in the crisis and that, 'Since we could not expect to have more than a marginal influence on [settlement] terms ... and since our position was highly vulnerable, we should seek to disengage ourselves so far as possible'. This may have gone too far. One factor that helped the Israeli victory was that many Egyptian troops were pinned down in Yemen, partly thanks to British policy. Certainly, Britain continued to have important interests in the Middle East, not least because of the importance of oil and the Suez Canal to the British economy. Wilson later called the war 'the biggest contributing factor to the devaluation' in November. But this very vulnerability reinforced the need to avoid 'taking sides' in the Arab–Israeli dispute.[80] Oil supplies seemed particularly vulnerable immediately after the war, when there was a short-lived, poorly enforced Arab oil boycott of the West. From this point there was a gnawing sense of vulnerability among ministers where oil was concerned, reinforced by the outbreak of civil war in Nigeria in July. A more immediate concern was the closure of the Suez Canal. The British were desperate to reopen it but few others, apart from Egypt, would make this a priority. It suited the Israelis to keep the Canal closed to pressurise Egypt; the Americans, less dependent on Canal traffic than the British, would not break with Israel on the issue.[81]

Disengaging Britain from the Arab–Israeli dispute did not prove easy. One dilemma centred on arms supplies. The OPD decided in November 1967 that, while it was happy to make money from arms, Britain should supply them in a 'balanced' way, minimising the supply of 'offensive' types.[82] This inevitably left room for interpretation and when, in 1968, the Israelis asked to buy 250 Chieftain tanks it provoked serious arguments in the OPD before it was agreed, in principle at least, to supply them. Healey backed the deal as likely to reinforce the 'balance' in the Middle East and benefit British industry. But the FO was concerned that it would offend the Arabs, harm British exports in Arab markets (much larger than Israel's), upset the military balance and retard peace efforts.[83] The issue ran on throughout the remainder of the government, as the FO succeeded in delaying an actual sale. It overshadowed a visit by the Israeli premier, Golda Meir, in June 1969 and became entangled with a proposal to sell Chieftains to Libya.[84]

Neither could the British resist the temptation to continue playing a diplomatic role in the Arab–Israeli dispute, with the FO particularly guilty of calling into question its own policy of disengagement. Brown's best-remembered success as Foreign Secretary came through working for a UN resolution on the Arab–Israeli conflict. In the wake of Israel's victory some observers hoped it would be possible to make a trade of 'land for peace' quite quickly: Israel would return conquered territories in return for Arab recognition of its right to exist. The Kuwaiti government urged London to take the lead in peace-making as a way to restore British standing among Arabs.[85] Brown went to a special UN session in mid-June and made a speech calling for the return of conquered territories, including East Jerusalem. This led to bitter complaints from the Israeli delegation in New York and from Crossman at home. Nonetheless, in mid-July President Johnson 'wished that we could find something for Wilson to do' in securing a settlement.[86] The chances for any initiative did not look good: Israel demanded face-to-face talks with the Arabs; the Arabs would neither recognise nor negotiate with Israel. But continuing border incidents between Israel and its neighbours increased the international pressure for a solution and UN efforts began in earnest in September. By then Anglo–Israeli relations seemed poor but Brown was typically unapologetic. In a meeting with ambassador

Remez in mid-October, he accused the Israeli government of stirring an anti-British campaign, was frank about his anxiety to open the Suez Canal and was insistent that Israel should talk.[87]

A 'land for peace' deal did indeed form the essence of UN Security Council Resolution 242, of 22 November, which was the result of a British initiative and which, while calling for Israeli withdrawal from conquered 'territories', did not insist that this should apply to all 'the territories' (the word 'the' being omitted). It was put forward because of the deadlock that grew around earlier efforts, a pro-Israeli draft by the USA and a pro-Arab one from India. The US ambassador to the UN, Arthur Goldberg, later insisted he 'was the principal drafter' of the eventual resolution, and told an interviewer that the 'British had about as much to do with it as you'.[88] But at the time Goldberg told the Israelis that London was not acting as a surrogate of Washington and even advised Eban to be wary of what a British resolution said. Eban visited London, to satisfy himself that the British were being even-handed, and he later had close contact with Lord Caradon, on whom the burden fell of finalising the resolution. Significantly, Eban felt that the resolution gave advantages to Israel through its very ambiguity: Israel could, for example, retain the conquered territories as long as there was no durable peace.[89] But the British were equally adept at selling their wording to the Arabs: in talks with the Egyptian foreign minister, Mahmoud Riad, Caradon laid emphasis on the importance of Israeli withdrawal to the resolution. The British ambassador, notes Riad, 'maintained good and cordial relations with everyone' and was helped by a long familiarity with the problem.[90] There was no way of enforcing the resolution except through further talks and it was far from an actual peace settlement, but it was unanimously approved by the Security Council, became the basis of all future attempts to achieve an Arab–Israeli settlement and showed that Britain could still influence world affairs through the use of diplomatic skill.

Peace proved impossible to achieve in the wake of Resolution 242. The UN appointed a mediator, Gunnar Jarring, but he made little progress at first. In 1968 Israel and Jordan began secret contacts, with London becoming a venue for talks between Eban and King Hussein. They achieved nothing, partly because Hussein could not promise to deliver general Arab agreement on a settlement.[91] In January 1969 the Soviets put forward proposals for a settlement and talks between the USA, USSR, Britain and France followed. Wilson saw these as a way of maintaining co-operation with France and, perhaps, helping Britain into the EEC but, while they dragged on into 1970, they achieved no breakthrough. In July 1969 and again in early 1970, Stewart favoured taking an initiative, building on the British success with Resolution 242, but other ministers felt that it was best to take a low profile in Middle

East affairs. Any British initiative seemed likely to be rejected by Israel anyway and, with an election approaching, Wilson was especially reluctant to risk alienating Jewish voters. It was one of the few issues that provoked arguments between him and Stewart in front of other ministers.[92]

Conclusion

On a visit to Saudi Arabia and the Gulf in January 1969 the newspaper chairman Cecil King found there were 'no bouquets for British policy'. Local rulers blamed the British for supporting Israel, quitting the Gulf and leaving a subversive government behind them in Aden. Tore Petersen sympathises with them, arguing that Labour 'seized every opportunity to dismantle the empire' in the Middle East and that, given the low financial cost of keeping forces in the Gulf, this retreat 'should be attributed to lack of will, not lack of power', while Diane Kunz makes the point that, by giving up their military presence in the region, the British reduced their ability to shape the policy of Arab countries on oil and perhaps lost the chance to prevent the problems in price and supply of the 1970s.[93] But an alternative view comes from John Wright, the senior economic adviser at the CO in 1966–8: 'it was not at all obvious … that we could keep down the price of oil in the long run by the use of force'. The Aden imbroglio and Britain's powerlessness during the Six Day War seemed to show that the country was unable to project military power in the region effectively. The expectation was that locals would turn against the presence of military bases in the long term, even if they appeared ready to accept them in the short term (Gibraltar and Cyprus proving special cases). A study by the Foreign and Commonwealth Office (FCO) Near Eastern Department in 1969 set out five principles for future British policy in the Middle East which, while they provoked some controversy in the FCO, identified a less forthright method of safeguarding interests. London should 'disengage' from the Arab–Israeli dispute and from intra-Arab arguments, it should support Iran as a pro-Western element in the region and, while seeking to protect British assets like oil, it should accept that Anglo-American companies might no longer dominate the oil industry in future.[94] Around the same time, a paper on the Mediterranean argued that Britain should operate through NATO, tying Malta and Cyprus into the Western defence system and even relaxing pressure to reopen the Suez Canal, because an open Canal would allow the Soviet navy easier access to the Indian Ocean.[95]

The Labour government, then, saw a shift from a policy built on a regional military presence, close ties to traditional rulers and opposition to Nasserism, to one that sought to protect British interests through a military withdrawal, acceptance that the days of sultans and sheikhs might be numbered, and a readiness to come to terms with radical leaders. The last was evident in the recognition of an NLF regime in Aden, the restoration of relations with Nasser and the end of the bases in Libya. But, as with so many other developments under Labour, the policy change was far from smooth or determined. Wilson himself was dubious about dealing with Nasser and, while he was less interested in the Middle East than in other issues, his support for Israel led him to back the ill-conceived 'Red Sea regatta'. In what has been called a display of 'Cabinet government at its best' – and in stark contrast to the 1956 Suez crisis – most other ministers had to unite against the Prime Minister to prevent bellicose action.[96] Yet, even after that, the FO, while it advocated 'disengagement' from the region's problems, also tried to take a leading role in Arab–Israeli peace efforts, especially in devising Resolution 242. The vexed question of arms sales confirmed that disengagement from the Arab–Israeli dispute was almost impossible for a country with such significant commercial interests. Furthermore, the attempt to deal with radical regimes, be it the NLF or Gaddafi, brought few dividends and the British found themselves reluctantly working with 'traditionalists', especially in the Gulf, where, contrary to expectations, the sheikhs held on to power quite successfully. The British later remained active in the Middle East in a military as well as a commercial sense, with the secondment of personnel to the Gulf states, training exercises and a number of military operations, beginning with the Dhofar campaign in Oman soon after Labour lost office. In retrospect, then, the government marked less a decisive break with the past than a halfhearted experiment with disengagement that deteriorated into continued military and diplomatic involvement in the region, albeit at a reduced level.[97]

Notes

I am grateful to my Nottingham colleague, Dr Spencer Mawby, for his comments on an earlier draft of this chapter.

Unless otherwise stated the place of publication is London.

1 Phillip Darby, *British Defence Policy East of Suez, 1947–68* (Oxford University Press, Oxford, 1973), 204–11, 279–80; C. J. Bartlett, *The Long Retreat: a short history of British defence policy, 1945–70* (Macmillan, 1972), 162–4.

2 Humphrey Trevelyan, *The Middle East in Revolution* (Macmillan, 1970), 218.

3 For background on Aden see: Glen Balfour-Paul, *The End of Empire in the Middle East: Britain's relinquishment of power in her last three Arab dependencies* (Cambridge University Press, Cambridge, 1991), chapter 3; R. J. Gavin, *Aden Under British Rule, 1839–1967* (Hurst, 1975); Fred Halliday, *Arabia Without Sultans* (Penguin, 1974), chapters 6 and 7;\ David Ledger, *Shifting*

Sands: the British in South Arabia (Chatto and Windus, 1983), very detailed on 1964–7; Karl Pieragostini, *Britain, Aden and South Arabia* (Macmillan, 1991).

4 Spencer Mawby, 'British special operations in Yemen, 1951–64', *Intelligence and National Security*, forthcoming; William Jackson, *Withdrawal from Empire: a military view* (Batsford, 1986), 214–23.

5 W. P. Kirkman, *Unscrambling an Empire* (Chatto and Windus, 1966), 160–2; Kennedy Trevaskis, *Shades of Amber* (Hutchinson, 1968), 223–5 and 229–48.

6 J. B. Kelly, *Arabia, the Gulf and the West* (Weidenfeld and Nicolson, 1980), 21–3; Liddell Hart Centre, King's College, London, Charles Johnston papers, 2/34, Johnston to Fisher (7 September 1970). Also critical is Ledger, *Shifting Sands*, especially 223–5.

7 Pieragostini, *Aden*, 192–9.

8 Public Record Office (PRO), CAB 128/39, CC14 (64) (11 December); CAB 148/17, OPD(64)16th (30 December); Pieragostini, *Aden*, 93–4.

9 Lord Wigg, *George Wigg* (Michael Joseph, 1972), 305 and 349–51; Barbara Castle, *The Castle Diaries 1964–70* (Weidenfeld and Nicolson, 1984), 14; *House of Commons Debates*, vol. 716, columns 1138–9.

10 PRO, PREM 13/113, Greenwood to Wilson (14 June), and Trend to Wilson (undated, regarding OPD(65)19th).

11 CAB 148/18, OPD(65)41st (23 September); CAB 148/22, OPD(65)133rd (22 September); PRO, PREM 13/113, Turnbull to CO (24 September); Bodleian Library, Oxford, Anthony Greenwood papers, MS. Eng. c. 43, Greenwood to Wilson (24 September), and MS. Eng. c. 48, Poyton to Greenwood (18 January); Pieragostini, *Aden*, 135–7, 145–6.

12 PREM 13/704, Beswick report on visit of 5–23 November.

13 British Library (BL), London, Aden High Commission files, R/20/D/216, Turnbull to Greenwood (16 February and 25 May 1965); CAB 158/54, JIC(64)77th (Final) (8 March 1965).

14 For example: CAB 159/43, JIC(65)1st (7 January), 5th (4 February) and 13th (25 March); PRO, DEFE 32/10, COS 7th/65 (4 February); DEFE 4/181, COS 9th/65 (16 February) and 183, COS 15th/65 (23 March).

15 Jackson, *Withdrawal*, 223–4 and 233–41; but especially Julian Paget, *Last Post: Aden 1964–7* (Faber and Faber, 1969), part 2 (statistical details from Annex D).

16 Tony Geraghty, *Who Dares Wins* (Little, Brown, Boston, 1992), 400–7; Tom Connor, *Ghost Force* (Weidenfeld and Nicolson, 1998), 128–37.

17 CAB 158/60, JIC(65)92nd (23 December); CAB 159/44, JIC(65)54th (22 December); Pieragostini, *Aden*, 124, 159–60.

18 Trevaskis, *Shades*, 237–8; Kelly, *Arabia*, 27.

19 PREM 13/704, Aden to CO (16 and 17 February); CAB 148/25, OPD(66)14th (2 March); Edward Short, *Whip to Wilson* (MacDonald, 1989), 267–8; Pieragostini, *Aden*, 176–8.

20 CAB 148/25, OPD(66)27th (25 May); CAB 128/41, CC26 and 29(66) (26 May and 16 June).

21 CAB 158/63, JIC(66)37th (25 May), CAB 158/64, JIC(66)64th (10 October), and CAB 158/64, JIC(66)74th (29 December); CAB 159/47, JIC(67)9th (27 February).

22 *House of Commons Debates*, vol. 737, column 1167; CAB 148/25, OPD(66)47th (2 December).

23 CAB 158/66, JIC(67)20th (3 March).

24 PREM 13/1295, Trend to Wilson (9 March), Brown–Nasser message (24 March); CAB 148/30, OPD(67)11th (10 March); CAB 128/42, CC13(67) (16 March).

25 CAB 128/42, CC15(67) (23 March).

26 CAB 128/42, CC18 and 30(67) (10 April and 11 May); PREM 13/1296, Aden to FO (15 April) and Shackleton to Wigg (3 May).

27 Trevelyan, *Middle East*, 211 and 222; PRO, FO 800/968, Brown–Trevelyan meeting (6 May).

28 PREM 13/1775, Wilson–Feisal meeting (10 May); Lyndon B. Johnson Library (LBJL), Austin, Meetings Notes File, box 1, memorandum for 24 May meeting.

29 PREM 13/1296, Aden to FO (8 June).

30 PREM 13/1297, Aden to FO (27 June, 10, 20 and 21 August); Trevelyan, *Middle East*, 228–34; Colin Mitchell, *Having Been a Soldier* (Hamish Hamilton, 1969), chapters 11–13.

31 For contrasting views of the collapse see: Kelly, *Arabia*, 37–41; Trevelyan, *Middle East*, chapters 4 and 5.

32 CAB 148/30, OPD(67)29th (5 September); PREM 13/1297, FO/CRO outward telegram (5 September); Richard Crossman, *The Diaries of a Cabinet Minister, Volume II: Lord President of the Council and Leader of the House of Commons 1966–8* (Hamish Hamilton and Jonathan Cape, 1976), 462; CAB 128/42, CC54(67) (7 September).

33 CAB 148/30, OPD(67)34th (27 October); CAB 128/42, CC62(67) (30 October); Crossman, *Diaries II*, 541.

34 CAB 128/42, CC68 and 69(67) (23 and 30 November).

35 Stephen Dorril, *MI6* (Fourth Estate, 2000), 729–35; Geraghty, *Who Dares*, 178–205; Connor, *Ghost Force*, chapter 8. For two contrasting general accounts see: Halliday, *Arabia*, chapters 9–11; Kelly, *Arabia*, chapter 3.

36 Ronald Hyam, 'Winds of change: the Empire and Commonwealth', in Wolfram Kaiser and Gillian Staerck, eds., *British Foreign Policy, 1955–64* (Macmillan, 2000), 202–3; Kelly, *Arabia*, 42–4; Trevelyan, *Middle East*, 264–6.

37 Halliday, *Arabia*, 398–418.

38 DEFE 4/205, DP 40/66 (2 September 1966); DEFE 4/211, COS 5th/67 (26 January); CAB 148/80, OPDO(67)7 (23 May).

39 CAB 148/30, OPD(67)1st (6 January); CAB 148/80, OPDO(67)8 (7 June).

40 CAB 128/39, CC49(65) (23 September); Balfour-Paul, *End*, 119–21.

41 BL, Aden High Commission files, R/20/D/409, McGarthy minute (5 May 1965), and see R/20/D/218, *passim*; CAB 158/58, JIC(65)41 (14 January 1966) and 42 (15 October 1965). On security in Bahrain see Anthony Parsons, *They Say the Lion* (Jonathan Cape, 1986), 114–17, 125–31.

42 CAB 159/46, JIC(66)49th (1 December) and 50th (8 December), and 47th, JIC(67)1st (5 January).

43 CAB 148/18, OPD(65)27th (26 May), 28th (2 June) and 29th (16 June); Castle, *Diaries*, 32–4 and 39–40.

44 PREM 13/2209, telegrams to FO (7–10 January); and see *Foreign Relations of the United States (FRUS), 1964–8*, vol. XXI (US Government Printing Office, Washington, DC, 1996), 230–3, 256–8, 274–6 and 280–1.

45 Paul Gore-Booth, *With Great Truth and Respect* (Constable, 1974), 377; PREM 13/2209, FO/CRO to posts (2 February).

46 FO 800/970, talks with Al-Sabah (26 February) and Zahedi (12 March).

47 PREM 13/3326, 'Derek' to Palliser (8 March) and see Graham to Youde (28 April 1969) for a statement of British policy.

48 Balfour-Paul, *End*, 126–35.

49 CAB 148/18, OPD(65)52nd (24 November).

50 CAB 148/25, OPD(66)34th (5 August), 39th (12 October) and 41st (29 October).

51 CAB 128/42, CC2 and 4–11 (19 January–9 March); CAB 130/312, MISC 137(67)1st–3rd (5 February–6 March); Robert Pearce, ed., *Patrick Gordon Walker: political diaries, 1932–71* (Historians' Press, 1991), 309–12.

52 CAB 128/43, CC16, 24 and 25(67) (29 February, 28 March and 2 April).

53 CAB 128/39, CC8(65) (8 February); CAB 129/120, C(65)18 (7 February).

54 PREM 13/1534, *passim*; John Darwin, *Britain and Decolonisation* (Macmillan, 1988), 308–9.

55 PREM 13/2125, Madrid to FO (19 December), Day to Palliser (27 June).

56 CAB 158/59, JIC(65)45 (5 August) and CAB 158/67, JIC(67)45 (25 August).

57 CAB 159/48, JIC(68)10th (29 February) and 17th (18 April) show reluctance to get involved in internal security; *FRUS*, vol. XXIV, 112–19 and 121–3.

58 PREM 13/2758, Stewart to Wilson (6 May); David Blundy and Andrew Lycett, *Qaddafi and the Libyan Revolution* (Corgi, 1988), 66–70; Denis Healey, *The Time of My Life* (Michael Joseph, 1989), 323.

59 CAB 128/44, CC42(69) (4 September); PREM 13/2758, Healey to Wilson (1 September), Stewart to Wilson (4 September).

60 CAB 128/44, CC52 and 61(69) (30 October and 18 December); CAB 148/91, OPD(69)20th, confidential annex (4 November) and 24th (11 December); PREM 13/2758, Trend to Wilson (3 November); PREM 13/3298, Stewart to Wilson (11 December).

61 PREM 13/1617, Stewart to Hadow (29 March 1967).

62 PREM 13/1617, Wilson to Eshkol (21 May) and FO to Washington (21 May); Abba Eban, *Personal Witness* (Putnam, New York, 1992), 360–1.

63 CAB 128/39, CC19(65) (30 March); CAB 129/120, C(65)49 (24 March).

64 David Watkins, *Seventeen Years in Obscurity* (Book Guild, Lewes, 1996), 113–16 (quote from 113); Harold Wilson, *The Chariot of Israel* (Weidenfeld and Nicolson, 1981). See also: Christopher Mayhew, *Time to Explain* (Hutchinson, 1987), 158–63; Dennis Walters, *Not Always With the Pack* (Constable, 1989), 156–61.

65 June Edmunds, 'The evolution of British Labour Party policy on Israel', *Twentieth Century British History*, vol. 11, no. 1 (2000), 24–9; Randolph and Winston Churchill, *The Six Day War* (Penguin, 1967), 38–43; Walter Laqueur, *The Road to War* (Penguin, 1968), 214–18.

66 Peter Paterson, *Tired and Emotional: the life of Lord George Brown* (Chatto and Windus, 1993), 88–91; FO 800/961, Wilson–Brown meeting (4 September 1966).

67 George Brown, *In My Way* (Golancz, 1971), 137–40; Thomas Brenchley, *Britain and the 1967 Arab–Israeli War* (DPhil, Oxford University, 1999), chapter 6.

68 CAB 128/42, CC61, 63 and 68(67) (26 October, 2 and 23 November); Crossman, *Diaries II*, 537 and 548.

69 PREM 13/1618, record of meeting (23 May); Brown, *My Way*, 136–7. For a detailed account of British policy-making between 23 May and 2 June see Robert McNamara, 'Britain, Nasser and the outbreak of the Six Day War', *Journal of Contemporary History*, vol. 35, no. 4 (2000), 619–39.

70 DEFE 32/11, COS–Healey meeting (23 May); PREM 13/1618, Healey to Wilson (24 May).

71 CAB 128/42, CC31(67) (23 May); Castle, *Diaries*, 257–8; Pearce, *Walker Diaries*, 314–16; also Patrick Gordon Walker, *The Cabinet* (Jonathan Cape, 1970), 138–52 for a 'disguised' account.

72 Eban, *Witness*, 377–9; PREM 13/1618, record of Wilson–Eban meeting (24 May).

73 CAB 128/42, CC31(67) (25 May); PREM 13/1618, FO to Paris (25 May); PREM 13/1858, Wilson to Johnson (25 May); Castle, *Diaries*, 259.

74 CAB 130/323, MISC 150(67)1st (25 May), and see 2nd and 3rd (26 May, including reports from Thomson and Brown on their visits); DEFE 4/218, COS 41st/67 (26 May), 42nd/67 (29 May) and DP49/67 (Final) (29 May); and CAB 129/130, C(67)88 (29 May) reviewing the political situation.

75 DEFE 32/11, COS–Healey meeting (30 May); CAB 128/42, CC33(67) (30 May); Castle, *Diaries*, 259–60; Crossman, *Diaries II*, 357–8; Pearce, *Walker Diaries*, 316.

76 PREM 13/1906, records of meetings (1–3 June); Robert McNamara, *In Retrospect* (Time Books, New York, 1995), 278; Lyndon Baines Johnson, *The Vantage Point: perspectives of the Presidency 1963–69* (Weidenfeld and Nicolson, 1971), 292–5; LBJL, National Security File, Country File, UK, box 210, officials' conversation (2 June).

77 CAB 128/42, CC36(67) (6 June); Harold Wilson, *The Labour Government 1964–1970: a personal record* (Weidenfeld and Nicolson, 1971), 398–9 (including quote); Eban, *Witness*, 400–1.

78 CAB 159/57, JIC(65)20th (18 March); CAB 159/62, JIC(66)24th (24 March); and CAB 159/66, JIC(67)26th (17 April).

79 Gore-Booth, *Great Truth*, 366–7; Crossman, *Diaries II*, 366.

80 CAB 128/42, CC46(67) (11 July); Castle, *Diaries*, 276; Wilson, *Government*, 400.

81 The oil and Canal issues featured on the Cabinet agenda for months: CAB 128/42, CC37–40, 43, 46, 52 and 53 (June–July); CAB 148/30, OPD(67)32nd (10 October).

82 CAB 148/30, OPD(67)36th (15 November).

83 CAB 148/35, OPD(68)20th and 21st (7 and 13 November); Richard Crossman, *The Diaries of a Cabinet Minister, Volume III: Secretary of State for Social Services 1968–1970* (Hamish Hamilton and Jonathan Cape, 1977), 251.

84 The Libyan deal was proposed before the overthrow of the monarchy, but created a major headache when Colonel Gaddafi seized power: CAB 128/44, CC27 and 61(69) (12 June and 18 December); CAB 148/91, OPD(69)5th (26 March), 6th (1 May) and 16th (15 October); Tony Benn, *Office Without Power: diaries 1968–72* (Hutchinson, 1988), 164; Crossman, *Diaries III*, 466–7, 513–14, 522, 685–6. Also PREM 13/2736, records of Meir visit (11–17 June).

85 PREM 13/1621, FO to Kuwait (15 June).

86 CAB 128/42, CC39 and 41(67) (15 and 22 June); Crossman, *Diaries II*, 392–3; Brenchley, *Britain*, 131–8 (and see Appendix E for text); LBJL, Tom Johnson's Notes of Meetings, meeting of President and advisers (18 July).

87 FO 800/969, FO to Tel Aviv (13 October).

88 LBJL, oral histories, Goldberg, interview 1 (23 March 1983), 10 and 17–18.

89 Eban, *Witness*, 455–9; also Gideon Rafael, *Destination Peace* (Stein and Day, New York, 1987), 187–90.

90 Mahmoud Riad, *The Struggle for Peace in the Middle East* (Quartet, 1981), 66; U Thant, *View from the UN* (David and Charles, 1978), 293. Sydney Bailey, *Four Arab–Israeli Wars and the Peace Process* (3rd edition) (Macmillan, 1990), 269–78, includes a full analysis of the resolution compared with others.

91 Eban, *Witness*, 496–8; PREM 13/2775, Wilson–Eban meeting (13 December).

92 CAB 128/44, CC39(69) (30 July); CAB 148/91, OPD(69)13th, confidential annex (28 July) and OPD(69)15th (8 October); PREM 13/2776/1, Maitland to Palliser (14 January), Trend to Wilson (25 July); Crossman, *Diaries III*, 598, 669–70, 786–7 and 873.

93 Cecil King, *The Cecil King Diary 1965–70* (Jonathan Cape, 1972), 235; Tore Tingvold Petersen, 'Crossing the Rubicon? Britain's withdrawal from the

Middle East, 1964–8', *International History Review*, vol. 22, no. 2 (2000), 333, 336–8 and 340; Diane Kunz, 'Anglo-American defence and financial policy during the 1960s', *Journal of Imperial and Commonwealth History*, vol. 27, no. 2 (1999), 228.

94 Wright in 'East of Suez', Institute of Contemporary British History seminar, 16 November 1990; PRO, FCO 49/260, PWP(69)7 (16 December 1969).

95 FCO 49/270, draft memorandum (11 December 1969).

96 McNamara, 'Six Day War', 638–9.

97 See Clive Jones and John Stone, 'Britain and the Arabian Gulf', *International Relations*, vol. 13, no. 4 (1997), 1–24.

5

The Atlantic alliance and détente

The years 1964–70 were troubled for the North Atlantic Treaty Organisation (NATO), marred by arguments over nuclear sharing and French
withdrawal from its military structure. The USA's involvement in Vietnam provoked fears among European governments that Washington
was neglecting their concerns. Relations between America, Britain and
Germany were disrupted in 1965–7 by arguments over the financial
costs of military forces on German soil and in 1967 there was a military
coup in Greece, threatening the alliance's democratic credentials. There
were also important shifts in NATO military strategy, with the adoption
of 'flexible response', and a move towards a greater political role for
the alliance, with the 1967 Harmel report on détente.

Michael Stewart explained Britain's aims within the alliance to the
Cabinet in 1965. They were to preserve NATO in the face of Gaullist
criticism, influence US behaviour, promote the relaxation of East–West
tension and come to terms with increasing German power while preventing German access to nuclear weapons.[1] These aims sometimes
provoked serious differences, even with close allies. Indeed, in the context of European security, at least down to the Czechoslovakian crisis of
1968, relations with allies proved more complex and challenging than
relations with the USSR. It should be noted at the outset that an attack
by the Soviet bloc in Europe was deemed unlikely because of the danger
of mutual nuclear obliteration. In 1965 the Joint Intelligence Committee
(JIC) ended the practice of opening its 'Weekly Survey of Intelligence'
with an item on Warsaw Pact intentions regarding hostilities. The JIC
was soon less concerned with Soviet bellicosity than with the impact of
the Vietnam War on détente. Even in 1968, when the USSR obtained
nuclear 'equality' with America, the JIC was confident the USA held
the upper hand in terms of military and economic power.[2]

Nuclear sharing

In reviewing his administration's early months in January 1965, Wilson claimed one major foreign success: 'Apart from anything else we have killed the MLF'.[3] The MLF, or Multilateral Force, originated around 1960 and was intended to overcome European criticism of the USA's monopolisation of the Western deterrent. State Department officials also believed that Germany would inevitably want nuclear weapons in future and that it was best to pre-empt this by forming a NATO deterrent in which Bonn shared. However, the idea of allowing Germany a 'finger on the nuclear trigger' provoked criticism within the alliance and the USSR demanded that the MLF be abandoned before negotiations on a global Non-Proliferation Treaty (NPT) could begin. De Gaulle disliked the MLF, partly because it was linked to US ambitions of ending the independent French and British nuclear deterrents. For the same reason the British were lukewarm about it, but, at the Nassau conference of December 1962 with President Kennedy, Harold Macmillan made ambiguous promises of support for the project as the price of obtaining Polaris missiles. Vital to MLF plans by 1963 was a mixed-manned surface fleet, a truly 'international' force rather than one based on the territory of particular members.[4] Britain's Ministry of Defence (MOD) saw the surface fleet as an unnecessary escalation of the arms race, vulnerable to Soviet attack. The Chief of the Defence Staff, Earl Mountbatten, 'considered it the greatest piece of military nonsense I had come across in fifty years'. But the Foreign Office (FO) feared outright opposition would alienate Washington and Bonn, and the Conservatives avoided a final decision on membership.[5]

Labour's position on nuclear sharing was wrapped up in the party's debate over the British deterrent. In 1960 the annual conference had famously voted for unilateral nuclear disarmament but the leader, Hugh Gaitskell, fought back the following year. Unity was rebuilt around the position that Britain would not replace its existing deterrent, the V-bombers, when they became redundant. Labour's 1964 election manifesto, however, promised only 'the renegotiation of the Nassau agreement' and did not rule out all forms of nuclear sharing, although it was critical of the MLF. In February in the Commons Denis Healey, as shadow spokesman on defence, refused to say whether Labour would cancel Polaris and it is likely he and Wilson decided to retain the missiles before entering office.[6] Wilson's memoirs say they kept Polaris in late 1964 because it 'was clear that production of the submarines was well past the point of no return', when in fact, as Lawrence Freedman has shown, it would have been possible to cancel Polaris at limited cost.[7] The missile system would not become operational until the late 1960s and the submarines could have been put to another use. The decision

to retain the system was probably influenced by ambitions of a continuing great power role, the desire to influence US nuclear policy and
the relatively low expense. However, it was also tied to the MLF controversy. Wilson, Healey and Foreign Secretary Patrick Gordon Walker
first implied that Polaris would be retained at an ad hoc committee
meeting, whose record suggests little discussion beyond the need to
contribute Polaris to an 'Atlantic Nuclear Force' (ANF). This was a
scheme the government developed as Britain's alternative to the MLF.[8]

Accounts of the ANF usually credit the plan to Healey,[9] but Wilson
boasted that he thought of the key element in his bath during the
general election campaign. Britain would commit its strategic weapons
to a joint NATO force for its lifetime, abandoning the right that
Macmillan had secured to withdraw British forces to meet 'supreme
national interests'. This concession was significant. By limiting Britain's
'independent' nuclear capability it would please those who wanted to
end this and it would bring Britain nearer to equality of status with
Germany. Once Wilson defined the basic idea, Gordon Walker developed
other features of the ANF, including its name.[10] The proposal was presented to the Cabinet on 26 November 1964 and with it, by implication,
the decision to retain Polaris, a point that created remarkably little difficulty. As Austen Morgan puts it, the new government 'conjured away
the idea of an independent nuclear deterrent with the ANF' and so
'abandoned its opposition to nuclear weapons'.[11] There is debate about
how seriously leading ministers took the ANF. Healey's memoirs, for
example, declare that it sank 'without trace, because nobody wanted
it'.[12] But Dick Taverne, Healey's Parliamentary Private Secretary, thought
that 'Denis would have accepted the ANF proposal if it had come off'
and this view has support from later historians. Gordon Walker even
called it the 'major foreign policy initiative' of the early months of the
government.[13] It fitted British needs well, as it offered a chance to
replace the MLF proposal and 'renegotiate' Nassau, without alienating
the Americans and Germans or scrapping Polaris. Also, the British
contribution would take the simple form of committing its strategic
weapons to the ANF, rather than participating directly in a 'mixed-
manned' element such as a surface fleet. Then again, Wilson showed
no great commitment to the ANF and, as will be seen below, Britain put
up no great fight for it when it ran into difficulties.

Having devised the ANF, the problem was to convince the USA to
support it. Wilson's memoirs emphasise the pressure he was still under
from America to agree to the MLF before he met President Johnson for
their first summit in December. Ambassador David Bruce urged this
and so did other US officials.[14] Nonetheless, before heading for
Washington Wilson said, 'time was on our side and against the Americans. We were not in a hurry for an agreement.' A German election was

due in September 1965 and, if there were no early agreement, the issue could be deferred for months.[15] There were actually some doubts about the MLF in Washington, especially from the President's National Security Adviser, McGeorge Bundy. But Johnson was reluctant to upset Germany's Chancellor, Ludwig Erhard, who favoured the MLF because it offered his country a degree of nuclear equality within the alliance. During the summit Johnson agreed the ANF should be discussed by NATO but only alongside the MLF. The USA would not particularly push either project, instead putting the onus on Britain and Germany to find a way forward.[16] Wilson's retrospective interpretation was that 'we had won the day', a claim repeated in other British accounts.[17] Certainly, without firm US support, and with a complex alternative now on the table, it would be difficult to make progress on the MLF. Many American studies agree that the summit spelt the end of the project while arguing that its demise was primarily due not to Wilson but to US doubts.[18] Yet in both British and American versions two essential points are largely ignored. First, as well as criticising the MLF, the British had put forward the ANF and the subsequent failure of this scheme must be explained. Second, Johnson made no final 'decision' about the MLF in the Washington talks and US support for a genuine form of nuclear sharing actually continued for another eighteen months, posing a continuing problem for Britain.

When Wilson reported to the Cabinet on 11 December he admitted the idea of a mixed-manned surface fleet was still on the table but emphasised Johnson's readiness to consider the ANF.[19] But even Gordon Walker saw the ANF as being, in part, a time-buying exercise. He wrote on 23 December, 'it would pay us if things drag on a bit, perhaps until the German elections. But it must look as if others, not we, are dragging our feet'.[20] In Bonn, in contrast, there was deep pessimism about the MLF, foreign minister Gerhard Schroeder complaining that Washington had lost interest in it. Significantly, however, Secretary of State Dean Rusk told him that US aims remained the same, even if tactics had changed, and stated that 'in our view the ANF proposals can leave room for the MLF substantially as it was initially conceived'. This had little effect in the short term because, as Wilson had predicted, the German elections forced Erhard to let the matter drift until September.[21] But there was every reason to expect renewed US–German pressure on London when the elections were over.

Over the following months the ANF/MLF controversy, though pushed into the background, continued to have international repercussions, not least on the NPT. Work on such a treaty was well under way in the FO, directed by the Minister for Disarmament, Lord Chalfont. Britain's desire to achieve an NPT had been strengthened by the first Chinese atomic test and worries that, in response to it, India would develop nuclear weapons. A key problem with the ANF was that the Kremlin saw it as no better than the MLF. The Soviet premier, Alexei Kosygin, told Wilson it would still give Germany control over nuclear weapons and so amounted to proliferation. Throughout 1965, despite British arguments to the contrary, the Soviets repeated that an NPT was incompatible with the ANF.[22] London also found itself at loggerheads with Washington and Bonn on the terms of the NPT. The USA suspected that Moscow pushed non-proliferation only so as to disrupt NATO by dividing Germany from its allies: it was natural for Bonn to dislike any agreement that permanently left it in an inferior position to London and Paris in the nuclear field. The USA and Germany opposed the tabling of the British draft in the disarmament talks, sponsored by the United Nations (UN), because the draft would have prevented a German share in any future 'European' nuclear force. The Germans also wanted the MLF/ANF issue to be resolved before an NPT was negotiated.[23] In August 1965, when the British refused to co-sponsor a US draft NPT at the disarmament talks, the differences became publicly obvious.[24]

An alternative route to nuclear co-operation was already being developed; this involved consultation ('software') rather than a sharing of weapons ('hardware'). In May 1965 the US Defense Secretary, Robert McNamara, proposed a NATO 'select committee' to look at an expanded alliance role in nuclear planning. This idea was accepted, despite some German scepticism, and studies took place over the next eighteen months.[25] But in the short term, once Erhard won the September elections, interest in a 'hardware' solution to NATO nuclear sharing was resuscitated. Wilson, in Cabinet on 7 December 1965, insisted the 'MLF was dead' but in Washington on 16 December he found it expedient to say that the ANF was still on the table.[26] A few days after that Erhard arrived in Washington and put a memorandum to Johnson stating that Germany was ready to discuss the ANF, but only if it had a proper mixed-manned element on the lines of the MLF.[27] Johnson and Erhard both sent Wilson a copy of this paper, the President commenting that there should be a serious response to it. But by now Wilson was determined to do nothing. He made his scepticism about a hardware solution clear in two cleverly worded replies, promising to study the German memorandum while hoping that progress would continue on McNamara's scheme for consultative machinery.[28] After this Johnson, increasingly concerned by the Vietnam War, showed little determination to press matters and, in mid-February 1966, when Erhard suggested talks at foreign minister level on NATO nuclear issues, Wilson instructed officials not to hurry a reply. The British general election provided a convenient excuse for further delay and Wilson had no desire to rekindle debate about nuclear issues before the polls closed. 'One of the more remarkable features of the parliament was the almost total disappearance of the independent nuclear deterrent as an issue between the parties.'[29] Despite his narrow majority in 1964 and Labour's divisions on nuclear questions when in opposition, Wilson had managed to retain Britain's deterrent without provoking domestic political controversy, partly by arguing that he was going to 'internationalise' the deterrent via the ANF. Once the March election was won he had no need for the ANF. Its final passing was, however, linked to a crisis that struck NATO that same month.

French withdrawal

In reviewing world events at the start of 1965, Nicholas Henderson, at the time Private Secretary to the Foreign Secretary, considered President de Gaulle a more important element than recent events in Vietnam, the USSR or China because he had an impact on so many important issues, from the MLF and the European Economic Community (EEC), to NATO and détente. Anglo-French relations in the 1960s can seem like a catalogue of adverse actions by de Gaulle: he vetoed two British bids to enter the EEC, condemned British reliance on the USA, pulled out of NATO and adopted an unhelpful approach to the 1967 Middle East war and Biafra. The JIC even learnt that de Gaulle made Britain his second most important intelligence target, after the USA but ahead of the USSR.[30] It was not all negatives. Britain and France did sometimes work together, criticising the MLF for example and developing technological projects, like Concorde. There were even some British ministers, like Richard Crossman, who felt de Gaulle's ideas for East–West détente and a less supranational EEC were to be welcomed. Crossman strongly objected to a memorandum, circulated by Stewart in January 1966, that criticised de Gaulle's policies. But FO fears seemed justified when, on 9 March, Wilson was formally told that France was quitting NATO's integrated command structure.[31] French withdrawal from NATO had long been predicted. In June 1965 there had been Anglo-American talks about how to deal with it: they would do nothing to provoke the General, but would work with the rest of NATO, act as if the alliance would last indefinitely and make clear that they were prepared for anything he might do. His decision to leave was much misunderstood at the time. Rather than retreating into isolationism he intended to alter relationships within the Western alliance, reducing US influence in Europe and paving the way for improved East–West relations while still remaining vigilant in the face of Soviet Communism.[32] He never ended France's commitment to the 1949 North Atlantic Treaty. Nonetheless, his semi-detached role raised the danger that he might pursue policies out of step with other Western powers, fears that increased when he visited Moscow in June. Withdrawal also caused administrative inconvenience because 100,000 NATO personnel and NATO headquarters had to be moved from France.

In Washington the State Department initially favoured a firm line but Johnson's response to de Gaulle was remarkably calm: 'when a man asks you to leave his home, you don't argue, you just get your hat and go'. There was a similar measured reaction, disguising some deep-seated anger, in the rest of NATO. In Bonn, the Atlanticists Erhard and Schroeder were well aware that France could not replace the USA as a guarantor of security, but recognised that they must strike a middle course between Washington and Paris because of the need to preserve the EEC.[33] In Britain, Denis Healey was typically robust, referring to the French President as 'a bad ally in NATO and a bad partner in the Common Market', for which he subsequently apologised in public. But Stewart told ministers that, despite the potential costs of French behaviour, a hostile response would simply worsen the crisis. The important point was to keep the alliance together. He also pointed out that French withdrawal would increase Britain's voice in NATO, even if it also benefited Germany.[34] The FO concentrated at first on drawing up a statement reaffirming the value of NATO, which was issued by the fourteen remaining members on 18 March. London was so quick to develop this proposal that US ambassador David Bruce feared his own government 'may give the impression of taking too passive a part', but the statement proved short and surprisingly insubstantial. In addressing the Commons on the crisis, Stewart responded to French policy by emphasising that an 'integrated organisation is essential to give life to the treaty' because 'the nature of modern conflict' meant that offensives could be launched very quickly. In the Overseas Policy and Defence Committee (OPD), however, he recognised the need to respond to some of de Gaulle's criticisms of the alliance by reforming NATO institutions and supporting East–West détente.[35]

The new situation might easily have rekindled the debate over German nuclear weapons. After all, West Germany, whose army had overtaken the size of the British in 1964, was of enormous importance to the alliance after de Gaulle's departure and could have demanded a share of nuclear 'hardware'. Instead, French withdrawal smoothed the way for a less ambitious system, of shared nuclear planning. Ironically, only days before the General's move, Wilson had declared himself 'totally opposed' to any 'hardware' arrangement with Germany in discussion with a US official, records of which were kept restricted in Whitehall.[36] After the French withdrawal, the State Department continued to study nuclear sharing and Johnson told Wilson that it was 'imperative' that the USA, Britain and Germany should 'stay as close as possible to each other' following the withdrawal; the Germans must not feel that they had been 'cast adrift' and so the nuclear issue might need to be addressed.[37] But Wilson was not going to pay the price of Western unity in the form of the MLF/ANF. When he met Erhard in May 1966, the need to take a common approach to NATO's problems was paramount and the issue of nuclear sharing was studiously avoided.[38] Eventually, in September, on another visit to Washington, Erhard conceded, 'Nobody was expecting a "hardware solution" any longer'. He lost office soon afterwards, but Willy Brandt, foreign minister in the new government, confirmed in December that Germany no longer wanted 'hardware'.[39] The NATO Council that month agreed to create a Nuclear Defence Affairs Committee to discuss nuclear planning. Under this was a seven-member Nuclear Planning Group, including Germany as well as the USA and Britain, which held its first meeting in April 1967.[40] By then the British had confirmed that Polaris would be 'assigned' to NATO but, since orders for firing would come directly from the Prime Minister, the much-trumpeted 'internationalisation' of the nuclear deterrent did not actually amount to much.[41]

Another side-effect of French withdrawal was that Britain, in 1968–70, became the leading force in developing a European defence identity. It has long been recognised that the British encouraged meetings between Western European defence ministers, the 'Eurogroup', which discussed the standardisation of weapons systems and prepared joint approaches to NATO Council meetings. Healey has been very much identified with this. What has not been clear is the way this evolved from a combination of de Gaulle's disruptive policy, the US government's long-standing desire to see Europe take on a greater share of the defence burden and the failure of Britain's 'second try' at EEC entry. In early 1968, in the wake of de Gaulle's veto, the British, with discreet US encouragement, decided to build links with the other EEC members in ways the General could not block. But the 'Eurogroup' took time fully to reach fruition and Healey's role in its genesis should not be exaggerated. Actually, the FO first suggested an initiative on West European defence co-operation, especially equipment procurement, in mid-1967, as part of the effort to enter the EEC. But the MOD was sceptical, fearing this would harm the cohesion of NATO while doing nothing to impress de Gaulle. Stewart's diaries show that, in early 1968, Healey was still not keen to push European defence co-operation if this was linked to maintaining pressure for EEC entry. After some progress in 1968 it was necessary to persuade the incoming Nixon administration to back the proposal and to win over sceptics who feared that a successful defence organisation could lead the USA to pull troops out from Europe. The first all-day meeting of European defence ministers was not held until September 1970, after Labour lost office.[42]

The colonels in Greece

The April 1967 coup by Greek colonels raised questions about whether a member could remain in NATO if martial law was introduced and parliament suspended. While it had always included one dictatorship, Portugal, the alliance liked to portray itself as liberal and democratic. But Greece was on the exposed periphery of NATO in the eastern Mediterranean, it had seen a civil war between the government and Communists in the 1940s and, largely thanks to differences over Cyprus, it had uneasy relations with a fellow NATO member, Turkey. There had been serious inter-communal violence between the Greek and Turkish communities in Cyprus in 1964 that died down just before Labour came to power. The FO wished to keep the situation as stable as possible and was ready to tolerate the colonels. The ambassador to Athens, Ralph Murray, advised the Foreign Secretary, George Brown, that, given NATO interests, bilateral trade and the vulnerability of Britons imprisoned in Greece, it was best to deal with the new regime and 'push them into a suitable political evolution'. Wilson realised that the colonels' triumph would add to his problems in managing the left at home and wanted to encourage Greek conservatives to oppose the colonels but Brown was reluctant to meddle in internal politics, pointing out that Britain had already come to terms with military coups in other allied states, Pakistan and Turkey.[43] The survival in office of the monarch, Constantine II, allowed the British and others to maintain diplomatic relations with Greece without having to recognise a 'new' regime.[44] But it did not prevent a new upsurge of communal tension in Cyprus, which threatened to erupt into a Greek–Turkish war in November. Despite being the former colonial power in Cyprus, the British let the USA take the lead in brokering a settlement. It is noteworthy, however, that just before the crisis broke Britain secretly informed Constantine that, if it would help secure a settlement, they were ready to transfer one of their sovereign base areas on Cyprus to Turkey.[45]

Constantine launched a counter-coup against the colonels on 13 December but botched it and was exiled. At first, in line with other NATO members, the British dealt with the post-monarchical regime while avoiding formal recognition.[46] But pressures grew to work more closely with the colonels, especially when the possibility arose of a major sale of naval vessels by the firm Vospers. In July 1968, Stewart, again Foreign Secretary, told the OPD that British policy had four aims: to encourage a move to constitutional rule, preserve Greece as an effective NATO ally, protect British interests in the country and retain influence over Greek foreign policy. He argued that, with the colonels secure in power and some signs of constitutional progress, the Vospers sale should be welcomed. But Barbara Castle, Crossman and others were less keen to compromise their principles and sought to delay a decision. Wilson

was in a difficult position, having recently talked publicly of the
'bestialities' of the colonels' regime.[47] In January 1969, despite continuing complaints from Crossman about the moral hypocrisy involved, some
important principles were decided that would govern future relations
with Greece. A 'tortuous' OPD meeting decided that arms sales should
go ahead on the understanding they were linked to NATO defence needs.
But co-operation via the Council of Europe was a different issue, since
that body had partly been established to protect human rights in post-
war Europe.[48] At the end of the year Britain duly decided to vote for
Greece's suspension from the Council and the colonels left the organisation before a formal vote was taken.[49] There was thus an expression
of distaste for the regime even if the British, in common with most
other NATO allies, were unwilling to pay a real price in terms of compromising their defence and commercial interests.

Offset costs and Anglo-German relations

The danger of a disintegration of NATO in 1966 seemed real, not only
thanks to de Gaulle but also because of growing differences between
the USA, Britain and Germany – the trio now very much at the centre
of alliance relationships – over so-called 'offset costs'. In 1964 the USA
had 262,000 personnel serving in Germany, while the British Army of
the Rhine (BAOR) comprised 51,000 troops. The Americans and British
were happy to pay the resource costs of these forces, in equipment and
salaries for example, but were unhappy with the exchange costs – the
expenditure in Deutschmarks needed to keep forces in Germany. The
problem had caused Anglo-German differences under Macmillan and
Germany had agreed in principle to 'offset' the foreign exchange costs
by buying military equipment from the USA and Britain. But such purchases fell well short of what Britain, in particular, believed to be fair
and the Conservatives had reduced the size of the BAOR (from 77,000
in 1957), with Macmillan sometimes threatening to cut it altogether. By
the mid-1960s, the West German economy was one of the strongest in
the world and no one believed war in Europe to be imminent, while the
USA and Britain both faced balance of payment difficulties.[50] The need
to reduce foreign exchange costs in Germany was an important element
in Labour's defence review in 1964–6.

Labour had inherited a vague arrangement, made under Douglas-
Home in July 1964, whereby Bonn agreed to offset British costs 'so far
as possible'. The issue was discussed at the first Wilson–Erhard summit
in March 1965 but there was currently a downturn in German growth,
it was an election year and Erhard felt he deserved some credit for
supporting sterling on the money markets. The British also knew that

any threat to reduce the size of the BAOR carried its own risks: it would upset all the NATO allies, including the USA; it would not save much money because the troops would have to be rehoused in Britain; and it might not be taken seriously, since everyone knew the troops were best based in Germany to face a Soviet attack. Neither side wished to upset the other and the two leaders simply agreed to address the problem in further talks. The forthcoming state visit to Germany by Elizabeth II, designed to symbolise post-war Anglo-German rapprochement, reinforced the need for an amicable settlement.

In April 1965 the Chief Secretary to the Treasury, Jack Diamond, negotiated a deal in Bonn that represented a compromise. The current agreement was extended to March 1967 and there was still no precise figure for the amount to be paid, but German purchases would offset about 70 per cent of foreign exchange costs. It was a compromise with which the British were soon ill at ease.[51] The balance of payments crisis of July 1966 led the government for the first time to talk publicly of reducing its NATO commitment if a better deal were not achieved. Despite some resistance from Stewart, the Chancellor of the Exchequer, James Callaghan, successfully pressed the Cabinet on 19 July to achieve a substantial 'offset' from Germany and himself flew to Bonn the next day to show that Britain meant business.[52]

Callaghan's talks led to the establishment of a joint commission to study the problem but this made slow progress and, on 10 August, he pressed the OPD for an early reduction of the BAOR. But the FO and MOD were gravely concerned about the political impact of any British withdrawal from Europe and there were similar feelings in Washington by August. Indeed, President Johnson, fearing an 'unravelling' of the alliance, put pressure on both his allies to begin talks with the USA on the problem. The British agreed to hold 'trilateral' talks, hoping to move quickly, but the Germans were unhappy to be pressured so strongly and it was only during a summit with Johnson that Erhard agreed to participate. Then the German Chancellor lost office and there was a long delay before a successor, Kurt Kiesinger, was appointed. Negotiations began in earnest only in January 1967, in London. Finally, in May, a complex compromise was reached which, among other items, provided for extra offset purchases from Britain by both the USA and Germany, and which still left $20 million per year for Britain to cover. There would be further offset negotiations under Labour but they would never be so divisive again.[53] The British realised that further argument with Germany might complicate their efforts to enter the EEC and, besides, there was an increasing desire for close co-operation with Germany on military and technological projects.[54]

Hubert Zimmerman has asked why the British made such a fuss, over so many years, about offset costs, 'without making a determined effort to break the deadlock': these costs were a small part of Britain's foreign exchange problem, the issue tarnished Britain's image as a good ally in NATO and the haggling may have adversely affected the currency markets. Zimmerman blames much of the problem on the obsession with the value of sterling. But troop costs were a two-way affair. The Germans themselves conceded the principle of offset and they too had it in their power 'to break the deadlock', by being more generous with their increasing wealth. They never did cover in full the windfall earnings they obtained from the presence of 51,000 British troops, who, in exchange terms, were little different to tourists. Alternatively, they could have done what Kiesinger apparently contemplated in January 1967: called the British bluff and told them to remove the BAOR. Except that this, too, revealed the two-way nature of relations because, as the Germans well knew, it could have triggered pressure for a US withdrawal and so ruined German security.[55]

The offset issue demonstrated the complexity of Anglo-German interactions in this period. Bilateral relations were at least as complicated and significant as those with France, touching on nuclear weapons, European integration and détente, as well as NATO and monetary issues. Before Labour took power, Gordon Walker feared 'a US alliance with Germany over our heads', which would reduce Britain's place in the Western alliance. Yet he also recognised that it was best to try to control Germany, not by opposition, but through 'a close association ... an openly clear and friendly relationship'. Oliver Wright, his Private Secretary, told Wilson that, 'How to promote movement in East–West relations and to make sense of ... NATO ... without alienating the Germans ... [was] the question of questions for our diplomacy', while Stewart circulated a Cabinet memorandum in 1965 arguing that there were 'compelling reasons of national interest ... to work constructively with the Germans'.[56] Nonetheless, it is difficult to sense any great improvement in Anglo-German relations under Labour, at least until the last months of the government. In some ways the high point of the early years was the Queen's state visit in 1965, while low points occurred in October 1967, when Chalfont hinted at cuts in the BAOR if Britain were not let into the EEC, and November 1968, when ambassador Herbert Blankenhorn was given a dressing down by Wilson over Bonn's refusal to revalue the Deutschmark. The FO may have been quite consistently aware of the need to placate Germany for the sake of British policy on the EEC and NATO, but the Treasury and MOD were more ready to bully the Germans over defence spending. It was difficult for Britain, in decline as a world power, to reconcile itself to the recovery of Germany to the point that it had become an important ally of the USA. Britain also had to accept that it was less important in German eyes than France, their EEC partner. Yet there was a real sense of friendship once the Social Democratic Brandt became Chancellor in 1969. When he visited London in March 1970, Wilson welcomed him with the remark that relations 'stood at an all-time high'.[57]

Détente and the Harmel report

Frederic Bozo has argued that de Gaulle's withdrawal from NATO and advances in détente in the later 1960s were inextricably linked: the General argued he would be freer to pursue détente outside NATO and this forced the other members to show he was wrong. Bozo's thesis certainly finds support in the British case. Downing Street was quick to urge that French withdrawal should be followed by efforts to relax East–West tension.[58] Actually, Britain had long been at the forefront of those hoping to reduce East–West tension, not least because it was so vulnerable to a Soviet nuclear assault. Advocates of détente were not necessarily interested in tolerating the existence of the Communist bloc. There was an element in British diplomacy that saw a relaxation of East–West tensions as a less dangerous way of *fighting* the Cold War than a policy of threats. In the 1950s Winston Churchill had urged summit meetings, security understandings and expanded trade with the USSR not only as a way to reduce the danger of a nuclear conflagration but also as a means of breaking up the Soviet bloc. By showing the benefits of capitalism, liberalism and peaceful co-operation, the West could bring about a withering of Communism.[59] Wilson's interest in détente was well established. He had worked to expand Anglo-Soviet commerce as President of the Board of Trade (1947–51) and visited the USSR regularly in the 1950s as a consultant for a timber company. At a speech in Belper in January 1964 he had talked of moving beyond co-existence to 'genuine co-operation' and, building on earlier Labour proposals for military disengagement in central Europe, urged the creation of a 'nuclear-free zone' there. He also visited Moscow twice as leader of the opposition.[60]

Labour's election victory coincided with the overthrow of the volatile Nikita Khrushchev by Leonid Brezhnev, who became party leader, and Alexei Kosygin, who became premier. Both were uninspiring, if competent, apparatchiks, whose foreign policy was, compared with that of Khrushchev, unadventurous. They were determined to retain Marxist–Leninist rule in Eastern Europe, made little attempt to heal the rift with China and built up massive military power. They were ready to contemplate détente with the West, but early plans for a US–Soviet summit came to nothing, mainly because of the Vietnam War. The British ambassador, Humphrey Trevelyan, was well aware that progress on an Anglo-Soviet level was dependent on broader developments in East–West relations. The theme of several of his early despatches to the new Foreign Secretary, Patrick Gordon Walker, was that London could not act in isolation where the USSR was concerned. In order to prevent tensions in the Atlantic alliance that the Soviets might exploit, policy towards the Eastern bloc had to be co-ordinated with NATO allies, especially Washington and – given the centrality of the division of Germany to the Cold War – Bonn. The best Britain could do was encourage the others to pursue détente, and to work to improve commercial, scientific and cultural Anglo-Soviet links.[61]

David Bruce predicted that, once elected, Wilson would seek both a close 'special relationship' and an 'honest broker' role between Washington and Moscow. Sure enough, soon after holding his first summit with Johnson, Wilson was boasting about his role as a 'stalking horse' for both superpowers in their relations with each other. After his first summit in Moscow the Prime Minister told President Johnson that, while the Soviets were not ready to talk directly to the USA at present, 'they may be ready to keep [a dialogue] going through us'.[62] He certainly tried to develop commercial links with the Soviets as well as regular meetings with their leaders but he never achieved anything dramatic or broke with general Western policy. Some British ministers were particularly keen on détente, notably Tony Benn, who, as Minister of Technology, planned to 'develop direct connections with the countries of Eastern Europe and encourage the operation of détente, in which I profoundly believed'. He had some limited success in fostering technological exchanges and was critical of the FO for not sharing his enthusiasm. Richard Crossman also favoured détente, telling Wilson it was wrong to let other allied states stand in the way of this, especially the Germans with their reluctance to deal with Walter Ulbricht's East Germany. 'In an atmosphere of Cold War', argued Crossman, 'Ulbricht [can] flourish. In an atmosphere of détente, conditions are created for an easing of the tyranny under which the East Germans suffer'.[63]

Even on a bilateral Anglo-Soviet level, however, there was no easy way to break the ideological divide and difficulties were generated more by Soviet rigidity than any reluctance about détente in the FO. The Kremlin gave Britain no special status as an East–West arbiter. Wilson's first summit in Moscow, for example, took more than a year to arrange. He first proposed a meeting in late 1964, hoping it might be in London, but the Soviets refused to contemplate this. Instead, foreign minister Andrei Gromyko was sent over in March 1965, by which time Vietnam loomed as a major problem.[64] Only in February 1967 – a year after Wilson's first visit to Moscow – would Kosygin venture to London. It proved difficult to expand trade, which remained heavily balanced in the Soviets' favour, and Moscow was even indifferent when Wilson urged that the two countries conclude a 'friendship treaty'.[65] The most persistent sore point in bilateral relations was the case of Gerald Brooke, a college lecturer arrested in the USSR in April 1965 for importing bibles. He was initially imprisoned for five years but in 1969 was threatened with further charges. In June, despite some disquiet, the Cabinet decided to exchange him for two spies, Peter and Helen Kroger, imprisoned in Britain since 1961. For *The Times* and *Daily Express* it was a sordid exchange of a naïve young man for two professional agents; for the *Guardian* and *Sun* there was little choice if an idealistic individual were to be spared further suffering. There was general agreement that the case exposed the true nature of the totalitarian state in the East.[66]

Records of Wilson's meetings in the USSR, in February 1966, July 1966 (an 'unofficial' visit linked to a trade fair) and January 1968, reveal the mixed nature of the relationship, with limited improvements in trade and technological links countered by Wilson's protests about Brooke and Soviet complaints about Britain's pro-Americanism, especially on Vietnam. Geraint Hughes has convincingly argued that Wilson, while he deluded himself into believing he had real influence on Moscow, took only an intermittent interest in détente and concentrated too narrowly on trade and summitry, while he had little grasp of broader security issues.[67] One proposal made by Wilson on the February 1966 visit was the establishment of a Kremlin–Downing Street 'hot-line', but it took until October 1967 for it to become operable, by which time de Gaulle had already secured such a link.[68] The FO Deputy Under-Secretary, Denis Greenhill, commented in early 1968 that, while there had been a 'striking improvement in the atmosphere and mechanics of Anglo-Soviet relations ... I cannot see that we are closer on funda-mentals'. Thanks to the invasion of Czechoslovakia that August there were no further Anglo-Soviet summits until Wilson returned to power in the mid-1970s, although he had planned to visit Moscow in July 1970 if he won the election.[69] One growing problem after Czechoslovakia was British concern about the size of the Soviet espionage operation in the United Kingdom, which was becoming too large for the security services to control. By September 1968 MI5 reckoned at least 137 Soviet officials were spies and the issue was raised with the Soviet ambassador in November.[70] The decision was taken under the Heath government in 1971 to expel 105 agents, sparking years of poor Anglo-Soviet relations just when the rest of NATO was warming to the détente policy that Britain had done much to inaugurate.

Labour's policy towards Eastern Europe was also unremarkable, more active than the Conservatives' perhaps, but less ambitious than that of France or even, by the end of the decade, West Germany. Ministerial visits to Eastern Europe were not that frequent; cultural contacts were fostered by the British Council but only on a modest budget; and, while individual politicians called for improved relations with East Germany, the official line was that West Germany was the only true Germany. Wilson saw no need to stir controversy on the last point, when there were so many other problems to face in Anglo-German relations. Only when Bonn itself sought to improve relations with East Germany did the British do the same.[71] Britain might ideally want to relax tensions in Europe but these tensions did not actually seem that threatening in the mid-1960s and London had other priorities, especially the main-tenance of the Anglo-American relationship and NATO, which militated against close relations with Moscow. The Prime Minister himself insisted that the main point of difference with de Gaulle on détente was that London believed this could be pursued only in a NATO context. Wilson may originally have had hopes of playing a mediatory role between the superpowers, but a paper by Stewart for the OPD in June 1968 showed a less ambitious, distinctly practical policy towards the USSR: Britain should be ready to talk, but must not 'run after' Moscow; trade and technological links should continue, but only if the benefits were reciprocal; cultural exchanges must be cost-effective; Soviet propaganda attacks must be met head on; and criticism in Britain of the Soviet police state should be 'discreetly' stimulated. As regards Eastern Europe, 'we must be careful not to appear to be driving wedges between them and the Soviet Union' but trade, technology, cultural exchanges and personal visits could all be used to encourage 'greater individual independence' by those under Soviet domination.[72]

Despite the problems in bilateral relations, some progress on détente did prove possible on a multilateral basis. Proposals for a European security conference had been pressed by the Soviets since the mid-1950s but were long treated with suspicion. Moscow seemed to want to detach the USA from Atlantic defence and to force Bonn to recognise East Germany. By the mid-1960s the atmosphere was becoming less dis-trustful, however, and even some West German leaders, notably Brandt, were sympathetic to the development of links to the Eastern bloc. In July 1966 the Warsaw Pact published its latest call for talks on all-European security, to create a system based on the peaceful settlement of disputes and the acceptance of existing European borders, including the division of Germany. This was still not in a form that appealed to the Western powers but, coming after de Gaulle's visit to Moscow, it added to the pressures for the alliance to study détente. Also, while the FO was sceptical about a security conference, Britain's interest in reducing defence costs led officials to favour an agreement on mutual troop withdrawals from central Europe by NATO and the Warsaw Pact.[73] In December 1966 the Atlantic Council responded to the increasing pressures for détente by asking a committee chaired by the Belgian Prime Minister, Pierre Harmel, to study the alliance's options. The

British played an unremarkable role in the committee's proceedings; they were determined to overcome French doubts and get a positive statement on détente, but keen not to upset Bonn on delicate issues like German reunification. In December 1967 the Council adopted the Harmel report, which accepted that NATO should have a role in developing détente with the Eastern bloc, complementary to its military function.[74]

This meeting proved important for the alliance in another way. It accepted that NATO should adopt a defensive strategy, known as 'flexible response', as the USSR could now match the USA in nuclear weapons. 'Flexible response' appeared to concede that it was no longer possible to threaten all-out nuclear war in the event of a Warsaw Pact attack. Instead, there would be a graduated escalation of conflict, beginning with a conventional phase and working through different levels of nuclear response, up to a strategic exchange. In fact, 'flexible response' was driven by political considerations. Western Europeans wanted to show that Washington could still defend them whereas the Americans needed to believe that a strategic nuclear exchange was not inevitable. Recent research suggests that it made little real difference on the operational side, where experts understood there would still be a rapid move to a strategic exchange.[75] Thus a study by the Chiefs of Staff in 1966 argued that the USSR's growing nuclear arsenal, married to the poverty of Western conventional forces, meant there must be a quick resort to tactical weapons; planning ought therefore to be based on deterring a war in the first place. But when Healey tried to write this logic into the February 1967 White Paper other ministers reacted badly, fearing the adverse public impact.[76]

In opposition, Labour had criticised NATO's reliance on nuclear weapons, but in order to make 'flexible response' viable a large number of conventional forces would have been required and Britain, as much as any European country, was trying to restrict spending on conventional forces. It was partly because of these problems that the British hoped Moscow would be interested in cutting its own troop levels in central Europe. The Atlantic Council, meeting in Reykjavik in June 1968, did propose talks with the Warsaw Pact on 'mutual balanced force reductions' but the Warsaw Pact had a clear conventional superiority in Europe and was not eager to bail NATO out of its difficulties. Healey doubted that a Soviet attack would actually be launched, yet he was at the forefront of attempts in 1969 to study how tactical nuclear weapons might work in practice, hoping that, if the Soviets knew that NATO had a viable nuclear strategy, this would further deter them from launching war. Unsurprisingly, such frank debate within the alliance over nuclear war stirred up some concern in the press in early 1970.[77]

Czechoslovakia and after

The Harmel report potentially paved the way for great advances in
détente but little happened in the short term. The Soviets showed no
enthusiasm for it, partly because it failed to embrace their ideas on
European security and partly because it adhered to a policy of continuing Western military strength. Hope was provided by the signature of
the NPT in July 1968. It had taken years to negotiate and was very
much dominated by the superpowers in the later stages, when Britain's
readiness to push for the NPT in the face of allied doubts was tempered
by the need to work with Germany more closely in NATO and on the
EEC application.[78] Many potential nuclear powers refused to sign but,
whatever its limits, the treaty represented one of the most important
East–West agreements to date and it was accompanied by a US–Soviet
promise to discuss limits on their strategic nuclear arsenals. The OPD
discussed a forthright policy to follow it up. Among other initiatives,
Britain should back a comprehensive test ban and make proposals for
limiting biological and chemical warfare.[79] But within weeks all the opti-
mism about détente was set back by events in Czechoslovakia. There
had been growing concern over events there since March 1968, when
Warsaw Pact leaders first criticised the liberalising policies of the new
party leader, Alexander Dubcek. Fears grew of possible Soviet intervention similar to that in Hungary in 1956 and, in mid-July, the issue
was brought to Cabinet. But, since the Czechoslovakians themselves had
not requested help, it was felt that any British action would be counter-
productive. Richard Crossman was shocked at the inactivity over a
situation that had parallels to Munich thirty years before, but the embassy
in Prague reported on 12 August that the worst was over. Czechoslovakia
could 'look forwards instead of backwards'. Then, on 20–21 August, the
Warsaw Pact invaded.[80]

Percy Cradock, a former diplomat, has analysed the failure to predict
the invasion and discerned a number of problems. NATO's policy of
'non-interference' meant some intelligence sources were not fully ex-
ploited; Warsaw Pact ciphers could not be read; and such intelligence
as was available was ambiguous, partly because Moscow itself was doubtful about an invasion until the last moment.[81] Many ministers were on
holiday on 21 August. Wilson and Stewart had to fly back to London to
condemn the invasion.[82] Britain did not want to go beyond other governments in expressing hostility towards Moscow, however. A sparsely attended
Cabinet meeting on 22 August was reluctant to let the situation damage
trade or do anything to threaten the status quo in central Europe, but
it was decided that no further ministerial visits to the Eastern bloc should
be arranged and that parliament should be recalled. There was an inevitable impact on certain high-profile links, such as a proposal for

computer sales to Romania and hopes of relaxing controls on East–
West trade. 'This is the price the Russians pay', noted Benn, 'and I am
afraid it is a price we will also pay in terms of orders'.[83] Not everything
was negative, however. There was some satisfaction in London that the
crisis had shown NATO to be united, had undermined de Gaulle's independent policy on détente and had weakened those voices in the USA
urging troop reductions in Europe. The British took advantage of the
situation to strengthen their own links to other European members of
NATO.[84] The invasion was not seen as signalling a return to a Soviet
Cold War policy and Stewart instructed British posts in late October
that détente must remain an aim, because 'in the longer term contact
with Eastern Europe is the principal means by which we can encourage
the liberal forces in those countries'. NATO allies took a similar line in
cancelling visits and reducing rather than completely cutting contacts.[85]
The Soviets were unapologetic, Brezhnev declaring in November that they
would act whenever the 'socialist community' was threatened. In December
Moscow even accused the British of exploiting the situation in Czechoslovakia to launch an anti-Soviet policy and subsequently complained
about a number of points, from British co-operation with Germany to
Healey's statements about the importance of nuclear defence to NATO.[86]
It was during these months that London also began to press the Soviets
to reduce their espionage activities and that the Brooke case reached its
critical point, all of which put bilateral relations in a depressing state.

Wilson has been accused of 'appeasement', in the style of Chamberlain,
over Czechoslovakia. Yet the course he took was no different to that
taken by the rest of NATO, which, after Hungary in 1956, knew it had
little influence behind the Iron Curtain. The whole alliance adopted a
low-key approach to the Prague Spring, made no contingency plans to
deal with a Warsaw Pact invasion of Czechoslovakia and stuck to verbal
condemnations when it occurred.[87] This allowed détente to recover quite
quickly. In January 1969, Richard Nixon's administration began with
the bold assertion that superpower relations were entering an 'era of
negotiations' and by the end of the year the USA and USSR had begun
talks on the Strategic Arms Limitation Treaty (SALT). Although excluded
from direct involvement, London felt it had a great interest in SALT
because a treaty would restrain the arms race, bolster the NPT and
prevent Britain falling even further behind the superpowers in the nuclear
arms race.[88] The impression of a return to 'business as usual' with the
Soviets was also seen in the relaxation of Western strategic trade restrictions against the Eastern bloc in mid-1969.[89]

The revival of links was very welcome to some in British government.
As ambassador to Moscow in 1968–71, Duncan Wilson questioned
whether Soviet policy was driven by Marxist–Leninist ideology so much
as by pragmatism. The ambassador was one of those who believed that,

by developing commercial links to the Soviet bloc, Britain would not only match French and German efforts in this direction but help to foster political change there.[90] Another diplomat who was interested in using détente to break up the Soviet bloc was the ambassador to Warsaw, Nicholas Henderson. Although he expected no dramatic immediate results, he pressed 'the idea of opening a dialogue with Eastern Europe', believing 'it was unfortunate to give the impression ... of regarding the whole place as but the poodle of the Soviet Union', especially when events like those in Czechoslovakia showed that East Europeans were far from reconciled to Communist rule.[91] By May 1969 ministerial visits to the USSR had been revived; Benn was due in Moscow to discuss technological links and Wilson asked him to urge better bilateral relations on Kosygin. Benn felt Stewart was unenthusiastic about the visit but the differences between them may have been only ones of degree. During an FO meeting in late July, Stewart hoped 'to return gradually and discreetly' to relations with the Warsaw Pact as they had been before Czechoslovakia.[92]

Progress on broader European security talks also proved possible in late 1969. The key moment was Brandt's election victory, followed by his talk of 'two Germanies in one nation', a concept that allowed him to deal with East Germany while denying that the German nation itself was divided. It was a development that Labour could only welcome and it increased the pressures on Britain to embrace détente more fully. In Cabinet on 11 December Benn complained that, with the Americans talking about SALT and Brandt beginning his *Ostpolitik*, 'Britain looked pretty negative'. But Stewart denied this was so, pointed out that the Soviets had continually ignored calls for talks on mutual balanced force reductions and promised to urge NATO to be forthcoming on European security.[93] The Atlantic Council shortly afterwards agreed to a European security conference but on certain conditions, such as US and Canadian involvement. At the next Council meeting, in May 1970, Stewart was one of those keenest to hold a security conference, although this might have been affected by electoral considerations.[94] Another positive sign was that tentative discussions were beginning on the future of Berlin between the four occupying powers, Britain, the USA, France and the USSR.[95] The last year of the Wilson government therefore saw real advances for détente, even if no agreements were possible before Labour lost office in June.

Conclusion

The British were largely successful in their NATO policies under Wilson. The MLF may have been destroyed by a combination of factors, but

Labour's determination to replace it with the ANF proved significant. As to the ANF, although it was a British creation, its failure need not be seen as a setback. There is no evidence that anyone in London mourned it and the fact is that, by late 1965, British aims either were not helped by it (as with the NPT) or could be achieved without it (as with nuclear consultation). On nuclear issues Britain could be satisfied by 1968 with a situation in which the NPT was signed, the Nuclear Planning Group had been created in NATO and the British nuclear deterrent preserved, without either stirring up domestic controversy or dividing the alliance. Britain had worked alongside the USA and Germany to keep NATO together in the face of de Gaulle's withdrawal in 1966 and the same three countries reached a compromise on offset payments, despite the complexities of the issue and the strong feelings involved. While the British did much to stir up arguments on the offset payments, they also increasingly recognised the need to work closely with Bonn. James Ellison has argued that the British application to enter the EEC helped to keep the Western alliance together at this point. It contributed to de Gaulle's isolation, disrupted his attack on NATO and improved Britain's standing in Europe. More generally, Ellison argues that Britain needs to be 'written back' into the history of NATO in the mid-1960s, where the focus is too often on the Franco-American rift and the growing significance of Germany. NATO was one place where Britain demonstrated its continuing importance to the USA, countering the negative effect of the withdrawal from east of Suez and Wilson's refusal to send troops to Vietnam. It is ironic that de Gaulle, the arch critic of the 'special relationship', did much to facilitate this. French withdrawal also encouraged the British to seek a negotiated settlement to the offset problem, support the Harmel exercise and develop the 'Eurogroup', all of which helped NATO both to survive and to evolve at a critical juncture.[96]

On détente, despite early hopes of a real British contribution, there were no great achievements and bilateral Anglo-Soviet relations became very difficult in 1968–9. In fact, the British failed to develop a comprehensive and consistent outlook on détente. While Benn was interested in trade and technological ties, other ministers were less keen; there was a tendency to focus on relations with the USSR while neglecting relations with other East European countries; and Wilson himself concentrated on improving the atmosphere of Anglo-Soviet relations at summit meetings rather than on developing a sophisticated approach to the relaxation of tensions. But the most significant problems for détente were caused by Soviet behaviour, especially over Czechoslovakia, rather than reticence on Britain's part. The Soviets courted de Gaulle rather than Wilson in the 1960s, were suspicious of British links to the USA and even seem to have singled London out for particular attack in the months following Czechoslovakia. Then again, British success on the

NATO front probably went hand in hand with slow progress on détente. As the FO always argued, and as Wilson accepted, progress on East–West relations was possible only in line with the rest of the alliance. By the end of the government, furthermore, the logic of this approach was being proven. While de Gaulle's unilateral bid for détente had come to nothing, Britain's insistence on working with its allies was paying off, with developments in train that would lead to agreements on Berlin, SALT and European security over the following years.

Notes

Unless otherwise stated the place of publication is London.

1 Public Record Office (PRO), CAB 128/39, CC49(65) (23 September).
2 CAB 158/60, JIC(65)87th (14 March) and CAB 158/69, JIC(68)10th (18 January); CAB 159/43, JIC(65)1st (7 January) and 22nd (27 May), and CAB 159/44, JIC(65)33rd (12 August).
3 Barbara Castle, *The Castle Diaries 1964–70* (Weidenfeld and Nicolson, 1984), 4.
4 On the MLF to 1964 see: Pascaline Winand, *Eisenhower, Kennedy and the United States of Europe* (St Martin's Press, New York, 1993), 203–43, 315–23, 332–50; Helga Haftendorn, *NATO and the Nuclear Revolution: a crisis of credibility, 1966–67* (Clarendon Press, Oxford, 1996), 126–45; Christoph Bluth, *Britain, Germany and Western Nuclear Strategy* (Oxford University Press, Oxford, 1995), chapter 3.
5 Donette Murray, *Kennedy, Macmillan and Nuclear Weapons* (Macmillan, 1999), chapters 5–7; John Baylis, *Ambiguity and Deterrence* (Oxford University Press, Oxford, 1995), 320–31. Quote from Philip Ziegler, ed., *From Shore to Shore: the diaries of Earl Mountbatten of Burma 1953–79* (Collins, 1979), 104.
6 This argument follows Andrew Pierre, *Nuclear Politics* (Oxford University Press, Oxford, 1972), 267–70 and 283–4. See also Labour Party manifesto, *The New Britain* (1964); *House of Commons Debates, Fifth Series*, vol. 690, column 480.
7 Harold Wilson, *The Labour Government 1964–1970: a personal record* (Weidenfeld and Nicolson, 1971), 40; Denis Healey, *The Time of My Life* (Michael Joseph, 1989), 302; Lawrence Freedman, *Britain and Nuclear Weapons* (Macmillan, 1980), 31–2; Peter Hennessy, *Cabinet* (Blackwell, Oxford, 1986), 145–7.
8 CAB 130/212, MISC 16/1 (11 November); CAB 21/6047, MISC 11/2 (9 November).
9 For example, Bluth, *Nuclear Strategy*, 99–100; Susanna Schrafstetter and Stephen Twigge, 'Trick or truth? The British ANF proposal, West Germany and US non-proliferation policy', *Diplomacy and Statecraft*, vol. 11, no. 2 (2000), 168.
10 PRO, FO 800/951, Gordon Walker diary memorandum (26 December); British Library of Political and Economic Science, London, Alastair Hetherington papers, 7/16 and 7/20, meetings with Wilson (22 October and 19 November).
11 CAB 128/39, CC11(64) (26 November); Richard Crossman, *The Diaries of a Cabinet Minister, Volume I: Minister of Housing 1964–6* (Hamish Hamilton and Jonathan Cape, 1975), 73; Austen Morgan, *Harold Wilson* (Pluto, 1992), 271.

12 Healey, *Time*, 304–5. See also: Philip Ziegler, *Wilson: the authorised life* (Weidenfeld and Nicolson, 1993), 209; Solly Zuckerman, *Monkeys, Men and Missiles: an autobiography 1946–88* (Collins, 1988), 375.

13 Geoffrey Williams and Bruce Reed, *Denis Healey and the Policies of Power* (Sidgwick and Jackson, 1971), 173; Schrafstetter and Twigge, 'ANF proposal', 161–84; FO 800/951, Gordon Walker diary memorandum (26 December).

14 Wilson, *Government*, 46; *Foreign Relations of the United States* (*FRUS*), 1964–8, vol. XIII (US Government Printing Office, Washington, DC, 1995), 120 and 126–32; PRO, PREM 13/103, record of meeting (dated 27 November); PREM 13/27, record of meeting (30 November).

15 Hetherington papers, 8/18, record of meeting (4 December).

16 PREM 13/104, records of meetings and memoranda (7 and 8 December); *FRUS*, vol. XIII, 121–2 and 146–56.

17 Wilson, *Government*, 50; Healey, *Time*, 305; Williams and Bruce, *Healey*, 174–5; Anthony Shrimsley, *The First Hundred Days of Harold Wilson* (Weidenfeld and Nicolson, 1965), chapter 7; and Edward Short, *Whip to Wilson* (MacDonald, 1989), 97.

18 For example: Philip Geyelin, *Lyndon B. Johnson and the World* (Praeger, New York, 1966), chapter 7; Thomas Schwartz, 'Lyndon Johnson and Europe', in H. W. Brands, ed., *The Foreign Policies of Lyndon Johnson* (College Station, 1999), 45–7; John Steinbruner, *The Cybernetic Theory of Decision* (Princeton University Press, Princeton, 1974), 285–310.

19 CAB 128/39, CC14(64) (11 December).

20 PREM 13/219, Gordon Walker to Wilson, Callaghan and Healey (23 December).

21 *FRUS*, vol. XIII, 169–79, quote from 173.

22 PREM 13/219, Kosygin to Wilson (6 January); PREM 13/603, Stewart–Gromyko and Wilson–Gromyko meetings (17–18 March); PREM 13/805, Stewart–Gromyko meetings (30 November and 2 December). On Labour's approach to the NPT see: J. P. G. Freeman, *Britain's Nuclear Arms Control Policy in the Context of Anglo-American Relations, 1957–68* (Macmillan, 1986), 196–208; also Alun Chalfont, *The Shadow of My Hand* (Weidenfeld and Nicolson, 2000), chapters 8–9.

23 FO 371/181387/45, record of meeting (8 March); FO 371/181388/91, Stark to Street (21 June) and 371/181388/97, Bonn to FO (5 July); *FRUS*, vol. XI, 193–6; Bluth, *Nuclear Strategy*, 161–3.

24 FO 371/181391/192, information telegram (14 August), 371/181391/203, Geneva to FO (17 August), and 371/181391/215, Geneva to FO (19 August); *FRUS*, vol. XI, 233–5; Freeman, *Arms Control Policy*, 209–21.

25 Bluth, *Nuclear Strategy*, 180–5; Paul Buteux, *The Politics of Nuclear Consultation in NATO* (Cambridge University Press, Cambridge, 1983), 37–44.

26 Castle, *Diaries*, 75; PREM 13/686, record of plenary (16 December).

27 *FRUS*, vol. XIII, 289–95; Hans-Peter Schwarz, ed., *Akten zur Auswartigen Politik der Bundesrepublik Deutschlands, 1966, Vol. II* (Oldenbourg, Munich, 1997), docs 466 and 469.

28 PREM 13/805, Erhard to Wilson (22 December), Johnson to Wilson (23 December) and replies (5 January).

29 PREM 13/805, Erhard to Wilson (5 February, delivered on 16 February), and Wright to Maclehose (16 March); D. E. Butler and Anthony King, *The British General Election of 1966* (Macmillan, 1966), 7.

30 Nicholas Henderson, *Inside the Private Office* (Academy, Chicago, 1987), 94–5;

CAB 159/46, JIC(66)35th (25 August 1966); and see P. M. H. Bell, *Britain and France, 1940–94* (Macmillan, 1997), chapter 10.

31 CAB 129/124, C(66)16 (28 January); Crossman, *Diaries I*, 442 and 445; Charles de Gaulle, *Lettres, Notes et Carnets* (Plon, Paris, 1987), 264–5.

32 *FRUS*, vol. XIII, 217–21 and see 233–5; Frederic Bozo, *Deux Strategies pour l'Europe: de Gaulle, les Etats-Unis et l'Alliance Atlantique* (Plon, Paris, 1996), especially chapter 5.

33 *FRUS*, vol. XIII, 335–8; Lyndon B. Johnson Library (LBJL), Austin, John Leddy oral history interview (for quote); Verena Salzman, *West Germany, the US and the Crisis of the Western Alliance, 1963–6* (PhD, Cambridge University, 1999), 167–77.

34 Wilson, *Government*, 244; CAB 128/41, CC17(66) (10 March); CAB 148/25, OPD(66)15th (9 March).

35 LBJL, National Security File (NSF), Country File, France, box 177, Bruce to Rusk (8 March); *British and Foreign State Papers, 1965–6* (Stationery Office, 1975), 560 (for NATO statement); *House of Commons Debates*, vol. 727, columns 554–7; CAB 148/25, OPD(66)18th (5 April); CAB 148/27, OPD(66)44th (1 April).

36 PREM 13/1273, unsigned letter to Maclehose (4 March).

37 *FRUS*, vol. XIII, 363–5, 374–5, 402–3, 417–19, 433–4; PREM 13/1044, Johnson to Wilson (23 May).

38 PREM 13/2559, Wilson to Johnson (27 May); Horst Osterheld, *Aussenpolitik unter Bundeskanzler Ludwig Erhard* (Droste, Frankfurt, 1992), 316–19.

39 *FRUS*, vol. XIII, 472; LBJL, National Security File, Country File, France, box 173, Paris to State (16 December).

40 See Buteux, *Nuclear Consultation*, chapters 2 and 3.

41 PREM 13/2571, Healey to Wilson (21 March) and reply (10 April).

42 James Ellison, 'Dealing with de Gaulle: Anglo-American relations, NATO and the second application', in Oliver Daddow, ed., *Harold Wilson and European Integration: Britain's second application to join the EEC* (Frank Cass, 2002), 181–3; Healey, *Time*, 316; PRO, DEFE 4/221, COS 65th/67 (31 August); Churchill College, Cambridge, Stewart papers, STWT 8/1/5, diary entries of 10 April and 1 May. Also Williams and Reed, *Healey*, 256–8; *FRUS*, vol. XIII, 695 and 766–7.

43 FO 800/968, Brown–Murray meeting (3 May); Ziegler, *Wilson*, 343–4, citing Wilson papers; PREM 13/2140, Brown to Wilson (1 May).

44 CAB 128/42, CC23(67) (27 April) and see CC28(67) (4 May).

45 CAB 128/42, CC68 and 69(67) (23 and 30 November); PREM 13/1372, Palliser to Maclehose (10 November); communication via Mountbatten (19 November).

46 CAB 128/43, CC9(68) (18 January); PREM 13/2140, FO/CRO to posts (30 January).

47 CAB 148/35, OPD(68)13th and 15th (12 July and 1 August); Castle, *Diaries*, 484–5; Richard Crossman, *The Diaries of a Cabinet Minister, Volume III: Secretary of State for Social Services 1968–70* (Hamish Hamilton and Jonathan Cape, 1977), 131–2 and 166–7.

48 CAB 148/91, OPD(69)2nd (30 January); Crossman, *Diaries III*, 346–7.

49 CAB 128/44, CC20, 21 and 58(69) (1 and 7 May, and 4 December).

50 Wolfram Kaiser, 'Money, money, money: the economics and politics of the stationing costs, 1955–65', in Gustav Schmidt, ed., *Zwischen Bundnissicherung und privilegierter Parnerschaft* (Brockmeyer, Bochum, 1995), 1–31.

51 Based on John W. Young, 'West Germany in the foreign policy of the Wilson government, 1964–7', in Saki Dockrill, ed., *Controversy and Compromise:*

alliance politics between Great Britain, Germany and the United States, 1945–67 (Philo, Bodenheim, 1998), 173–5 and 181–6.

52 PREM 13/934, Callaghan to Wilson (14 July), and Stewart to Callaghan (18 July); James Callaghan, *Time and Chance* (Collins, 1987), 200–1.

53 Based on Young, 'West Germany', 187–9. See also Haftendorn, *NATO*, 251–90.

54 See especially PREM 13/1526, Trend to Wilson (27 July).

55 Hubert Zimmerman, 'The sour fruits of victory: sterling and security in Anglo-German relations during the 1950s and 1960s', *Contemporary European History*, vol. 9, no. 2 (2000), 225–43.

56 Robert Pearce, ed., *Patrick Gordon Walker: Political Diaries, 1932–71* (Historians' Press, 1991), 299–300; PREM 13/343, Wright to Wilson (24 October 1964); CAB 129/122, C(65)119 (5 August). For a contemporary perspective see Donald Watt, *Britain Looks to Germany: a study of British opinion and Germany Since 1945* (Wolff, 1965).

57 PREM 13/3222, record of meeting (5 March). For discussions see: Gustav Schmidt, 'Vom Anglo-Amerikanischen Duopol zum Trilateralismus', *Amerikastudien*, vol. 39 (1994), 73–109; Sabine Lee, *Victory in Europe: Britain and Germany since 1945* (Longman, 2001), chapter 5.

58 Frederic Bozo, 'Détente versus alliance: France, the United States and the politics of the Harmel report', *Contemporary European History*, vol. 7, no. 3 (1998), 343–60; PREM 13/1043, Palliser to Wilson (11 March), Wilson to Stewart (15 March) and Wilson to Johnson (29 March).

59 See John Young, *Winston Churchill's Last Campaign: Britain and the Cold War, 1951–5* (Clarendon Press, Oxford, 1996); Brian White, *Britain, Détente and Changing East–West Relations* (Routledge, 1992).

60 Ziegler, *Wilson*, 56–8, 65–6, 89–93 and 149–50; Ben Pimlott, *Harold Wilson* (Harper Collins, 1992), 292–3 and 307–8; Belper speech quoted in G. E. Noel, *Harold Wilson and the New Britain* (Gollancz, 1964), 148, 169 and 173–4.

61 Richard Bevins and Gregory Quinn, 'Blowing hot and cold: Anglo-Soviet relations', in Wolfram Kaiser and Gillian Staerck, eds., *British Foreign Policy 1955–64: contracting options* (Macmillan, 2000), 229–32.

62 Cyrus Sulzberger, *An Age of Mediocrity: memoirs and diaries, 1963–72* (Macmillan, New York, 1973), 110; Hetherington papers, 8/12, meeting with Wilson (11 January 1965); PREM 13/1216, Wilson to Johnson (26 February 1966).

63 Tony Benn, *Office Without Power: diaries 1968–72* (Hutchinson, 1988), 17 and 84, and see 18–21; PREM 13/343, Crossman to Wilson (11 August 1965).

64 PREM 13/98, Washington to Moscow (9 December); PREM 13/603, especially Wright to Wilson (8 January) and Stewart to Wilson (16 March).

65 The fullest discussion is G. A. Hughes, *Harold Wilson, the USSR and British Foreign and Defence Policy in the Context of East–West Détente* (PhD, King's College, London, 2002), especially 104–12 and 306–10 (trade), and 204–7 and 261–70 (friendship treaty).

66 CAB 128/44, CC20, 30 and 33(69) (1 May, 26 June and 22 July); Gill Bennett and Keith Hamilton, eds., *Documents on British Policy Overseas, Series III, Volume 1: Britain and the Soviet Union, 1968–72 (DBPO)* (Stationery Office, 1997), 135–8 and 165–9; Denis Greenhill, *More by Accident* (Wilton 65, York, 1992), 127–9; all newspapers from 25 July 1969.

67 PREM 13/1216, records of meetings (22–24 February 1966); and PREM 13/1218, record of meetings (16–18 July 1966); PREM 13/2402, records of meetings (22–24 January 1968); Hughes, *Wilson*, 126–31, 171–5, 184–9 and 261–70. Full records of Kosygin's 1967 visit in PREM 13/1840.

68 PREM 13/2376, *passim*.

69 PREM 13/2402, Greenhill to Gore-Booth (29 January); PREM 13/3429, *passim*.

70 PREM 13/2009, Stewart to Wilson (27 September); *DBPO*, 91–3.

71 Josef Korbel, *Détente in Europe* (Princeton University Press, Princeton, 1972), 60–6; Henning Hoff, 'The GDR factor in British foreign policy, 1955–73', paper given to the International History workshop, Cambridge University, 1998, 13–14.

72 PREM 13/902, Palliser to Maclehose (4 June 1966); *DBPO*, 48–57 and see 58–64.

73 PREM 13/902, Stewart to Wilson (20 June) and Palliser to Morphet (30 June).

74 For a full account of the Harmel talks see Haftendorn, *NATO*, chapter 5.

75 John Duffield, 'The evolution of NATO's strategy of flexible response: a reinterpretation', *Security Studies*, vol. 1, no. 1 (1991), 132–56; Francis Gavin, 'The myth of flexible response: US strategy in Europe during the 1960s', *International History Review*, vol. 23, no. 4 (2001), 847–75.

76 DEFE 4/207, 56th/66, annexed paper COS 2039 (17 October); CAB 148/30, OPD(67)3rd (30 January); Richard Crossman, *The Diaries of a Cabinet Minister, Volume II: Lord President of the Council and Leader of the House of Commons 1966–68* (Hamish Hamilton and Jonathan Cape, 1976), 215–16.

77 Based on: Williams and Reed, *Healey*, 252–62; Michael Carver, *Tightrope Walking: British defence since 1945* (Hutchinson, 1992), 87–90; Haftendorn, *NATO*, chapter 8.

78 Chalfont, *Shadow*, 115–16; Freeman, *Nuclear Arms*, chapter 9.

79 CAB 148/35, OPD(68)13th (12 July); CAB 148/37, OPD(68)50th (8 July). Britain later tabled a biological warfare convention at the UN (Cmnd 4113, 1969). British preparations for chemical–biological warfare focused on defensive measures, but a lethal chemical was being developed in 1965 for 'retaliatory' use: PREM 13/3464, Healey to Wilson (8 November 1965).

80 CAB 128/43, CC36(68) (18 July); Crossman, *Diaries III*, 143; Modern Records Centre, University of Warwick, Coventry, Richard Crossman papers, MSS 154/3/LPO/20/37–8, Prague to FCO (12 August).

81 Percy Cradock, *Know Your Enemy: how the Joint Intelligence Committee saw the world* (John Murray, 2002), 247–56.

82 PREM 13/1993, Chalfont note, FO to Moscow and Downing Street statement (all 21 August); Michael Stewart, *Life and Labour* (Sidgwick and Jackson, 1980), 221–2.

83 CAB 128/43, CC38(68) (22 August); *DBPO*, 69–80; Benn, *Office*, 97–100.

84 PREM 13/1994, FO to UKDEL, NATO (30 August); CAB 148/35, OPD(68)17th (25 September); Crossman, *Diaries III*, 199–200.

85 *DBPO*, 85–90 (quote from 85) and see 138–57; Korbel, *Détente*, 95–8.

86 *DBPO*, 93–110, 115–26.

87 Bernard Levin, *The Pendulum Years* (Quartet Books, 1989), 127–31; John McGinn, 'The politics of collective inaction', *Journal of Cold War Studies*, vol. 1, no. 3 (1999), 111–38.

88 PREM 13/2569, Zuckerman to Wilson (25 June), Burrows statement (16 July); PREM 13/3131, Zuckerman to Wilson, Trend to Wilson (both 20 January 1970).

89 CAB 148/91, OPD(69)18th (28 July).

90 Sean Greenwood, *Britain and the Cold War* (Blackwell, 2000), 177–8; and see *DBPO*, 100–10, 127–9, 179–87 and 211–14.

91 Nicholas Henderson, *Mandarin: the diaries of Nicholas Henderson* (Weidenfeld and Nicolson, 1994), 20–2.

92 Benn, *Office*, 166–7 and 169; *DBPO*, 157–64.
93 CAB 128/44, CC60(69) (11 December); Benn, *Office*, 218 and see 228.
94 CAB 128/45, CC24(70) (28 May); Stewart, *Life*, 161 and 228.
95 PREM 13/3221, *passim*.
96 Ellison, 'Dealing with de Gaulle', 173 and 181–4; James Ellison, 'Just another problem: Britain's part in Johnson's policy towards Europe', LSE International History seminar, 5 December 2001; and see Brown's arguments in CAB 148/30, OPD(67)38th (29 November).

6

The European Economic Community

Britain's absence from the European Economic Community (EEC) at its creation has been seen as a key error of post-war governments.[1] When the 'Common Market' was founded by the Treaty of Rome in 1957 it included three of the largest West European economies – France, West Germany and Italy – as well as Belgium, the Netherlands and Luxembourg. In fact, there were understandable reasons why London did not embrace European integration. Not only was Britain's sense of separation from the continent deepened by the Second World War, but also the country depended on *global* trade, with special links to the Commonwealth. Unlike France, which had been invaded by Germany three times since 1870, Britain felt no urge to 'pool' sovereignty as a way to control German power. In the mid-1950s, however, the Conservative governments did seek a free trade area (FTA) with the nascent EEC, so as to secure access to the continental economies without compromising Commonwealth trade. When, in 1958, France's new leader, Charles de Gaulle, vetoed the FTA, Britain founded the European Free Trade Association (EFTA) with six smaller West European countries. This was a defensive measure, mainly comprised of small economies, never likely to match the economic and political potential of the EEC. In 1961, encouraged by the USA, which wanted to see a strong anti-Communist Europe, Macmillan launched the first application for membership. But Britain's very closeness to the Americans helped ensure another de Gaulle veto in 1963.[2]

Pressure for a 'second try', 1964–6

When Labour entered office another bid to 'enter Europe' seemed unlikely.[3] In 1962 Hugh Gaitskell had attacked the Macmillan application, saying it ended 'a thousand years of British history', and used the issue to restore his relations with the Labour left. Under him, Labour set five conditions for entry, concerning safeguards for the Commonwealth, EFTA,

142

agriculture, national economic planning and independence in foreign policy.[4] The 1964 Conservative manifesto admitted membership was 'not open to us in existing circumstances' and, while the Liberals remained keen on entry, Wilson, with his small majority, was unlikely to risk party unity for the uncertainty of another application. Labour's manifesto stated 'that the first responsibility of a British Government is still to the Commonwealth' and hoped to reinvigorate the Commonwealth as a focus of British trade. Before becoming Foreign Secretary, Patrick Gordon Walker even wrote, 'In certain circumstances the EEC might break up. This would not be bad for us: but we must not ... appear to want it'.[5] While he held office there were no signs of movement on the EEC, although he accepted the Foreign Office (FO) line that Britain should seek inclusion in any new talks about European political unity. Even Britain's EFTA partners found themselves poorly treated when, only days after the election, the government introduced its 15 per cent surcharge on imports. This action was symptomatic of a general incoherence in policy towards the Association, which simply lacked significance for London.[6] When Michael Stewart succeeded Gordon Walker there was no major change and the EEC was barely touched upon when Wilson held his first summit with de Gaulle, in April 1965. The meeting was primarily intended to establish a sound working relationship with Paris, an aim that ambassador Patrick Reilly believed it achieved, in the face of de Gaulle's continuing belief that Britain was hopelessly pro-American.[7]

Whatever the difficulties of a 'second try', there were good reasons why the possibility became real in 1965. Britain's economic performance contrasted with healthy growth on the continent; other than France, the members of the EEC – known as the 'Friendly Five' – were in favour of British entry; and support for entry was especially strong in the FO and George Brown's Department of Economic Affairs (DEA). One diplomat (and later Labour 'Euro-sceptic'), Bryan Gould, felt that the FO 'lost sight of its proper role as the defender of British interests' when it became a 'proselytiser for the European ideal', but he recognised that the temptations of such a course were strong: membership might provide Britain with a revived international significance, especially if a common political outlook developed. Despite the 1963 veto, key officials, like Con O'Neill (ambassador to the EEC in 1963–5), also believed British interests would be better defended inside the EEC, because policies on trade and agriculture could then be shaped directly. With de Gaulle securely in power and the EEC in its 'transitional' period of creation, the situation was not a hopeful one and in an initial review of policy towards Europe with Stewart, key officials urged that Britain must avoid 'increasing and dangerous isolation in Europe', by mending relations with EFTA following the surcharge and maintaining military involvement on the continent. Stewart's first speech on Europe referred to possible EEC talks on political unity and said Britain was ready to join in these, there being 'no reason ... to think that we can go less far than the members of the Community ... in promoting European unity'. This did not significantly depart from Gordon Walker's position, but it was said in public and sounded positive.[8] In his memoirs Stewart wrote that two factors made him more sympathetic to entry: evidence that Commonwealth countries wanted trade deals with the Community; and the need to counter de Gaulle's bid to create an exclusivist, anti-American Europe. His Permanent Under-Secretary, Paul Gore-Booth, believed 'nothing short of a new attempt at membership ... could break down the wall between Europe and ourselves'. At the DEA Brown and his Permanent Secretary, Eric Roll, were keen 'pro-marketeers', and the Department initiated its own study of British–EEC relations in early 1965.[9]

Elsewhere in Whitehall there was less 'pro-European' feeling. The Treasury became fearful of the effect of entry talks on the position of sterling. The Board of Trade was headed by one leading 'anti-marketeer' on the 'right', Douglas Jay, and the Ministry of Agriculture by another, Fred Peart. Western Europe was now a more important source of trade than the Commonwealth, but Jay and Peart argued that entry to the EEC would increase domestic food prices and adversely affect the balance of trade. At a ministerial committee on 25 March 1965, it was agreed that a new application was impossible at present and that priority must be given to global attempts to reduce trade barriers through the so-called 'Kennedy round'. But this did not mean that entry was ruled out. Talks on the Kennedy round, which had been initiated in 1962, were progressing slowly, at the headquarters of the General Agreement on Tariffs and Trade (GATT), in Geneva. They promised Britain the possibility of sweeping tariff reductions on a global scale, but there were serious differences between the USA, which hoped to achieve a halving of tariffs across the board, and the EEC states, which were unwilling to reduce agricultural tariffs because this would ruin their plans for a Common Agricultural Policy (CAP). The March meeting noted that EEC membership would give free access to a large market and that there was a danger of EFTA and Commonwealth states striking a deal with the Community themselves. Nigeria was already seeking a special trade arrangement.[10] In May–June Wilson chaired a small committee on strengthening Commonwealth trade which, pressed by Jay, looked at a form of free trade arrangement. But it was felt that British industry itself could not accept free trade on some items (such as textiles) and that developing countries would much prefer a deal with the EEC to one with Britain.[11]

Some ministers were concerned that Brown and Stewart were developing a pro-market policy without fully informing the Cabinet. But even some of those later deemed 'anti-marketeers' could see logic in an application: Tony Benn, the Postmaster General, believed the 'real choice is whether we go in with Europe or ... become an American satellite'. In such a debate the position of the Prime Minister was crucial but, as always, Wilson's views are hard to fathom. His family and personal links were more with the Commonwealth and the USA than Europe, but he had never shown much emotion in his anti-Europeanism and, throughout his career, took the pragmatic line on the EEC in public that the conditions of entry were more important than the principle. His official biographer argues his main concern was that Europe 'should not be allowed to breach party unity', which explains his attempts to play down the issue before the 1966 election.[12] Thus in June 1965, when Jay and Peart tried to circulate a Cabinet memorandum on the detrimental impact of entry on food prices and trade, Wilson prevented them. Yet in December he also opposed an attempt by Stewart, with Brown's support, to circulate a memorandum favouring entry.[13]

Nonetheless, there were signs that the Prime Minister was prepared to be active on Europe. In March 1965 he was impressed by arguments from Stewart in favour of 'bridge-building' between the EEC and EFTA. This fell far short of EEC membership but could have involved institutional links and a free trade arrangement; and the Prime Minster played a personal role in the project, circulating a Cabinet paper to promote it. He shared the FO's concern about an 'inward-looking', protectionist yet economically powerful Community.[14] Helen Parr has shown that 'bridge-building' in 1965 was a tactical exercise with four aims: to counter French domination of the EEC; to keep EFTA tariff reductions in line with the EEC and so forestall a growing rift in Europe; to prevent other EFTA members defecting to the EEC; and to open a debate in Cabinet that might open the way to an entry bid.[15] It also served to answer those who wanted a more positive policy, without offending those who did not. But, as in the mid-1950s FTA talks, the Six would be conceding more than they gained by allowing access to their 'common market'. Feedback from continental posts in May–June suggested EEC scepticism about 'bridge-building' and by September the initiative had run up against a daunting obstacle: the EEC became embroiled in the 'empty chair crisis', when de Gaulle pulled French representatives out of meetings, partly because he objected to the organisation's supranational elements. The pursuit of 'bridge-building' then seemed unwise, since it would exacerbate internal EEC differences: Wilson had told the Commons in July that it was 'not for us to take sides ... still less to exploit' differences in the Community.[16]

In early 1966 there was still confusion about the Prime Minister's intentions. In February Crossman believed that, for Wilson, 'the difficulties of staying outside Europe and surviving as an independent power are very great compared with entering on the right conditions'. However, Benn wrote, 'Harold is afraid ... that to cut our world commitments would be a preamble to our admission to the Common Market which he does not favour'.[17] All three of his major biographies see him as having become favourable to entry by mid-1966, but are vague on the precise time and Wilson's motivations.[18] It is possible to surmise why he should have become favourable to entry at this time: opinion polls and business interests wanted this; the value of the Commonwealth was undermined by the divisions over Rhodesia and Kashmir; and a pro-market line would remove the danger of Edward Heath, the new Conservative leader, making capital of the issue.[19] Exactly when he became favourable to entry is something even government papers fail to clarify but, logically, his moves towards membership *after* the March 1966 election make sense only if he had at least become open to membership *before* that date. It is significant that in January 1966, while resisting pressure for the issue to be taken to Cabinet, he agreed with Brown and Stewart that 'a move into Europe' should be studied by a group of officials under Eric Roll.[20] It may also be significant that, even when the empty chair crisis came to an end, Wilson made no attempt to revive the 'bridge-building' initiative, even though he was urged to do so by Jay. Instead, the options now became full membership or nothing.[21] There are also signs that Wilson was considering the tactical side of entry talks around election time, with an expectation that the empty chair crisis had opened the way for a deal with de Gaulle. In conversations with the newspaper chairman, Cecil King, Wilson laid emphasis on the fact that 'the French are intent on maintaining a separate foreign and defence policy, which fits in best with British ... interests'. This also made him reluctant to side too closely with the Friendly Five against de Gaulle, in the way the FO might have preferred. In December 1965, concerned at the crisis in the EEC, the FO advocated a 'declaration of intent', saying Britain was ready to accept the Treaty of Rome. This would have reinforced the image of Britain as a 'good European' and would have strengthened the morale of the Friendly Five in the empty chair crisis. But Wilson wrote on a memorandum from Stewart, 'Why should we find the acceptance of French conditions "dangerous" since they reject supranationality...? These ought to help us'.[22]

In the March election Wilson stuck to his pragmatic course, focusing on the terms, not the principle, of entry. His speech at Bristol on 18 March was balanced between statements about the potential benefits of membership and the need to protect British interests in any entry terms. The speech was enlivened by a jibe at Heath with an anti-European flavour: Wilson accused the Conservative leader of rolling 'on his back like a spaniel' because, a few days earlier, Heath had welcomed a statement from Paris that suggested British entry was possible.[23] Labour's manifesto, however, stated that Britain 'should be ready to enter the ... [EEC], provided essential British and Commonwealth interests are safeguarded', a wording which suggested the principle of an application had already been decided. For a time, his even-handed approach continued. He appointed Jay and Peart to a new Cabinet committee on relations with Europe, but he also created an unofficial 'minister for Europe', George Thomson, and accepted Michael Palliser as his new Private Secretary for foreign affairs. Palliser was the son-in-law of Paul-Henri Spaak, the Belgian statesman and 'father of Europe', and made his pro-market feelings clear at the outset, but Wilson assured him that 'we shan't have any problems over Europe'. Palliser later made the telling comment that Wilson was approaching Europe 'in his usual devious crab-like fashion so it was almost impossible to know what his views were'.[24]

The new Cabinet committee first met on 9 May, with Wilson in the chair, when it received a report from Roll's group of officials. This ruled out any early initiative because of the probability of French opposition and it was agreed that, for the moment, studies should simply continue in Whitehall. Burke Trend, the Cabinet Secretary, helped defeat the idea that Britain should make a 'declaration of intent' to sign the Treaty of Rome because it seemed pointless to do so if entry were deemed impossible. The situation was complicated by de Gaulle's recent withdrawal from NATO and the British economy needed to be strengthened ahead of entry.[25] In fact, de Gaulle and British economic weakness were to dog the 'second try' over the next eighteen months and were all too apparent when the French premier, Georges Pompidou, visited London in early July. The visit provided an opportunity to explore French thinking, but Pompidou refused to be drawn on British entry, preferring to urge devaluation. Foreign minister Maurice Couve de Murville advised the British to consider some form of association, short of membership, but this was something that never interested Wilson. There were good practical reasons for his attitude: association would mean accepting some of the costs of full membership without all the benefits. Yet it is significant that, having earlier given up on 'bridge-building', he now ruled out this other 'halfway house' solution. Once again, the issue was full membership – or nothing – and Wilson did not even want officials to study the 'association' option when one minister suggested this.[26]

Despite the unpromising situation, which ought to have confirmed that there was currently no way into the EEC, the ensuing sterling crisis made an entry bid more likely. True, the crisis seemed to justify French doubts about British readiness for entry, but it also justified those who argued that the EEC was a potential source of economic salvation in the long term. Furthermore, it forced Wilson to move the disgruntled Brown to the FO. The newcomer was quite capable of upsetting Europeans with his undiplomatic antics: he put his arm round President de Gaulle, called one senior French minister 'a frog' and dismissed Spaak as someone who 'counted for nothing'. But the new Foreign Secretary also saw 'a vigorous ... policy towards Europe' as central to British well-being. It might pave the way for a managed devaluation of sterling and a restructuring of the Western alliance, including a reduction in British expenditure east of Suez and 'a *partnership* between the US and a united Europe'. And he would not be put off by predictions of another veto.[27] Parr sees the July 1966 crisis as central to the decision for a 'second try'. The crisis confirmed the impossibility of pursuing a major role in the world while providing growth and welfare at home, and it provoked a sense of desperation only months after the election. This traumatic event does most to explain why the government launched the 'second try' precisely when it did, despite the obvious danger of another veto. The fact that this shift was a pragmatic, short-term reaction to a crisis, however, also meant that there was no broad, well considered adjustment of Britain's international role. The position east of Suez remained in place for a time and the government continued to emphasise the defence of sterling, even though an EEC application made it more likely that devaluation would occur because the Six would want Britain to resolve its balance of payments problems and the British themselves needed to prepare for competition within the Common Market.[28]

Application and veto, 1966–7

Whatever the timing of Wilson's conversion to the idea, there can be no doubt that he pursued entry with tenacity after October 1966. By then various official studies were complete and he decided ministers should discuss them in a weekend session, on 22 October, at Chequers. In the morning, the Joint Permanent Secretary of the Treasury, William Armstrong, said that devaluation might be necessary before entry. According to Benn, Brown became 'quite hysterical' at this and there was 'a great row'. But the Prime Minister arranged that ministers alone would meet in the afternoon, when it was agreed that he and Brown should explore membership through a 'probing' visit to EEC capitals. This appeared a positive move but also bought time before a final decision was needed. The economic arguments were deemed to be balanced but politically, Brown and Stewart argued, there was little alternative to membership if Britain were to remain a significant power. Nevertheless, to placate the sceptics, it was decided to study two alternatives to membership: 'going it alone' and a proposal, associated with US Senator Jacob Javits, for a North Atlantic Free Trade Area, between the USA, Canada and Britain. According to Wilson and Brown, their joint probe was designed to defend the interests of both the pro- and anti-marketeers, with the latter seeing the Prime Minister as a defender of their interests.

It was clear, even to many of the 'antis', that in fact Wilson had moved in favour of entry, but only two ministers (Minister of Power Richard Marsh and Scottish Secretary William Ross) opposed the probe. Crossman and Healey consoled themselves with the thought that de Gaulle would veto the attempt anyway.[29]

After the Cabinet formally approved the probe, it was announced by Wilson to the Commons on 10 November. Even Crossman, no enthusiast for EEC membership, believed that the entry bid must be made with determination or not at all. In Cabinet on 9 November, James Callaghan, the Chancellor, emphasised that an application would be a morale booster for industry, just when the introduction of mandatory sanctions against Rhodesia was likely to create economic unease.[30] In some ways the prospects for entry looked better than for Macmillan in 1961. There was widespread consensus in support from the three main political parties, most daily newspapers (the exception being the *Daily Express*), industrialists and City finance houses. Public opinion also seemed favourable. As Anne Deighton argues, some of 'the most potent challenges Harold Wilson faced … came … from sources closer to him (within the Party and the Cabinet)'. In Cabinet, a right-winger, Jay, was the most persistent opponent but within the Parliamentary Labour Party (PLP) it was the leftist Tribune Group that was most identified with opposition. Then again, the March election had brought in many new MPs who were well disposed to entry, the Trades Union Congress supported an application as likely to safeguard jobs and the party conference, despite its radicalism elsewhere, backed EEC entry in 1967.[31]

In the wake of the probe's launch, Brown declared the 'juggernaut had started to roll and nothing could … stop it'. Yet, when he met de Gaulle in December, he faced the General's usual arguments that Britain was too Atlanticist, a global trading power, likely to alter the Community's existing character. Ambassador Reilly saw this as further evidence that de Gaulle was 'extremely sceptical' about a British application and hoped to discourage one.[32] Brown and Wilson went on anyway. By early 1967 the entry bid was closely wrapped up in the government's post-July 1966 economic strategy and thus central to its political fate. It was, perhaps, Wilson's self-deluding, confident side that led him to believe he could break down the main barrier, in Paris. But when he told the Economic Policy (Steering) Committee that he would 'free-wheel' in talks with de Gaulle, 'and take my own line when it comes to negotiations', he showed there was no sophisticated 'plan' for overcoming another veto.[33]

One way in which Wilson tried to pave the way for entry was to emphasise British prowess in technology. Projects like the Anglo-French Concorde airliner and Jaguar fighter-bomber were evidence of Britain's value to European partners if they wished to match US competition in high technology. Wilson was identified with talk of the 'white heat' of technological revolution and had created a Ministry of Technology. There were fears of a 'brain drain' across the Atlantic, British industry was in the middle of a wave of mergers in order to compete on a global scale and the country spent proportionately more on research and development than any other country with the exceptions of the USA and USSR. Yet, even here, there was no magical 'key' to the European door, partly due to Britain's own behaviour. While it developed some European projects, it also retained strong transatlantic links, buying the US Hercules and Phantom aircraft for example. Labour even tried to pull out of developing the Concorde soon after the party took office, as part of a general effort to concentrate technological efforts on profitability rather than 'prestige projects'. But the original agreement, signed by the Conservatives in 1962 (partly with the intention of helping the first EEC application), meant that the French could have gone on with the project alone, while suing Britain for half the cost. Ultimately Concorde was completed but there were similar British doubts about the European Launcher Development Organisation (ELDO), founded in 1962 with the intention of developing space rockets, and Britain finally quit this in 1968. In his Guildhall speech of 14 November 1966, Wilson urged the creation of a European Technological Community (ETC) and he was certainly persistent on this theme in 1967. But he never fleshed the ETC out in detail, de Gaulle expressed no interest in it and it was undermined by Britain's attitude towards projects like ELDO, which the Europeans actually valued. One official was clear the ETC was primarily useful from the 'card-playing angle', so it 'does not matter if we are a bit vague'; the government must 'keep the carrot dangling ... until we are safely in the EEC'. But, Michael Stewart later complained, 'the trouble with the technological initiative was that it always seemed to change shape when one tried to grapple with it'.[34]

The probe began with a visit to Rome in mid-January 1967, which set the pattern for future visits. Wilson and Brown gave assurances about their commitment to a European future, enquired about potential problems, such as the CAP, and explored the likely reaction to an application. The Italians, in return, made it clear that, while they favoured British membership, there were limits to what they would do to pressure de Gaulle. But when Castle raised the last point in Cabinet, Wilson merely remarked, 'Well, Paris will show'. It was hoped France might find it impossible to issue a veto, especially if the Friendly Five were united and Wilson could convince the General that Britain was genuinely committed to a European future.[35] The most striking fact about the Paris talks of 24–25 January was that de Gaulle did not issue a veto. However, he was again critical of British links to the USA, was concerned to set up the CAP and was unimpressed by Wilson's argument that EEC enlargement would foster technological co-operation. Ambassador Reilly concluded that de Gaulle was reluctant to humiliate his guest and create a crisis, especially with a French general election looming, but hoped instead to dissuade Wilson from making an application.[36] The fact that no veto was issued allowed the probe to continue to Brussels, Bonn and the Hague, ending in Luxembourg on 7–8 March. The visits more than confirmed that the CAP was likely to prove costly to Britain, as an industrial nation with an efficient agricultural sector. But arguably the agricultural problem made it vital to enter quickly, so as to influence the policy's financial details. Yet even the Germans would give no promises to force de Gaulle to accept enlargement. Thus, while the probe confirmed Wilson's desire for membership and conditioned the Cabinet to an entry bid, it also highlighted the possible difficulties.[37]

Wilson now circulated a lengthy report to ministers. He portrayed this in his memoirs as an example of openness, and certainly Cabinet ministers debated the EEC at length, but, whatever the length of talks, Jay felt various ruses were used to ensure that anti-market views did not receive a proper hearing.[38] In Cabinet on 21 March Healey and Castle again pointed out that de Gaulle was likely to veto an application, but Brown was keen to try to enter before the CAP was finalised.[39] Eager to press forward before the Whitsuntide parliamentary recess and now openly favouring an application, Wilson held a series of Cabinet meetings in April on the details of entry, with such subjects as regional policy and capital movements, agriculture, constitutional issues and the Commonwealth.[40] 'We shall go into Europe on a wave of exhaustion', complained Castle, who concluded that 'Harold and George have so cleverly set the scene that it will be impossible … to come to any decision but to have a try'. Discussion of the broad principle of entry was avoided and any alternatives were ruled out: 'going it alone' was seen as a recipe for a continuing decline of British influence, while an Atlantic free trade area would mean US domination. The implication was that the country *had* to enter the EEC if it was to remain a force in the world, a point underlined by Burke Trend when he argued that, even if de Gaulle issued a veto, London must continue to press its case. Jay found little support among anti-marketeers for the idea of threatening Wilson with their resignation.[41] There was also a series of meetings of the PLP, where Wilson won approval for an application.[42]

At the end of April ministers held another weekend meeting. Whatever the importance of the July 1966 crisis in making EEC membership more attractive, the economic implications of entry were viewed, even by pro-marketeers, as unpredictable. The antis felt they would be costly; certainly in the short term, food prices would rise and sterling would be vulnerable. In the long term, however, there could be gains from greater competitiveness in a larger market. Part of the discussion – kept separate from the rest of the record and restricted – concerned the relationship between entry and devaluation. It had long been argued that they were linked, but Wilson perhaps hoped this would not be the case and Callaghan set out all the problems with devaluation, including global monetary instability and losses to overseas holders of sterling. The discussion also drew a direct link between entry and retreat from east of Suez: in order to make the economy competitive, it was said, one option was to make 'cuts in defence expenditure overseas greater than those now in contemplation (a course which would be entirely consistent with entry…)'. But essentially the 'pro' case again turned on political gains, the argument being that Britain faced increasing irrelevance, even in US eyes, if it remained outside the Community. Both Jay and Benn reckoned the voting was thirteen to eight in favour; Crossman put it at ten to seven, with six neutrals who were willing to back Wilson so long as he acted quickly and decisively.[43]

The decision to make an application was confirmed by Cabinet on 2 May, with Wilson making it clear that, following negotiations, they might still reject entry if the terms were not right.[44] In the Commons debate that followed, it was evident that the party was less than united on the issue, as fifty Labour MPs opposed an application. But, with Conservative and Liberal support, Wilson was able to obtain a massive majority of more than 400. Lord Chalfont now became 'Mr Europe', to manage the negotiations. Nonetheless, de Gaulle remained the obvious barrier and on 16 May told a press conference that British membership would upset the existing balance in the EEC and that London should seek 'association'. Some believed it amounted to a veto but Palliser advised Wilson to 'bash on, regardless', arguing that the press conference was 'a war of nerves – to see whether your nerve is as strong as the General's'. Wilson agreed.[45] Brown told a new ministerial committee on the application that, to make life difficult for de Gaulle, they must reduce their conditions for membership below Macmillan's and seek swift negotiations.[46] To avoid antagonising de Gaulle, the Americans remained publicly silent about their support for British entry. There were already signs that enlargement might be detrimental to good Anglo-American relations in that, during the last phase of the Kennedy round in May, the British tended to steer a course closer to the Europeans so as not to upset the chances of EEC entry.[47]

At this point Wilson still apparently believed that he could win over de Gaulle. But at Versailles on 19–20 June, the General's line was the same as ever: Britain was too close to the USA and was not committed to a European future. The best argument Wilson could put to the Cabinet was that the General appeared depressed and might resign himself to enlargement![48] After this Wilson himself seems to have become pessimistic about the application (it virtually disappears from his lengthy memoirs) and reverted to the line he had earlier criticised, that Britain's best course was to rely on pressure from the Friendly Five to force entry. But by now there was plenty of evidence of the limits to the influence of the Five. The most vocal support for Britain came from the Dutch foreign minister, Joseph Luns, but the Netherlands was too weak, politically and economically, to force any change in Paris. This could only, perhaps, be achieved by the Germans, but they were repeatedly reticent about tackling de Gaulle. In April, for example, when the premier of Northern Ireland, Terence O'Neill (cousin of Con O'Neill), visited Bonn, even the anglophile foreign minister, Willy Brandt, expressed 'the hope that London understood that one could not go on throwing oneself against a brick wall on behalf of British entry'.[49] The British were therefore forced back on dubious tactics that merely accented the desperation of their case. The prime example was when Brown, unable to present the application directly to the EEC, because the French might refuse to accept it, submitted one instead to the ministers of the Six when they were all gathered at a meeting of the Western European Union (WEU) on 4 July.[50] Wilson continued to make enthusiastic statements about Europe, even telling a French minister he 'did not exclude the eventual creation of a European currency'.[51] For Palliser, the need to enter the EEC was made more urgent by the July 1967 decision on withdrawal from east of Suez and the ensuing US disappointment with Britain: 'we cannot afford to reach a position where the Americans have discarded us as a useful world ally before we have managed to join the Community and thereby to begin the process ... of transforming Western Europe into a force for world ... influence'.[52]

The situation did not seem entirely hopeless. In August, Jay and a less vocal anti-marketeer, Bert Bowden, were removed from the Cabinet; and in September the EEC Commission reported in favour of enlargement. Ireland, Denmark and Norway, all close trading partners of Britain, were also keen to join. The US embassy even judged that British tactics were 'intelligent and effective': by showing a keenness to talk and submitting a straightforward application, with few conditions, they had solidified support among the Friendly Five and put de Gaulle on the defensive. But it did not take long for the situation to unravel. Influenced by French doubts, the Commission left the timing of negotiations open and even suggested that there should instead be 'pre-negotiations' to explore differences, an idea the British feared could lead to endless preliminary talks.[53] In October there were rumours de Gaulle would veto, whatever the risks of sparking a crisis. He came close to asking Reilly to withdraw the application, which only convinced Palliser that the General was on the defensive but which may have been further evidence that he wanted to avoid humiliating the British. Meanwhile, Wilson made another vain attempt to persuade the Germans to pressurise de Gaulle, when Chancellor Kurt Kiesinger visited London late in the month.[54] A few days later, there was another incident that suggested desperation. In the so-called 'Chalfont affair', the Minister for Europe, known as a Wilson confidant but probably speaking without his direct approval, told journalists in an 'off-the-record' talk that Britain would not accept another 'No'; they might reconsider existing commitments in Europe if it happened. The press interpreted this to mean that British troops could be pulled out of Germany.[55]

In a press conference on 27 November 1967 de Gaulle delivered the *coup de grâce*. Armed by the devaluation of sterling shortly before, the President criticised Britain's 'extraordinary insistence and haste' in seeking entry and argued that it was too weak for such a challenge.[56] The British leader, who had earlier hoped for entry without devaluation, now faced a double defeat: devaluation and the door to Europe slammed in his face. Of course, Wilson was never an idealistic pro-European, but this did not soften the blow. His confidence about finding a way past de Gaulle had proved misplaced and his logic that Britain had to join the EEC in order to remain a major influence in world affairs had put the country's foreign policy in an impasse: the logic might well be true, but the route to Europe was blocked. For a time Britain did not give up. Irrepressible, Brown hoped the Friendly Five might yet tackle de Gaulle at a forthcoming EEC Council of Ministers. When Wilson and Brown met on 28 November they were reluctant to let de Gaulle dictate events, rejected any alternative short of full membership and, as a matter of principle, wanted the Six as a whole – not just France – to decide the fate of the application. The Cabinet accepted such tactics, although Healey successfully pressed for a review of future policy. The Foreign Secretary, with a curious mixture of naivety and arrogance, even complained to Brandt, 'Willy, you must get us in so we can take the lead'. But on 19 December, faced by a dogged Couve de Murville, EEC ministers decided they could not consider the application further.[57] There were suggestions from ministers that officials were to blame for the fiasco and, in his memoirs, Brown was especially critical of Reilly. Yet the ambassador never hid the problems facing an application. Following the Versailles summit he had even warned that, if London tried to force de Gaulle into a decision during the next six months, it was likely to result in a veto. Ministers, especially Brown, had been just as guilty of over-optimism. The conclusion of an FO post mortem was that a veto had always been seen as possible, but that an application was pressed for the potential political rewards, which included the provision of a meaningful international role for Britain.[58] This argument explains why Brown continued to insist that the second application remain 'on the table', ready to be taken up when de Gaulle departed.[59] Indeed, ironically, with the acceleration of the withdrawal from east of

Suez occurring at this point, it became even more essential to secure a European role.

Application revived, 1968–70

In early 1968 Brown, before resigning, still hoped that the Friendly Five might force de Gaulle to back down; the Benelux countries put proposals for links between the Friendly Five and the four applicants for membership, Britain, Ireland, Denmark and Norway. There were hopes in particular of continuing talks on technological co-operation and on security questions. But in Cabinet on 18 January Wilson, while still interested in technological projects, questioned the wisdom of pushing the Five into dispute with Paris and preferred to let the British economy strengthen. Other ministers disliked 'hanging about in the ante-chambers ... waiting to be rebuffed', as Benn put it. Little came of the Benelux proposals, opinion polls moved against entry and there was disappointment in February when Kiesinger met de Gaulle and agreed to sign a joint declaration with him. Its content was innocuous but, for Reilly, it symbolised a return 'to business as usual in the Community'.[60] There was a Cabinet review of foreign policy in February, which represented a compromise between Brown and his critics. They argued that entry was unlikely while de Gaulle held office. He pressed the case that, with the retreat from east of Suez now irreversible, British interests must focus on Europe. The aim should be to enter the EEC as part of a broader policy that built up a strong, cohesive Europe allied to the USA. The level of debate seems to have been poor, with Healey the only one seriously doubtful about continuing to press membership.[61] In a real sense policy remained unchanged despite the veto: the timetable might have been set back, but the second application was still 'on the table' and relations with the Friendly Five continued to be cultivated. One significant area, which Benn helped develop in 1968 as Minister of Technology, was co-operation with Germany and the Netherlands on a project to produce enriched uranium via the centrifuge process. This marked a further effort by London to exploit its technological strength in Europe, but another aim was to break Germany away from a possible nuclear partnership with France. The centrifuge project raised complex technical questions and a formal agreement was not signed until March 1970, by which time there was a better prospect of EEC entry anyway.[62] Another joint European project was the Jaguar multi-role combat aircraft, developed with Germany, Italy and the Netherlands.

The process of keeping the application 'on the table' carried its own dangers. Reilly left the Paris embassy in September 1968 and his successor was a Conservative politician, Christopher Soames, a former Cabinet

minister, married to Churchill's daughter, Mary. A more high-profile
appointment could hardly be imagined and he had high hopes of what
might be achieved, though Palliser and a former ambassador, Gladwyn
Jebb, 'tried to drum into him that he must not expect a change of heart
in de Gaulle and that all that could be done was to wait for his ...
departure'.[63] In early 1969 an attempt by Soames to work with the
General backfired embarrassingly though, as in Reilly's day, London
was more to blame than the ambassador. On 4 February the two met
and de Gaulle presented some ideas that, on the surface, appeared
dramatic, though they were actually developments of thoughts he had
explored before. Building on his dislike of supranationalism in the EEC
and of US domination, as well as earlier suggestions about British
'association' with the EEC, he suggested London and Paris might work
towards a free trade arrangement in Western Europe, such as Britain
had long wanted, but with agriculture included. This would be dominated by the larger powers (including Germany and Italy) and could be
accompanied by a winding down of NATO. Frederic Bozo has convincingly argued that the approach was a serious initiative, as Soames
himself believed, an attempt by the General to achieve his hopes of
ending US 'domination' of Western Europe and maximising French
influence. But in London there were fears that this was a trap. Any
Anglo-French talks about ending the EEC and NATO would, if discovered, split Britain from the Friendly Five and offend Washington.
Furthermore, Wilson was due to meet Kiesinger on 12 February and
now faced a dilemma. Should he tell the Chancellor about de Gaulle's
ideas, risking French wrath, or keep quiet and risk the Germans finding
out later? It was decided to give the Germans an account of the Soames
interview and, having told Bonn, it was impossible not to inform other
European capitals too. Soon the story was in the press and the French,
who denied the British version of events, were livid. Wilson's account
reflects his annoyance at poor FO advice on the 'Soames affair' and
certainly the FO had no desire to become involved in Gaullist attempts
to 'sabotage' the Community, such as may have appealed to London in
the 1950s. But again Wilson and his ministers must share responsibility
for what occurred. Castle admits that, when the policy was first explained
to the Cabinet, she and Crossman 'hadn't really been listening to Michael
[Stewart]. He is the easiest man not to listen to we have ever met'.[64]

The Soames affair occurred at a delicate time, coinciding with
President Nixon's European tour and overshadowing Wilson's attempt
to improve relations with Kiesinger.[65] Yet it was not the only problem to
trouble Anglo-French relations. Immediately before the affair broke, the
FO had been redoubling its efforts to stay close to the Friendly Five, by
making greater use of the WEU, a security organisation created in 1955.
It included Britain and all the Six and could serve as a forum for

political–security talks between them. Stewart was well aware, as he told the Cabinet on 11 February 1969, that the French had already boycotted some informal WEU meetings because of the British attempt to use them as a link to the EEC, pending full membership. But he was not too concerned: if France did not attend, it would emphasise de Gaulle's isolation and foster the impression that political integration demanded British involvement. Now Stewart intended to initiate talks in the WEU on the Middle East. Predictably, when the talks were held, on 14 February, the French stayed away, creating another 'empty chair' situation. Only months later, however, prospects became more hopeful with de Gaulle's sudden resignation, on 28 April, following his defeat in a referendum. He had long been seen as the main barrier to EEC enlargement and his departure immediately raised expectations about the 1967 application being taken up.[66] Although the new President, Pompidou, was a Gaullist, Anglo-French relations soon saw signs of improvement, especially with the appointment of the anglophile Maurice Schumann as foreign minister. It is also worth noting that, while nothing came of the idea, some consideration was given by Britain (even before de Gaulle's resignation) to co-operate on nuclear weapons with France.[67]

The possibility of reviving the application was discussed in Cabinet on 22 July. One worry now was that enlargement might occur only at the price of the Friendly Five conceding a costly financing method for the CAP, which would increase the financial burden of membership to Britain. Significantly, Wilson took the view that the principle of entry was already decided and that there was no need, yet, to review policy: 'we mustn't have a change of stance … but we oughtn't to be over-eager'.[68] In a further discussion on 25 September, however, Stewart was keen to move quickly. A summit of EEC leaders had been planned and it was felt that membership talks might open in mid-1970. But, with a general election looming, others were worried about the opinion polls. Wilson again struck a middle course, using his old formula of being ready to enter on the right terms, but this time he leant towards caution. He was concerned about the polls, ready to make a full study of the economic costs of entry and, thanks to the beneficial impact of devaluation, said Britain was now strong enough survive the challenge of either entry to, or exclusion from, the EEC. He also noted that an election might be over before serious negotiations began.[69]

In October the pro-market cause was given another boost with the election of a new German Chancellor, Willy Brandt, a long-time advocate of EEC enlargement. But, even before this, Soames was confident a wave was rising that would carry Britain into the Community, with Pompidou ready to open negotiations.[70] These developments culminated in a breakthrough summit of Community leaders, at the Hague in December, where it was agreed to settle the financing of the CAP

while also opening talks on enlargement.[71] The position was not all
positive for Britain. The operation of the CAP would be settled *before*
enlargement, so that Britain could not shape the financial deal; and
de Gaulle's departure had led to a new enthusiasm for supranational
schemes, including monetary union.[72] None of this worried the Planning
Department of the Foreign and Commonwealth Office (FCO), which,
in a report on British aims in Europe over the next decade, looked
forward not only to an enlarged EEC but also greater co-operation on
foreign and defence policy, with moves 'towards a Federal State'.[73] In
contrast Wilson, interviewed on the BBC's *Panorama* programme on 12
January, adopted a balanced approach, saying entry must be on the
right terms with no 'great federal constitutions'.

There is evidence that Wilson was still personally favourable to entry,
if understandably reluctant to let it upset his re-election chances. When,
at a meeting on 19 January 1970, Benn suggested that the EEC should
not be 'an all or nothing issue' he found 'this was not welcome either to
Roy Jenkins or to the PM himself'. A few days later Maurice Schumann
was in London for a remarkably friendly visit. It was planned to begin
entry negotiations in the summer, keeping them uncomplicated and
quick.[74] Nonetheless in February, following two Cabinet discussions at
which there was grave concern over the economic cost of membership,
the government published a White Paper that predicted food prices
rising as much as 26 per cent, while the exchange cost might be over a
billion pounds. It was hardly calculated to win the electorate over and
Wilson's official biographer concludes that, while 'he was not yet retreating from his support for British entry ... he was placing on record the
fact that a line of retreat existed'.[75] His tactic until the election was to
depict Heath as someone who favoured entry at any price, while Labour
would fight for British interests. But, apart from electoral considerations, Wilson was also probably preparing for the entry negotiations
themselves where, in order to extract the best possible terms, he had to
create the impression that Britain might not join if treated ungenerously.
There was therefore a need to address an EEC 'audience' as well as a
domestic one.[76] Crossman was convinced that Wilson, like Stewart, was
'still fanatically convinced of the need to go in', adding (with no sense
of irony) that 'Harold will go for things which ... are unpopular, because
he thinks them right'. Yet the Prime Minister kept to his balanced
approach. When in late March the Minister without Portfolio, Peter Shore,
publicly attacked the principle of membership, the Prime Minister was
upset but refused to reprimand him.[77]

During the election campaign the Conservative manifesto actually
asserted that there was 'a price we would not be prepared to pay' for
entry. Heath was well aware of the danger of suggesting otherwise,
especially after Enoch Powell emerged as an anti-marketeer, focusing

on the likely loss of sovereignty.[78] There was little to choose on Europe between the two main parties for the voter and only over the following few years would it become clear that, while Heath was determined to push into Europe, Wilson was ready to shift to an apparently 'anti-market' stance, though actually his argument was that Heath's terms were not good enough and must be renegotiated. One account has argued that, if he had won in 1970, Wilson would not have entered the EEC. But this is based on the idea that he was 'a Commonwealth man' and presumes that the Labour Party, if re-elected, would have become deeply divided over Europe. Both are questionable assumptions.[79] There were plenty of signs that, if re-elected, Wilson would have taken Britain in: he sounded out Roy Jenkins, an ardent pro-European, about becoming Foreign Secretary; the FO placed entry at the centre of its plans for future policy if Labour had been re-elected; and the Prime Minister agreed that, despite the election, a date should be set to begin entry talks as early as 30 June – giving no time for post-election second thoughts. When Stewart wrote an article on British policy for the American journal *Foreign Affairs* it emphasised the desire to enter the EEC and looked forward to speedy negotiations.[80] Finally, it is worth noting that, for all his renowned lack of idealism about the EEC, Wilson privately declared in 1969, 'I have never ruled ... out' a European federation, even if he did not 'consider it likely in the short-term'.[81]

Conclusion

If there is a fundamental reason why Labour made an EEC application it is that there seemed no viable alternative base for maintaining a prominent international role. From the start, the government took the FO line that Britain should not be excluded from talks on political co-operation in Western Europe and, while Wilson pursued 'bridge-building' in 1965, by mid-1966 he came to see full membership of the EEC as the best option. Alternatives such as 'association' were ruled out; the political case for entry seemed strong. The Commonwealth was divided, the USA did not treat Britain as an equal and a 'going it alone' policy seemed to promise only irrelevance. The economic case was always less clear because, while the short-term costs would undoubtedly be substantial, the long-term dynamic gains were impossible to quantify. There were always doubts about whether de Gaulle would let the British in, but the July 1966 sterling crisis catapulted Labour into a premature effort and the decision to withdraw from east of Suez, taken while the 'second try' was under way, reinforced the logic of seeking entry to provide the country with an international role. This was why the second British application remained 'on the table' after de Gaulle's veto, to be taken up once he resigned. There were 'anti-marketeers' in the party, but Wilson outmanoeuvred them and no leading ministers resigned over the issue.

   Ultimately, indeed, Wilson's policy on European integration can be seen as quite successful. It is often forgotten that the second application eventually succeeded, being adopted by Heath and carrying Britain 'into Europe' in 1973. Piers Ludlow has shown that the very launch of the second application strengthened feeling among the Friendly Five in favour of enlargement, so that de Gaulle's 1967 veto was a Pyrrhic victory. The French themselves recognised, over the following few years, that the atmosphere in the Community had become so poisoned that it was necessary to allow Britain inside if the organisation were to move forward. As Helen Parr puts it, even in 1967 'the British ... won the long-term war' in that everyone knew 'that Britain would accede to the European Community once de Gaulle was gone'. Clive Ponting adds that Wilson achieved the 'object of making the EEC a largely bipartisan issue and not a matter of controversy in 1970'. But Ponting also highlights the reason why this remarkable consensus in the British body politic did not last. For, as on other issues, 'the government seemed to be adopting increasingly Conservative policies' and on Europe backbenchers would take their revenge in opposition, dividing Labour on this more than any other issue.[82]

Notes

Unless otherwise stated the place of publication is London.

1 The thesis of, for example: Anthony Nutting, *Europe Will Not Wait* (Hollis and Carter, 1960); Richard Mayne, *The Recovery of Europe* (Weidenfeld and Nicolson, 1970); Roy Denman, *Missed Chances* (Cassell, 1996).
2 Based on John W. Young, *Britain and European Unity* (Macmillan, 2000), chapter 1. See also: Piers Ludlow, *Dealing With Britain: the Six and the first UK application* (Cambridge University Press, Cambridge, 1997); Jacqueline Tratt, *The Macmillan Government and Europe* (Macmillan, 1996); Wolfram Kaiser, *Using Europe, Abusing the Europeans* (Macmillan, 1996).
3 For brief reviews of policy in 1964–70 see: Roger Broad, *Labour's European Dilemmas* (Palgrave, 2001), 54–74; Clive Ponting, *Breach of Promise: Labour in power 1964–1970* (Hamish Hamilton, 1989), chapter 12; Hugo Young, *This Blessed Plot: Britain and Europe from Churchill to Blair* (Macmillan, 1998), 181–209. Uwe Kitzinger, *The Second Try* (Pergamon, 1968) is a collection of documents. Fuller are: Oliver Daddow, ed., *Harold Wilson and European Integration: Britain's second application to join the EEC* (Frank Cass, 2002), see chapter 1 on historiography; Helen Wallace, *The Domestic Policy Making Implications of the Labour Government's Application for Membership of the EEC, 1964–70* (PhD, University of Manchester, 1975), still useful on the policy machine; but the fullest account based on archival evidence is Helen Parr, *Harold Wilson, Whitehall and British Policy Towards the European Community, 1964–7* (PhD, Queen Mary College, London, 2002).

4 Brian Brivati, *Hugh Gaitskell* (Richard Cohen, 1996), chapter 17; Philip Williams, *Hugh Gaitskell* (Jonathan Cape, 1979), chapter 25.

5 Lord Gladwyn, *Memoirs* (Weidenfeld and Nicolson, 1972), 355–70 (on Liberals); Robert Pearce, ed., *Patrick Gordon Walker: political diaries, 1932–71* (Historians' Press, 1991), 301.

6 Public Record Office (PRO), FO 371/177374/130, FO to posts (23 October), and 371/177374/121, interdepartmental paper, 'October 1964'; Clive Archer, 'Britain and Scandinavia: their relations within EFTA, 1960–68', *Co-operation and Conflict*, vol. 11 (1976), 19–21.

7 FO 371/184286/139, Reilly to Stewart (23 April).

8 Bryan Gould, *Goodbye To All That* (Macmillan, 1995), 54–5, 73–5, quote from 75; PRO, PREM 13/306, Stewart to Wilson (12 February); speech to British Chamber of Commerce, Brussels (11 February). Parr, *Whitehall*, 45–65, includes a valuable look at thinking in Whitehall in early 1965.

9 Michael Stewart, *Life and Labour* (Sidgwick and Jackson, 1980), 162–3; Paul Gore-Booth, *With Great Truth and Respect* (Constable, 1974), 350; George Brown, *In My Way* (Gollancz, 1971), 207–15; Eric Roll, *Crowded Hours* (Faber and Faber, 1985), 172–3 and chapter 11.

10 PRO, CAB 130/227, MISC 48/1st (25 March); Donna Lee, *Middle Powers and Commercial Diplomacy: British influence at the Kennedy trade round* (Macmillan, 1999), chapters 4 and 5; and on Commonwealth trade, Philip Alexander, 'From imperial power to regional powers', in Daddow, ed., *Wilson*, 190–4, 201–2.

11 CAB 130/229, MISC 56, especially MISC 56/3rd (14 June); PRO, PREM 13/183, Trend to Wilson (28 May), Jay to Wilson (3 June), with responses from ministers (11–14 June). Commonwealth trade ministers met in June 1966 with little result: PREM 13/773, Jay to Wilson (20 June 1966).

12 Barbara Castle, *The Castle Diaries 1964–70* (Weidenfeld and Nicolson, 1984), 18, 20, 33; Tony Benn, *Out of the Wilderness: diaries 1963–67* (Hutchinson, 1987), 204; Philip Ziegler, *Wilson: the authorised life* (Weidenfeld and Nicolson, 1993), 130–1.

13 PREM 13/904, Jay to Wilson (15 June), Stewart to Wilson (10 December), Reid to Maclehose (28 December 1965); Douglas Jay, *Change and Fortune* (Hutchinson, 1980), 361.

14 PREM 13/306, Stewart to Wilson (3 and 18 March); CAB 129/121, C(65)51 and 52 (26 March), and 73 (11 May).

15 Parr, *Whitehall*, 66–80.

16 FO 371/182346/79, Statham minute (3 June); FO 371/182348/163, Marjoribanks to O'Neill (20 September) and 371/182348//190, Robinson to Statham (18 October); *House of Commons Debates*, vol. 716, column 1141.

17 Richard Crossman, *The Diaries of a Cabinet Minister, Volume I: Minister of Housing 1964–66* (Hamish Hamilton and Jonathan Cape, 1975), 461; Benn, *Wilderness*, 392.

18 Ziegler, *Wilson*, 240–2; Ben Pimlott, *Harold Wilson* (Harper Collins, 1992), 433–5; Austen Morgan, *Harold Wilson* (Pluto, 1992), 295.

19 Wolfram Kaiser, 'Party games: the British EEC applications of 1961 and 1967', in Roger Broad and Virginia Preston, eds., *Moored to the Continent: Britain and European integration* (Macmillan, 2001), especially 70–2, emphasises domestic politics. But it is not obvious Wilson needed an entry bid soon after the 1966 election win to put the Conservatives on the defensive, still less to unite Labour.

20 Wilson raised the idea of sending a 'prominent person' around EEC capitals but the FO felt this made sense only if accompanied by a 'declaration of

intent' to enter. PREM 13/904, Brown to Wilson (18 January); PREM 13/905, Stewart to Wilson (21 December, 26 January and 3 February).

21 PREM 13/905, Jay to Wilson (3 February).

22 Cecil King, *The Cecil King Diary, 1965–70* (Jonathan Cape, 1972), 57–8, 67; PREM 13/904, Wilson minute on Stewart to Wilson (10 December, including draft declaration of intent); and see PREM 13/905, Wright to Wilson (1 February).

23 David Butler and Anthony King, *The British General Election of 1966* (Macmillan, 1966), 110–14; speech reproduced in Kitzinger, *Second Try*, 108–12.

24 Churchill College Archive, Cambridge, British Diplomatic Oral History Project, Michael Palliser interview, 14. Palliser's predecessor had been sceptical about an entry bid: PREM 13/905, Wright to Wilson (28 January).

25 CAB 134/2705, E(66)1st (9 May) and papers 2–3 (4 and 6 May); PREM 13/905, Trend to Wilson (6 May); Crossman, *Diaries I*, 512–13.

26 PREM 13/1509, record of luncheon (8 July); PREM 13/907, Wilson to Bottomley (27 July); Roll, *Crowded Hours*, 172–3; Maurice Couve de Murville, *Une Politique d'Etrangere* (Plon, Paris, 1971), 416–19.

27 Peter Paterson, *Tired and Emotional: the life of Lord George Brown* (Chatto and Windus, 1993), 212–13; Alun Chalfont, *The Shadow of My Hand* (Weidenfeld and Nicolson, 2000), 118; FO 800/981, paper attached to Maclehose to Gore-Booth (16 August) (original emphasis).

28 See Helen Parr, 'Gone native: the Foreign Office and Harold Wilson's policy towards the EEC', in Daddow, ed., *Wilson*, 75–94.

29 CAB 130/298, MISC 126(66)1st (22 October); CAB 134/2705, E(66)3rd (22 October); Benn, *Wilderness*, 480; Brown, *My Way*, 205–6; Castle, *Diaries*, 177–9; Richard Crossman, *The Diaries of a Cabinet Minister, Volume II: Lord President of the Council and Leader of the House of Commons 1966–68* (Hamish Hamilton and Jonathan Cape, 1976), 81–5; Denis Healey, *The Time of My Life* (Michael Joseph, 1989), 329–30; Jay, *Fortune* (Hutchinson, 1980), 365–6; Richard Marsh, *Off the Rails* (Weidenfeld and Nicolson, 1978), 96; Harold Wilson, *The Labour Government 1964–1970: a personal record* (Weidenfeld and Nicolson, 1971), 380–1.

30 CAB 128/41, CC53, 54 and 55(66) (1, 3 and 9 November); Castle, *Diaries*, 181, 183; Crossman, *Diaries II*, 101, 104–6, 116–17.

31 Anne Deighton, 'The Labour Party, public opinion and the second try', in Daddow, ed., *Wilson*, 39–55, quote from 39; and, in same volume, Philip Lynch, 'The Conservatives and the Wilson application', 56–74, and Neil Rollings, 'The Confederation of British Industry and European integration in the 1960s', 115–32. On pressure groups see Robert Lieber, *British Politics and European Unity* (University of California Press, Berkeley, 1970), chapter 9; and on Labour, L. J. Robins, *The Reluctant Party* (Hesketh, Ormskirk, 1979), 47–54 and 62–9.

32 King, *Diary*, 95–6; PREM 13/1475, record of meeting (16 December) and Reilly to Brown (22 December and see 4 January); Brown, *My Way*, 219–20.

33 Crossman, *Diaries II*, 191.

34 Based on John Young, 'Technological co-operation in Wilson's strategy for EEC entry', in Daddow, ed., *Wilson*, 95–114. On particular projects see: John Costello, *The Battle for Concorde* (Salisbury, 1971), chapters 4–7; Robert Baker, *ELDO: British policy and the politics of European co-operation, 1961–9* (MPhil, Queen Mary College, London, 2001), chapters 5–9. Quotes from PRO, HF2/20, Garvey to Jenkyns (7 December 1966); PREM 13/2113, Palliser to Maitland (22 July 1968).

35 PREM 13/1475, records of meetings (16–17 January); Wilson, *Government*, 419–27; CAB 128/42, CC2(67) (19 January); Castle, *Diaries*, 210–11.
36 PREM 13/1475, Reilly to Brown (4 January); PREM 13/1476, records of meetings (24–25 January) and Paris to FO (26 January); CAB 128/42, CC3(67) (26 January); Wilson, *Government*, 428–36.
37 PREM 13/1478, probe 'master' records; Wilson, *Government*, 437–41, 470–7.
38 Wilson, *Government*, 477–7, 495–7; Jay, *Fortune*, 381–4.
39 CAB 128/42, CC14(67) (21 March); Crossman, *Diaries II*, 285; Castle, *Diaries*, 236–7; Jay, *Fortune*, 383.
40 CAB 128/42, CC17, 20, 21, 22 and 24(67) (6–27 April).
41 Castle, *Diaries*, 239, 241–5 and 247, quotes from 242 and 244; Crossman, *Diaries II*, 303, 311, 317–18, 320–1 (321 on Trend); Jay, *Fortune*, 384–7.
42 Labour History Archive, Manchester, minutes of the PLP (16 March, 6, 20, 27 April and 11 May).
43 CAB 128/42, CC25 and 26(67) (30 April); CAB 128/46, CC(67)25th (30 April), 'No Circulation Record'; Benn, *Wilderness*, 496; Castle, *Diaries*, 247–50; Crossman, *Diaries II*, 332–6; Jay, *Fortune*, 387–9.
44 CAB 128/42, CC27(67) (2 May); Castle, *Diaries*, 250–1; Crossman, *Diaries II*, 339; Jay, *Fortune*, 390–3.
45 Charles de Gaulle, *Discours et Messages, Volume V, Vers le Terme, 1966–9* (Plon, Paris, 1970), 155–73; PREM 13/1482, minutes written on O'Neill to Gore-Booth (18 May).
46 CAB 134/2803, EUR(M)(67)1st (24 May).
47 *Foreign Relations of the United States* (*FRUS*), 1964–8, vol. XIII (US Government Printing Office, Washington, DC, 1995) 579–80; Donna Lee, 'Endgame at the Kennedy round', *Diplomacy and Statecraft*, vol. 12, no. 3 (2001), 115–38.
48 PREM 13/131, record of meetings (19–20 June); CAB 128/42, CC41(67) (22 June); Wilson, *Government*, 522–6.
49 John W. Young, 'The Netherlands in Britain's strategy for EEC entry', in Nigel Ashton and Duco Hellema, eds., *Unspoken Allies: Anglo-Dutch relations since 1780* (Amsterdam University Press, Amsterdam, 2001), 241–54; Terence O'Neill, *The Autobiography* (Hart-Davis, 1972), 90–1; Katherine Boehmer, 'Germany and the second British application to the EEC', in Daddow, ed., *Wilson*, 211–26.
50 CAB 128/42, CC44 and 45(67) (3–4 July). Labour could have 'reactivated' the 1961 application but Brown urged a new one: PREM 13/1479, Brown to Wilson (21 March), Palliser to Wilson (22 March).
51 PREM 13/1507, Wilson–Debre meeting (17 July); and see PREM 13/1436, Kaldor memorandum (12 January 1967), looking at a single currency.
52 PREM 13/2636, Palliser to Wilson (7 July).
53 PREM 13/1485, Nield to Wilson (6 October) gives a full review of thinking at this point; *FRUS*, vol. XIII, 630–1.
54 PREM 13/1485, G.F. (for Palliser) to Wilson (6 October); PREM 13/1486, records of Kiesinger meetings (23–25 October), Palliser to Wilson (25 October), Paris to FO (2 November).
55 PREM 13/1498, *passim*; Chalfont, *Shadow*, 121–5; John Dickie, *Inside the Foreign Office* (Chapmans, 1992), 171–5. Wilson had made veiled threats himself: PREM 13/1479, Wilson–Brandt meeting (13 April). And he continued to talk of 'putting the fear of God' into Kiesinger: PREM 13/2627, Maitland to Palliser (11 October 1968).
56 De Gaulle, *Vers le Terme*, 227–47. Ironically, the British at first expected

devaluation would help the application: PREM 13/1487, Brown to Wilson (24 November).

57 PREM 13/2646, Palliser to Maitland (28 November); CAB 128/42, CC69(67) (30 November); CAB 129/134, C(67)187 (28 November); Willy Brandt, *People and Policies* (Collins, 1978), 162–3.

58 PREM 13/1483, Reilly to Gore-Booth (28 June); PREM 13/1484, Chalfont to Brown (19 July); PREM 13/1487, Maitland to Palliser (11 December) and Palliser to Nield (12 December).

59 PREM 13/1488, Brown to Wilson (19 December); CAB 128/42, CC73(67) (20 December).

60 CAB 128/43, CC9 and see 10(67) (18 and 25 January); Benn, *Office Without Power: diaries 1968–72* (Hutchinson, 1988), 20–1; Castle, *Diaries*, 364, 378–9; PREM 13/2107, Paris to FO (17 February).

61 CAB 128/43, CC15(67) (27 February); CAB 129/135, C(68)42 (23 February); Castle, *Diaries*, 382–3.

62 Susanna Schrafstetter and Stephen Twigge, 'Spinning into Europe: uranium enrichment and the development of the gas centrifuge, 1964–70', *Contemporary European History*, vol. 11, no. 2 (2002), 253–72; Benn, *Office*, 124–5, 127–8, 182 and 246.

63 Miles Jebb, ed., *The Diaries of Cynthia Gladwyn* (Constable, 1995), 342; Churchill College, Cambridge, Christopher Soames papers, 49/2, personal note (28 March 1968).

64 For accounts of the affair see: Uwe Kitzinger, *Diplomacy and Persuasion* (Thames and Hudson, 1973), 45–58; Bernard Ledwidge, *De Gaulle* (Weidenfeld and Nicolson, 1982), chapter 22; Young, *Blessed Plot*, 200–7; Dickie, *Foreign Office*, 166–71. For British evidence see: CAB 128/44, CC9 and 10(69) (20 and 27 February); PREM 13/2628, *passim* (5 February–1 March); Castle, *Diaries*, 605–6, 610; Richard Crossman, *The Diaries of a Cabinet Minister, Volume III: Secretary of State for Social Services 1968–1970* (Hamish Hamilton and Jonathan Cape, 1977), 373–4, 378–9; Joe Haines, *The Politics of Power* (Cape, 1977), 74–81; Wilson, *Government*, 609–11, 617–18. For French views see: Frederic Bozo, *Deux Strategies pour l'Europe* (Plon, Paris, 1996), 206–8; Couve, *Politique*, 427–9; Michel Debre, *Gouverner Autrement: memoires, vol. IV, 1962–70* (Albin Michel, Paris, 1993), 266–71.

65 Wilson's Bonn visit was designed to maintain momentum for EEC entry: PREM 13/2672, Palliser to Maitland (22 July 1968); PREM 13/2675, records of talks (12–13 February).

66 CAB 128/44, CC8, 9 and 20(69) (11 and 20 February, 1 May).

67 This followed a French sounding in Washington about nuclear co-operation. Heath, the Conservative leader, had shown an interest in Anglo-French nuclear co-operation but the government would do nothing that would upset NATO: PREM 13/2097, Palliser to Maitland (23 December 1968); PREM 13/2560, Hartles to Youde (29 May 1969); PREM 13/2489, Stewart to Wilson (17 October 1969); PREM 13/2652, Graham to Youde (7 November 1969).

68 CAB 128/44, CC33 and 35(69) (16 and 22 July); Benn, *Office*, 192; quote from Crossman, *Diaries III*, 586.

69 CAB 128/44, CC45(69) (25 September); Benn, *Office*, 203; Castle, *Diaries*, 711; Crossman, *Diaries III*, 653.

70 PREM 13/2630, Youde to Wilson (2 October), Paris to FCO (10 October); also Jeremy Thorpe, *In My Own Time* (Politico's, 1999), 189.

71 CAB 128/44, CC58(69) (4 December); Kitzinger, *Diplomacy*, chapter 2.

72 PREM 13/2631, FCO to Paris and reply (18–19 November), O'Neill to Private Secretary (12 December).

73 PRO, FCO 49/257, draft memorandum (25 November 1969).
74 Benn, *Office*, 226–8; PREM 13/3208, record of meeting (23 January).
75 CAB 128/45, CC5 and 6(70) (3 and 5 February); *Britain and the European Communities: an economic assessment* (Cmnd 4289, February 1970); Castle, *Diaries*, 758–9; Ziegler, *Wilson*, 337–8.
76 On negotiating strategy: PREM 13/3201, Nield to Moon (19 March). On the two 'audiences', see Wallace, *Policy Making*, 348.
77 CAB 128/45, CC14(70) (26 March); Castle, *Diaries*, 782–3; Crossman, *Diaries III*, 811–12 (including quote), 874–5. Shore's speech in Donald Watt and James Mayall, *Current British Foreign Policy, 1970* (Temple Smith, 1971), 221–3.
78 John Campbell, *Edward Heath* (Jonathan Cape, 1993), 246–8, 273; Simon Heffer, *Like the Roman* (Phoenix, 1998), 529–31, 546–8.
79 Denman, *Missed Chances*, 230–2.
80 David Owen, *Time to Declare* (Michael Joseph, 1991), 161–2; Churchill College, Cambridge, Michael Stewart papers, 9/7/28, 'Future Policy Proposals', sent Stewart to Shore (13 May 1970); PREM 13/3201, Moon to Tickell (19 May); Michael Stewart, 'Britain, Europe and the Alliance', *Foreign Affairs*, vol. 48, no. 4 (1970), 655–9.
81 PREM 13/2560, handwritten minute before Youde to Barrington (3 June).
82 Parr, *Whitehall*, 265; Piers Ludlow, 'A short-term defeat: the Community institutions and the second British application', in Daddow, ed., *Wilson*, 135–50; Ponting, *Breach*, 214.

7

Southern Africa

Fear of racial conflict was an important factor in 1960s politics, both domestic and international. One study foresaw 'race war' becoming 'the major preoccupation of mankind', as non-whites felt increasingly disadvantaged economically. Even Lord Caradon, Britain's ambassador to the United Nations (UN), feared 'a division of the world on racial lines with all the Africans and ... Asians and the Russians (and the Communist Chinese too) on the one side and the Western powers on the other, leading to a break-up of the multiracial Commonwealth and a race conflict in Africa'.[1] In retrospect, such fears seem terribly exaggerated. Developing countries were too weak and poor to threaten the existing international order. In 1963 thirty-six states formed the Organisation of African Unity (OAU), but over the following years they failed to maintain a united front on such problems as Rhodesia and Biafra. Yet racial problems had an impact on Britain because of its imperial past. At home the government was criticised for restricting Commonwealth immigration and, while it also introduced a Race Relations Act to tackle discrimination, tension was stirred in 1968 by Enoch Powell's warning of race warfare if immigration did not stop. Overseas, the government faced particular problems because of the policies of two imperial offspring: South Africa and Rhodesia.

South Africa

Most African countries were totally opposed to South African 'apartheid', the system of racial segregation developed since 1948. Arguments over it had led to South Africa quitting the Commonwealth in 1961 and there was growing pressure in the UN for a trade embargo to bring the system down. Britain was in a difficult position here, because while it wanted to work with the Commonwealth and UN, it also had a mutually beneficial relationship with South Africa. The Royal Navy used the Simonstown naval base, strategically placed on the Cape of Good Hope;

166

South Africa was a firm ally against Communism; it controlled valuable mineral deposits, including gold and diamonds; and there was considerable British investment there.[2] Labour came to office with a promise to end arms sales to South Africa, which had continued under the Conservatives despite a 1963 UN resolution. But the new government soon found its principles had to be compromised. It did introduce quite a strict embargo, but with one major exception: an order for sixteen Buccaneer aircraft went through. The decision has been seen as evidence that Wilson was ready to 'sell out' moral principles as soon as he won office. But there were a number of compelling reasons for it. The Buccaneers had been ordered before the UN resolution, they had partly been paid for and the South Africans would have reacted angrily to cancellation. They might put pressure on the colonies of Bechuanaland (which later became Botswana), Basutoland (Lesotho) and Swaziland, which were largely surrounded by South African territory, or they could terminate the Royal Navy's use of Simonstown. Above all, however, South Africa was Britain's fourth largest export market, worth £300 million per year, much of which could be endangered if a 'buy non-British' policy were adopted. The case helped obscure the fact that policy on arms was much tighter than that of the Conservatives. It is significant, for example, that Labour did not pursue a possible sale of Bloodhound missiles, worth £11 million: policy was not completely driven by economic self-interest, therefore.[3] It should also be noted that the Buccaneers were for navy use and unsuited to internal suppression. True, they could have been used to counter a UN economic blockade of South Africa, but Britain was determined to avoid such a policy anyway, for reasons similar to those that had guided the debate over arms sales. Economic warfare would damage British trade and investments, harm the remaining southern African colonies and, thanks to the high self-sufficiency of South Africa, probably fail in its aim.[4]

The restrictions on arms sales created a Cabinet crisis in December 1967, when Wilson was weakened by the devaluation of sterling. The Foreign Office (FO), Commonwealth Relations Office (CRO) and Ministry of Defence (MOD) were keen to revive arms sales as a way to maintain defence co-operation with South Africa. Such co-operation seemed to be endangered following the decision, taken as part of the withdrawal from east of Suez, to end the permanent Royal Navy presence at Simonstown (while retaining the right to use it in wartime). The Confederation of British Industry also wanted to resume arms sales in order to boost trade. But Wilson expressed doubts about a change in the Overseas Policy and Defence Committee (OPD) in September 1967 because of the possible adverse impact on the party and Commonwealth.[5] The Foreign Secretary, George Brown, encouraged the South Africans to expect a change of policy but in the OPD on 8 December Wilson was again able to prevent a decision.[6] James Callaghan, who had just resigned as Chancellor of the Exchequer, then publicly suggested a revival of sales and sparked a furore in the party and press. The formidable grouping of Brown, Callaghan and the Defence Secretary, Denis Healey, seemed on strong ground: the need to boost balance of payments was currently paramount. But Wilson, the astute tactician, decided to re-assert his authority, in the wake of the devaluation debacle, by fighting on an issue where he could claim the moral high ground. A Cabinet meeting on Friday 15 December was, according to Healey, 'the most unpleasant meeting I have ever attended'. Then, over the weekend, Brown alienated his supporters because of extremely detailed press reports about events, which were attributed him. In fact, Wilson himself had been happy to leak details to friendly editors only days before; he even told Alasdair Hetherington, of the *Guardian*, that it did not matter if Brown resigned. But at the next Cabinet meeting there was consensus that unity had to be demonstrated behind Wilson if the government were to survive. The result was that Wilson's links to the left were strengthened, his relations with Brown and Healey worsened and policy towards South African arms was left unchanged.[7]

The need to balance moral outrage over apartheid against more practical considerations was evident elsewhere. For example, the govern-ment consistently abstained in UN Security Council votes on the issue against South Africa's control of South-West Africa (which later became Namibia), control of which it had obtained in 1919. London was critical of the October 1966 decision to put South-West Africa under UN control, arguing that this simply could not be enforced.[8] Once again, economic interests reinforced such a policy. In the late 1960s the British relied, in part, on South-West Africa for supplies of uranium, something the OPD was told only in 1970.[9] But Wilson was tougher when it came to sporting links. South Africa pressed England not to select the South African-born coloured player, Basil d'Oliveira, for the team's 1968–9 cricket tour and cancelled it when he was selected. The following year opposi-tion mounted in Britain against a South African cricket tour of England. The issue was debated in Cabinet and threatened to become a concern in the forthcoming general election until, in May, the Cricket Council was prevailed upon to cancel the tour.[10] On South Africa, then, Wilson struck a balance that proved to be tolerable, adopting a moral stance on arms sales and sport while doing nothing that would seriously damage British interests. It proved much less easy to find a balance where Rhodesia was concerned and one factor that complicated decision-making was the fear that action against that rebellious country might provoke tension with South Africa.

Rhodesia's road to illegal independence

Lying on South Africa's border, Southern Rhodesia (which later became Zimbabwe) was a British colony that, in 1923, was granted a wide degree of internal self-government under the domination of white settlers. In 1961 a new constitution was published, on the basis of which Rhodesians argued independence should be granted. This promised eventual black equality, but the franchise depended on property rights and educational attainment, and it would have taken decades for blacks (about 90% of the population, but generally poor) to elect a government of their choice. Furthermore, whites could always amend the constitution if they seemed likely to lose control. Suspicion that the whites would seek to hold on to political power increased when the hard-line Rhodesian Front won the December 1962 general election. The British Conservative government refused to grant independence in these circumstances. Two black parties, the Zimbabwe African National Union of Ndabaningi Sithole and the Zimbabwe African People's Union of Joshua Nkomo, began a campaign of armed resistance but were weakened by internal divisions and the detention of their leaders. In 1964 the situation was becoming critical, because neighbouring black countries were gaining independence: Malawi on 6 July; and Zambia on 24 October – days after Labour's election win. Meanwhile, in April, Ian Smith had become Rhodesian prime minister, making 'hard-liners' determined to win independence. From the start, therefore, Labour faced the possibility of a unilateral declaration of independence (UDI), which would have lacked a legal basis without a formal grant from Britain.[11]

It has been said that Wilson 'inherited an almost impossible position' on Rhodesia, as Southern Rhodesia was generally known after 1964. The Rhodesian Front had developed a siege mentality that made it difficult to reason with, and in Smith they had a blinkered, if deter-mined and devious, leader. His outlook can be sensed from his later, absurd claim that Labour might have granted independence but 'Wilson was dedicated to appeasing his "comrades" in the OAU and the UN'.[12] Britain had little influence inside Rhodesia, as it had allowed it to govern itself so long, and some Britons were sympathetic to the Rhodesian whites, yet world opinion and democratic sensibilities meant it was im-possible to concede independence without some promise that majority rule would follow. The Commonwealth, OAU and certain British domestic groups – the Labour Party, Liberals, anti-apartheid movement and British Council of Churches – were determined on majority rule. Wilson was strongly anti-racist: the only time that his Private Secretary, Oliver Wright, saw him lose his temper was over the treatment of black leaders in Rhodesia. The Labour leader had said during the 1964 election cam-paign that Rhodesia should not be granted independence 'so long as the government of that country remains under the control of a white minority' and the principle of 'no independence before majority rule' (NIBMAR) would haunt him thereafter.[13] He immediately backed away from it, because it removed any real basis for discussion with Smith. What in fact became policy, as it had effectively been for the Conservatives, was 'unimpeded progress' to majority rule. Even if the whites were allowed to dominate political life for a while, there must be a firm promise that they would eventually concede change.

Wilson's small parliamentary majority made it difficult for him to run risks but he tried to use a mixture of pressure and diplomacy to prevent Smith unilaterally declaring independence. Since the whites already had all the privileges they could want, the pressure had to include threats rather than inducements, but these should not drive Smith into illegality. Wilson began, in late October, by warning that UDI would carry a price to pay in the form of economic sanctions and international isolation, but this had little impact. In a long exchange of letters with Downing Street, Smith refused even to talk face to face at first.[14] He preferred to concentrate on solidifying his domestic position, and held a referendum on 5 November that demonstrated white support for independence, though not necessarily 'unilaterally'. Then, in January 1965 the funeral of Winston Churchill forced him to come to London, where he reluctantly met Wilson for the first time. Wilson reported to the Cabinet afterwards that Smith was preparing for UDI, but that he would try to claim he had been provoked into it. It was at this point that the British seriously began to study how to put economic pressures on Rhodesia.[15] The pattern of Wilson's first administration was established, with the British trying to stave off a crisis, while Smith avoided a deal, appearing reasonable but preparing for UDI. Each side wanted to be able to blame any final break on the other but in Salisbury (which is now Harare) policy was driven by stronger emotions than in London and the very sterility of the negotiations probably encouraged the urge for full independence.[16]

In an early analysis Elaine Windrich accused Wilson of abandoning Labour's opposition policies and becoming caught, like the Conservatives, in a hopeless middle position: unwilling to grant independence to a racially based state, but also unable (or unwilling) to take effective measures against Smith, the British government sought a compromise 'that would paper over the more apparent differences between the two sides'. It is a view echoed by others. Barbara Castle complained that Wilson 'was engaged in an extraordinary show of vacillation', one moment threatening the Rhodesians, 'the next sending … emissaries scurrying round' in search of compromise, in a process that 'weakened his own authority and strengthened Smith's'.[17] The first emissaries were the Commonwealth Secretary, Arthur Bottomley, and the Lord Chancellor,

Lord Gardiner, who went to Rhodesia in March, where they discovered a highly charged atmosphere, with black nationalists eager to see majority rule and white Rhodesians terrified by the prospect.[18] From Wilson's viewpoint, however, it was a success to defer UDI as long as possible, delaying a crisis in which unpleasant, and economically costly, decisions would have to be made. He also probably hoped to stave off a crisis until after the next British election. The need to avoid UDI was strengthened by early studies of economic sanctions, which concluded that pressure from Britain alone would have a limited effect, whereas Rhodesia could cut power supplies to Zambia and so threaten its copper production, on which British industry relied.[19] It was possible at this time to believe that Smith's preparations for UDI were a bluff. Jack Johnston, the British High Commissioner in Salisbury, found it difficult to predict what exactly Smith wanted: he was 'a slippery customer ... perfectly capable of denying anything he may have said ... and believing in his own denial'. The British were even uncertain about whether Smith genuinely believed in UDI, or was pushed along by 'hard-liners'.[20] Indeed, the feeling that Smith might be split from the hard-liners and make a settlement persisted as an element in Wilson's thinking for years.

In May 1965, London put forward the 'five principles' as the basis for any settlement: there should be 'unimpeded progress to majority rule'; no 'retrogressive amendment' to the constitution; an immediate strengthening of black political rights; moves to end racial discrimination; and evidence that a settlement 'was acceptable to the people of Rhodesia as a whole'.[21] (In January 1966 a sixth principle was added. It stated that neither the minority nor the majority should oppress each other in future.) The principles merely codified the main elements of existing policy, seeking steady progress towards majority rule without fulfilling NIBMAR. But they tied Britain's hands in future talks and in a sense made agreement less likely, because they went beyond what the Rhodesia Front would accept. They certainly did not bring any immediate diplomatic progress. At the June Commonwealth conference, there were demands for a constitutional conference to prepare for majority rule, but Wilson avoided any firm undertakings. In July, Bottomley's deputy, Cledwyn Hughes, visited Rhodesia but did little more than exchange views. Meanwhile, Smith's preparations for UDI continued. In May he won a resounding election victory, the Rhodesian Front taking every white seat in parliament. In July he also began to establish a diplomatic presence abroad, appointing a representative to Portugal, a right-wing dictatorship that was trying to hold on to its African colonies, one of which, Mozambique, bordered on Rhodesia. It was a further sign of weakness in Britain's position that the FO was reluctant to create a crisis with Portugal because it was an ally in the North Atlantic Treaty Organisation and a net importer of British goods.[22]

There were flaws in Smith's position, too. South Africa was unenthusiastic about the creation of another white supremacist state, because this would undermine its own attempts to portray apartheid as a 'unique' system that did not threaten its neighbours. London and Washington even hoped that South Africa would help to dissuade Smith from UDI.[23] There were also doubts about UDI from within Smith's government. Rhodesia's Central Intelligence Organisation, under Ken Flower, warned that UDI would be unsustainable in the long term if, as expected, economic sanctions were introduced against the country.[24] Nonetheless, in September 1965, on the basis of reports of Rhodesian Front discussions, Johnston became anxious that 'the last act in this Greek tragedy' was beginning. Wilson, now aware that a crisis might not be forestalled beyond the election, told the Cabinet that Britain would continue to use diplomatic efforts to avoid UDI. Nothing would be done to allow Smith 'to plead any action of ours in justification' of such action. But there would be no retreat on points of principle and contingency plans for UDI would continue to be prepared.[25] The 'war book' included financial measures, legal steps to take over Rhodesia's government and action in the UN. According to Castle, the Prime Minister, in Cabinet on 7 October, 'seemed almost to relish the fight'. But ministers were only too aware that it would be difficult to bring Smith down quickly and that the economic damage to Britain, through the loss of cheap Rhodesian tobacco supplies and disruption of the Zambian copper industry, would be serious. Also, as Crossman argued, assuming the powers of the Rhodesian government would be a purely symbolic step.[26] In talks of 7–11 October, when Smith came to London and again insisted on independence, there was complete deadlock, and the CRO concluded that 'we and Rhodesia are completely clear ... where we both stand; but we are polls apart'.[27]

With the unwelcome decision looming, Wilson engaged in one of those dramatic acts of personal diplomacy that characterised his premiership. On 21 October he announced to a tense Cabinet his decision to fly to Salisbury. Crossman had the impression that he genuinely hoped to forestall UDI rather than simply pin the blame on Smith, but a telegram, sent to Johnston before the Cabinet meeting, suggests that more than one consideration was at work: 'this idea ... is designed to play the Ace of Spades in order to avert UDI, but is also based on wider considerations concerning the Commonwealth, Parliament here and public opinion generally'.[28] On 25 October Wilson began five long days of talks in Rhodesia, which came to focus on the proposal for a royal commission to discuss the terms of independence. There were daunting technical problems about how such a group would take decisions, the precise proposals it would consider and how its recommendations might be put to the Rhodesian people, especially to blacks.[29] With difficulty, Wilson won Cabinet approval for one variation of the scheme.[30] But, typically, Smith backed off from agreement and, on 5 November, declared a state of emergency. Until late in the day, he may have feared that Britain would take military action, an idea that was being particularly pressed by, of all people, the Archbishop of Canterbury, Michael Ramsey. Ken Flower believed that, in October, it 'was still a question of who would call whose bluff first' and was astonished when, in a public statement on 30 October Wilson (for reasons discussed below) ruled out military action.[31] There was some last-minute manoeuvring to save the royal commission proposal, with Wilson still eager to reach a compromise, but UDI was announced on 11 November 1965.[32] In an atmosphere of preparing for war, Britain then carried through its threatened constitutional and economic measures against Rhodesia.[33]

One account concludes that the government 'came through the initial test on Rhodesia reasonably successfully'. If anything, Wilson improved his standing, at home and abroad, with his attempts to prevent UDI and escaped any blame when it came. Also, because he refused to respond violently to UDI, the Rhodesian question caused him no harm in the March 1966 election. Crossman was impressed by the way the Prime Minister carried public opinion while Healey believed that Wilson 'showed great tactical skill in handling the early stages of the … crisis over Southern Rhodesia'.[34] Instead, it was the Conservatives who were divided on the problem: in a parliamentary vote on oil sanctions on 21 December they had split three ways: most abstained, alongside their leader, Edward Heath, but fifty MPs on the imperialist right voted against sanctions, while thirty-one liberal-internationalist Conservatives sided with the government. Wilson was ruthless in exploiting the situation and deliberately exaggerated the differences with Heath, which were not actually that great.[35] The threat from the Conservatives proved of lesser concern than that from those who wanted tougher action. However successful he had been in pinning the blame for the crisis on Smith, Wilson faced immediate criticism over the lack of tough action to end the rebellion. On 3 December, the OAU called on its members to break off diplomatic relations with Britain if it did not act to end UDI by 15 December. Among several states that did break off relations were two Commonwealth members, Tanzania and Ghana. Then, on 16 December, when Wilson spoke at the UN, twenty African delegations walked out. Continued pressures from the Commonwealth led to a special conference of its leaders in January, in Lagos, Nigeria, where Wilson was pressed to use force. He successfully asked to be given time for economic sanctions to take effect and was thus able to minimise international criticism at election time.[36] But, in contrast to the careful diplomatic manoeuvres of his first term, Wilson's second would be marked by greater Commonwealth discontent, desperate bids at compromise with Smith and personal failures for the Prime Minister.

The failure of coercion

Debate still rages around what Britain hoped to achieve through sanctions against Rhodesia. William Rodgers, a junior minister at the
Department of Economic Affairs, which co-ordinated the policy, was
'absolutely convinced that sanctions wouldn't work' and that others
deluded themselves into believing they would. But what did 'work' mean?
Destroying white Rhodesia? Forcing it to compromise? Something else?
Jeremy Fielding, for example, argues that sanctions were designed to
impress world opinion and relieve pressure for more extreme action,
such as military force or economic warfare against South Africa.[37] For
black Africans, British action always seemed halfhearted, influenced by
economic self-interest and a feeling that the issue was unimportant.[38]
British officials have argued that the point of sanctions was not to bring
the white regime down but to persuade Smith to talk or to replace him
with an alternative leader who would. Paul Gore-Booth, Permanent Under-
Secretary at the FO, wrote that 'we could only do our best to impede
the Rhodesian economy and ... see whether the process would bring
about a settlement consistent with the ... Six Principles'. Joe Garner,
the Permanent Under-Secretary at the CRO, said that his department
favoured sanctions not in order to ruin the Rhodesian economy but 'in
the hope of provoking a situation in which the regime would be compelled to yield to a moderate government'. This fits with the argument
of Grant Hugo that the only logical purpose of sanctions could have
been to create 'a situation where the Rhodesian government would
prefer – or would be compelled by their own ruling class – to make
political concessions in order to curtail economic losses'.[39] Ben Pimlott
is among those who believe the initial aim of the British was to bring
about Rhodesia's 'collapse', but makes the important suggestion that
the purpose of sanctions became less ambitious over time. This logic is
also apparent in the most detailed account of sanctions policy, by Evan
Fountain. On the basis of archival material he believes that, whatever
the flaws in the policy, sanctions were intended seriously by the Wilson
government but that the exact purpose changed. Before November
1965 it was hoped that the threat of sanctions would deter UDI. When
UDI came there was little choice other than to introduce sanctions,
which had been threatened for months and which were preferable to
the use of force. Until about April 1966 it was hoped that they might
bring the Smith regime down; thereafter they were seen as an adjunct
to diplomatic pressure on Smith for a settlement.[40]

For several months after UDI, indeed, the hope was that Smith could
be toppled. In November 1965, Burke Trend, the Cabinet Secretary,
drafted a policy directive that began: 'The general objective is to bring the
downfall of the Smith regime and a return to constitutional government

... with a view to the resumption of progress towards majority rule as quickly as possible', while a memorandum from Bottomley drew a distinction between the 'war aim' of Smith's overthrow and 'peace aims', concerned with restoring constitutional rule. In January 1966, Wilson told the US President, Lyndon Johnson, 'we want to bring Smith down and bring him down quickly' and, to achieve this, Trend recommended a mixture of economic pressures, propaganda, encouragement of Smith's opponents and, eventually, the deployment of military forces. But it was always important to the British to ensure that there was no breakdown of order in Rhodesia and that both races were given an opportunity to live together peacefully, and this acted as a brake on extreme action. A period of direct rule by the Governor of Rhodesia was foreseen, perhaps lasting years, before majority rule was introduced. In planning all this, Wilson was well aware of the need to satisfy at least four different 'constituencies': a memorandum of 23 November 1965 said that long-term policy must be 'acceptable to British opinion ... rally the moderates in Rhodesia ... satisfy other Commonwealth governments ... and not give rise to undue attack at the United Nations'. However, as Fountain argues, it did not take long for the government to shift its aim and to see sanctions as a way to encourage a diplomatic settlement. By June 1966, Wilson was telling the US Secretary of State, Dean Rusk, that sanctions 'would force Smith into real negotiation'. The hope was that he would break away from the hard-liners and agree to restore constitutional rule. It was clear to Rusk that this might involve concessions to Smith that delayed majority rule for some time. This change, from wanting to be rid of Smith, to being ready to deal with him if a compromise could be struck, came about because of weaknesses in any policy of coercion, which must now be explored.[41]

One weakness, already recognised in early 1965, was the position of Kenneth Kaunda's Zambia. It was the only independent black African state bordering on Rhodesia, a fact that underlines the geographical strength of Rhodesia's position. Most of its other neighbours were under friendly regimes: Portuguese-controlled Mozambique, South Africa, and South African-ruled South-West Africa. To the west, Botswana, which became independent in September 1966, was sparsely populated. If military action were to be taken against Rhodesia, it would have to be launched from Zambia, which was also important in any economic embargo. Zambia, however, was vulnerable to counter-pressure, as it was dependent on Rhodesia for coal and for electricity for example, the latter from the Kariba dam, on their shared border.[42] Furthermore, Britain needed those power supplies to keep flowing because Zambian mines were the source of a third of its copper supplies. When Britain introduced an oil embargo against Rhodesia, one of the first results, on 18 December 1965, was that Zambia lost oil supplies that previously

passed through Rhodesia. Britain (later with Canadian and US assistance) had to launch an airlift to help. One potential method of breaking
the stranglehold, which Kaunda and Tanzania's Julius Nyerere proposed, was to build a thousand-mile railway between their countries.
But British officials doubted its economic viability and it would take
years to build. As a result the Chinese, in one of their few successful
forays into African politics, agreed to fund it.[43]

In late November 1965, Kaunda asked the British to send aircraft to
protect Zambia and troops to seize control of the Kariba dam. The
British agreed to send a squadron of Javelin fighters, not only to deter
a Rhodesian attack, which was seen as unlikely, but also to prevent the
more bellicose African states from despatching forces there. To Kaunda's
dismay, Britain refused to send a substantial ground force, still less one
that would deploy on the Rhodesian border, for fear of sparking a war.
He in turn refused the offer of a purely token British battalion though
he did accept the Javelins.[44] Relations with Zambia became, in themselves, a complex problem for the British, with Kaunda pressing them
for firm action but concerned by his country's exposed predicament.
He favoured military action because he believed it would resolve matters
quickly and remove any danger of a full-scale race war in southern
Africa and was exasperated when Britain did not agree. But he would
not enforce a full embargo on Rhodesia, because it made sense for
Zambia to bear the brunt of the economic war only if it was prosecuted
wholeheartedly and aimed at NIBMAR. On neither count did British
policy deliver.[45]

When UDI occurred, Rhodesia was deemed to be in 'rebellion' and
Britain assumed legal responsibility as the colonial power. The British
Governor, Humphrey Gibbs, remained in place, but Smith's government was declared to hold no legal authority and Rhodesian officials
were requested by London not 'to further the success of the rebellion'.
But, since Smith's ministers refused to be sacked by Gibbs, and since
Britain advised Rhodesian officials to avoid violence, the government
in Salisbury easily maintained its authority. The paucity of British
constitutional weapons was underlined by the so-called 'Battle for the
Queen', in which Wilson tried to exploit the symbolic importance of
the monarchy to those white Rhodesians who considered themselves
'British'. Elizabeth II had made it clear before UDI that she would not
remain the head of state of an illegal regime and that she supported
Wilson's policy on Rhodesia. But even here the wily Smith was able to
turn matters to his advantage. When, in October 1965, Wilson took a
letter to Salisbury from the Queen urging a settlement, the Rhodesian
premier read it out at a banquet as if he were in personal contact with
her! He insisted that Rhodesians could be loyal to the crown while despis-
ing her present government. As one biography of the Queen points

out, 'Gibbs' beleaguered survival ... was a nagging reminder of Smith's illegitimacy in the eyes of the world' and the sense of loyalty to the crown, especially among Rhodesia's armed forces, was such that Smith did not dare declare a republic until 1970.[46] Nonetheless, British constitutional measures had little role in ending UDI.

A far more potent threat would have been the use of force. The failure to act militarily drew much criticism from black African states. Since the Second World War, the British had been ready to use force against the Egyptians at Suez, Chinese Communists in Malaya and the Mau-Mau in Kenya. Why not against whites in Rhodesia? Some in Britain agreed. Among Cabinet ministers, Barbara Castle later complained that 'Harold sold the pass by making it clear he would not use force to bring the illegal regime to heel' and, in retrospect, even a moderate like James Callaghan regretted force was not used, though how this would have squared with his contemporary determination, as Chancellor, to restrict defence spending is unclear.[47] It is important to note that, as seen with the deployment of Javelins in Zambia, Wilson *was* ready to consider certain military options. There were plans to attack Rhodesian power supplies if Smith had cut electricity to Zambia from the Kariba dam. The British also stood ready to send troops into Rhodesia if Smith's regime collapsed or if Smith agreed to it. What was out of the question, as Wilson made clear to the Commons in December 1965, was the launch of a full-scale invasion against armed opposition. Neither did Britain want anyone else to attempt this. Sending British aircraft to Zambia was partly designed to prevent an Egyptian-led military intervention and, according to Cecil King, the newspaper chairman, Wilson said that, if Egypt did make a move, aircraft from HMS *Eagle* in the Indian Ocean would bomb Zambia's airfields. Wilson even suggested that Rhodesian commanders should be told that British deployments in Zambia were aimed not at them but at their opponents.[48]

Wilson's personal aversion to war, fear of stirring race problems at home and a lack of enthusiasm for any costly military operations all contributed to the decision against force, and there may be something in the black African suspicion that, for British policy-makers, there were limits to the importance of Rhodesia. Castle recalled that 'the issue on which I came nearest to resigning from the government was Rhodesia' but she also noted that 'I was often isolated in Cabinet'. However, there were always formidable practical arguments against armed intervention in Rhodesia and experts were against such a course long before Labour took power. Indeed, ministers were presented with the problems within days of taking office in October 1964. Intervention should be avoided because of the dangers of a 'major and perhaps prolonged operation of war', from which it would 'be politically difficult to withdraw once committed'; clashes with Rhodesians of British stock 'would be a most repugnant task for our forces'. Instead, UDI should be met by economic and political sanctions.[49] Considerable work was done in the months after UDI to clarify British views on military intervention, but the basic conclusion remained the same. To be certain of success, an invasion would require a pre-emptive air strike and the deployment of five brigades, but this would take three months to prepare, deplete British war stocks (ruling out any similar operation for two years) and use up all available air transport. Neither could it be isolated from other possible commitments. This was at a time when forces were still heavily involved in Borneo and Aden, and in fact only two brigades were available for action. Other problems with military action included the unreliability of Zambian security and, again, the effect on troops' morale of fighting white Rhodesians.[50] It is not clear exactly how important the last factor was, relative to others, partly because, even among themselves, the British downplayed it. Thus, when giving an explanation of the military problems to the Liberal leader, Jo Grimond, Healey deliberately avoided the issue. But Ian Smith claimed that the Javelin squadron commander in Zambia promised he would not attack Rhodesia and one account talks of 'a near mutiny in the regiment' when the Special Air Service (SAS) thought they might be sent to Rhodesia (because Rhodesians had fought alongside the SAS in Malaya in the 1950s).[51]

The British did keep military action under review. In October 1966 the Cabinet again ruled that an invasion was impracticable. In June 1967 a plan was drawn up to introduce forces in the event of a coup against Smith, but no further work was done because a coup seemed unlikely.[52] A plan for a coup against Smith had been drawn up in the CRO in early 1966 but it relied on finding support among the Rhodesian military, who would have to carry it out, as well as the Governor and civilian leaders, who would set up an interim government, and it was not attempted. It may be suspected that the British exaggerated the difficulties, but in December 1965 the US Joint Chiefs of Staff also studied the problems of an invasion and found them formidable.[53] This still leaves one important question. Notwithstanding the problems of using force, why did Wilson *publicly* rule it out, instead of letting the Rhodesians believe it was an option, so creating uncertainty in their minds? Ken Flower argues that Wilson's statement on 30 October 1965, that there would be no 'thunderbolt', finally persuaded Smith to proceed with UDI. Even Denis Healey, who believed the actual use of force was impossible, felt that Wilson had committed a 'classic strategic blunder' in his statements. Indeed, in a conversation with Cecil King, Wilson conceded, 'Perhaps the criticism is justified'. Yet, even here, it is possible to defend him. Pressure to clarify the position on military action was intense in late 1965 and likely to become even stronger if it were not categorically ruled out. Also, as Joe Garner pointed out, 'an implied threat would have rebounded when the Africans realized that it had never been intended'. Furthermore, the British had already privately told Smith that force would not be used.[54]

Even in the intelligence field, the British were less than supreme. Ahead of UDI the Joint Intelligence Committee (JIC) produced an accurate prediction of its likely effects. There would be: a 'passionate and emotional' reaction among black Africans; pressure on Britain to take military action; limited support for Rhodesia from South Africa and Portugal; and problems for the Zambian economy. Economic sanctions would have 'a serious but not ... crippling effect'; it would be hard for Smith to back down once UDI occurred; and the white regime would collapse only after long-term economic pressure. But none of this suggested reliance on 'covert' sources and intelligence work in Rhodesia was evidently poor.[55] Inadequate political guidance, organisational problems and a lack of sources on the ground seem to have combined to produce an underestimation of Smith's determination to pursue independence and an overestimation of the chances of him being replaced internally. As with the military, there may also have been some resistance to working against Rhodesia: Tom Bower talks of an officer who 'sympathised with Rhodesia's whites' and was dilatory about finding anyone to launch a coup against Smith.[56] Rhodesia became 'a high political priority' for MI6 but it took time to build a presence in central Africa and even the Government Communications Headquarters found it difficult to obtain information, because the Rhodesians relied on landlines rather than signals for their communications. Some information was evidently gathered from Flower, who made some personal visits to London. But Dick White, the head of MI6, soon feared deceit by him.[57] While no great admirer of Smith, the spy chief proved quite adept at countering certain British activities, using leaks to the *Daily Telegraph*. Flower also directed his own propaganda campaign against Wilson, which evidently included smears about his leftist leanings and relationship with Marcia Williams. Again, Zambia was a weak point. In 1966 Kaunda had to sack most of his special branch officers because of fears they were leaking information to the Smith regime; next year, a five-man spy ring was rounded up.[58] Wilson even discovered problems on his own doorstep: papers were passed to a Rhodesian agent for a time in 1967 by a typist in the Cabinet Office. On the subversive side, British radio propaganda was broadcast from Francistown in Bechuanaland. But the effort was dogged by inefficiency at first and by Rhodesian 'jamming' later.[59]

With constitutional measures ineffective and force ruled out, coercion came to rely primarily on economic sanctions. Britain knew that support for multilateral action would be easy to obtain and, on 20 November 1965, the UN had called for economic sanctions to be introduced.

Rhodesia became the first post-war example of the use of a sanctions policy by the international community to force political change. The British themselves began with a wide but limited range of economic sanctions, including the suspension of development aid, expulsion from the sterling area and a ban on purchases of Rhodesia's key export, tobacco. Then, on 1 December, Wilson announced a package that amounted to a ban on 95 per cent of trade with Rhodesia, and he told President Johnson, 'We have ... decided to go for the quick economic kill'.[60] There was another tightening-up of regulations at the end of January 1966, effectively ending all trade links. UN sanctions were voluntary at first but this suited the British because mandatory sanctions could have created a precedent for moves against South Africa.[61]

Wilson's most famous utterance about Rhodesia, one that would haunt him for the rest of his career, was his statement to the January 1966 Commonwealth conference that sanctions would end UDI in 'weeks not months'. Perhaps he had little choice but to say this. After all, other measures were unlikely to work, UN pressure made sanctions unavoidable anyway and he needed both to neutralise Commonwealth pressures for the use of force and to prevent Rhodesia complicating his chances of re-election. Then again, there is evidence that he really believed sanctions would succeed and, in the view of the official biographer, 'was succumbing to his natural over-optimism'. On 3 January he told Castle that Britain had underestimated its own strength in 1965: sanctions were biting, Smith was desperate. A few days later he took a similar line at an OPD meeting.[62] While he was well aware of the emotional element that drove the Rhodesian Front, Wilson may have believed, as a rational and pragmatic individual leading a nation whose very lifeblood was international trade, that Rhodesians could be induced to talk under economic pressure. Yet, as seen above, studies in 1965 had predicted that sanctions would take time to work and that Rhodesia could counter with far worse damage to Zambia. The situation may have looked optimistic in January, but only for a short time. The Rhodesians put great effort into breaking sanctions and, in some ways, were better off than before. On the financial side, for example, when their assets in London were seized, they retaliated by defaulting on their debts and by directing private investment by ordinary Rhodesians into the domestic economy, which consequently benefited by £100 million or more.[63] Furthermore, Britain itself was damaged by the actions it took. For example, Rhodesian tobacco supplies had to be replaced with purchases outside the sterling area, to the detriment of the balance of payments and, while the Americans gave some help with tobacco supplies, they would not cover the whole loss. By 1968 the cost of the Rhodesian problem to Britain's balance of payments was estimated at £30 million per year.[64]

The scale of difficulty in relying on economic pressure was revealed by oil sanctions, which were introduced on 21 December 1965. Their introduction was delayed because Wilson needed to ensure they had US support, something he established only at his summit meeting with Johnson that month. The British also needed time to prepare for a Rhodesian counter-embargo against Zambia.[65] On 9 April, the UN also approved the Beira patrol, through which the Royal Navy could forcibly prevent oil reaching Rhodesia via the traditional route for such imports. This accompanied Wilson's victory in the so-called 'Battle of Beira', when British pressure led to a Greek tanker sailing away from the Mozambican port without unloading its cargo of oil.[66] Once more, how-ever, studies in 1965 had shown that, while oil sanctions might have a demoralising impact on Rhodesia, they would take time to work, could be evaded (through South Africa and alternatives to the Beira route through Portuguese territory) and would encourage counter-measures against Zambia.[67] Sure enough, the Rhodesians were able to import refined oil products through South Africa and Portuguese territory, which raised the issue of taking measures against them. But, as seen above, South Africa was too important to the British economy for tough action against that country to be contemplated, while sanctions against Portugal made no sense if Rhodesia could get supplies via South Africa. Wilson actually sometimes suggested targeting Portugal but was repeatedly opposed by other ministers.[68]

Wilson suspected for a time that the source of oil supplies was the French company Total, but in February 1968 it became clear that much 'sanctions busting' was done by two UK companies, British Petroleum and Shell. Nevertheless, as publicly revealed in the Bingham report ten years later, Commonwealth Secretary George Thomson, instead of pub-licising the issue and invoking the law, connived with the companies in an operation by which Rhodesia would be appear to be supplied with oil by Total.[69] There has inevitably been speculation about what Wilson knew. He later claimed that, while suspicious about breaches of the oil sanc-tions, he did not know the scale. Even his official biographer feels this is a weak defence, since the Prime Minister's duty was to seek the truth. It is evident that he did see an account of Thomson's 21 February 1968 meeting with oil executives but it arrived in Downing Street only in mid-March, when Wilson was preoccupied with George Brown's resignation. Yet there is other evidence in the prime ministerial files, including a minute to Wilson on 22 April 1968 saying that BP and Shell had broken sanctions.[70] The behaviour of these companies made little difference to Rhodesia's survival, but it was quite hypocritical for London to continue calling on other countries to enforce sanctions. The scandal confirmed the extent of Britain's failure to put Smith under sustained pressure. By the time the UN introduced comprehensive mandatory sanctions in May

1968 the whole policy was in tatters, with most leading industrial nations quite happy to trade with Rhodesia clandestinely. The OPD acknowledged in March 1968 that Rhodesia was receiving all the oil it needed; but by then ministers felt obliged to maintain the Beira patrol because terminating it would merely emphasise the scale of the sanctions failure.[71]

The failure of diplomacy

Whatever reliance Wilson placed on international support, Rhodesia was primarily a British responsibility. The USA gave diplomatic support, backed sanctions and helped ease some economic costs of UDI but, given its heavy involvement in Vietnam, expected Britain to carry much of the burden of defending Western interests in Africa.[72] European allies and the Commonwealth also looked to London to take a lead. Pushed to the fore, the Cabinet agreed only six weeks after UDI that it would be unwise to demand 'unconditional surrender' and that, while diplomatic recognition of Smith's government was impossible, indirect talks with Smith through the Governor were acceptable. At this point the aim of any talks was to replace the illegal regime and it was revealed during the March 1966 British general election that a CRO official, Duncan Watson, was in Salisbury, for talks with Gibbs.[73] Around election time, however, weaknesses in the coercive side of policy pointed the British government to greater reliance on negotiations. Whereas in the early months after UDI sanctions were meant to bring Smith down, with diplomacy smoothing the way for this, after the election, with sanctions limited in their effect, it was hoped to negotiate a deal with Smith himself. The logic was set out by Michael Stewart, the Foreign Secretary: 'Since the use of force was ruled out, we must seek a negotiated settlement. It was unlikely that sanctions would compel the illegal regime to surrender; they might, however, in time induce the regime to agree to a settlement which could be reconciled with our six principles'.[74] Sanctions, then, had become a partner of diplomacy, a means of pressuring Smith to compromise. Wilson's overall aim remained that of securing 'unimpeded progress' to majority rule but his methods and the precise terms of a settlement were flexible.

Reports in February 1966 suggested that, contrary to Wilson's early hopes, sanctions were not crippling Rhodesia. The Prime Minister himself, preoccupied with the election, now talked of a 'long haul' rather than a 'quick kill'; and if economic sanctions were not working quickly and military force was ruled out, then diplomacy emerged as an obvious option.[75] For a time, however, various alternatives were explored which show Wilson's flexibility. In March–April an attempt was made to persuade South Africa to push Smith into a settlement, but unfortunately this coincided with the 'Battle of Beira', when British tactics upset the South Africans. In any case, even if the South Africans did not welcome UDI, neither were they willing actively to 'take sides' against Rhodesia. With the British election over, Kaunda told Wilson, 'we now expect very vigorous action on your part' and, in a sign of their readiness at this point to consider various possibilities, the British did suggest a complete closure of the Zambian–Rhodesian border as a way to tighten the economic pressure on Smith. But Kaunda feared the impact of such a step on Zambia itself and would not agree.[76] This was also the time that a coup against Smith was studied but, like armed invasion, ruled out. Instead of vigorous action, the British reverted to the only option they had left themselves, diplomacy backed by continuing economic pressure. Hints from Smith that he would negotiate without conditions led Oliver Wright to visit Salisbury in mid-April, with only a small group of ministers being informed.[77] The full Cabinet was told on 28 April and, while Castle in particular feared the compromises that might follow, it was agreed to open 'talks about talks' with Rhodesia, the understanding being that these were not actual 'negotiations' and did not imply recognition of the rebel regime.[78]

A new ministerial committee, Rhodesia 'X', was created to have oversight of the negotiations and Wright, who had now left Number 10, led the British delegation. But the talks, which oscillated between London and Salisbury from May to August, failed to achieve anything other than criticism of Britain from African states. They were finally ended when the Rhodesian government took steps to increase its powers of detention. With another Commonwealth conference looming, the break was not unwelcome to London.[79] The full Cabinet had a lengthy discussion on 1 September 1966, when, after considering more radical suggestions, including full support for NIBMAR, ministers confirmed the current policy of voluntary UN sanctions and a readiness to talk on the basis of the six principles.[80] However, only days later, Commonwealth leaders gathered in London and were so vociferous in their demands for firm action that they forced British policy to change. To pacify the delegates, the Cabinet agreed that, if UDI were not terminated before December, the policy of NIBMAR would be adopted by Britain and that the UN would be asked to introduce mandatory sanctions. Sanctions should be 'selective', however, so as to avoid demands for economic warfare against South Africa. These moves kept the Commonwealth together and raised the prospect of a complete break with Smith, which was counter to Wilson's existing policy. But they also made the danger of economic warfare with South Africa all the greater and led Wilson into another active diplomatic phase.[81]

Wilson's retreat in the face of Commonwealth outrage ought to have helped his diplomatic efforts at a settlement, at least in the short term.

Logically, Smith should have been concerned by the prospect of mandatory sanctions and anxious to negotiate meaningfully. But a mission
to Salisbury in September 1966 by the Commonwealth Secretary, Herbert
Bowden, and the Attorney General, Elwyn Jones, found little basis for
negotiation.[82] Nor did Smith show interest in a range of proposals that
followed. Rather, it was Wilson who seemed increasingly desperate for
a settlement. A deeply reluctant Bowden was induced to return to Salisbury
in November and there was a last-minute decision that both prime ministers should meet face to face once more. As in the weeks before UDI,
Wilson wanted to avoid passing the point of no return. In Cabinet on
29 November Castle led the doubters, but the summit conference was
approved. Smith apparently decided to talk because he believed, in the
light of Wilson's evident desperation, that a favourable deal might be
struck and there was some movement towards a compromise by both
leaders.[83] On board HMS *Tiger*, off Gibraltar on 2–4 December, they
discussed a series of alterations to the 1961 constitution that would have
kept white rule for many years but with safeguards against retrogressive
constitutional change.[84] It was more than Smith had been offered before
and the British Cabinet, meeting on 4 December, accepted it as the
best way to end UDI, though it might have split the Commonwealth.
When Castle complained about the terms, Wilson, who had already described it as a choice of evils, said it was the best deal Britain could get
'for the voluntary winding-up of the rebellion by the rebels themselves'.
It was not possible to dictate 'surrender' terms. But Smith's memoirs
confirm that he did not push the deal strongly on his return home and
that he wanted a unanimous agreement from his Cabinet on what was
done. Such tactics put the decision in the hands of hard-liners and
agreement was rejected.[85] Wilson had not lost too much through this
diplomatic failure: Commonwealth and party unity were preserved and
Smith was again seen as unreasonable, without any need for an embarrassing compromise. But, in light of the promises to the Commonwealth
conference, Britain now had to commit itself to NIBMAR and ask the
UN for selective mandatory sanctions, which were introduced on 16
December 1966, all of which made a negotiated settlement with Smith
improbable. When Cabinet reviewed the situation there was no great
hope of ending UDI at an early date. Policy really had settled into a
long haul, with the hope that sanctions would eventually create
opposition to Smith and so foster conditions for a settlement, but with
diplomacy unable to serve much immediate purpose.[86]

There was little movement for most of 1967. In June–July a former
High Commissioner to Salisbury, Lord Alport, was sent to explore the
situation in Rhodesia, and in November the Commonwealth Secretary,
George Thomson, followed, but to no avail.[87] Repeatedly the existing
policy, relying on sanctions to bring some change in Rhodesia, was

confirmed despite the flaws in the sanctions regime.[88] In view of the problems, serious thought was even given to 'disengaging' Britain from its legal responsibility for the problem, effectively letting it be tackled by the UN. This may seem an unusual, even craven idea but actually it had been around for some time. A month after UDI, Stewart had advised Wilson that there were only two alternatives for Britain in Rhodesia: using force or handing the problem to the UN. The use of sanctions was likely to be too slow in bringing Smith down and would create dangers, FO planners predicted, of 'a crisis in British domestic opinion, Commonwealth break-up, racial warfare, Communist penetration, damage to our economy or prestige and a conflict of British interests over South Africa or Portugal'. This was not advice that Wilson was disposed to take. When the option was raised again in March 1966 Burke Trend opposed it, at least as an immediate option, arguing it would be 'a public admission of failure'. It was considered several times thereafter, including November 1966, ahead of the *Tiger* talks, when Trend again opposed it, insisting 'there is no sudden and dramatic move which would enable us to transfer ourselves from the centre of the stage to the back row of the United Nations' chorus'.[89] In late 1967 the OPD decided seriously to study 'disengagement' but it did not hold the field for very long.[90] The hopelessness of dealing with Smith was confirmed by his execution of three blacks in March 1968 in defiance of international pleas for clemency. This generated considerable outrage and led Wilson to tell the OPD that the idea of 'terminating our special jurisdictional responsibility' was out of the question. Instead, in yet another sign of his flexibility, he pushed for stricter sanctions enforcement, before others pointed out that this would provoke arguments with all the Western nations that were breaching sanctions.[91]

A toughening of the sanctions policy did take place in the wake of the executions. On 29 May the UN introduced comprehensive mandatory sanctions, a step that was accepted by Britain, whose own sanctions were already 'comprehensive'. However, it did spark renewed concern that there might now be calls for measures against South Africa and it did nothing to move Smith.[92] Soon Wilson returned to the logic that, if the Rhodesia problem were to be solved, diplomacy was the only real option. He employed two unlikely 'special envoys', his lawyer, Lord Goodman, and a press baron, Max Aitken, to fly to Salisbury in August 1968 and pave the way for another summit.[93] It was agreed that Smith should meet Wilson in October, this time aboard HMS *Fearless* at Gibraltar, but on the basis of the ideas explored on *Tiger* almost two years before. Even Stewart was sceptical about talks and Wilson argued rather lamely in Cabinet that Britain had always agreed to look at honourable pro- posals for a settlement and that nothing was lost through negotiation.[94] In five days of talks in mid-October, Wilson went as far as ever to

compromise, agreeing that the Smith regime should hold power throughout the 'transitional' period to majority rule. But there was still great
Rhodesian reluctance to give up their existing constitution before they
were absolutely certain what would replace it, with special concern about
the safeguards Britain demanded over future constitutional change.[95]
Castle told Wilson that she would resign if the negotiations 'go the wrong
way' ('I would resign myself', he cheerfully replied). Sure enough,
despite further weeks of talks on the details, with Thomson again
visiting Salisbury, the Rhodesian Cabinet again rejected the deal.[96]

Persistently, in fact, the Rhodesian Front showed that it would accept
no settlement that threatened to end white rule, even many years in
future, and it is difficult to see what Wilson gained on this occasion,
either from the talks themselves or from his willingness to leave the
Fearless deal 'on the table'. Rhodesian intransigence had already been
amply demonstrated, the Conservatives were unable to make capital on
Rhodesia and he simply ran the risk of dividing his Cabinet, the Labour
Party and the Commonwealth by seeming to renege, yet again, on the
NIBMAR pledge. At best he had impressed moderate opinion with a
readiness to negotiate, but now any negotiations seemed useless and in
1969–70 even Wilson took little interest in tackling the issue. In February
1969 a new Rhodesian constitution was published that effectively put
back black equality for decades. This suggested that compromise had
been useless all along and that Wilson had merely tainted himself by
his willingness to contemplate a deal. Smith's declaration of a republic
in March 1970 provided a final insult to Wilson's government, which
was quite unable to end UDI before itself losing office, although the
issue had little impact on the 1970 election campaign. In the last few
years of the government any deal with Smith was unlikely because he
knew he might get a better deal from the Conservatives.

Conclusion

Southern Africa's problems underlined the way Labour compromised
its original promises and principles, in a way no other region did. Wilson
hated racism, in opposition his party promised to end arms sales to
South Africa and during the 1964 election campaign he had shown
sympathy for NIBMAR in relation to Rhodesia. But, as on so many
issues, his government tried to escape contradictory pressures by finding a middle way between high principle and the loss of its soul. Just as
there was a compromise on race policy at home, based on tighter immigration control and action against racial discrimination, so the approach
to southern Africa accepted the existence of white supremacist states in
the short term, while signalling that they could never be treated as full

members of the international community. Commercial self-interest, re-inforced by security considerations and the local strength of South Africa's position, made it difficult to indulge Labour's loathing for apartheid. Even the restrictions on arms sales came to be questioned by some ministers. Rhodesia was a far more complex challenge that absorbed a considerable amount of ministerial energy, especially in 1964–8, and one on which any overall assessment of the government's international policy must dwell. In the first phase, Britain could not prevent UDI, but Wilson did make Smith appear unreasonable, and then showed a combination of vigour and moderation that kept the Commonwealth together and did no harm in the 1966 election. But, if this was a period of qualified success, and even if one accepts that the inheritance from the Conservatives was a difficult one, it is easy to see subsequent policy as a failure. Wilson, who took a leading role on the Rhodesian issue, seemed inconsistent in aim, veering between threats and compromise, reacting to events rather than controlling them. He never could find the right mix of coercive elements and diplomatic inducements to end the 'rebellion'.

Robert Good judges that British policy followed 'a set of negative guidelines' and so resulted in 'a complete impasse: no force; no con-frontation with South Africa; and no sell out'. Yet, while highlighting the muddle and failure, Good also recognised that Wilson himself succeeded in avoiding a breach with any of his 'constituencies', be it the Labour Party or public opinion at home, the UN or even the Common-wealth abroad. Joe Garner also considered that, while policy was blighted by Wilson's tactical switches, 'he stoutly upheld ... the main lines of his policy, namely resistance to illegality ... together with readiness to reach ... an honourable settlement'.[97] This is stating the case in lofty terms: Kaunda, Castle and others would not have seen a settlement on the *Fearless* terms as 'honourable'. But the need to face several 'constitu-encies', the limits to any policy of coercion and the doggedness of the Rhodesians combined to produce a formidable problem. Britain could probably have ended UDI quickly only by risking an actual invasion, perhaps linked to an internal coup, or by outright economic warfare; either option would have been financially costly, had no guarantee of quick success, and could have triggered conflict with South Africa. It simply was not worth running such grave risks, especially when all long-term analyses suggested UDI would eventually fail anyway. The problem was that, in the short term, economic sanctions were insufficient to cripple the Rhodesian economy and turn whites against Smith. Sanctions did not even induce the Rhodesian Front to negotiate an end to UDI on generous terms, the aim on which Wilson came to focus after the 1966 election but which was complicated by the adoption of NIBMAR that December. Richard Crossman recognised that behind all the tactical shifts in Wilson's policy, the leaps between tough rhetoric and desperate bids at negotiation, there was a broad consistent hope: 'It's winning that matters here, whether by settlement or by defeating Smith'. But when Wilson lost office in 1970, Smith was still there.

Notes

Unless otherwise stated the place of publication is London.

1 Ronald Segal, *The Race War* (Penguin, 1967), 13; Churchill College, Cambridge, Michael Stewart papers, STWT 9/5/4, Caradon to Wilson (3 June 1966).

2 For background see: Ritchie Ovendale, 'The South African policy of the British Labour government, 1945–51', *International Affairs*, vol. 59, no. 1 (1982–3), 41–58; Geoffrey Berridge, *Economic Power in Anglo-South African Diplomacy* (Macmillan, 1981), chapter 2.

3 Based on John Young, 'The Wilson government and the debate over arms to South Africa', *Contemporary British History*, vol. 12, no. 3 (1998), 62–86.

4 Public Record Office (PRO), CAB 148/18, OPD(65)15th (12 March); CAB 148/20 OPD(65)48th (8 March).

5 CAB 148/30, OPD(67)30th (14 September); PRO, PREM 13/2400, Rogers to Wilson (12 September); PRO, DEFE 24/154, *passim*; Richard Crossman, *The Diaries of a Cabinet Minister, Volume II: Lord President of the Council and Leader of the House of Commons 1966–8* (Hamish Hamilton and Jonathan Cape, 1976), 476–9.

6 PREM 13/2400, Palliser to Maitland (19 November), Brown to Wilson (7 December) and FO to Pretoria (8 December); CAB 148/30, OPD(67)39th (8 December).

7 CAB 128/42, CC70, 71 and 72(67) (14–18 December); Denis Healey, *The Time of My Life* (Michael Joseph, 1989), 334–6; British Library of Political and Economic Science, London, Alastair Hetherington papers, 13/1, meeting with Wilson (13 December). For other accounts by those involved see: George Brown, *In My Way* (Gollancz, 1971), 172–4; Barbara Castle, *The Castle Diaries 1964–70* (Weidenfeld and Nicolson, 1984), 336–42; Crossman, *Diaries II*, 602–8; John Silkin, *Changing Battlefields* (Hamilton, 1987), 78–9; Harold Wilson, *The Labour Government 1964–1970: a personal record* (Weidenfeld and Nicolson, 1971), 470–6. The fullest academic discussion is Tim Bale, '"A deplorable episode"? South African arms and the statecraft of British social democracy', *Labour History Review*, vol. 62, no. 1 (1997), 22–40.

8 PREM 13/3128, FO/CRO outward telegram (29 October 1966), brief for Wilson (25 April 1967).

9 PREM 13/3128, note by Ministry of Technology (19 March 1970), Benn to Wilson (26 March).

10 CAB 128/45, CC19(70) (30 April); James Callaghan, *Time and Chance* (Collins, 1987), 261–3; Denis Howell, *Made in Birmingham* (Queen Anne Press, 1990), 200–9; D. R. Thorpe, *Alec Douglas-Home* (Sinclair Stevenson, 1996), 396–9.

11 For background see: James Barber, *Rhodesia* (Oxford University Press, Oxford, 1967); Robert Blake, *A History of Rhodesia* (Eyre Methuen, 1977); and Frank Clements, *Rhodesia* (Collins, 1969).

12 Clive Ponting, *Breach of Promise: Labour in power 1964–1970* (Hamish Hamilton, 1989), 144; Ian Smith, *The Great Betrayal* (Blake, 1997), 100.

13 Churchill College Archive, Cambridge, British Diplomatic Oral History Project, Oliver Wright interview, 12–13; Wilson to Mutasa (2 October 1964) quoted in Elaine Windrich, *Britain and the Politics of Rhodesian Independence* (Croom Helm, 1978), 31.

14 *Southern Rhodesia: documents relating to negotiations ... November 1963–November 1965* (Cmnd 2807, 1965), 42–56; PREM 13/85 and 86, *passim*.

15 Wilson, *Government*, 73–5; Smith, *Betrayal*, 80–7; PREM 13/534, Wilson–Smith meeting (30 January); CAB 128/39, CC6(65) (1 February); CAB 148/18, OPD(65)6th (29 January).

16 This logic follows Barber, *Rhodesia*, chapter 13.

17 Windrich, *Britain*, 7; Barbara Castle, *Fighting All the Way* (Weidenfeld and Nicolson, 1993), 360–1.

18 CAB 148/18, OPD(65)13th (5 March); CAB 129/120, C(65)40 (10 March); Smith, *Betrayal*, 88–91.

19 CAB 148/18, OPD(65)10th (17 February) and OPD(65)17th (24 March); CAB 148/20, OPD(65)40th (15 February) and OPD(65)54th (18 March).

20 PREM 13/535, Salisbury to CRO (15 and 23 April).

21 PREM 13/537, CRO memorandum (25 May) and Salisbury to CRO (28 May).

22 PREM 13/567, Stewart to Wilson (11 September).

23 Library of Congress, Washington, DC, Averell Harriman papers, box 576, Trimble to Harriman (8 October).

24 Ken Flower, *Serving Secretly* (John Murray, 1987), 29, 38–40, 43–4.

25 PREM 13/538, Salisbury to CRO (11 and 12 September); CAB 128/39, CC47(65) (12 September).

26 CAB 128/39, CC50(65) (7 October); CAB 148/18, OPD(65)42nd (2 October) and OPD(65)43rd (7 October); Castle, *Diaries*, 60–1; Richard Crossman, *The Diaries of a Cabinet Minister, Volume I: Minister of Housing 1964–66* (Hamish Hamilton and Jonathan Cape, 1975), 344.

27 PREM 13/540, CRO to Ottawa (11 October); see *Southern Rhodesia* (Cmnd 2807), 69–95, for records of the talks; Wilson, *Government*, 146–9; Smith, *Betrayal*, 91–5.

28 CAB 128/39, CC52(65) (21 October); Crossman, *Diaries I*, 355–6; PREM 13/542, CRO to Salisbury (20 October).

29 *Southern Rhodesia* (Cmnd 2807), 102–35; fuller records in PREM 13/543. See also: Wilson, *Government*, 153–68; Windrich, *Britain*, 48–53; Alan Megahey, *Humphrey Gibbs, Beleaguered Governor* (Macmillan, 1998), 101–4.

30 CAB 128/39, CC56(65) (2 November); Castle, *Diaries*, 62–3; Crossman, *Diaries I*, 367–8.

31 Smith, *Betrayal*, 99; Megahey, *Gibbs*, 104–6; Owen Chadwick, *Michael Ramsey* (Oxford University Press, Oxford, 1990), 242–8; Flower, *Serving*, 51, 283–5, 286–91.

32 CAB 128/39, CC58 and 59(65) (9–10 November); Castle, *Diaries*, 65–7; Crossman, *Diaries I*, 375; *Southern Rhodesia* (Cmnd 2807), 136–43; Smith, *Betrayal*, 98–107.

33 CAB 128/39, CC60, 61 and 62(65) (11–18 November).

34 Ponting, *Breach*, 159; Crossman, *Diaries I*, 432; Healey, *Time*, 331.

35 Mark Stuart, 'A party in three pieces', *Contemporary British History*, vol. 16, no. 1 (2002), 51–88.

36 CAB 128/41, CC1(66) (18 January); Wilson, *Government*, 195–6; communiqué, 12 January, in *British and Foreign State Papers, 1965–6* (Stationery Office, 1975), 535–9.

37 Rodgers quoted in Austin Mitchell and David Wienir, eds., *Last Time: Labour's lessons from the sixties* (Bellew, 1997), 181; Jeremy Fielding, *The Currency of Power: Anglo-American economic diplomacy and the making of British foreign policy, 1964–8* (PhD, Yale University, 1999), 146–50.

38 For example, Dickson Mungazi, *The Cross Between Rhodesia and Zimbabwe* (Vantage, New York, 1981), chapter 4.

39 Paul Gore-Booth, *With Great Truth and Respect* (Constable, 1974), 331; Joe Garner, *The Commonwealth Office 1925–68* (Heinemann, 1978), 393; Grant Hugo, *Britain in Tomorrow's World* (Chatto and Windus, 1969), 116–17.

40 Ben Pimlott, *Harold Wilson* (Harper Collins, 1992), 381–2, 450, 457; Evan Davis Fountain, *Purposes of Economic Sanctions: British objectives in the Rhodesian crisis, 1964–6* (DPhil, Oxford University, 2000), *passim*, but especially 264–71.

41 PREM 13/546, Trend to Wilson (17 November); CAB 130/254, MISC 100/A/9 (23 November); PREM 13/1114, Trend to Wilson (5 January); *Foreign Relations of the United States* (*FRUS*), 1964–8, vol. XXIV (US Government Printing Office, Washington, DC, 1999), 886–8, 908–11; Wilson, *Government*, 180–1; Fountain, *Purposes*, chapters 6 and 7.

42 On Zambia's predicament see: Robert Good, *UDI: the international politics of the Rhodesian rebellion* (Faber, 1973), chapter 4; Jon Pettmann, *Zambia: security and conflict* (Friedmann, Lewes, 1974), chapters 4 and 5.

43 Castle, *Fighting*, 361–2; Richard Hall, *The High Price of Principles: Kaunda and the white south* (Hodder and Stoughton, 1969), chapter 14.

44 CAB 128/39, CC65 and 66(65) (29–30 November); Douglas Anglin, *Zambian Crisis Behaviour* (McGill-Queen's University Press, Montreal, 1994), 126–39.

45 See Hall, *High Price*, 121–5.

46 Ben Pimlott, *The Queen* (Harper Collins, 1996), 346–54, quote from 350.

47 Castle, *Fighting*, 385; Callaghan, *Time*, 145.

48 *House of Commons Debates*, vol. 720, columns 360 and 538; Cecil King, *The Cecil King Diary, 1965–70* (Jonathan Cape, 1972), 43–5; DEFE 32/10, COS meeting (3 December 1965).

49 Castle, *Fighting*, 384, 386; CAB 130/206, MISC 4/2 (27 October) and MISC 4/3 (28 October).

50 See especially: CAB 148/25, OPD(66)1st (6 January); CAB 148/26, OPD(66)4th (5 January); DEFE 4/194, COS 2nd/66 (11 January, confidential annex); DEFE 4/195, COS 8th/66 (8 February); DEFE 24/72, DP6/66 (5 February); PREM 13/1116, 'Rhodesian Contingency Planning' (16 February).

51 PREM 13/545, Healey–Grimond meeting (11 November); Smith, *Betrayal*, 111–12; Ken Connor, *Ghost Force: the secret history of the SAS* (Weidenfeld and Nicolson, 1998), 115–17.

52 CAB 128/46, CC(66)50th (13 October); DEFE 32/10, COS 57th/66 (20 October) and DEFE 32/11, COS 65th/67 (22 June 1967).

53 PREM 13/1117, Trend to Wilson (9 March 1966); *FRUS*, vol. XXIV, 868–70.

54 Flower, *Serving*, 51; Healey, *Time*, 332; King, *Diary*, 45; Garner, *Commonwealth Office*, 392–3; PREM 13/543, Salisbury to CRO (29 October).

55 CAB 158/60, JIC(65)69th (1 October). The JIC remained sceptical about the impact of sanctions: CAB 158/61, JIC(66)19th (2 March), CAB 158/62, JIC(66)29th (29 March) and CAB 158/67, JIC(67)34th (11 May). See also Percy Cradock, *Know Your Enemy: how the Joint Intelligence Committee saw the world* (John Murray, 2002), 226–8.

56 Tom Bower, *The Perfect English Spy: Sir Dick White and the secret war, 1935–90* (Heinemann, 1995), 342–4; Garner, *Commonwealth Office*, 391 and 393.

57 Bower, *English Spy*, 356–8; Nigel West, *The Friends* (Weidenfeld and Nicolson, 1988), 167.

58 Stephen Dorril and Robin Ramsay, *Smear! Wilson and the secret state* (Fourth Estate, 1992), 95–6; Hall, *High Price*, 125, 181–5.

59 Nigel West, *A Matter of Trust: MI5, 1945–72* (Weidenfeld and Nicolson, 1982), 206–8; British Library of Political and Economic Science, London, George Wigg papers, 4/68, Wigg to Wilson (11 February, 6 April 1966) on Francistown.

60 CAB 128/39, CC66(65) (30 November); *FRUS*, vol. XXIV, 850.

61 PREM 13/1118, Rogers to Wilson (15 April).

62 Philip Ziegler, *Wilson: the authorised life* (Weidenfeld and Nicolson, 1993), 236; Castle, *Diaries*, 90; CAB 148/25, OPD(66)1st (6 January).

63 Smith, *Betrayal*, 112; Flower, *Serving*, 62.

64 PREM 13/1756, Graham to Wilson (17 October 1968).

65 CAB 148/18, OPD(65)51st (17 November); CAB 128/39, CC68, 70 and 71(65) (7, 14 and 16 December); PREM 13/548, Wilson–Johnson meeting (16 December).

66 See especially Good, *UDI*, 132–45.

67 CAB 148/18, OPD(65)51st (17 November); CAB 148/24, OPD(65)182nd (14 November); PREM 13/564, Trend to Wilson (16 November).

68 For example: CAB 148/30, OPD(67)33rd (18 October); CAB 148/33, OPD(67)73rd (15 October); CAB 148/35, OPD(68)7th (28 March); CAB 148/36, OPD(68)23rd (26 March).

69 Ponting, *Breach*, 249–55; *Report on the Supply of Petroleum … to Rhodesia* (FCO, 1978).

70 PREM 13/3437, Palliser to Wilson (22 April); Ziegler, *Wilson*, 319; Pimlott, *Wilson*, 455–7.

71 PREM 13/3438, FCO Sanctions Unit report (10 October 1969); Flower, *Serving*, chapter 4; CAB 148/35, OPD(68)5th (8 March 1968).

72 On US policy see: Anthony Lake, *The 'Tar Baby' Option: American policy toward Southern Rhodesia* (Columbia University Press, New York, 1972), chapters 3 and 4; Thomas Noer, *Cold War and Black Liberation* (University of Missouri Press, Columbia, 1985), chapters 8 and 9; Gerald Horne, *From the Barrel of a Gun: the US and the war against Zimbabwe* (North Carolina University Press, Chapel Hill, 2001), chapter 4.

73 CAB 128/39, CC72(65) (21 December); PREM 13/1117, report by Watson (March); Windrich, *Britain*, 76–84.

74 CAB 134/3167, R(X)(66)9th (3 August); see also Fountain, *Purposes*, 218.

75 See especially PREM 13/1116, Hughes to Wilson (8 February), Trend to Wilson (10 February) and Wilson to Hughes (11 February); PREM 13/1117, Balogh to Wilson (7 March), Trend to Wilson (23 March).

76 PREM 13/1117, Trend to Wilson (9 March and 2 April); PREM 13/1118, Verwoerd to Wilson (15 April) and FO to Cape Town (18 April); PREM 13/1119, Pretoria to FO (20 April). On Zambia see: PREM 13/1118, Kaunda to Wilson (7 April); PREM 13/1120, Kaunda to Wilson (6 May).

77 PREM 13/1119, CRO to Salisbury (20 April); Pretoria to FO (20 April), records of ministerial meetings (21 and 26 April) and Pretoria to FO (24 April); CAB 130/284, MISC 111(66)1st (25 April) and paper 1 (22 April).

78 CAB 128/41, CC21(66) (28 April); Castle, *Diaries*, 119–20.

79 The talks may be followed through CAB 134/3167, R(X)1st–10th (May–August), and 11th (31 August) reviews the situation; Windrich, *Britain*, 86–92.

80 CAB 128/41, CC44(66) (1 September); Castle, *Diaries*, 162–4; Crossman, *Diaries II*, 19–20.

81 CAB 134/3167, R(X)(66)12th and 13th (7–8 September); CAB 128/41, CC45 and 46(66) (10 and 16 September); Wilson, *Government*, 277–87; Castle, *Diaries*, 166–7; Crossman, *Diaries II*, 28–30; communiqué, 15 September, *State Papers, 1965–6*, 597–602.

82 CAB 128/41, CC48(66) (29 September).

83 CAB 134/3167, R(X)(66)16th–19th (25 October–28 November); CAB 128/41, CC50, 55, 60, 61 and 62(66) (13 October–1 December); Castle, *Diaries*, 182–3, 189–94; Crossman, *Diaries II*, 114–15 and 138–43; Smith, *Betrayal*, 120–3, 126.

84 PREM 13/1133, records of talks; *Rhodesia: proposals for a settlement* (Cmnd 3159, 1966); *Rhodesia: documents relating to proposals for a settlement* (Cmnd 3171, 1968); Wilson, *Government*, 309–17; Smith, *Betrayal*, 126–31.

85 CAB 128/41, CC63(66) (4 December); Castle, *Diaries*, 195–8; Crossman, *Diaries II*, 146–9 (quote from 147); Smith, *Betrayal*, 129–32.

86 CAB 128/41, CC66(66) (13 December); Castle, *Diaries*, 201–2; Crossman, *Diaries II*, 162.

87 CAB 128/42, CC38, 51, 60 and 65(67) (13 June, 24 July, 23 October and 14 November); Castle, *Diaries*, 266, 281–2 and 312–13; Windrich, *Britain*, 105–17.

88 For example, PREM 13/1738, Trend to Wilson (7 February); PREM 13/1739, Trend to Wilson (6 June); and PREM 13/1741, Trend to Wilson (6 October).

89 PREM 13/547, Wright to Wilson (7 December 1965) and attached FO paper; PREM 13/1117, Trend to Wilson (9 March 1966); PREM 13/113, Trend to Wilson regarding R(X) meeting (18 November 1966).

90 CAB 148/30, OPD(67)39th (8 December); CAB 148/33, OPD(67)89th and 93rd (5 December).

91 CAB 148/35, OPD(68)5th (8 March); Crossman, *Diaries II*, 697–8; PREM 13/2320, Trend to Wilson (7 and 19 March).

92 CAB 128/43, CC30(68) (30 May).

93 Arnold Goodman, *Tell Them I'm On My Way* (Chapmans, 1993), 219–20; Brian Brivati, *Lord Goodman* (Richard Cohen, 1999), 194–7; and documents in PREM 13/2323 and 2324.

94 CAB 128/43, CC40(68) (8 October); PREM 13/2324, Wilson–Stewart meeting (12 September); Castle, *Diaries*, 527; Richard Crossman, *The Diaries of a Cabinet Minister, Volume III: Secretary of State for Social Services 1968–1970* (Hamish Hamilton and Jonathan Cape, 1977), 215–17.

95 CAB 128/43, CC41(68) (15 October); PREM 13/2327, full record of talks (19–23 October); *Report of the Discussions Held on Board HMS Fearless* (Cmnd 3793, 1969); Smith, *Betrayal*, 143–6; Wilson, *Government*, 567–70.

96 Castle, *Fighting*, 387; CAB 128/43, CC43, 45 and 46(68) (24 and 31 October, 12 November); PREM 13/2330, record of Thomson visit (4–16 November).

97 Good, *UDI*, 296; Garner, *Commonwealth Office*, 397.

8

The Nigerian civil war

The Nigerian civil war of 1967–70 was virtually forgotten over following decades. But at the time it was compared, as a moral problem, to Vietnam and it is still possible to read claims about the 'deliberate starvation and slaughter of the Ibo people … significantly helped by the British government'. The exact scale of suffering in the conflict is difficult to gauge. Figures of around 50,000–100,000 deaths are supported by Red Cross estimates but at the time the claim that several millions were dying of starvation was widely believed, partly thanks to the effective propaganda campaign of the secessionist regime in the eastern region of Biafra.[1] Wilson called it 'a terrible problem for a Government in a democratic country', but had no doubt that it was right to back Nigerian unity. 'Britain's international prestige, to a greater extent than for any other external power, [became] tied to the outcome of the civil war', because London was a key supplier of arms to the federal government.[2] British policy was vilified by anti-war groups in Europe and America, and the issue affected relationships with the Commonwealth, the Organisation of African Unity (OAU) and individual countries, particularly the USSR, France and Nigeria itself. Indeed, in 1968–70, the civil war was the most consistently significant foreign policy issue facing the government and helps to illustrate that, even after the decision to withdraw from east of Suez, Britain could not escape commitments born of its imperial past.

African independence and Nigeria, 1964–6

The bulk of the Empire in Africa had been granted independence by 1964 and the mid-1960s saw freedom for Gambia (1965), Botswana, Lesotho (both 1966) and Swaziland (1968). The newly independent states needed to establish workable political and administrative systems in the wake of colonial rule and develop their economic potential in the face of poverty, illiteracy and rapid population growth. Some found stability through the domination of one individual, such as Julius Nyerere, who led Tanzania from 1961 to 1985. Other governments succumbed to military coups. Army officers, being educated as well as armed, often saw themselves as potential national saviours. An early victim was Kwame Nkrumah, a leading figure in the non-aligned movement, who had led Ghana to self-rule in 1957 as a 'model' of colonial independence. He was overthrown on 24 February 1966 by the army and police, while abroad on a Vietnam peace mission. The coup, largely unopposed, brought to power General Joseph Ankrah. From exile in Guinea, Nkrumah accused the British, Americans and others of involvement. Britain certainly gained from events since Ankrah's junta restored diplomatic relations, recently broken off by Nkrumah over the Rhodesia episode, and it also expelled Soviet personnel.[3] But Nkrumah produced no evidence of British involvement and the Joint Intelligence Committee (JIC) had predicted in June 1965 that there was 'little likelihood' of Nkrumah losing power over the next year: 'the armed forces are unlikely to precipitate a coup'. The British had been approached more than once to help a coup, most recently in March 1965, but the Commonwealth Relations Office (CRO) argued that, however welcome Nkrumah's departure might be, 'we have not yet gone to the lengths of involvement in plots to secure the overthrow of any Commonwealth government', and Wilson agreed.[4] More persistent rumours of involvement in Nkrumah's overthrow focused on the US Central Intelligence Agency.[5]

An African country where East and West competed for influence was the Congo, where civil war broke out after independence from Belgium in 1960. By 1964 the main problem, the secession of the province of Katanga, had been resolved in favour of the central government, which was backed by the West. But other rebellions continued and in November 1964 there was a crisis over the maltreatment of Western hostages, including a number of Britons, held by rebels in Stanleyville. This crisis figured in several Cabinet discussions at the start of the Wilson government. It led the Belgians and Americans to launch a rescue operation that was followed by a massacre of rebels by government troops and an outcry from other African states over such 'imperialist' intervention. Britain provided the rescue mission with staging facilities on Ascension Island but managed to escape serious criticism.[6] In 1965 the situation stabilised under a pro-Western military strongman, Joseph Mobutu, but the Congo was an ominous example of the danger of fragmentation within African states along ethnic lines, made more dangerous by economic inequalities, military involvement in politics and external intervention. Part of the colonial inheritance was a system of borders between African countries that made little sense in terms of geographical and ethnic realities. But calling the borders into question risked provoking instability and bloodshed throughout the continent and the OAU was determined to respect existing territorial divisions.

When Nigeria gained independence from Britain in 1960, it seemed in a promising position, but it soon fell victim to the twin threats of military coup and regional secession. It was one of the largest African countries in geographical area and, at almost 55 million, was the largest sub-Saharan state in terms of population. Because oil had been discovered in the east of the country in 1958, Nigeria was potentially wealthy and it had a federal constitution that sought to balance regional interests. There was a coalition government under Abubakar Balewa. But Nigeria, like the Congo, had deep ethnic, religious and economic divisions. There were dozens of tribal groups but south-west Nigeria, including the capital Lagos, was populated mainly by the Yoruba; the south-east, the wealthiest region, mainly by the Ibos; the north of Nigeria, mainly by the Hausa and Fulani. The British had divided Nigeria into north and south for administrative purposes in 1899 and with good reason. The north was principally dry grassland, populated by Moslems, and included more than half Nigeria's population; the south was tropical jungle and many of its people had embraced Christianity. But in 1939 the south was itself divided into Eastern and Western regions and by 1960 three political parties existed in Nigeria, largely reflecting this administrative division of the country. In 1962 there were problems when the Western Nigerian leader, Obafemi Awolowo, was imprisoned. Then, in 1964–5, intimidation was used to ensure the victory of pro-government candidates in elections. None of this quite prepared Nigerians for the bloodbath that occurred on 15 January 1966 – only days after the Lagos Commonwealth conference – when Abubakar and other leaders were assassinated during a coup led by mainly Ibo, middle-ranking officers. It followed months of disturbances in Northern Nigeria, in which Ibos had been attacked, and it brought General Johnson Aguiyi-Ironsi, an Ibo, into power. A military government was established, which soon alienated northerners by promoting Ibos to key positions and proposing reforms that would limit the north's political predominance.

On 29 July 1966, after further disturbances in the north, Ironsi was himself overthrown and murdered. After a few days Lietenant-Colonel Yakubu ('Jack') Gowon, the army chief of staff, emerged as an acceptable leader to most of the officer corps. Although a northerner, he was from a minority group, the Ngas, and a Christian. He had no previous political experience and no charisma but seemed a well meaning, trustworthy individual. He hoped to hold the country together through constitutional changes to the federal system, including the sub-division of the three main regions into smaller units. In mid-September 1966, however, there was a further outbreak of violence in the Northern region. Several thousand Ibos were killed and tens of thousands became refugees. After these 'northern massacres' constitutional talks ground to a halt and the military governor of the Eastern region, Lieutenant-Colonel Chukwuemeka Ojukwu, began to plan a breakaway state, though his real intention may have been to replace Gowon as leader of Nigeria. The Oxford-educated Ojukwu, who had been appointed governor of the Eastern region under Ironsi, had never accepted the leadership of Gowon and held him in contempt, just as the Sandhurst-trained Gowon never trusted Ojukwu, believing him to be more an ambitious politician than a soldier.

British policy and the outbreak of war, 1966–7

Accounts of the war, mostly published near the time, are rarely neutral and begin with diametrically opposed views of its origins. For those who see it as a war for Biafran independence, Nigeria was a colonial creation whose unity was in tatters by 1966. Gowon's government lacked legitimacy and independence offered Ibos the only way to find security. Others see it as a war against secession, similar to the American Civil War, with the modest Gowon an unlikely Lincoln. Pro-federal accounts point to the unity that was maintained by the Lagos government through two and a half bitter years of conflict; they see Ojukwu as a rebel and point out that 40 per cent of Eastern Nigerians were non-Ibos, unsympathetic to the Biafran state. Such works also take strongly different views of British policy. To pro-Biafrans, Britain had been responsible for foisting an unwelcome unity on the disparate peoples of Nigeria in order to exploit them, it actively dissuaded Gowon from compromising with Ojukwu in 1966–7 and, from the outset, armed the federal forces. In the Biafran enclave, one of its leaders later recalled, the 'name "Harold Wilson" became a curse among the people, both living and dying'.[7] Yet pro-federal accounts see London as dithering over whether to back Gowon at first and failing to provide sufficient arms during the war, while Nigerian tactics were unfairly vilified by British MPs and the press. One study of Nigerian foreign policy judges that 'Britain's policy of neutralism at the outset of the civil war, and later lukewarm support for the federal side … had a chilling effect on Nigeria–British relations'. Both sides, however, agree that in 1968–70 Michael Stewart was a key federal supporter. One pro-Biafran account even states that 'throughout the war the best statements of Federal policy are to be found in the speeches of Mr. Michael Stewart'.[8] Unsurprisingly, the official record reveals British policy to have been more nuanced than either pro-Biafran or pro-federal accounts portray.

In 1964–5 Labour's relations with the Abubakar regime had been cordial. Nigeria was nominally non-aligned but in practice pro-Western in its foreign policy and did not criticise Wilson much on Rhodesia.[9]

When trouble came in 1966, Britain certainly wished to preserve 'One Nigeria' and the High Commissioner, Francis Cumming-Bruce, advised Gowon against seeking a dissolution of the federation. Faced by numerous problems elsewhere, the USA left Britain to take the lead on the issue.[10] But London did not want to be pushed into a position of being the main supporter of the Federal Military Government (FMG) and thought was given to establishing a Commonwealth peacekeeping force.[11] Also, the British did seriously back attempts at compromise between Gowon and Ojukwu. Malcolm MacDonald, Wilson's 'roving ambassador' in Africa, was important for shuttling between the two sides. Largely thanks to MacDonald, the Ghanaian leader, General Ankrah, was encouraged to invite Gowon and Ojukwu to talks at Aburi in January 1967. Here they seemed close to agreement on a loose federation and this might have been the ideal solution for safeguarding British interests, because it would have preserved a single economic entity while avoiding a war. Wilson minuted that it was 'another good job of work by Malcolm'.[12] But the Aburi accords proved stillborn. The FMG could not accept the concessions to Ojukwu on regional autonomy, especially after he publicly gloated over the deal on returning to the Eastern capital, Enugu. The agreements were, in any case, ambiguous on key points and had been intended by Gowon (who seems to have been comprehensively outwitted by his rival) as a first step to a full agreement rather than the blueprint for autonomy that Ojukwu deemed them to be.[13] Although Ojukwu later bitterly criticised British policy, he was quite happy with their mediation at this point. Indeed, both he and Gowon pressed for MacDonald to return.[14]

Attempts at mediation went on and the Biafrans were evidently hopeful that the new British High Commissioner, David Hunt, who arrived in February 1967, would be sympathetic to them. Hunt, a self-confident individual with considerable experience of Commonwealth problems, had served in Nigeria before and knew Wilson from Oxford days. He arrived with instructions to urge continued negotiations on Gowon and avoid firm promises of British support if secession occurred. Yet Ojukwu was disappointed at his first meeting with Hunt, in Enugu on 14 March, when it became clear that Britain would not back secession either. A few days later Ojukwu sent Wilson word that, if a loose federation could not be agreed, secession would occur. This led the British to make contingency plans for the evacuation of their citizens, an understandable priority after events in the Congo.[15] By April secession was virtually a fact. Ojukwu had stopped sending Eastern tax revenues to the central treasury and Gowon responded with a partial blockade. But on 12 May the Commonwealth Secretary, Bert Bowden, told the Overseas Policy and Defence Committee (OPD) that the ideal solution for Britain was still a united Nigeria in which all the regions willingly participated. Secession would threaten the security of the 3,500 British subjects in the Eastern region and put investments at risk, especially in the oil industry.[16]

On 27 May 1967 Ojukwu finally proclaimed the independence of 'Biafra'. He was confident that the Ibos were behind him and he had an efficient army, not much smaller than the federal one. For finance, he demanded that oil companies, principally Shell and British Petroleum (BP) (acting in Nigeria as a single enterprise), pay revenue to Enugu rather than Lagos. Bowden told the Cabinet that oil supplies were a priority – inevitably, given that there was a danger of war in the Middle East at this point – and a refusal to pay Ojukwu could lead to supplies being cut. But initially London tried to avoid a decision on the royalties issue, so as not to upset the FMG. It was not the only sign of British caution. They began to evacuate subjects from the Eastern region and did not rule out diplomatic recognition of Biafra, although they waited to see whether other countries recognised it first. Hunt, the 'man on the spot', was more forthright. He had become a firm opponent of Ojukwu, blaming his ambition for the gathering crisis and arguing that British attempts to discourage Gowon from force were tantamount to support for secession.[17] Only on 5 July did war break out. By then the Six Day Arab–Israeli War had made oil an even more precious commodity to the British, and Shell–BP had just decided that it would be wisest to pay Ojukwu the royalties he demanded. The British government understood the dilemma, but disliked the decision.[18] Indeed, it may have been the Shell–BP action that convinced Gowon he must completely blockade the Eastern region and invade it.

The course of the war, 1967–70

Before focusing on British policy, the main features of the Nigerian civil war need to be sketched. The Biafran's best chance of victory came in August 1967, when its army struck towards Lagos. But within weeks they were in retreat and, arguably, defeat was already no more than a matter of time. Not only did federal armies capture the Biafran capital in October, they also landed on the southern coast, cutting off access to the sea and pushing into oil-producing areas. The strategically placed port of Bonny, which controlled sea access from Biafra, fell as early as 25 July. Port Harcourt, with Biafra's oil terminals, chief harbour and main airport, followed in May 1968. Ojukwu was then reduced to holding a land-locked enclave with limited food supplies, and contact with the outside world was possible only through a few airstrips, most famously Uli. Yet the war continued, partly because of external factors. At first it seemed that, in terms of foreign support, the federals had a clear advantage. The OAU supported a settlement based on existing borders and some African states, notably Egypt, gave military support. The USSR, keen to find influence in Africa, also backed Gowon with arms supplies and Nigeria became an unusual example of Moscow and London taking the same side in a major international conflict during the Cold War. In the USA the Johnson administration continued to let the British take the lead on the issue but, faced by rising domestic concern, it also posed as a 'neutral' in the conflict and imposed an arms embargo on both sides. When Richard Nixon became President he took a more visible role in humanitarian relief efforts but effectively retained a 'neutral' policy.[19] Ojukwu, however, won support from three right-wing governments, whose interests in southern Africa pointed them to dividing black Africans wherever possible. South Africa, Rhodesia and Portugal all provided Biafra with financial assistance. More important, from July 1968 de Gaulle emerged as Ojukwu's saviour, with military supplies flown in via two former French colonies, the Ivory Coast and Gabon, both of which also extended diplomatic recognition to Biafra. The British believed de Gaulle was motivated by a desire to reduce 'Anglo-Saxon' influence in West Africa, where there were many former French colonies but Nigeria was the largest country. A dramatic Nigerian reaction to de Gaulle was deemed unlikely because of Lagos' desire for a trade deal with the European Economic Community (EEC), which would require French approval.[20]

An important factor in the conflict was its humanitarian dimension. By arguing that the federals blocked aid and claiming that over a million Biafrans were starving, Ojukwu created an image of a federal govern-ment bent on genocide. Images of people reduced to living skeletons filled the Western media after mid-1968, winning sympathy for Biafra among the European and US public. Even two former British colonies, Tanzania and Zambia, recognised Biafra in 1968, because of doubts about the viability of the Nigerian federation and fears of a humanitarian disaster. The federals denied any intention of genocide and argued malnutrition was as much due to Ojukwu's resistance as their imposition of a blockade, itself a legitimate method of waging war. Lagos blamed Western humanitarian groups for effectively taking sides and prolong-ing the conflict, by providing Biafra with sympathy, aid and an element of legitimacy. The International Committee of the Red Cross took on famine relief in April 1968, but Nigerian sensitivities over sovereignty made it a delicate relationship. In June 1969 the FMG fell out with the Red Cross and itself took over the co-ordination of relief.[21] Western exasperation was such that some governments began to supply an illegal 'air bridge' into Uli. The amount that could be carried was limited, since flights were possible only at night, but attempts to arrange a land 'bridge' or daytime flights proved impossible. Lagos, again insisting on its sovereign rights, would allow 'legal' supplies to Biafra only along federal-controlled routes, so that no arms could be smuggled at the same time. But Ojukwu wanted flights to be outside federal control, partly because he *was* flying arms in, partly because he wanted to assert Biafran 'sovereignty' and partly because, he claimed, the federals might use flights as cover for an air attack.

'Neutrality', economic interests and arms sales

A few days after Biafra's declaration of independence, Gowon warned Wilson and other leaders that recognition would 'amount to interference in the internal affairs of my country and will be regarded as an unfriendly act'. In this early phase it has been said that 'British policy seemed to be out of gear if not totally immobilized'.[22] Indeed, it took several months to settle into a consistently pro-federal line. While clearly sympathising with the federals and supplying them with arms, Britain adopted a 'neutral' line in public pronouncements and did not categorically rule out recognition of Biafra. Like the USA, Britain kept its consulate in Enugu open until October, when it was closed because of Biafran harassment.[23] Bowden explained the 'neutrality' policy for the Cabinet on 11 July:

> We were seeking to avoid a commitment to either side in the hostilities and, though we had supplied arms to the Federal Military Government in respect of orders which had been accepted before recent events, we had not agreed to meet a further request from them for further substantial supplies of arms. Our current assessment was that ... the Federal Military Forces might eventually be victorious, but only after a considerable time.[24]

It has been argued that the British backed Gowon because they believed he could put down any secession quickly, but Hunt vigorously denied this in his memoirs, and Bowden's Cabinet statement shows that a long war was expected.[25] The Biafran offensive of August 1967 surprised Gowon and the British, and there was evidently some difficulty in assessing Ojukwu's intentions, compounded by poor intelligence from the local MI6 station, which had failed to develop sources among the Biafran leadership.[26] Frederick Forsyth has asked why London was not more open to Biafran secession: there was evidence that the peoples of Nigeria might never live peacefully together; recently created federations in Central Africa and the West Indies broke up with London's approval; and British economic interests throughout Nigeria might have been safeguarded through a negotiated dissolution. But as the former colonial power, responsible for establishing the federal system many decades earlier and with an interest in maintaining the territorial integrity of other ex-colonies, Britain was never likely to back armed secession. Stewart's memoirs lay particular stress on the dangers of the Biafran example provoking the break-up of other African states on tribal lines.[27]

Substantial economic interests also led Britain ideally to prefer 'one Nigeria'. Apart from the investment in oil led by Shell–BP, British firms dominated the local banking system and London was the home of the United Africa Company, which, through its retail, plantation and processing interests was responsible for over a third of Nigerian trade. Furthermore, around a tenth of British oil imports came from Nigeria in 1966 and Britain accounted for half the foreign investment there.[28] But Kenoye Eke is probably right to argue that 'Britain's fence-sitting diplomacy', in the early stages of the war, 'was influenced by the extensive British interests in Nigeria's oil industry ... which was then under Biafran control'.[29] Even if its long-term economic interests were better guaranteed by a strong federal government, in the immediate term it was the Biafrans who controlled most of the oil and could intimidate the producers. The local Shell–BP manager was imprisoned by Ojukwu for a time – hence the period of indecision about who should be paid oil royalties. Gowon showed he was prepared to be tough on oil himself: he extended the economic blockade to include oil tankers and attacked Bonny, with its oil terminal, as soon as possible. It was after the fall of Bonny that the Labour government advised Shell–BP to pay all oil royalties to Lagos.[30] From the viewpoint of British economic interests, it proved a wise decision. Shell–BP was able to resume its oil exports in October 1968, five months after the federal capture of Port Harcourt. However, oil operations remained vulnerable to Biafran attack, an attack on a pumping station in July 1969 provoking particular concern in the Cabinet.[31]

On the issue of arms supplies, the Wilson government has received intense criticism. It has been said that 'British military and other support of Nigeria increasingly dictated the pace and duration of the war' and that, whoever else interfered in the war, Britain's was the 'crucial intervention'. Without it, 'the conflict would not have lasted as long as it did in spite of the other interventions'.[32] Even while Britain claimed to be 'neutral', pre-war armament orders from Nigeria were still being fulfilled. Reports of this surfaced in the press as early as 9 August 1967, leading Forsyth to question whether there ever really was a 'neutral' phase of British policy. But papers relating to a visit to Lagos by George Thomas, Minister of State at the CRO, confirm that supplies were linked either to pre-war orders or, as with anti-aircraft guns, they were for well defined defensive purposes. Requests for aircraft and fast patrol boats were rejected, one CRO official commenting, 'we have leant over backwards to stick to the principle of non-intervention in Nigerian affairs'.[33] Clearly, 'neutrality' was an ambiguous concept where Nigeria was

concerned. London may have seen itself as 'neutral' but it is unsurprising that critics felt otherwise. The problem for the British was that,
paradoxically, it would not have been a 'neutral' act to end arms ship-
ments to the FMG because, as Wilson said to Hunt, 'Nigeria was a fellow
Commonwealth country in difficulties ... we had equipped her in the
first place and ... a refusal would be equivalent to intervention in favour
of the rebels'. But there was room for the federals, too, to be upset
about British policy. Hunt was critical of London's desire to limit arms
sales, arguing that it might even drive Lagos into nationalising the oil
industry. Worried by the strains in bilateral relations, Wilson assured
Gowon, on 16 July, that Britain would supply 'material of types similar
to those you have obtained in the past'.[34]

The British reviewed their arms policy in August but confirmed Wilson's
line. The federals should be supported as the legitimate government,
but only given 'reasonable quantities of types similar to those supplied
in the past', such as rifles and ammunition, not sophisticated weapons.
At this point, it should be noted, following JIC analyses of the initial
Biafran advances, the British had come to doubt that there would be
any clear 'victory' in the war. The CRO was now open to a negotiated
settlement, one paper arguing that, to protect its economic interests,
Britain needed to maintain the economic unity of Nigeria rather than
any particular political system. The paper also correctly predicted that
a long war would put Britain under pressure to supply large quantities
of arms, which would provoke public criticism.[35] Over the following
months, however, for reasons discussed below, peace talks failed to achieve
any breakthrough and in November a shift of arms policy occurred. By
then the federals were advancing on Port Harcourt and their eventual
victory seemed more certain. George Thomson, the new Commonwealth
Secretary (not to be confused with George Thomas, his junior minister),
told the Cabinet that 'British interests would ... now be served by a
quick [federal] victory'. Arguments for a 'quick kill' were based on evidence
that a negotiated settlement was unlikely, that relations with Lagos, though
strained, were far friendlier than with Biafra and that oil would begin
to flow again once Port Harcourt fell. Nonetheless, while mortars and
submachine guns were now sent to Nigeria, alongside some armoured
cars, the FMG was still denied aircraft and other highly destructive
weapons.[36] British parliamentary and public criticism of arms supplies
caused particular bitterness on the federal side, souring relations between
the two countries, because 'all that was happening was the issue of export
permits for the arms bought in the open market by the Federal government, just as the Biafrans were doing elsewhere'. There was also annoyance
in Lagos that Britain put limits on the types of arms supplied.[37]

The British government defended its supply of arms to the federals
on the grounds that they were justified in fighting secession, that supplies

gave Britain some influence over Lagos, that others could easily provide the arms if Britain did not and that it was better to end the war quickly than encourage Biafran intransigence.[38] Another factor was fear that, if Britain did not arm the federals, then they would become reliant on the USSR. George Thomas recalls Gowon saying, in July, that because Britain was reluctant to provide aircraft and bombs, 'you are driving us into the hands of the Communists'. The first Soviet jet aircraft arrived in August, and one study judges that 'the Nigerians demonstrated ... diplomatic skill ... when they asked the Soviet Union for help, after Britain had initially dithered ... Britain had no alternative but to follow suit'.[39] In fact, it was not as simple as that. The British still refused to supply fighter aircraft, arguing they were unnecessary to meet the threat from the Biafrans, whose bomber force comprised two old B-26s. Also, the shipment of Soviet arms did not create any panic in London, nor lead to any immediate change in arms policy. The JIC warned, in August, that the Soviets 'would be prepared to make a considerable investment in military aid to Nigeria if they considered there were good prospects of successfully increasing their influence in the area'. But the OPD was told on 15 September that the Nigerians had too few pilots to make good use of Soviet aircraft.[40] So the first Soviet supplies had no great effect on policy-making in London. Over the long term, however, the knowledge that the USSR could replace it as a supplier probably deterred Britain from considering an arms embargo. Gowon warned Wilson in June 1968, in a bitter letter about pro-Biafran feeling in Britain, that, if arms supplies ended, 'I shall have no alternative but to obtain weapons I need from any available sources', and Wilson told President Nixon the following year, 'If we were to turn our backs on the Federal Government, we should only drive them into the hands of the Russians'.[41]

To many in Britain, supplying arms on any basis was morally wrong, no matter what the links between the two countries, the dangers of secession and the possibility of Nigeria buying arms elsewhere. An important element in the domestic debate was that Stewart and other ministers appeared dishonest in statements to the Commons about the scale of British arms supplies. These ministers argued, with various degrees of consistency, that Britain had been Nigeria's 'traditional supplier' of arms before 1967 and that any quantitative growth in supplies was because the federal armed forces had also grown in size. But some MPs and newspapers were never convinced and official Nigerian trade figures, revealed in 1969, suggested a different picture. Whereas Britain had supplied most Nigerian arms imports in 1963, it provided less than 40 per cent in the years 1964–6, so that the term 'traditional supplier' had become inaccurate. Yet it supplied nearly half in 1967 and by 1969 was covering almost all federal requirements. Britain's importance as a wartime supplier therefore cannot be disputed, especially since it was supplying small arms, ammunition and armoured cars, which were ideally suited to what was essentially an infantry war, and it was certainly providing a higher percentage than in peacetime.[42] Furthermore, some British training aircraft were adapted for military operations. Indeed, Nigerian air force pilots preferred converted Provost trainers to more sophisticated types and, while they would not provide these to the FMG directly during the war, the British did provide information on countries that might sell them second-hand.[43]

Then again, the government line on arms supply was not completely dishonest. Across the years 1964–6 as a whole, Britain was easily the Nigerians' largest supplier and the official Nigerian wartime trade figures were not exhaustive. They omitted all Soviet arms, for example. Also, Britain was in a difficult position because other pre-war suppliers of Nigerian arms *did* decide to enforce an embargo after 1967. This was true, for example, of the USA, Belgium and the Netherlands. Thus the Nigerians relied on Britain even more. Wilson continued to insist that Britain was the 'traditional supplier' and Stewart argued that denying arms to the FMG would effectively mean 'siding with the secessionists'. They also pointed out that the war lasted beyond 1968 only because of French supplies.[44] It should be noted that contemporary calls for a UN arms embargo on both sides were unrealistic. Apart from the problems with policing such an arrangement, the UN itself was not ready to act in an 'internal' dispute and, if it had tried to do so, the USSR would have vetoed any action.[45]

Public debate and humanitarian aid

If the British media and backbenchers had really wanted to shape policy on Nigeria they should have developed a clear view in the first six months of war, when the official line was flexible. Instead, they were largely indifferent at that time and so allowed policy to become clearly pro-federal. Only in mid-1968 did Biafra suddenly replace Vietnam as a moral cause for many critics of the government. In June, Violet Bonham Carter, the Liberal peer, was 'haunted by the appalling tragedy of Biafra', describing it as 'this massacre by starvation – the worst human tragedy since Hitler'. A number of Conservative MPs felt strongly on the issue and there was pressure to end arms sales at the 1968 and 1969 Labour Party conferences. Criticism of the government thus ranged across the political spectrum. It also included some undeniably 'Establishment' figures. The Archbishop of Canterbury, Michael Ramsey, seconded a motion in the House of Lords by Labour peer Fenner Brockway, the leading anti-colonialist campaigner, calling for the end of arms deliveries.[46] In September 1968 Brockway became the leader of an umbrella Committee for Peace in Nigeria. The Catholic Church also pressed for aid to Biafra. Among the media there was pro-Biafran opinion in *The Times* and even pro-Labour newspapers like the *Guardian*. Television reports often appeared pro-Biafran, too.[47] The weekly *Spectator* became a consistent advocate of the Ibo cause, not least through the pen of Auberon Waugh, who co-wrote a book entitled *Biafra, Britain's Shame* and who fought a by-election on a 'Save Biafra' ticket.[48] Some critics, such as the journalist Frederick Forsyth, became unashamedly pro-Biafran; others, such as Leonard Cheshire, the Second World War pilot and founder of the Cheshire Homes, were motivated only by humanitarian concern.[49]

Even some of Wilson's allies were sympathetic to the Biafrans. His legal adviser, Lord Goodman, considered Biafra the 'first difference' that began their estrangement, while James Griffiths, a loyal member of the Cabinet in 1964–7, now sent letters to his former colleagues, pleading with them to prevent a 'final solution'.[50] As on other foreign policy issues, it helped that the Conservative leadership was generally close to the government position. But Wilson escaped outright defeat at the 1968 annual conference only by accepting a composite resolution that arms sales would be halted 'if there is a possibility of ending the civil war by stopping the supply'.[51] Within the government itself, too, there were doubts about policy. George Thomas, the Minister of State at the Commonwealth Office, was a Christian pacifist who considered resignation over arms supplies to the federals.[52] It has been said that at Cabinet level there was 'only token dissent from a few members' and, certainly, at a meeting on 24 October 1968, Lord Gardiner, the Lord Chancellor, was 'demolished' when he supported an arms embargo. But Nigeria was on the agenda of nearly half the Cabinet meetings in May–December 1968 and concern was expressed about public attitudes, arms policy and famine in Biafra. Discussions became very difficult for Wilson at times. On 5 December 1968, even Callaghan joined Castle, Crossman and others in pressing for a reconsideration of policy because of the arms and humanitarian problems, which had gravely upset the parliamentary party. To quell dissent, Wilson talked of securing an international arms embargo, probably well aware that, given Soviet and French attitudes, this would be impossible to achieve. There was another lengthy discussion five days later, the day before a major Commons debate on the issue. Here Thomson and Stewart emphasised that secession was the key issue, that the federals were being helpful on relief and that Gowon's military policy was not aimed at genocide, while Wilson raised the possibility of going to Nigeria himself.[53]

One result of the upsurge of popular concern was that the agenda of the British government changed. It now had to defend its policies in public, give more thought to humanitarian relief and show greater interest in diplomatic efforts to settle the war. On several occasions in June 1968 the British urged Gowon to minimise civilian casualties and to allow medical supplies to Biafra.[54] It is clear from official papers that this new-found concern was the result of parliamentary pressure, but also that it represented the other side of the coin to arms supplies. The CRO and Foreign Office (FO) believed that, only by urging the FMG to be moderate and by improving Britain's relief provision, could the government keep the public tolerant of arms supplies for Gowon.[55] In early July, Wilson asked John Hunt, leader of the 1953 ascent of Mount Everest (and no relation of the High Commissioner in Lagos), to head a team to explore Nigeria's relief needs and advise on British assistance. Typically, Ojukwu refused to meet them.[56] On 27 August 1968, in a Commons debate, the government was caught out by the strength of feeling on Biafra, and was forced to 'talk out' the debate without a vote.[57] After this it appointed Major-General Henry Alexander to join a team of international observers to monitor federal army operations. They found no evidence of genocide but this did little to reassure public opinion since the team operated at the invitation of the FMG.[58] There was also renewed pressure on Gowon to be generous about peace talks and relief supplies, with Lord Shepherd being sent to Lagos to argue the case. 'We … needed to demonstrate', he wrote, 'that, if … there were a final holocaust … we had done all we could to prevent it'.[59] Pressure on Gowon to avoid civilian casualties was now consistent but the provision of British humanitarian assistance was not that remarkable. Although, by July 1969, Britain had provided $7.5 million in relief aid to Nigeria–Biafra, this was dwarfed by US assistance (ten times as much) and behind that of West Germany ($23 million), Norway ($13 million) and the Netherlands ($10 million).[60]

The diplomacy of war

Alongside its humanitarian activities, Britain became involved in several diplomatic efforts to end the war, but its role was undercut by its pro-federalism. In June 1968 Ojukwu, who had been gratuitously insulting the ex-colonial power for the past year, listed its policy first among the 'obstacles in the way of peace'.[61] British peace attempts, rather than being determined and sustained, appear more like publicity exercises, designed to neutralise criticism at home: 'when opposition was beginning to become serious the government would decide to take an initiative and defuse the situation'.[62] A negotiated settlement was never going to be easy because, while the federals were primarily determined to retain 'one Nigeria', Ojukwu was most anxious to secure independence. Outside negotiators tried to secure compromises on the basis of guaranteeing

Ibo security within a single state. But no proposal appealed equally to the two sides and negotiations were complicated by the issue of diplomatic recognition, the FMG being determined to deny the Biafrans the equality of status they craved. The same distrust pervaded attempts to secure the narrower aim of a cease-fire. The Biafrans seemed to want any cease-fire to be a respite, to give them time to prepare for a revived military struggle, but the federals were determined that any cease-fire should lead to a lasting agreement that ended the secession, a desire which took the two sides back to their fundamental disagreement over Nigerian unity.[63]

In late 1967 the Commonwealth Secretary-General, Arnold Smith, began to sound out both sides on a settlement that would preserve Nigerian unity. The British were reluctant to become directly involved at this point, partly because intervention by the ex-colonial power might be unwelcome to the OAU. But the Cabinet was told in October that Britain was trying to persuade the federals, 'on the basis of their victories, to negotiate from strength and in the hope of avoiding massacres'.[64] In February 1968 Smith's efforts seemed to be bearing fruit and a British contribution to a Commonwealth peacekeeping force was again discussed. The CRO and Ministry of Defence backed a British contribution, not least because peace would safeguard Britain's oil interests, but some ministers on the OPD feared it could become a large-scale, lasting commitment. (This, it should be remembered, was before public concern had really mounted about Nigeria.) Eventually it was agreed to contribute to a force only on conditions that Richard Crossman, at least, believed made it impossible. Not only was a force to be time-limited to six months, but it should include contributions from Ghana and India, and be half financed by Canada.[65] A press leak then undermined Smith's efforts and the talks broke down.[66] London was the venue for another exchange between federal and Biafran representatives on 6–15 May, chaired by Smith, which led to a formal conference in Kampala, Uganda, on 23 May. But this, too, came to nothing. Ntieyong Akpan, head of the Biafran civil service, subsequently confirmed that Ojukwu kept his delegation 'under strict instructions to be rigid' and 'to break up the discussions at the earliest opportunity'. The federal side, having just taken Port Harcourt, was also determined to offer little.[67]

Soon after this failure the upsurge of concern in Britain over the war began and the government began to be more direct in the search for peace. In late June, Lord Shepherd, Minister of State at the CRO, visited Lagos and told Gowon that since the federals had now effectively won, it made sense to negotiate from strength, avoiding the dangers of the Ibos shifting to a guerrilla war strategy. But the FMG insisted that there could be no cease-fire until the Biafrans recognised 'one Nigeria'. On 30 June Ojukwu, seizing another opportunity to criticise Britain, unflatteringly compared Shepherd to Chamberlain at Munich.[68] Repeated efforts by the OAU also failed to bring peace and some African countries became more tolerant of diplomatic action by the ex-colonial power.[69] In early December 1968, after an approach from the Ivory Coast government, the British even suggested to Gowon that they might send a junior minister to meet Ojukwu and pave the way for peace talks. Gowon was unenthusiastic.[70] This was the time of the Cabinet meetings, discussed above, at which even moderate ministers questioned policy and Wilson now became deeply concerned about the possibility of defeat over policy on Nigeria. He wrote an extraordinarily pessimistic letter to Stewart, arguing that 'having once tasted blood, [Cabinet opponents] would subject other issues from Greece to Germany and through Vietnam to the same treatment'. Downing Street and the FO might soon lose control of foreign policy.[71]

Just as he indulged his penchant for personal diplomacy at critical points in Rhodesia and Vietnam, so Wilson now conceived of a mission of his own to Nigeria. His aims were typically immodest. He would visit Ojukwu, bring him to a meeting with Gowon and then arrange a cease-fire and peace talks. In December 1968 Shepherd flew to Lagos to arrange this, telling Gowon that Wilson's mission was essential if British support for the FMG were to be maintained. At the same time Biafran representatives were asked whether Ojukwu might meet a British minister (Wilson was not named). But both sides realised that Wilson was trying primarily to resolve his domestic problems. Ojukwu issued another public statement opposing talks and Gowon refused to receive the Prime Minister.[72] Shepherd subsequently reported that the FMG resented British initiatives and instead expected their unconditional support. It was a line similar to that of High Commissioner Hunt, who feared any ministerial contact with Ojukwu would be seen as a major change in British policy, provoke a crisis with Lagos and encourage Biafra to continue fighting.[73] Wilson was left disappointed, his thunder stolen by Fenner Brockway, who, accompanied by James Griffiths, made a 'private' visit to Nigeria and helped secure a Christmas truce.

It was not long before Wilson returned to the charge, however, with a visit to Lagos in March 1969 that became the most high-profile British peace initiative of the war. The issue had cast its shadow over the Commonwealth prime ministers' meeting in January, which Gowon did not attend.[74] Then, in February, feelings were stirred up by the bombing of civilian targets in Biafra. British dockworkers had refused to load arms bound for Nigeria and it seemed the incoming Nixon administration might be pro-Biafran.[75] In early March another Commons debate was due, with the Conservative front bench now apparently sympathetic to a UN arms embargo. The government urged Gowon to ensure further civilian targets were not hit but concern again mounted in Cabinet. On

12 March there was a serious clash between Stewart, who had circulated another memorandum defending the arming of the FMG, and his critics. Some adopted a moral position but Castle, more practically, pointed out that hopes of a 'quick kill' had repeatedly failed and Crossman, drawing parallels to the birth of Israel, argued that the FO had consistently underestimated the Biafrans.[76] The prime ministerial visit was announced the following day, having been arranged during a visit by Denis Greenhill to Lagos, which had itself been planned by Wilson and Stewart several days before, in anticipation of a crisis. But on this occasion Wilson's attempt to wrong-foot his opponents, by announcing the visit during the Commons debate, backfired. News of the visit leaked beforehand. It did not really matter because, while the debate was the most difficult to date, the expected backbench revolt did not fully materialise. Thirty-four Labour MPs opposed the government line on the war, alongside the Liberals and twenty Conservatives, but most Conservatives abstained and the government majority was 170. With the debate over, the value of the visit was unclear and the timing hardly seemed ideal, with arguments over trade union reform at their height. Castle considered that Wilson was simply 'indulging in his near-fatal weakness for gestures as a substitute for action'.[77] But Stewart told the Cabinet that the visit would be used to press Gowon on several fronts: to negotiate, to help relief efforts more and to guarantee the future safety of Ibos. Wilson was quite frank that he also hoped to defuse the continuing domestic concern in Britain.[78]

In the event, the visit of 27–31 March 1969 proved most important for improving relations with the FMG. To impress the critics, an aircraft loaded with relief supplies was taken along, for Ibos in federal-controlled territory, and with government encouragement Leonard Cheshire, well known for his charity work, made a secret visit to Biafra to try to discover if they were open to a settlement. There were hopes of a Wilson–Ojukwu meeting, primarily to discuss relief, but it never materialised. Instead, there was a tortuous exchange between the British and Biafrans about a possible meeting, in which each side seemed most concerned with avoiding the blame for failure. Wilson, influenced by Nigerian sensibilities, refused to meet Ojukwu in any country recognising Biafra, but Ojukwu wanted a meeting in Biafra itself.

For reasons of security, and to counter the impact of a recent Soviet naval visit, Wilson and Gowon held some of their meetings on HMS *Fearless*. They discussed the military situation, a possible cease-fire, relief problems and ways to improve public handling of the federal case. Gowon insisted there would be no recriminations against Ibos after the war, though he firmly resisted Wilson's appeals for an amnesty to include Ojukwu. Wilson in turn resisted any relaxation in the types of weapons Britain supplied. But the atmosphere was good and there were no arguments. While in Nigeria, Wilson toured the war zone and on his way home, keen not to upset the OAU, he also visited its President, Haile Selassie.[79] All in all, David Hunt and his staff 'felt that this very successful visit set the seal on our endeavours of the past two years'. Nigerians, in retrospect, saw this as the point at which trust was re-established between London and Lagos after the strains of Britain's earlier 'neutralism'. Wilson reported to the Cabinet that he had been deeply impressed by Gowon's sincerity and that Britain should adhere to its 'one Nigeria' policy. The Prime Minister's own doubts about that policy, stirred by the December Cabinet debates, now seem to have been stilled.[80]

The end of the war

Following Wilson's visit no one could guess how long the war would drag on and it continued to spark periodic crises. Federal attempts to stop flights into Uli led to a Swedish relief aircraft being shot down on 5 June 1969 and for a time there was a rift between Gowon and the Red Cross, which provoked another outbreak of public anguish in Britain. In the wake of this crisis, however, Gowon became more forthcoming on relief flights into Biafra and this helped Wilson avoid another parliamentary embarrassment when the war was debated on 10 July.[81] In mid-September, Lagos scored again in the propaganda war by agreeing not to attack daylight relief flights. It was Ojukwu who rejected a deal because, he claimed, the agreement would be used as a cover to attack Uli.[82] A few months later, amid claims that a third of Biafrans were starving, there was yet another inconclusive debate in Cabinet. Castle and Crossman attacked government policy after Stewart tabled another memorandum defending it. Crossman again insisted that Biafra had done enough to win its independence but Tony Benn thought 'it is very difficult to see how we could support Biafra', not least because Ojukwu was 'in effect starving the Biafrans as a political weapon'. A further parliamentary debate was imminent and Wilson was becoming as agitated over the situation as he had been twelve months before. He sent another emissary, Under-Secretary at the Foreign and Commonwealth Office (FCO) Maurice Foley, to Lagos, where he received a frosty response for urging another attempt at talks with Ojukwu. Neither was Gowon impressed by an idea, which had become something of a personal fad for Wilson, that the Royal Air Force (RAF) might handle relief flights into Biafra. If agreement could not be reached on Red Cross flights, asked the Nigerian leader, why would Ojukwu, with his contempt for the British, accept the RAF?[83] Gowon's toughness did nothing to help Wilson with his problems in the Commons, where it seemed rebel left-wingers might ally with the Conservatives to defeat the government. Coincidentally, reports of the

My Lai massacre, of Vietnamese villagers by US troops, accentuated the moral outrage over Western policy towards the developing world. Wilson had little choice other than to defend his government's policy and, in the event, rose to the occasion. On 8 December he opened the debate with a speech that 'represented for me the results of a great deal of heart-searching'; he insisting the federals were ready to agree adequate relief supplies and blamed Ojukwu for preventing a deal.[84] At a meeting of the 'inner Cabinet' the possibility of a defeat was discussed. But again, the government's majority proved better than expected, even if the rebellion against the government, with eighty-six Labour MPs involved, was the biggest ever on Nigeria.[85]

Still the war continued to create difficulties for Wilson. A report in December from the British defence attaché in Lagos, Colonel Robert Scott, was deeply critical of the tactics and leadership of the federal forces, as well as their failure to destroy the Uli airstrip, but he was impressed by Biafran resilience and was still uncertain how long the war would last. The report was leaked to the *Sunday Telegraph*, sparking a lengthy court case under the Official Secrets Act. Yet ironically it was published in mid-January, just when Biafra suddenly collapsed.[86] In late December 1969 federal forces, so criticised in Scott's report, launched an offensive that rapidly overran the beleaguered enclave. On 11 January 1970 Ojukwu fled to the Ivory Coast. A few days later, Biafra surrendered. The first British journalists into the war zone found masses of surrendered soldiers and tens of thousands of malnourished civilians, but no massacres.[87] Instead, Gowon followed a policy of reconciliation and allowed food aid into Biafra; he also exposed Ojukwu's earlier claims of genocide as lies. Even some of the FMG's critics were impressed by the victor's magnanimity.[88] According to Denis Greenhill, Stewart was so relieved at the sudden victory that it 'made him temporarily incapable of work' and FCO staff had to consult his doctor.[89] Wilson was keen to be seen to be active in tackling humanitarian problems at this point, urging moderation on Gowon, keeping in close touch with Nixon and sending John Hunt on another mission to Nigeria to plan British relief efforts.[90] For weeks it was feared that Ojukwu might embarrass the government by trying to enter Britain. The issue even reached the Cabinet, where some were keen to deny him entry, but Callaghan, now Home Secretary, saw no legal grounds to do so; in the event, the problem never materialised.[91]

Conclusion

The federal victory was complete, a fact that helped ensure there were no further attempts at secession, even if Nigeria found it difficult to achieve domestic stability. For the British government, national interests seemed to have been safeguarded. Economically, Shell–BP still dominated the Nigerian oil industry, investments remained safe and a healthy trade relationship continued. Politically, Nigeria again pursued a foreign policy that was nominally 'non-aligned' but in actual fact sought good relations with the West, while Moscow was unable to exploit its wartime arms supplies to secure any lasting foothold.[92] For the Prime Minister the war was neatly removed from public view some months before the 1970 general election. Any conclusion must, however, take account of moral questions about the conduct of policy. These were arguably more complex than those concerning the Vietnam and Rhodesia problems, because in Nigeria the British government seemed responsible, especially through arms sales, for thousands of deaths in a questionable political cause. The early attempt at 'neutrality', the effort to disguise the scale of arms sales and Wilson's near panic over policy in December 1968 all indicated unease, even at the heart of the policy machine, about backing the FMG.

In a long war, however, 'neutrality' was never really an option. Britain, as the ex-colonial power and major supplier over many years, could deny arms to Gowon only at the cost of, effectively, backing Ojukwu. Ending arms sales would have pleased the critics but was unlikely to end the killing in Nigeria and the potential costs of such a policy were daunting: Soviet penetration of Africa, a complete rift with Lagos and, if armed secession had eventually succeeded, a disturbing precedent for the rest of Africa. Even Crossman felt that the outcome of the civil war proved 'the wisdom and foresight of Harold Wilson and Michael Stewart', but Wilson's official biographer was less effusive: 'the best had probably been made of what was a thoroughly bad job'. A fuller judgement came from John St Jorre in an early account of the war. Britain had 'no practicable alternative' to its general policy, but it was executed in a 'confused, guilt-ridden and deceptive' way. The supposed early 'neutrality', the dishonesty over arms supplies and the fitful attempts at peace-making with 'ministers continually dashing off to Lagos' had all combined to make it 'a courageous policy cravenly presented'.[93] That telling conclusion could be drawn about other elements in British foreign policy under Wilson.

Notes

Unless otherwise stated the place of publication is London.

1 Simon Courtauld, *To Convey Intelligence: The Spectator* (Profile Books, 1999), 127 (quote); Patrick Davies, *Use of Propaganda in Civil War: the Biafra experience* (PhD, University of London, 1997).

2 Harold Wilson, *The Labour Government 1964–1970: a personal record* (Weidenfeld and Nicolson, 1971), 557; John Stremlau, *The International Politics of the Nigerian Civil War* (Princeton University Press, Princeton, 1977), 298.

3 Kwame Nkrumah, *Dark Days in Ghana* (Lawrence and Wishart, New York, 1968), 49; Geoffrey Bing, *Reap the Whirlwind* (MacGibbon and Kee, 1968), 416–29; Bob Fitch and Mary Oppenheimer, *Ghana* (Monthly Review Press, New York, 1966), 3–8.

4 Public Record Office (PRO), CAB 158/57, JIC(65)27th (18 June), and see CAB 159/43, JIC(5)19th (6 May); PRO, PREM 13/2677, Snelling to Wright and reply (25–26 March).

5 Bing, *Whirlwind*, 430–6; John Stockwell, *In Search of Enemies* (Deutsch, New York, 1978), 201; *Foreign Relations of the United States* (*FRUS*), 1964–8, vol. XXIV (US Government Printing Office, Washington, DC, 1999), 442–3, 447, 453–4, 457–61, quote from 457; and see David Rooney, *Kwame Nkrumah* (Tauris, New York, 1988), 249–54.

6 CAB 128/39, CC11(64) (26 November); Terence Lyons, 'Keeping Africa off the agenda', in Warren Cohen and Nancy Tucker, eds., *Lyndon Johnson Confronts the World* (Cambridge University Press, Cambridge, 1994), 257–60.

7 Key pro-Biafran texts include: Arthur Nwanko and Samuel Ifejika, *The Making of a Nation: Biafra* (Hurst, 1969), especially 283–5 on Britain; Frederick Forsyth, *The Making of an African Legend* (Penguin, 1969); and, more moderate, Suzanne Cronjé, *The World and Nigeria: the diplomatic history of the Biafran war* (Sidgwick and Jackson, 1972). Quote from Ntieyong Akpan, *The Struggle for Secession* (Frank Cass, 1972), 150.

8 Pro-federal accounts include: Rex Niven, *The War of Nigerian Unity* (Rowman and Littlefield, Totowa, NJ, 1971); John Oyinbo, *Nigeria: crisis and beyond* (Knight, 1971), quote from 107; Kenoye Eke, *Nigeria's Foreign Policy Under Two Military Governments, 1966–79* (Edwin Mellen, Lewiston, 1990), quote from 133.

9 Eke, *Foreign Policy*, 131–5.

10 CAB 128/41, CC41(66) (2 August); *FRUS*, vol. XXIV, 624–6.

11 PREM 13/1661, CRO to Lagos (31 October) and Canberra to CRO (14 November).

12 PREM 13/1661, Lagos to CRO (27–29 December, 2 and 6 January; Wilson minute on last); Clyde Sanger, *Malcolm Macdonald* (McGill-Queen's University Press, Montreal, 1995), 413–16.

13 Zdenek Cervenka, *The Nigerian War* (Bernard and Graefe, Frankfurt, 1971), 38–41, 265–73; A. H. M. Kirk-Greene, *Crisis and Conflict in Nigeria, Volume 1: 1966–7* (Oxford University Press, Oxford, 1971), 75–82, 312–72; Akpan, *Secession*, 49–54.

14 PREM 13/1661, Lagos to CRO (28 and 30 January).

15 David Hunt, *On the Spot: an ambassador remembers* (Peter Davies, 1975), 172–3, 177–9; PREM 13/1661, Ojukwu to Wilson (16 March), Healey to Wilson (22 March). For an alternative account by Hunt see: 'Diplomatic aspects of the Nigerian civil war', in *Diplomacy and Statecraft*, vol. 3, no. 1 (1992), 5–22.

16 CAB 148/30, OPD(67)19th (12 May).

17 CAB 128/42, CC33, 35 and 37(67) (30 May, 1 and 8 June); PREM 13/1661, Lagos to CRO (12 June).

18 CAB 128/42, CC45(67) (6 July).

19 Bassey Ate, *Decolonization and Dependence: the development of Nigerian–US relations* (University of Colorado Press, Boulder, 1987), chapters 2 and 3; Lyons, 'Keeping Africa', 274–6.

20 PREM 13/2259, Lagos to Commonwealth Office (1 August) and Paris to FO (5 August).

21 See *Face aux Blocs: la Croix-Rouge International dans le Nigerie en Guerre* (Red Cross, Geneva, 1973).

22 Philip Ziegler, *Wilson: the authorised life* (Weidenfeld and Nicolson, 1993), 338, citing Wilson papers; John St Jorre, *The Nigerian Civil War* (Hodder and Stoughton, 1972), 296–7.

23 Cronjé, *World*, 24–5; Stremlau, *Civil War*, 65–6; and on the consulate see PREM 13/1662, *passim* (12 September–9 October).

24 CAB 128/42, CC46(67) (11 July); Barbara Castle, *The Castle Diaries 1964–70* (Weidenfeld and Nicolson, 1984), 276.

25 St Jorre, *War*, 295–6; Forsyth, *Legend*, 160–2 and 175–6; Cronjé, *World*, 29–30 and 40–5; for the counter arguments see Hunt, *Spot*, 179–81.

26 Tom Bower, *The Perfect English Spy: Sir Dick White and the secret war, 1935–90* (Heinemann, 1995), 356; and see Anthony Verrier, *Through the Looking Glass* (Cape, 1983), 271–5.

27 Forsyth, *Legend*, 172–5; Michael Stewart, *Life and Labour* (Sidgwick and Jackson, 1980), 238–40. For discussions of British support for Nigeria see: Cronjé, *World*, 326–46; St Jorre, *War*, 297–305.

28 Okwudiba Nnoli, 'The Nigeria–Biafra conflict', in Joseph Okpaku, ed., *Nigeria: dilemma of nationhood* (Greenwood Press, Westport, 1972), 129–41.

29 Eke, *Foreign Policy*, 133, note 15.

30 CAB 128/42, CC53(67) (27 July). See also Cronjé, *World*, 30–1; Stremlau, *Civil War*, 74–6; Verrier, *Looking Glass*, 277–80.

31 CAB 128/44, CC39(69) (30 July); Cronjé, *World*, 144–59.

32 Nnoli, 'Nigeria–Biafra', 141, 143. Similarly, Cronjé, *World*, 325–6.

33 Forsyth, *Legend*, 162–4, 173, 176–9; PREM 13/1662, Forster to Palliser (7 July) and record of Thomas–Gowon meeting (8 July); and see Cronjé, *World*, 32–5.

34 Hunt, *Spot*, 194; PREM 13/1662, Lagos to CRO (13 July) and CRO to Lagos (16 July).

35 CAB 148/30, OPD(67)29th (5 September); CAB 128/42, CC54(67) (7 September); PREM 13/1662, Thomas to Wilson, and attached CRO memorandum (18 August), but see 'Nigeria' memorandum (23 August).

36 CAB 148/30, OPD(67)37th (23 November); CAB 128/42, CC68(67) (23 November).

37 Niven, *War*, quote from 151; Eke, *Foreign Policy*, 133.

38 For example: CAB 128/43, CC30 and 34(68) (30 May and 4 July); Wilson, *Government*, 555–6.

39 George Thomas, *Mr. Speaker* (Century Publishing, 1985), 105–6; Cervenka, *War*, 105.

40 CAB 159/47, JIC(67)34th (17 August), and see CAB 159/46, JIC(66)33rd (11 August) and CAB 159/48, JIC(68)1st (4 January); CAB 148/30, OPD(67)29th (15 September).

41 PREM 13/2258, Gowon to Wilson (1 June); PREM 13/3009, Wilson to Nixon (7 August).

42 Cervenka, *War*, 107–8 and 318–25; Cronjé, *World*, 45–65.

43 PREM 13/2260, Lagos to FCO (28 October), Wilson–Enaharo meeting (8 November); Forsyth, *Legend*, 171–2; Verrier, *Looking Glass*, 277.

44 Cervenka, *War*, 105; Wilson, *Government*, 555–6, 560; Stewart, *Life*, 239.

45 Cervenka, *War*, 108–9.

46 Mark Pottle, ed., *Daring to Hope: the diaries and letters of Violet Bonham Carter* (Weidenfeld and Nicolson, 2000), 349, 351; Cronjé, *World*, 175–80; Labour

Party, *Conference Report, Blackpool 1968*, 260–5, and *Brighton, 1969*, 212, 222; Owen Chadwick, *Michael Ramsey* (Oxford University Press, Oxford, 1990), 251–5.

47 For analysis of the media see W. A. Ajibola, *Foreign Policy and Public Opinion: a case study of British policy over the Nigerian civil war* (Ibadan University Press, Ibadan, 1978), chapters 4–6, also chapters 7 and 8 on pressure groups.

48 Courtauld, *Convey Intelligence*, 127–8; Auberon Waugh and Suzanne Cronjé, *Biafra, Britain's Shame* (John Murray, 1969).

49 Forsyth, *Biafra*; Richard Morris, *Cheshire* (Viking, 1990), 379–80.

50 Arnold Goodman, *Tell Them I'm On My Way* (Chapmans, 1993), 252–3; National Library of Wales, Aberystwyth, James Griffiths papers, file B11, letters to Shepherd (19 August 1968, including quote), Thomson (29 August 1968), and Stewart (8 July 1969).

51 Cronjé, *World*, 164–75, on Conservatives; Craig Wilson, *Rhetoric, Reality and Dissent: the foreign policy of the British Labour government, 1964–70* (PhD, Washington State University, 1982), 148–59, on Labour.

52 Thomas, *Mr. Speaker*, 106; and see E. H. Robertson, *George: a biography of Viscount Tonypandy* (Marshall Pickering, 1992), 183–4.

53 Clive Ponting, *Breach of Promise: Labour in power 1964–1970* (Hamish Hamilton, 1989), 230; CAB 128/43, meetings 30–4, 36, 43 (the 24 October meeting), 46, 49 (5 December) and 50 (10 December) all included Nigeria; Castle, *Diaries*, 566–7 (5 December); Richard Crossman, *The Diaries of a Cabinet Minister, Volume III: Secretary of State for Social Services 1968–1970* (Hamish Hamilton and Jonathan Cape, 1977), 236 (24 October) and 282–3 (5 December).

54 PREM 13/2258, Lagos to Commonwealth Office (6 June), Wilson–Enaharo meeting (12 June) and records of Shepherd–Gowon meetings (21–22 June).

55 The CRO and FO also wanted to pursue a Commonwealth peacekeeping force, but were resisted by other ministries. PREM 13/2258, Thomson to Wilson (16 June), Trend to Wilson (17 June); CAB 130, MISC(68)1st (18 June).

56 John Hunt, *Life is Meeting* (Hodder and Stoughton, 1978), 232–41; *Nigeria: British relief advisory mission* (Cmnd 3727, 1968).

57 Wilson, *Government*, 560–1; Cronjé, *World*, 75–8; Stremlau, *Civil War*, 264–5; generally on parliamentary concern see Ajibola, *Foreign Policy*, chapters 9 and 10.

58 Cervenka, *War*, 87–93; Cronjé, *World*, chapter 5.

59 PREM 13/2260, documents of 22–29 September (quote from undated Shepherd report to Thomson).

60 Joseph Thompson, *American Policy and African Famine* (Greenwood Press, New York, 1990), 130.

61 Akpan, *Secession*, 135, and see 143–6.

62 Ponting, *Breach*, 230; see also Forsyth, *Legend*, 189–90.

63 See Cronjé, *World*, 68–74.

64 Arnold Smith, *Stitches in Time* (Deutsch, 1981), 86–9; Stremlau, *Civil War*, 146–9; CAB 128/42, CC58(67) (11 October).

65 CAB 148/35, OPD(68)3rd (14 February) and OPD(68)7th (28 March); Richard Crossman, *The Diaries of a Cabinet Minister, Volume II: Lord President of the Council and Leader of the House of Commons 1966–68* (Hamish Hamilton and Jonathan Cape, 1976), 682–3 and 744.

66 Smith, *Stitches*, 91–4; Stremlau, *Civil War*, 159–65.

67 Akpan, *Secession*, 137–8; Smith, *Stitches*, 94–9; Stremlau, *Civil War*, 166–74.

68 PREM 13/2258, records of Shepherd–Gowon talks (21–22 June); Stremlau, *Civil War*, 174–9.

Young

69 On OAU efforts see: Cervenka, *War*, 96–99 and 101–3; Stremlau, *Civil War*, chapter 7.

70 PREM 13/2261, documents of 2–6 December.

71 PREM 13/2261, Wilson to Stewart (6 December) and Palliser to Maitland (9 December).

72 PREM 13/2261, FCO to Lagos (10 December); PREM 13/2262, documents of 11–12 December; PREM 13/2263, Shepherd–Gowon meeting (13 December).

73 PREM 13/2263, Shepherd to Stewart (16 December); PREM 13/2817, Lagos to FCO (26 December).

74 CAB 128/44, CC4(69) (16 January); PREM 13/2817, 'David' to Palliser (10 January).

75 See Cronjé, *World*, 114–22; Stremlau, *Civil War*, 297–303.

76 CAB 128/44, CC11 and 12(69) (6 and 12 March); Castle, *Diaries*, 617–18; Crossman, *Diaries III*, 409.

77 PREM 13/2817, Wilson–Stewart telephone call (7 March); PREM 13/2818, Lagos to FCO (11 March); Castle, *Diaries*, 625 and 628; Crossman, *Diaries III*, 414–15.

78 CAB 128/45, CC14(69) (25 March); Wilson, *Government*, 623–5.

79 PREM 13/2819, Wilson–Gowon meetings (28–30 March), Addis Ababa to FO (1 April) and Biafran press statement (1 April); PREM 13/2820, Hunt to Stewart (10 April, reviewing the visit); PREM 13/2825, documenting attempts to meet Ojukwu (19–31 March); Wilson, *Government*, 626–40; Cronjé, *World*, 122–9; Akpan, *Secession*, 150–1.

80 Hunt, *Spot*, 199 (including quote); PREM 13/2820, Hunt to Tebbit (5 April); Olajide Aluko, *Essays on Nigerian Foreign Policy* (Allen and Unwin, 1981), 45; CAB 128/44, CC15(69) (3 April).

81 CAB 128/44, CC30, 31 and 32(69) (26 June, 3 and 10 July). There was another abortive attempt to meet Ojukwu: PREM 13/2821, documents of 1–16 July.

82 CAB 128/44, CC43(69) (11 September).

83 CAB 128/44, CC55 and 57(69) (20 and 27 November); PREM 13/2822, Youde to Graham (19 November), Youde to Williams (3 December), Foley–Gowon meeting (6 December); Tony Benn, *Office Without Power: diaries, 1968–72* (Hutchinson, 1988), 215; Castle, *Diaries*, 733–4; Crossman, *Diaries III*, 746–7.

84 Wilson, *Government*, 729–32; *House of Commons Debates*, vol. 793, columns 39–62.

85 CAB 134/3118, PM(69)20th (9 December); Castle, *Diaries*, 738; Cronjé, *World*, 181–6.

86 *Sunday Telegraph*, 13 January (reproduced in Cervenka, *War*, 305–17). On the prosecution see: Jonathan Aitken, *Officially Secret* (Weidenfeld and Nicolson, 1971); David Hooper, *Official Secrets* (Secker and Warburg, 1987), chapter 9.

87 Max Hastings, *Going to the War* (Macmillan, 2000), 59–63; Churchill College, Cambridge, Michael Stewart papers, press cuttings file for January 1970.

88 Goodman, *Tell Them*, 254; Fenner Brockway, *The Colonial Revolution* (Hart-Davis MacGibbon, 1973), 352.

89 Denis Greenhill, *More By Accident* (Wilton 65, York, 1992), 139.

90 PREM 13/3375, Wilson note (10 January), Wilson–Nixon telephone call (12 January); and see Henry Kissinger, *White House Years* (Little, Brown, Boston, 1979), 416–17. On relief efforts see: Wilson, *Government*, 744–50; Hunt,

    Meeting, 242–6; *Nigeria: the problem of relief in the aftermath of the Nigerian Civil War* (Cmnd 4275, 1970); CAB 128/45, CC1(70) (13 January).
91 CAB 128/45, CC4 and 14(70) (22 January and 26 March); Benn, *Office*, 256; Castle, *Diaries*, 787; Crossman, *Diaries III*, 889–90.
92 Stremlau, *Civil War*, 377–9.
93 Crossman, *Diaries III*, 779; Ziegler, *Wilson*, 340; St Jorre, *War*, 304.

9
Conclusion

All governments have their successes and setbacks on particular international questions. Labour's approach to the Confrontation, the threat to Hong Kong or the 1966–7 crisis in the North Atlantic Treaty Organisation (NATO) may be counted as successes; the alienation of India in 1965 and the farcical invasion of Anguilla in 1969 as obvious negatives. But what of the overall record? Even Michael Palliser feared the government's foreign policy had to be considered 'one of failure: inability to sustain the … position East of Suez; no real influence … over Vietnam; inability to overcome the resistance of White Rhodesia…; British interests further damaged by the Six-Day war…; and, finally, failure to achieve entry into the EEC'.[1] Palliser speaks from the perspective of a professional diplomat and assesses 'success' in terms of maintaining and wielding diplomatic influence. But even on alternative measures, the government's record seems unimpressive. In terms of fulfilling its original aims, for example, cuts in overseas aid, divisions in the Commonwealth, the low profile taken in the talks on the Non-Proliferation Treaty after 1965 and criticism of British policy at the United Nations (UN) on issues like Aden and Rhodesia seemed a world away from the October 1964 manifesto. From a partisan perspective, the left in particular felt dismayed, believing that Wilson abandoned any socialist idealism in favour pragmatism and an obsession with wrong-footing the Conservatives. 'Our foreign policy', complained Richard Crossman in 1967, 'is virtually the same as the Tories', adhering to the US alliance and even extending to taking over 'the Tory determination to get into the Common Market … in order to keep Britain great'.[2] Bowing down to US interests over British Guiana and the Diego Garcia base (touched on in Chapter 1) were two particularly cynical betrayals of socialist ideals in the view of the left. Labour ministers long clung to hopes of a 'great power' role, maintained the nuclear deterrent and defended British commercial interests in the tradition of previous governments.

Yet Wilson never claimed to pursue a 'socialist' foreign policy. Britain's international policy is usually bipartisan in nature and events on the world scene are notoriously unpredictable. The post-war traditions of foreign policy based on the Atlantic alliance, Commonwealth co-operation and a gradual retreat from Empire had been built by Clement Attlee's Labour administration in 1945–51 and still commanded support across much of the party. The 1964 manifesto was sparse on detail where international matters were concerned and even where it did have something to say, as on the future of nuclear weapons, it was usually ambiguous, as such documents are. On some issues the government did show real differences from the Conservatives. The cancellation of TSR-2, restrictions on arms sales to South Africa, the treatment of the federal government in South Arabia and the withdrawal from South-East Asia were all bitterly criticised by the opposition at the time. Ben Pimlott is more generous than Palliser on the government's international policy, and makes three important points in this regard. First, it *is* possible to draw a favourable overall judgement on these years. The general avoidance of conflict, the eventual withdrawal from east of Suez, the turn towards Europe and the isolation of Rhodesia can all be counted in the government's favour. Second, Pimlott argues that, for all his supposed pragmatism and tactical shifts, Wilson actually stuck to certain principles doggedly. Some were harmful to Britain in the long term, such as maintaining the value of sterling. Others included anti-Communism, pro-Americanism and anti-racism. Finally, Pimlott points out that many well established criticisms of Wilson's policies 'cancel each other out' because of their subjectivism. For some he was too pro-American, for others too eager for détente. Some felt he was too slow to embrace the European Economic Community (EEC), while others condemned him for applying. The left wanted to sever links with South Africa yet in 1967 key ministers wanted to revive arms sales. Often policy dissatisfied people simply because Wilson was trying to find an acceptable balance.[3]

Contradictory pressures from domestic and international 'constituencies' were all too apparent on Vietnam, Rhodesia and Biafra but on none of these problems was there a disastrous failure and no particular international problems did the government great damage. Even in Aden, where the government came closest to humiliation, there was ultimately a remarkable escape. During a meeting to discuss election tactics in March 1970, Michael Stewart was even able to report 'that foreign affairs had been going rather well', with no crises and no military casualties for some time.[4] Biafra, Rhodesia, Vietnam and controversial plans for a South African cricket tour – none had any significance by election time.

In a wider sense, however, international policy may have had a profound impact on the fortunes of the government. If one accepts that memories of the 1967 devaluation crisis and its aftermath cost Labour the election in 1970, then decisions in the earlier period on sterling parity and defence expenditure, themselves affected by the need to placate allies, preserve the Commonwealth and maintain global influence, loom even larger in the story of the Wilson governments. One possible line of defence for the government is that its inheritance from previous administrations was a poor one. This was especially the case on Aden, Rhodesia or the terms of the German 'offset' arrangement. More broadly, the Conservatives between 1951 and 1964 had failed to match their international ambitions to national resources. After Suez, the Macmillan governments tried to maximise status and influence through the US alliance, a world role and the possession of nuclear weapons, but they could not escape continuing pressures for decolonisation, balance of payments problems and the failure to enter the EEC. British policy became reactive rather than pro-active in dealings with the outside world. Hoping to arrest the decline in their ability to shape the international environment, the British were unable to adapt promptly to the changes around them.[5] In terms of the country's economic predicament, the warning signs of a breakdown were already there: Britain's share, even of Commonwealth trade, was falling; competitiveness was declining compared with Western Europe and Japan; and there was a sterling crisis in 1960–1.[6]

Until 1964 the system somehow survived without a major crisis and the Conservatives were able to avoid definitive decisions on a raft of problems – devaluation, defence cuts, Rhodesian independence, the cancellation of TSR-2 – leaving Labour to inherit them. At that point, underlying balance of payment problems and daily political realities combined to put the new government in an extremely difficult, perhaps impossible, position. After all, it also had a narrow majority, a complex military–political situation to deal with in the Confrontation and a major ally, the USA, urging that it remain east of Suez and maintain the value of sterling. Then again, all the evidence is that key ministers in the new government were wedded to both a world role and sterling parity, at least at first, and that, even with a safe majority, they would have taken time to adjust their fundamental outlook. It may be that the Conservatives left behind an unenviable position in areas like Aden and Rhodesia, but Labour chose to maintain the broad strategy that it inherited on monetary policy and a global defence posture, alongside the Atlantic alliance, pretensions of a 'special' status in Washington, the possession of nuclear weapons and a commitment to decolonisation. In 1965–6 there actually were many people, in all three main political parties, urging a retreat from east of Suez but the government was slow to respond. Referring to this period in his memoirs, Wilson himself acknowledged the failure, saying that he should not have clung to the east of Suez role 'when facts were dictating a recession…. Others of my colleagues, left-wing and pro-European alike, were wiser in their perceptions'.[7] Even if one accepts that Wilson and Healey came to accept the inevitability of retreat within months of taking office, and that the Confrontation was the main factor holding them back, they still contrived to project an image of reluctance and indecision in cutting back on commitments.

A better defence of the Wilson Cabinets is that they had to cope with the end of previous post-war certainties of economic growth, currency stability and substantial state expenditure. Massive changes in the world economy would soon bring 'stagflation', the end of the Bretton Woods system and the abandonment of Keynesian economics. This posed a grave challenge to governments across the Western world. Social unrest and political uncertainty were considerable in the USA, France and Italy in 1968–9, on a scale far worse than in Britain, and few could see through the fog of uncertainty created by the breakdown of old realities. The overarching problems faced by the government were so vast as to have overwhelmed anyone. If one adds other factors over which Labour had little control, such as the declining value of Commonwealth trade and the unhelpful attitude of Charles de Gaulle, it was an unenviable position. As David Watt expressed it, 'Economic weakness brought on the with-drawal from east of Suez; and this in turn reduced British importance to the United States. Britain's influence in Europe was effectively negated by the French. The Commonwealth ... was a broken reed'.[8] But, again, even if it is agreed that the Wilson governments faced overarching problems beyond their control, it is still necessary to ask how well they managed their response to the challenge.

Ironically, it was the very breakdown of old realities that provided the government with one great reason to be remembered. Although critics complained about the government's adherence to a traditional policy of pro-Americanism, anti-Communism and support for NATO and nuclear defence, it also oversaw a turning point in Britain's inter-national posture. The shift from a world role to a European focus was symbolised by the July 1967 defence decisions, alongside the second application for membership of the EEC, talks later carried forward by Edward Heath. Unfortunately, partly because of the scale of the prob-lems facing policy-makers, this shift appears less as a self-conscious step, for which the government should be praised, than a hesitant reaction to circumstance. Helen Parr notes that decisions on the EEC, devalu-ation and withdrawal from east of Suez were each taken 'within its own specific context and did not represent a planned, nor an inevitable, transition'. In April 1967, the Cabinet took 'two of the most radical decisions in post-war policy-making' – to withdraw from Malaysia–Singapore by 1975 and to apply to the EEC – without any attempt to link the two directly in the relevant meetings.[9]

One of the decision-makers, Patrick Gordon Walker, later acknowl-edged the hesitation, doubt and confusion surrounding the east of Suez decision and its apparent separation from the debate on Europe. 'The

Cabinet looks as if it were pushed ... by unforeseen events into an unwelcome conclusion. Factors and policies that were clearly linked were
not correlated.' He also defended the government's record, however,
arguing that 'all questions before the Cabinet are in some degree inter-
acting' and that, even if it cannot be traced through the written record,
the debate on the EEC did affect the east of Suez decision.[10] Undoubtedly,
certain policy-makers, especially pro-Europeans like Brown, Jenkins and
Palliser, believed a choice should be made between the world role and
Europe, and they had some success in pushing this line after 1966. But
they were a minority and, while they might be praised for their foresight, they too were at the mercy of events: in 1967–8, just as it became
possible to devalue and hasten the withdrawal from east of Suez, the
road into Europe was blocked by de Gaulle. Other ministers were less
clear of the choice that should be made. Left-wingers like Richard
Crossman and Barbara Castle were keen to withdraw from east of Suez
but did not accept EEC membership as an equal necessity and even
moderates like Denis Healey and James Callaghan exhibited little enthusiasm for the 'Common Market'.

The scale of the changes in world affairs and Britain's declining
ability to shape its own future helps to explain the sense of doubt and
inconsistency that enveloped other policy decisions. John St Jorre's
comment on British policy towards Nigeria, that it was 'a courageous
policy cravenly presented', could equally be made about other areas.[11]
Wilson's determination to end Rhodesia's illegal independence while
avoiding war in southern Africa was obscured by his sudden diplomatic
shifts and the failure to develop a convincing sanctions policy. Given
the diverse pressures, the government's policy on Vietnam – vocal support for US policy but no direct involvement – was perfectly defensible.
But Wilson's hasty peace initiatives in 1965 and his criticism of certain
US actions suggested a less certain approach. In the Arab–Israeli dispute the British sought 'disengagement' but themselves compromised
this through arms sales, the ill-fated proposal for a 'Red Sea regatta'
before the Six Day War (which forced Wilson and his Foreign Secretary
into an abrupt retreat from their favoured policy) and involvement in
four-power talks afterwards.

There were genuine problems with steering a constant line. There
always are. Different constituencies need to be satisfied. Aims conflict.
The future is hard to predict. If the Aden imbroglio suggested it was
wise to come to terms with Arab radicalism, then events in Libya in
1969–70 showed that you might win little gratitude for pursuing such a
line. Furthermore, on some areas the government did show consistency,
most notably over resisting Indonesia in the Confrontation, maintaining
NATO in the face of French withdrawal, opposing of the Multilateral
Force and standing by Gibraltar and Hong Kong. Accusations of a general

'lack of will' are unfair. True, there may have been a tendency in some areas, especially the Gulf and Singapore, to exaggerate the dangers of nationalism and hasten the process of retreat, but Aden and Libya were good examples of the potential problems of backing traditional elements for too long. The government was quite capable of showing bravery and toughness when it wanted. Despite domestic opposition and a few moments of doubt, Wilson did support Gowon during the Nigerian civil war, refused to break with the Americans over Vietnam and even remained quite consistent after 1966 in seeking entry to the EEC. Indeed, with their overstretched resources, the British sometimes exhibited considerable bravado. They promised to defend Kuwait but could have done little to prevent an Iraqi invasion; they sent a single warship to Hong Kong in 1967 when the Chinese could have launched an army of millions against it. But there was often a sense of policy being made in haste, with limited thought about consistency or even consequences. Seeking an orderly withdrawal from Aden while undermining the morale of the federal government; making the preservation of NATO a priority while threatening troop cuts if Germany did not offer larger 'offset' payments; negotiating with the Smith regime while insisting it had no legal status; talking of 'neutrality' in Nigeria while arming one side; making an EEC application when it was always likely to be vetoed: none of these suggested that the links between different aspects of policy were thought through in a proper strategic way.

One factor that helped generate inconsistency was, of course, the personal approach of the Prime Minister. In one of the few previous attempts to consider the international record of the Wilson governments, Chris Wrigley noted that a major problem was 'to disentangle style and substance. While its essential continuity with that of previous … governments was often disguised by newsworthy sudden initiatives by Harold Wilson, so were its achievements'.[12] David Watt once suggested that the 'painful series of economic and political retreats' of the Wilson years were 'made more humiliating by Wilson's own tendency to grandiose pretensions of power and statesmanship'.[13] The difference between ambition and reality remained a problem, partly because the Prime Minister still aimed at greatness for the country and had pretensions to play a major role on the world stage. It would be wrong to lay too much emphasis on one individual. Even the most energetic Prime Minister must rely on others for advice. Wilson could not dominate all areas of policy and it has been seen that in certain areas he took only intermittent interest. In East–West relations, for example, for all his ambitions of a major role, he interested himself in trade and summitry to the detriment of a broad, strategic approach. But this was part of the problem. While cherry-picking the areas where he might intervene, it was the Prime Minister who insisted on a high international profile,

stole the headlines and interfered across a broad range of policy.[14] He
chaired most key committees in the international sphere, took some
decisions without reference to the Foreign Office and liked to believe
that he had a special standing in the world's major capitals. He may
have been no worse than Macmillan in the frequency of his interventions and the sudden personal initiatives may even have tailed off after
1968, but Wilson did much to set the tone of the government in world
affairs, helped by the electoral misfortunes of Patrick Gordon Walker
and the docility of Michael Stewart – even if the latter's readiness to
accept a place in the 'second rank' for Britain became widely accepted
in 1968–70, when Wilson's interest in foreign affairs dimmed somewhat.
George Brown was more of a challenge to Wilson as Foreign Secretary,
but he was defeated in the bitter arguments over arms to South Africa
and the acceleration of the withdrawal from east of Suez, after which he
soon departed.

The Prime Minister had many gifts that were well suited to diplomacy. He was energetic, flexible, tactful in personal discussion, able to
grasp details and ingenious at finding a compromise. Yet his character
was such as to accentuate the sense of uncertainty in policy, not least
because it was frequently hard to fathom why he took particular decisions
and, even when he did provide an explanation, he was not always consistent or trustworthy. Thus it is still difficult to say exactly why and
when he decided to pursue EEC membership. Even if he did hold certain
principles, Wilson was often obsessed with tactics, even when dealing
with major issues, and would shift his position in a bewildering way that
gave an impression of aimlessness. The versatility of his approach to
Rhodesia, for example, helped to obscure the fact that there was quite
a consistent aim to end the illegal status of the Smith regime and ensure
unimpeded progress to majority rule. One element of this was his tendency to launch sudden diplomatic initiatives, often with the intention,
as Chris Wrigley has noted, of addressing his various 'constituencies' at
home and abroad. Early in the government, such enthusiasm, imagination and apparent decisiveness could impress critics but over time they
grew tiring and actually became a focus of criticism.[15]

Wilson liked to compare himself to a rugby player breaking out of a
scrum. He used this image with Alasdair Hetherington, editor of the
Guardian, when discussing the idea of 'bridge-building' between the
EEC and the European Free Trade Association, and again with Barbara
Castle, when explaining why he launched the Davies peace mission in
Vietnam.[16] But it is significant that both these initiatives were short term
and soon forgotten. His Walter Mitty side helped accentuate the separation of ambition and achievement. He once talked of organising the
'biggest horse trade in history' with a settlement of the Vietnam War
linked to a deal on nuclear arms control.[17] He repeatedly believed that

he could achieve breakthroughs with personal diplomacy, ending Rhodesia's unilateral declaration of independence through meetings with Smith, resolving the Biafran secession through mediation between Gowon and Ojukwu, settling Vietnam in talks with Kosygin. But all the personal diplomacy, even if it often resulted in quite friendly encounters and the odd low-level agreement, rarely produced anything dramatic. He never did achieve a special status in Washington or Moscow but instead presided over a decline in the significance (though not, it seems, the quality) of the Anglo-American relationship and some difficult years in Anglo-Soviet relations.

Robert Rhodes James once wrote that 'Wilson's skill in the 1964–70 government was to give the appearance of great changes without in fact making any of substance'.[18] In fact, the Prime Minister deployed considerable skill to obscure or downplay the most substantial changes that did occur, perhaps because they were unwelcome to many of his supporters. The chief importance of his 1960s governments was not their essential continuity with post-war tradition, though there was consistency in many areas, but the fact that they presided over a major evolution in Britain's world position. Thanks to a certain re-learning of the lessons of the Macmillan years, Labour and Conservative front benches came to agree that the Commonwealth was of little value as a pillar of British influence and that power was best rebuilt in a European context. Britain's own value to the USA was very much in decline in 1966–8, even if personal relations among officials remained close. Above all, Britain's military influence in the world waned as bases were closed and political commitments liquidated. If the Attlee governments had laid the basis for post-war policies down to the mid-1960s, then the Wilson governments presided over the recasting of those policies to fit Britain's subsequent role as a primarily European power, still closely allied to the USA but as one middle-sized power among many, relying on non-military sources to maintain influence in the world. The problem was that, because so few ministers saw the nature of these changes clearly, the government did seem to embrace them reluctantly, with confusion and uncertainty in decision-making, interspersed by Wilson's attempts to 'break out of the scrum', which were actually no more than tactical bids to escape particular dilemmas. Wilson was only too well aware at such points of the various contradictory pressures facing him, but he never did publicly articulate a clear, forward-looking perspective on Britain's place in the world. Ironically, in 1970 Britain actually was left with international ambitions that did, after decades of overstretch, match resources to aims. A determination to abandon positions east of Suez, to maintain influence through non-military means, to accept a place in the 'second rank', to encourage détente and to focus on a European future created a sustainable policy in terms of both affordability and achievability. Yet this position was achieved more by muddle and a collapse of alternatives than any long-term vision.

Notes

Unless otherwise stated the place of publication is London.

1 Michael Palliser, 'Foreign policy', in Michael Parsons, ed., *Looking Back: the Wilson years 1964–70* (University of Pau Press, Pau, 1999), 28.
2 Richard Crossman, *The Diaries of a Cabinet Minister, Volume II: Lord President of the Council and Leader of the House of Commons 1966–8* (Hamish Hamilton and Jonathan Cape, 1976), 181–2.
3 Ben Pimlott, *Harold Wilson* (Harper Collins, 1992), 561–6.
4 Tony Benn, *Office Without Power: diaries 1968–72* (Hutchinson, 1988), 249.
5 See specially Anne Deighton, 'British foreign policy-making: the Macmillan years', in Wolfram Kaiser and Gillian Staerck, eds., *British Foreign Policy 1955–64: contracting options* (Macmillan, 2000), 3–17.
6 Catherine Schenk, 'Shifting sands: the international economy and British economic policy', and Christopher and Gillian Staerck, 'The realities behind Britain's global defence strategy', in Kaiser and Staerck, eds., *British Foreign Policy*, 19–31 and 33–53.
7 Harold Wilson, *The Labour Government 1964–1970: a personal record* (Weidenfeld and Nicolson, 1971), 243.
8 David Watt, 'Introduction', in W. R. Louis and Hedley Bull, *The 'Special Relationship'* (Oxford University Press, Oxford, 1986), 12.
9 Helen Parr, *Harold Wilson, Whitehall and British Policy Towards the European Community, 1964–7* (PhD, Queen Mary College, London, 2002), 355; Helen Parr, 'Gone native: the Foreign Office and Harold Wilson's policy towards the EEC', in Oliver Daddow, ed., *Harold Wilson and European Integration* (Frank Cass, 2003), 88.
10 Patrick Gordon Walker, *The Cabinet* (Jonathan Cape, 1970), 130–3.
11 John St Jorre, *The Nigerian Civil War* (Hodder and Stoughton, 1972), 304.
12 Chris Wrigley, 'Now you see it, now you don't: Harold Wilson and Labour's foreign policy', in R. Coopey, S. Fielding and N. Tiratsoo, eds., *The Wilson Governments, 1964–70* (Pinter, 1993), 123.
13 Watt, 'Introduction', 12.
14 I am grateful to Geraint Hughes for discussing these points.
15 Wrigley, 'Now you see it', 125–7.
16 British Library of Political and Economic Science, London, Alastair Hetherington papers, 9/5, meeting with Wilson (5 May 1965): Barbara Castle, *The Castle Diaries 1964–70* (Weidenfeld and Nicolson, 1984), 45.
17 Hetherington papers, 12/15, meeting with Wilson (8 June 1966).
18 Robert Rhodes James, *Ambitions and Realities* (Weidenfeld and Nicolson, 1972), 60.

Select bibliography

Unless otherwise stated, for books the place of publication is London.

Primary sources
Official sources

Great Britain
Public Record Office, Kew
CAB 128   Cabinet minutes.
CAB 129   Cabinet memoranda.
CAB 130   Cabinet committees (miscellaneous).
CAB 134   Cabinet committees (standing).
CAB 148   Defence and Overseas Policy Committee.
CAB 158   Joint Intelligence Committee memoranda.
CAB 159   Joint Intelligence Committee minutes.
DEFE 4   Chiefs of Staff minutes.
DEFE 10   Ministry of Defence committees.
DEFE 24   Defence secretariat registered files.
DEFE 25   Chief of Defence Staff files.
DEFE 32   Chiefs of Staff, Secretary's standard file.
FCO   Foreign and Commonwealth Office series.
FO 371   Foreign Office (FO) correspondence.
FO 800   FO private papers collections.
FO 953   FO Planning Department 1964–6.
PREM 13   Prime Minister's Office.

Oriental and India Office Collections, British Library, London
R/20/D   Aden High Commission 1962–7.

Political parties
Conservative Party archives, Western Manuscripts Department, Bodleian Library, Oxford: Leader's Consultative Committee ('shadow Cabinet'); and Parliamentary Foreign Affairs Committee.
Labour History Archive, Manchester: Parliamentary Labour Party minutes.
Labour Party conference reports (annual).
Labour Party election manifestos.
Labour Party National Executive Committee minutes (published pre-1967 by Harvester Press microfilms as *Archives of the British Labour Party, Part I: NEC minutes since 1900*; post-1967 from Labour History Archive, Manchester).

Parliament
Command papers.
Hansard, House of Commons Debates.

Published documents
Bennett, Gillian and Hamilton, Keith, eds., *Documents on British Policy Overseas, Series III, Volume I: Britain and the Soviet Union, 1968–72* (Stationery Office, 1997).
Hyam, Roger and Louis, William, eds., *The Conservative Government and the End of Empire, 1957–64* (two volumes, Stationery Office, 2000).
Watt, Donald and Mayall, James, *Current British Foreign Policy, 1970* (Temple Smith, 1971).

United States
National Archives, College Park, Maryland
Nixon Presidential Materials Project.
Record Group 59, State Department, central files and lot files.

Lyndon B. Johnson Library, Austin, Texas
Administrative History of the State Department.
National Security File.
White House Central Files: Confidential File; and Countries series.

Published documents
Documents of the National Security Council (University Publications of America microfilms, Frederick, Maryland, supplements published since 1987).
Foreign Relations of the United States, volumes for 1964–8 (US Government Printing Office, Washington, DC, since 1995).
Memoranda of the Special Assistant for National Security Affairs: McGeorge Bundy to President Johnson, 1963–6 (University Publications of America microfilms, Frederick, Maryland, 1987).
Herring, George C., ed., *The Secret Diplomacy of the Vietnam War: the negotiating volumes of the Pentagon Papers* (University of Texas Press, Austin, 1983).

West Germany
Schwarz, Hans-Peter, ed., *Akten zur Auswartigen Politik der Bundesrepublik Deutschland*, volumes for 1964–70 (Oldenbourg, Munich, 1996–2000).

France
De Gaulle, Charles, *Discours et Messages, Volumes IV, 1962–5*, and *V, 1966–9* (Plon, Paris, 1970).
De Gaulle, Charles, *Lettres, Notes et Carnets* (Plon, Paris, 1987).

Private papers collections

Bodleian Library, Oxford (Western Manuscripts Department): George Brown (by kind permission of Mrs Frieda Warman-Brown); Paul Gore-Booth; Anthony Greenwood (by kind permission of Lady Greenwood); and Con O'Neill and Harold Wilson (partially opened).
British Library of Political and Economic Science, London: Arthur Bottomley; Anthony Crosland; Alastair Hetherington; and George Wigg.
Churchill College, Cambridge: Patrick Gordon Walker; Andrew Gilchrist; Frank Roberts; Christopher Soames (by kind permission of Lady Soames); and Michael Stewart.

Hartley Library, University of Southampton: Earl Mountbatten of Burma.
House of Lords Record Office, London: Lord Shackleton.
Library of Congress, Washington, DC: Averell Harriman.
Liddell Hart Centre, King's College, London: Alexander Bishop; and Charles Johnston.
Lyndon B. Johnson Library, Austin, Texas: George Ball; and Francis Bator.
Modern Records Centre, University of Warwick, Coventry: Richard Crossman; Frank Cousins; and Lord Elwyn-Jones.
National Library of Wales, Aberystwyth: James Griffiths; Cledwyn Hughes (by kind permission of Lord Cledwyn); George Rendel (by kind permission of Miss Rosemary Rendel); and Lord Tonypandy (George Thomas).
Public Record Office, Kew: George Brown (FO 800); Robert Bruce Lockhart (FO 800).
Truman Library, Independence, Missouri: Philip Kaiser.
Virginia Historical Society, Richmond: David Bruce diaries.

Oral history projects

British Diplomatic Oral History Project, Churchill College Archive, Cambridge.
Brook Publications, 'Seventies Archive', British Library of Political and Economic Science, London.
Lyndon B. Johnson Library, oral histories.

Memoirs and diaries

Benn, Tony, *Out of the Wilderness: diaries 1963–67* (Hutchinson, 1987).
Benn, Tony, *Office Without Power: diaries 1968–72* (Hutchinson, 1988).
Blankenhorn, Herbert, *Verstandnis und Verstandigung: Blatter eines politischen Tagebuchs, 1949–79* (Propylaen, Frankfurt, 1980).
Brown, George, *In My Way* (Gollancz, 1971).
Cairncross, Alec, *The Wilson Years: a Treasury diary, 1964–69* (Historians' Press, 1997).
Callaghan, James, *Time and Chance* (Collins, 1987).
Castle, Barbara, *The Castle Diaries 1964–70* (Weidenfeld and Nicolson, 1984).
Castle, Barbara, *Fighting all the Way* (Weidenfeld and Nicolson, 1993).
Chalfont, Alun, *The Shadow of My Hand* (Weidenfeld and Nicolson, 2000).
Crossman, Richard, *The Diaries of a Cabinet Minister, Volume I: Minister of Housing 1964–66* (Hamish Hamilton and Jonathan Cape, 1975).
Crossman, Richard, *The Diaries of a Cabinet Minister, Volume II: Lord President of the Council and Leader of the House of Commons 1966–68* (Hamish Hamilton and Jonathan Cape, 1976).
Crossman, Richard, *The Diaries of a Cabinet Minister, Volume III: Secretary of State for Social Services 1968–1970* (Hamish Hamilton and Jonathan Cape, 1977).
Flower, Ken, *Serving Secretly* (John Murray, 1987).
Gore-Booth, Paul, *With Great Truth and Respect* (Constable, 1974).
Greenhill, Denis, *More By Accident* (Wilton 65, York, 1992)
Healey, Dennis, *The Time of My Life* (Michael Joseph, 1989).
Heath, Edward, *The Course of My Life* (Hodder and Stoughton, 1998).
Henderson, Nicholas, *Inside the Private Office* (Academy, Chicago, 1987).
Henderson, Nicholas, *Mandarin: the diaries of Nicholas Henderson* (Weidenfeld and Nicolson, 1994).
Hunt, David, *On the Spot: an ambassador remembers* (Peter Davies, 1975).

Hunt, John, *Life is Meeting* (Hodder and Stoughton, 1978).
Jay, Douglas, *Change and Fortune* (Hutchinson, 1980).
Jenkins, Roy, *A Life at the Centre* (Macmillan, 1991).
Johnson, Lyndon Baines, *The Vantage Point: perspectives of the Presidency 1963–69* (Weidenfeld and Nicolson, 1971).
King, Cecil, *The Cecil King Diary, 1965–1970* (Jonathan Cape, 1972).
Kissinger, Henry, *The White House Years* (Little, Brown, Boston, 1979).
Longford, Frank, *The Grain of Wheat: an autobiography* (Catholic Book Club, 1974).
Mayhew, Christopher, *Time to Explain* (Hutchinson 1987).
Owen, David, *Time to Declare* (Michael Joseph, 1991).
Parsons, Anthony, *They Say the Lion* (Jonathan Cape, 1986).
Pearce, Robert, ed., *Patrick Gordon Walker: political diaries, 1932–71* (Historians' Press, 1991).
Roberts, Frank, *Dealing With Dictators* (Weidenfeld and Nicolson, 1991).
Short, Edward, *Whip to Wilson* (MacDonald, 1989).
Smith, Ian, *The Great Betrayal* (Blake, 1997).
Stewart, Michael, *Life and Labour* (Sidgwick and Jackson, 1980).
Trevelyan, Humphrey, *The Middle East in Revolution* (Macmillan, 1970).
Trevelyan, Humphrey, *World's Apart: China 1953–5; Soviet Union 1962–5* (Macmillan, 1971).
Wigg, Lord, *George Wigg* (Michael Jose\ph, 1972).
Wilson, Harold, *The Labour Government 1964–1970: a personal record* (Weidenfeld and Nicolson, 1971).
Yew, Lee Kuan, *From Third World to First* (Harper Collins, 2000).
Zuckerman, Solly, *Monkeys, Men and Missiles: an autobiography 1946–88* (Collins, 1988).

Secondary sources

Books

Balfour-Paul, Glen, *The End of Empire in the Middle East: Britain's relinquishment of power in her last three Arab dependencies* (Cambridge University Press, Cambridge, 1996).
Bartlett, C. J., *The Long Retreat: a short history of British defence policy, 1945–70* (Macmillan, 1972).
Bower, Tom, *The Perfect English Spy: Sir Dick White and the secret war, 1935–90* (Heinemann, 1995).
Centre d'etudes en literature et civilisation de langue anglaise, *Cercles: the Wilson Years, 1964–70* (University of Rouen, 1999).
Cradock. Percy, *Know Your Enemy: how the Joint Intelligence Committee saw the world* (John Murray, 2002).
Cronjé, Suzanne, *The World and Nigeria: the diplomatic history of the Biafran war* (Sidgwick and Jackson, 1972).
Daddow, Oliver, ed., *Harold Wilson and European Integration: Britain's second application to join the EEC* (Frank Cass, 2002).
Darby, Phillip, *British Defence Policy East of Suez, 1947–68* (Oxford University Press, Oxford, 1973).
Dockrill, Saki, *Britain's Retreat from East of Suez: the choice between Europe and the world?* (Macmillan, 2002).
Dumbrell, John, *A Special Relationship: Anglo-American relations in the Cold War and after* (Macmillan, 2001).
Foot, Paul, *The Politics of Harold Wilson* (Penguin, Harmondsworth, 1968).

Freeman, J. P. G., *Britain's Nuclear Arms Control Policy in the Context of Anglo-American Relations,, 1957–68* (Macmillan, 1986).

Garner, Joe, *The Commonwealth Office 1925–68* (Heinemann, 1978).

Good, Robert, *UDI: the international politics of the Rhodesian rebellion* (Faber, 1973).

Greenwood, David, *The Economics of the East of Suez Decision* (Aberdeen University Press, Aberdeen, 1973).

Haftendorn, Helga, *NATO and the Nuclear Revolution: a crisis of credibility, 1966–67* (Clarendon Press, Oxford, 1996).

Hennessy, Peter, *The Prime Minister* (Allen Lane, 2000).

Jones, Matthew, *Conflict and Confrontation in South East Asia: Britain, the US, Indonesia and the creation of Malaysia, 1961–5* (Cambridge University Press, 2002).

Kaiser, Wolfram and Staerck, Gillian, eds., *British Foreign Policy 1955–64: contracting options* (Macmillan, 2000).

Kelly, J. B., *Arabia, the Gulf and the West* (Weidenfeld and Nicolson, 1980).

Lapping, Brian, *The Labour Government 1964–1970* (Penguin, 1970).

Logevall, Fredrik, *Choosing War: the lost chance for peace and the escalation of war in Vietnam* (University of California Press, Berkeley, 1999).

Mayhew, Christopher, *Britain's Role Tomorrow* (Hutchinson, 1967).

Miller, J. D. B., *Survey of Commonwealth Affairs: problems of expansion and attrition, 1953–69* (Oxford University Press, Oxford, 1974).

Morgan, Austen, *Harold Wilson* (Pluto, 1992).

Morgan, Kenneth, *Callaghan: a life* (Oxford University Press, Oxford, 1997).

Paget, Julian, *Last Post: Aden 1964–7* (Faber and Faber, 1969).

Parsons, Michael, ed., *Looking Back: the Wilson years 1964–70* (University of Pau Press, Pau, 1999).

Paterson, Peter, *Tired and Emotional: the life of Lord George Brown* (Chatto and Windus, 1993).

Pickering, Jeffrey, *Britain's Withdrawal from East of Suez* (Macmillan, 1998).

Pieragostini, Karl, *Britain, Aden and South Arabia* (Macmillan, 1991).

Pimlott, Ben, *Harold Wilson* (Harper Collins, 1992).

Ponting, Clive, *Breach of Promise: Labour in power 1964–1970* (Hamish Hamilton, 1989).

Shlaim, Avi, Jones, Peter and Sainsbury, Keith, *British Foreign Secretaries Since 1945* (David and Charles, London, 1977)

Shrimsley, Anthony, *The First Hundred Days of Harold Wilson* (Weidenfeld and Nicolson, 1965).

St Jorre, John, *The Nigerian Civil War* (Hodder and Stoughton, 1972).

Stremlau, John, *The International Politics of the Nigerian Civil War* (Princeton University Press, Princeton, 1977).

Subritzky, John, *Confronting Sukarno: British, American, Australian and New Zealand diplomacy in the Malaysian–Indonesian confrontation, 1961–5* (Macmillan, 2000).

Williams, Geoffrey and Reed, Bruce, *Denis Healey and the Policies of Power* (Sidgwick and Jackson, 1971).

Windrich, Elaine, *Britain and the Politics of Rhodesian Independence* (Croom Helm, 1978).

Young, Hugo, *This Blessed Plot: Britain and Europe from Churchill to Blair* (Macmillan, 1998).

Ziegler, Philip, *Wilson: the authorised life* (Weidenfeld and Nicolson, 1993).

Articles, chapters and working papers

Bale, Tim, '"A deplorable episode"? South African arms and the statecraft of British social democracy', *Labour History Review*, vol. 62, no. 1 (1997), 22–40.

Creevy, Matthew, 'A critical review of the Wilson government's handling of the D-notice affair 1967', *Intelligence and National Security*, vol. 14, no. 3 (1999), 209–27.

Dobson, Alan, 'The years of transition: Anglo-American relations 1961–7', *Review of International Studies*, vol. 16 (1990), 239–58.

Dockrill, Saki, 'Britain's power and influence: dealing with three roles and the Wilson government's defence debate at Chequers in November 1964', *Diplomacy and Statecraft*, vol. 11, no. 1 (2000), pp. 211–40.

Dockrill, Saki, 'Forging the Anglo-American global defence partnership: Harold Wilson, Lyndon Johnson and the Washington summit, December 1964', *Journal of Strategic Studies*, vol. 23, no. 4 (2000), 107–29.

Dumbrell, John, 'The Johnson administration and the British Labour government: Vietnam, the pound and east of Suez', *Journal of American Studies*, vol. 30 (1996), 211–31.

Easter, David, 'British intelligence and propaganda during the Confrontation, 1963–6', *Intelligence and National Security*, vol. 16, no. 2 (2001), 83–102.

Ellis, Sylvia, 'Lyndon Johnson, Harold Wilson and the Vietnam War', in Jonathan Howell, ed., *Twentieth Century Anglo–American Relations* (Macmillan, 2001), 180–204.

Gordon Walker, Patrick, 'The Labor Party's defense and foreign policy', *Foreign Affairs*, vol. 42, no. 3 (1964), 391–8.

Jones, Matthew, 'A decision delayed: Britain's withdrawal from South East Asia reconsidered, 1961–8', *English Historical Review*, vol. 67, no. 472 (2002), 569–95.

Kaiser, Wolfram, 'Party games: the British EEC applications of 1961 and 1967', in Roger Broad and Virginia Preston, eds., *Moored to the Continent: Britain and European integration* (Macmillan, 2001).

Kunz, Diane, 'Lyndon Johnson's dollar diplomacy', *History Today*, vol. 42 (April 1992), 45–51.

Kunz, Diane, 'Anglo-American defence and financial policy during the 1960s', *Journal of Imperial and Commonwealth History*, vol. 27, no. 2 (1999), 213–32.

McIntyre, David, 'Britain and the creation of the Commonwealth secretariat', *Journal of Imperial and Commonwealth History*, vol. 28, no. 1 (2000), 135–58.

McNamara, Robert, 'Britain, Nasser and the outbreak of the Six Day War', *Journal of Contemporary History*, vol. 35, no. 4 (2000), 619–39.

Petersen, Tore Tingvold, 'Crossing the Rubicon? Britain's withdrawal from the Middle East, 1964–8', *International History Review*, vol. 22, no. 2 (2000), 318–40.

Pickering, Jeffrey, 'Politics and "Black Tuesday": shifting power in the Cabinet and the decision to withdraw from "East of Suez"', *Twentieth Century British History*, vol. 13, no. 2 (2002), 144–70.

Rees, Wyn, 'British strategic thinking and Europe, 1964–70', *Journal of European Integration History*, vol. 5, no. 1 (1999), 57–71.

Roy, Raj, 'The battle for Bretton Woods: America, Britain and the international financial crisis of October 1967–March 1968', *Cold War History*, vol. 2, no. 2 (2002), 33–60.

Schrafstetter, Susanna and Twigge, Stephen, 'Trick or truth? The British ANF proposal, West Germany and US non-proliferation policy', *Diplomacy and Statecraft*, vol. 11, no. 2 (2000).

Schrafstetter, Susanna, and Twigge, Stephen, 'Spinning into Europe: uranium enrichment and the development of gas centrifuge, 1964–70', *Contemporary European History*, vol.11, no. 2 (2002), 253–72.

Steininger, Rolf, '"The Americans are in a hopeless position": Great Britain and the war in Vietnam, 1964–5', *Diplomacy and Statecraft*, vol. 8, no. 3 (1997), 237–85.

Stewart, Michael, 'Britain, Europe and the Alliance', *Foreign Affairs*, vol. 48, no. 4 (1970), 648–59.

Straw, Sean and Young, John W., 'The Wilson government and the demise of TSR-2', *Journal of Strategic Studies*, vol. 20, no. 4 (1997), 18–44.

Wrigley, Chris, 'Now you see it, now you don't: Harold Wilson and Labour's foreign policy', in R. Coopey, S. Fielding and N. Tiratsoo, eds., *The Wilson Governments, 1964–70* (Pinter, 1993).

Young, John W., 'West Germany in the foreign policy of the Wilson government, 1964–7', in Saki Dockrill, ed., *Controversy and Compromise: alliance politics between Britain, Germany and the United States, 1945–67* (Philo, Bodenheim, 1998).

Young, John W., 'The Wilson government and the Davies peace mission to North Vietnam', *Review of International Studies*, vol. 24 (1998), 545–62.

Young, John W., 'George Wigg, the Wilson government and the 1966 report into security in the diplomatic service and GCHQ', *Intelligence and National Security*, vol. 14, no. 3 (1999), 198–208.

Young, John W., 'The Netherlands in Britain's strategy for EEC entry', in Nigel Ashton and Duco Hellema, eds., *Unspoken Allies: Anglo-Dutch relations since 1780* (Amsterdam University Press, 2001), 241–54.

Young, John W., 'The Wilson government's reform of intelligence co-ordination, 1967–8', *Intelligence and National Security*, vol. 16, no. 2 (2001), 133–51.

Zimmerman, Hubert, 'The sour fruits of victory: sterling and security in Anglo-German relations during the 1950s and 1960s', *Contemporary European History*, vol. 9, no. 2 (2000), 225–43.

Theses

Baker, Robert, *ELDO: British policy and the politics of European co-operation, 1961–9* (MPhil, Queen Mary College, London, 2001).

Brenchley, Thomas, *Britain and the 1967 Arab–Israeli War* (DPhil, Oxford University, 1999).

Donohoe, Michael, *The Wilson Government's Vietnam Peace Initiatives, 1964–7* (MPhil, Oxford University, 1997).

Easter, David, *British Defence Policy in South East Asia and the Confrontation, 1960–66* (PhD, London School of Economics, 1998).

Ellis, Sylvia, *Anglo-American Relations and the Vietnam War, 1964–8* (PhD, University of Newcastle, 1999).

Fielding, Jeremy, *The Currency of Power: Anglo-American economic diplomacy and the making of British foreign policy, 1964–8* (PhD, Yale University, 1999).

Fountain, Evan Davis, *Purposes of Economic Sanctions: British objectives in the Rhodesian crisis, 1964–6* (DPhil, Oxford University, 2000).

Hughes, G. A., *Harold Wilson, the USSR and British Foreign and Defence Policy in the Context of East–West Détente* (PhD, King's College, London, 2002).

Parr, Helen, *Harold Wilson, Whitehall and British Policy Towards the European Community, 1964–7* (PhD, Queen Mary College, London, 2002).

Percox, David, *'Circumstances Short of Global War': British defence, colonial internal security and decolonisation in Kenya, 1945–65* (PhD, University of Nottingham, 2001).

Rippingale, Simon, *Hugh Gaitskell, the Labour Party and Foreign Affairs, 1955–63* (PhD, University of Plymouth, 1996).

Roy, Rajarish, *The Battle for the Pound: the political economy of Anglo-American relations, 1964–8* (PhD, London School of Economics, 2000).

Salzman, Verena, *West Germany, the US and the Crisis of the Western Alliance, 1963–6* (PhD, Cambridge University, 1999).

Twine, Christopher, *Anglo-American Relations and the Vietnam War, 1964–7* (PhD, University of Wales, Aberystwyth, 2000).

Wilson, Craig, *Rhetoric, Reality and Dissent: the foreign policy of the British Labour government, 1964–70* (PhD, Washington State University, 1982).

Index